"I've never seen greater courage th... this particular book."

"Michael Medved has vital things to say about the suppurations of modern Hollywood. . . . It's all down in his book *Hollywood vs. America*."

—WILLIAM F. BUCKLEY

"Even Medved's opponents are likely to recognize that his indictment of Hollywood films, network television and rock and roll music in the book is a focused, comprehensive and painstakingly researched analysis."

—PUBLISHERS WEEKLY

"Enthralling. . . . Memorable. . . . The book is required reading—never hysterical but always provocative."

—LOS ANGELES TIMES

"In tones of impassioned outrage and trenchant sarcasm, it amasses dozens upon dozens of examples supporting the thesis that Hollywood is out of touch with the rest of America. . . . In a crazy town, Michael Medved is insanely sane."

—INSIGHT

"Brilliant cultural criticism . . . intelligent, readable and right on the mark. . . . There is no doubt that Michael Medved's *Hollywood vs. America* is one of the most important books of the 1990s."

—MOVIEGUIDE

"An eloquent and feisty book. Whether Hollywood's dream merchants clean up their acts or continue their slide into mass-media nihilism, they can no longer claim ignorance of their sins."

—CHRISTIANITY TODAY

"*Hollywood vs. America* is fascinating reading, a must-read for parents who are concerned not only with their children's present entertainment options, but for their future choices, as well as what kind of world they will inherit."

—PREVIEW (DALLAS)

"A good and useful book. . . . I know of no one else who has shown so conclusively that obscenity, indecency, and anti-family, anti-military, anti-religious messages are persisted despite the fact that they are bad box office."

—AMERICAN SPECTATOR

"David slung that stone at Goliath, Luke Skywalker flew in the face of the empire, and Michael Medved is going after Hollywood. In his recent pop manifesto *Hollywood vs. America*, the feisty, mustached cohost of PBS's 'Sneak Previews' aims his great guns at the entertainment industry."

—BOSTON GLOBE

"The book carefully and systematically examines the destructive messages that are being transmitted by what is called 'entertainment.' . . . Citing dozens of recent examples from the Hollywood media, as well as surprising statistics from reliable polls and studies, Medved supports his controversial belief that the entertainment industry is not fulfilling its mandate to provide the people with what they want."

—BOOKS OF THE WEEK

"Combines eye-opening research, encyclopedic detail, and sophisticated analysis to explain how Hollywood's alienation from traditional values is itself alienating American moviegoers and television viewers."

—COMMENTARY

"Middle America appears to love him, agreeing wholeheartedly with his critiques—anti-violence, anti-gore, anti-sleaze—of contemporary films. . . . Medved marshals statistics and facts in rebutting Hollywood's characteristic reactions to criticism."

—LOS ANGELES DAILY NEWS

"An authoritative accounting of the many sins of Babylon by the Pacific."

—BOSTON HERALD

"Medved's brilliantly argued polemic makes a persuasive and heartfelt case for a 'cultural environmental movement' to turn Hollywood from its current degradation."

—MONA CHAREN, SYNDICATED COLUMNIST

"[Medved] is articulating a widely felt rage. . . . I'm glad he wrote the book. If nothing else, it reminds us that we aren't merely consumers of popular culture. By our action, or inaction, we help to create it."

—MINNEAPOLIS STAR TRIBUNE

"Insightful. . . . No one has more conclusively shattered these myths than movie critic Michael Medved in his newest book, *Hollywood vs. America*. And that's just one of the many valuable, eye-opening contributions this book makes to the raging debate over the 'culture war.'"

—NEW YORK GUARDIAN

"Must reading. . . . A hard-hitting look at the impact of the deterioration of entertainment industry fare."

—CHRISTIAN PARENTING TODAY

"It's refreshing to find an articulate advocate for audiences who are fed up with Hollywood's bent toward messages of death and destruction. . . . Medved trots out so many polls and consumer surveys that it's hard to dispute his contentions."

—SAN FRANCISCO CHRONICLE

"A provocative new book. . . . Mr. Medved's book sinks a few good blows in Hollywood's liberal bias—most noticeably in its contempt for mainstream religion."

—THE ECONOMIST (LONDON)

"Love him or hate him, Michael Medved has been kind enough to rekindle a long overdue debate."

—TORONTO STAR

"Armed with a subtle wit, a truckload of irrefutable statistics and the relentlessness of a jackhammer, Medved sets out to prove that Hollywood has lost faith with its audience. . . . This is one of the most important books of the year."

—CBS RADIO NETWORK

Also by Michael Medved

HOLLYWOOD VS. AMERICA

Michael Medved

HarperPerennial
A *Division of* HarperCollins*Publishers*

A hardcover edition of this book was published in 1992 by HarperCollins Publishers/Zondervan.

HOLLYWOOD VS. AMERICA. Copyright © 1992 by Michael Medved. All rights reserved. Printed in the United States of America. No part of this book may be used or reproduced in any manner whatsoever without written permission except in the case of brief quotations embodied in critical articles and reviews. For information address HarperCollins Publishers, Inc., 10 East 53rd Street, New York, NY 10022.

HarperCollins books may be purchased for educational, business, or sales promotional use. For information please write: Special Markets Department, HarperCollins Publishers, Inc., 10 East 53rd Street, New York, NY 10022.

First HarperPerennial edition published 1993.

Designed by C. Linda Dingler

The Library of Congress has catalogued the hardcover edition as follows:

Medved, Michael.
    Hollywood vs. America : popular culture and the war on traditional values / Michael Medved. —1st ed.
        p. cm.
    Includes index.
    ISBN 0–06–016882–X (cloth)
    1. Motion pictures—Moral and ethical aspects. 2. Television broadcasting—Moral and ethical aspects. 3. United States—Popular culture—Moral and ethical aspects. I. Title. II. Title: Hollywood versus America.
PN1994.M379   1992
302.23'43'0973—dc20

92–52604

ISBN 0-06-092435-7 (pbk.)
93 94 95 96 97 ❖/HC 10 9 8 7 6 5 4 3 2 1

For my own true beloved DIANE
who taught me that wholesomeness
and happiness need not be boring

Only the morally courageous are worthy of speaking to their fellow men for two hours in the dark. And only the artistically incorrupt will earn and keep the people's trust.

—FRANK CAPRA, *THE NAME ABOVE THE TITLE*, 1971

Contents

Acknowledgments

My appreciation goes first to Lissa Roche, director of seminars at Hillsdale College, who invited me to lecture at that altogether extraordinary Michigan campus in March of 1989. She later made a transcript of the talk I gave on that occasion ("Hollywood vs. Religion") and published it in the college's journal of ideas *Imprimis,* which reaches a circulation of more than 400,000. A subsequent lecture for Hillsdale's Shavano Institute ("Popular Culture and the War Against Standards," November 1990) received similar treatment, and both pieces eventually found their way into *Reader's Digest* and other publications.

In this way, Lissa's insistence (over my strenuous initial objections) that my lecture themes should reach a larger audience began the process that led to this book; for that, I thank her, and offer additional thanks for the invaluable research assistance she provided during the last twelve months. I am also grateful to her father-in-law, George Roche, president of Hillsdale College, for his friendship and his sound advice to me at a recent crossroads.

My friend Carolyn Joy Johnston, whose infectious enthusiasm for a range of good causes contaminates everyone she meets, worked tirelessly to help me with research; Marla Matzer, a frequent writer for *Premiere* magazine, also contributed generously of her time and insight in gathering background material for this book.

Our neighbors Judd and Denise Magilnick deserve special recognition: Judd's computer assistance at all hours of the day and night, and his extraordinary understanding of every aspect of the entertainment business, played a major role in completion of this manuscript. I constantly marvel over my good fortune in seeing our two growing families, with our wives linked by more than thirty years of friendship, living only two doors apart.

I can never sufficiently express my appreciation to my friend and teacher, Rabbi Daniel Lapin. In addition to his enormous contributions to the Jewish people at large and to our own neighborhood community, he provided significant encouragement for this project along with perceptive suggestions at key points in the creative process.

Richard and Arthur Pine have now been my literary agents for more than seventeen years; the fact that this sort of long-term relationship is increasingly unusual in the book business makes me cherish my association with them all the more. Richard's input has played an important role in helping this project take shape, and in keeping the author at work and on track.

Hugh Van Dusen, my patient editor at HarperCollins, displayed both understanding and insight to a remarkable degree, and demonstrated devotion beyond the call of duty by interrupting his Maine vacation to facilitate the completion of this project. John Sloan, my editor at Zondervan, offered understanding and imagination in an unusually sensitive stage of the writing.

Additional appreciation is in order to my PBS partner and pal of seven years, Jeffrey Lyons, whose loyalty and decency are in every way examplary; to my long-suffering and dedicated producer at "Sneak Previews," Nicolette Ferri; to assorted Medveds around the world—including Renate, David, Jon, and Ben—for their warm support; to Rob Cain, for thorough, prompt, and invaluable computer analysis; and to Dan Johnson, whose assistance and idealism have meant so much to my ability to address the pop culture issues that I care about most.

Finally, to those two people who have been closest to this project, and to every other endeavor in a busy life—

Harry Medved, my coauthor on three previous books, is a true Hollywood insider by virtue of his work for the Screen Actors Guild and as managing editor of *Screen Actor* magazine; he also happens to be one of the most considerate and generous human beings on the planet. We often disagree on both substantive and trivial matters, but we always manage to work together. His passionate interest in this book and his everyday assistance during all stages of its composition contributed immeasurably to my ability to finish the job. Surely it is one of life's most precious blessings that my best friend—and most valued colleague—also happens to be my kid brother.

My other "best friend" is, of course, my wife, Dr. Diane Medved. At times, the job of a movie critic can become so disorienting that it becomes especially valuable to share your home with a clinical psychologist; when the popular culture inflicts toxic doses of weirdness, my favorite therapist helps to keep me sane (most of the time). She is also an ideal mother, a peerless playmate, an organizational genius, and a gifted writer who constantly took time from her own fourth book to read, react, and rewrite, as this project gradually emerged. For all this, for our beautiful children, and for the last eight years of unparalleled happiness, I am forever in her debt.

Preface to the
Paperback Edition

An Accident of Timing

"In this world there are only two tragedies," wrote Oscar Wilde in 1892. "One is not getting what one wants, and the other is getting it."

Since the publication of *Hollywood vs. America*, I've definitely been savoring the second tragedy.

In writing this book I wanted to stir up controversy—to assault the smug complacency of the entertainment establishment and to help push Hollywood in a more responsible direction. However, the passionate intensity of the public response to my work—both positive and negative—far exceeded my expectations.

In part, the polarized nature of this reaction stemmed from an accident of timing: a few months *after* I turned in this manuscript to my editor, while the publisher worked to set my words in type, the Vice President of the United States surprised this author (and the rest of the country) by delivering a series of partisan political speeches in which he attacked the values of the mass media. Much to my chagrin, this meant that *Hollywood vs. America* appeared in print at precisely the moment that the national press raged with the astonishingly bitter charges and counter-charges between Dan Quayle and Murphy Brown.

In retrospect, even the former Vice President's most devoted admirers should recognize that he made a mistake in his attempt to raise serious issues of media accountability in the midst of a hard-fought election campaign. The context for his often thoughtful statements made it all too easy for skeptical reporters to dismiss them as desperate and distracting ploys by a failing political candidate. Even if many Americans felt sympathetic to Mr. Quayle's basic concern over the excesses of the entertainment industry, they failed to see a connection between the issues he addressed and his role as a national office-holder. What federal program could the Vice President possibly suggest to curb the media irresponsibility he so stridently decried? As a longtime foe of big government, he could hardly endorse some ambitious new Washington bureaucracy designed to approve future plot twists on "Murphy Brown."

No Conservative Monopoly

Moreover, Mr. Quayle's implicit suggestion that only conservatives worried over the destructive impact of the popular culture struck a false chord with the American public. Citizens of all political persuasions express these concerns; Tipper Gore, for one, warned of the anti-social messages in popular music years before the Vice President voiced his dissatisfaction with contemporary TV. For the last five years, the most militant and effective congressional critic of violence on television has been a liberal Democrat—Senator Paul Simon of Illinois. In October 1992, in the last weeks of the presidential campaign, a *Newsweek* poll showed an astonishing consensus on the question of the entertainment industry's irresponsible excesses. Eighty percent of a representative sample believed that movies today contain too much sex and violence. Eighty percent of the country might never agree that Elvis is dead—but they share the conviction that Hollywood has gone too far.

This concern remains all but universal today, long after the electoral triumph by the Democratic ticket. Attempts by some of President Clinton's more fervent show business supporters to interpret his victory as a vote of confidence in the entertainment industry makes no sense at all. The American people rejected the Bush-Quayle ticket because they disapproved of the leadership in Washington, not because they approved of the leadership in Hollywood. The Democratic plurality in the presidential race in no way signified a repudiation of calls for greater accountability on the part of the mass media; very few of the 43.7 million voters who cast their ballots for Bill Clinton felt they were providing Hollywood with a mandate for more violence and foul language in motion pictures or television.

The president-elect made an unmistakable effort to underscore that point in an interview with *TV Guide* just a week after election day. "The cumulative impact of the banalization of sex and violence in the popular culture is a net negative for America," Bill Clinton declared. "I think the question is, what can Hollywood do, not just to entertain, but to raise the human spirit."

Meanwhile, a group of the new president's closest associates published a collection of policy proposals called *Mandate for Change* in which they provided further evidence that Washington's concern over media messages would not disappear along with the Bush administration. Their book, strongly endorsed by Mr. Clinton himself, specifically cites the role of the entertainment industry in promoting family disintegration and suggests that the Chief Executive should initiate a "broad national discussion" of media responsibility. The authors declare, "It is fairly well established that educational programming accelerates early learning and that televised violence exacerbates aggressive behavior."

Fresh Developments and Updated Statistics

These new developments in a new administration point up one of the inevitable hazards for any book like *Hollywood vs. America*: the author's best efforts to keep his work comprehensive and current will be constantly overtaken by fresh developments and updated statistics.

For instance, in this book (which was completed in May 1992) I report on figures for motion picture attendance for the year 1991—which plunged to their lowest levels since 1976. The year-end numbers for 1992 provided even more striking evidence of audience alienation, as attendance continued to decline and *plunged to a sixteen-year low* and to its lowest level ever in terms of percentage of our population. Nor could Hollywood's apologists explain these declines as a simple shift from theatrical attendance to home video viewing, since video rentals fell off sharply in 1991, and then remained flat in 1992. In the traditionally "recession-proof" entertainment industry, which has enjoyed some of its most successful seasons in past periods of economic distress, these figures suggest a general (and intensifying) dissatisfaction with the content of the popular culture, rather than the temporary impact of financial hard times.

"The summer movie season is on, but moviegoers are decidedly turned off. . . . Many moviegoers say this summer's crop is one of the worst ever," *The Wall Street Journal* reported on August 6, 1992, at the height of Hollywood's busiest time of year. CinemaScore, the universally respected Las Vegas–based company that polls opening night audiences across the country to gauge their reaction to new motion pictures, confirmed that Hollywood's "grades" declined for the third year in a row. CinemaScore president Edward Mintz described public reaction to Hollywood's offerings for the summer of 1992 as "very disappointing," "ugly," and "a disaster."

One of the films that bucked the downward trend and became a gigantic 1992 hit in both theatrical release and home video also served to illustrate one of the major points in this book. *Sister Act*, the fast-moving, though formulaic, Whoopi Goldberg comedy, showed a more affectionate attitude toward the Roman Catholic church than any other film of recent years; audiences found themselves amused and uplifted by its story of a Reno lounge singer whose life and values are positively transformed when she is forced to hide out in a convent. The picture earned some $140 million in domestic box office gross, stunning all observers by placing fourth on the list of the year's top money makers, and outpacing all other nonsequels in 1992.

At the same time that the unexpected success of *Sister Act* illustrated the public's eagerness to embrace entertainment with a more sympathetic attitude toward conventional faith, other high-profile projects illustrated the self-destructive nature of Hollywood's underlying hostility to organized religion. The hugely talented Steve Martin starred in *Leap of Faith*, in which he played a greedy and hypocritical faith healer and evangelist who sets up his revival tent to prey on the unsuspecting citizens of "Rustwater, Kansas." *Leap of Faith* represented only the latest (and one of the most expensive) installments in the long series of earnest epics about crooked clergy, which I describe in Chapter 4 of this book, and like virtually all of its predecessors it proved an unequivocal flop at the box office—emerging as one of the most conspicuous commercial disappointments of Hollywood's Christmas season.

Another failed 1992 film—the sorry sequel *Alien*^{3}—provided a recent and particularly telling example of the industry's astonishing propensity for gratuitous insults toward religious believers, also discussed in Chapter 4. In *Alien*^{3}, heroine Sigourney Weaver finds herself marooned on an outer-space penal colony populated entirely by brutal, hardened, sex-starved, and foul-mouthed criminals. At one point, an inmate helpfully informs her, "You know, we're all fundamentalist Christians here."

Enhancing or Inhibiting Success

I do not suggest that this utterly unnecessary jab at religious traditionalists *guaranteed* the failure of *Alien*^{3}, any more than I suggest that *Sister Act's* relatively benign view of Catholicism *guaranteed* its success. Social and cultural messages are only one element—among many—in determining the public's response to a motion picture release. In the case of *Alien*^{3}, no one organized a boycott of the picture because of its glancing and gratuitous insults to Christian believers; moviegoers found an abundance of far less subtle reasons to avoid this thoroughly loathsome and inept motion picture. To suggest, however, that a picture's ideological orientation has no impact at all on its public reception is every bit as illogical and extreme as the notion that this element will singlehandedly assure triumph or failure.

The more balanced and moderate view suggests that the underlying attitudes toward religion and other institutions that turn up in movies can help to create a level of comfort—or discomfort—in the mass audience, and thereby enhance or inhibit a motion picture's success.

Imagine for a moment that *Sister Act* had gone out of its way to deride Catholic beliefs and institutions, as did *Nuns on the Run* (1990), another recent comedy with a strikingly similar plot but a radically different tone. Even with that hostile tone, the Whoopi Goldberg vehicle still might have reached a mass audience, but it's hard to imagine that its final box-office take would have been as formidable as it was if Catholics had felt consciously offended by the film.

Questioning Elements, Not Condemning Essence

In the same sense that a controversial message can damage a project without utterly dooming it, questioning one element in a film isn't the same as condemning its essence.

Reviewers and moviegoers will often find fault with an aspect of a film while still appreciating its strengths in other areas. Criticizing a movie's musical score, set design, editing, or ideological emphasis isn't the same as dismissing the overall piece of work as worthless or dangerous.

In this context, the titles mentioned in *Hollywood vs. America* are in no way intended as a laundry list of projects I dislike; any such comprehensive catalogue of feeble or tasteless movies would no doubt run even longer than this book's 380 pages.

Hollywood vs. America is, rather, a description of underlying attitudes in the popular culture that have helped to alienate a significant segment of the public. At times, those attitudes turn up in motion pictures of great artistic distinction; at others, they appear in projects of irredeemable awfulness. It is, in fact, the pervasive nature of these themes that makes them such a profound problem for Hollywood; although the quality of craftsmanship in today's motion pictures is hugely variable, their underlying attitudes are not.

That is why this book will frequently cite some annoying element in movies whose overall artistry or entertainment value I otherwise respect. In the case of *The Little Mermaid* and *E.T.*, for instance, I strongly endorsed both pictures at the time of their initial release— even selecting *E.T.* for my retrospective "Sneak Previews" list of "The Best Films of the 1980s." When I respectfully refer to both titles in the chapter in this book entitled "Kids Know Best," I do so not because I have reconsidered my previous praise, but because these movies illustrate the way that even some of today's finest family films will reinforce Hollywood's ubiquitous notion that children are always wiser and more sensitive than their parents.

Countless examples from Hollywood's glory years might serve to illustrate the way that even the most magnificent projects can occasionally feature destructive biases or irresponsible messages. Consider the history of the industry's lamentably racist past: no one would deny the fact that the movie industry of the '30s and '40s, despite its many virtues, regularly offered insulting and stereotypical portrayals of African-Americans and other minorities.

Gone With the Wind (among many other titles) clearly reflected some of these unfortunate attitudes.

To make this observation is not to condemn *Gone With the Wind* as a "bad" film or to question its status as a masterpiece. *Birth of a Nation* displayed even more obvious and poisonous racial hatred but is still recognized as a timeless and hugely influential artistic achievement. Nevertheless, any comprehensive examination of Hollywood's history of bigotry must include some mention of such brilliant and seminal films rather than focusing exclusively on embarrassing little Stepin Fetchit comedies.

In the same way, my discussion of the self-destructive excesses of today's Hollywood makes a point of touching upon some of the very best (as well as some of the very worst) work that the entertainment industry currently offers the public.

Influential, Not All-Powerful

In responding to the swelling chorus of criticism from the public, Hollywood's leadership often employs disingenuous rhetoric that seeks to blur essential distinctions. For instance, the defenders of the show business status quo automatically equate any challenge to the industry's current directions with a call for censorship—as if a plea for corporate responsibility amounts to some all-out assault on the First Amendment.

When it comes to discussions of the long-term impact of popular culture, the Hollywood apologists resort to similarly dishonest tactics—deliberately confusing the argument that the entertainment industry is influential with the assumption that it is all-powerful.

This confusion stands behind one of the most common attacks on anyone who suggests that popular culture might be damaging the fabric of this society. According to this line of reasoning, the industry's critics contradict themselves whenever they contend on the one hand that Hollywood is out of touch with America and then assert on the other that the mass media help to shape the values of the public. If we say that most people in this country remain more committed to religious faith, traditional families, and old-fashioned patriotism than contemporary films and TV shows might suggest, then how can we claim that this material exerts an important influence on public attitudes?

Upon closer examination, this objection makes no sense; it is the logical equivalent of suggesting that all TV commercials for *unsuccessful* political candidates are, by definition, complete wastes of resources with no impact on the electorate. Since the other guy ended up with more votes on election day, doesn't this show that the losing candidate squandered all the money he spent for his media campaign? According to such reasoning, no one can claim that Ross Perot's expensive and popular infomercials influenced the American people, since 81 percent of the votes for President of the United States went to his two rivals.

This is nonsense, of course: the fact that Perot failed to convince *everyone* in this country can hardly be taken as evidence that he convinced *no one*.

Similarly, the nature of media impact is never a simplistic all-or-nothing proposition; to say that Hollywood's messages have *some* influence on the public is not to claim that they are the *only* influence. In this light, the stubborn survival of traditional values in no way contradicts the notion that they are under attack, nor does the resilience of those values among most Americans prove that the media have played no role whatever in undermining them.

The limited and complex character of popular culture's effect on society at large is discussed in Part V of this book, with particular attention (pages 259–60) to the apparent inability of the entertainment establishment to bring the rest of the country in line with its point of view. This "evidence" of media impotence or irrelevance is, however, so easily distorted or misunderstood that it bears further examination here.

The example of television advertising provides the most useful model for understanding the way that repeated images and messages in popular entertainment can alter the way we think and act.

By now, most Americans are familiar with the intensive multimedia campaign for the Lexus automobile, yet how many of the hundreds of millions who have been exposed to this material will ever actually buy one of these cars? Given the substantial cost of this luxury vehicle, only the smallest fraction of all those who see the commercials will ultimately do what the media messages urge them to do and drive home from a dealer with a gleaming new Lexus.

Does this mean that the advertising campaign is useless and ineffective? Hardly. The purpose of most mass media efforts is to work a long-term, cumulative change in images and perceptions of a given product. The Lexus ads are not only intended to persuade some wealthy, middle-aged consumer to go out and buy the car as soon as possible, but they are also designed to plant the idea in younger viewers that this automobile is a desirable status symbol, a suitable trophy to crown future success. On the simplest level, the car commercials increase public awareness of a relatively new product, forcing us all to recognize that this once exotic import is an increasingly common fact of life on the highways of America.

Nearly all the available research suggests that the media sell violence and other forms of socially destructive behavior in much the same way they sell cars. Only a miniscule percentage of all pop culture consumers will be directly and immediately influenced to imitate what they see on screen, but for nearly everyone else Hollywood's messages help to redefine what constitutes fashionable or desirable conduct. If nothing else, repeated exposure to media images serves to alter our perceptions of the society in which we live and to gradually shape what we accept—and expect—from our fellow citizens.

The advertising model also serves to clarify one of the persistent and troubling questions about the impact of popular culture: if Hollywood's irresponsible obsessions contribute to the social problems around us, then why is it that even among those people who repeatedly patronize the most violent and degrading forms of mass entertainment, only a tiny handful ever become ax murderers or serial rapists?

The Lexus ad again provides an answer: repeated exposure to a television commercial doesn't mean you will automatically buy the car.

An advertising campaign needs to influence only a puny percentage of its potential viewers to make a big difference to the car company, and popular culture needs to change perceptions of only a small segment of its vast audience to make a significant difference to society. Even a marginal increase in the number of violent criminals can damage the quality of life—and intensify the climate of fear—for all law-abiding members of society.

As this book attempts to make clear, Hollywood's impact on society is subtle and gradual, not gross, dramatic, or instantly apparent. That is why responsible observers will focus on the question of cumulative impact, rather than singling out conspicuous but isolated examples of offensive material.

During more than 300 press interviews concerning this book and its message, I frequently have been asked to cite one particularly obnoxious example of the sort of motion picture or TV show that I find objectionable. I always refuse to comply with this request because what troubles me is no one movie, one television program, or one popular song. It is, rather, the hundreds of thousands of regularly repeated messages, the sheer weight of this material as it piles up over months and years of daily consumption, that should give us pause.

No single piece of entertainment represents a serious threat to our civilization, but the cumulative impact of this material (which assaults the average American more than thirty hours each week) plays an obvious and inevitable role in shaping the perceptions and values of this society.

More Diversity, Not Less

This distinction between a focus on individual instances of offensiveness and a general concern for the values of the popular culture is essential to understanding the conclusions reached in this book.

I never argue that Hollywood should altogether eliminate violent or profane or sexually graphic motion pictures, but I do believe that the industry currently makes too many of them. Sixty-one percent of all movie releases are rated "R" at the most recent count; to suggest that this percentage is much too high is not to insist that "R" movies have any place whatever in the movie mix. At the same time, "G"-rated family films now comprise only 2 percent of the titles released each year, offering parents precious few opportunities to enjoy an evening (or afternoon) at the theater with their children. Urging Hollywood to increase the range of these family-friendly alternatives does not amount to a demand that the industry only create movies like *Aladdin* and *Homeward Bound*. Diversity is one of the obvious glories of this society, and it is surely appropriate for the industry to provide very different sorts of entertainment for different audiences. In readjusting our media menu, the princes of the popular culture should strive for more diversity, not less.

Providing a more responsive—and responsible—range of pop-culture alternatives will not only serve the cause of decency and sanity, but will also advance the commercial interests of the entertainment industry.

One of the most startling and controversial aspects of the research for this book is the evidence it provides that Hollywood's obsession with sleaze and gore hurts rather than helps its pursuit of profit.

This contention received powerful confirmation in an independent analysis by one of the industry's most respected consulting firms just a few weeks after my work was published. According to a detailed report for subscribers from Paul Kagan Associates, Inc.: "There is an underexploited segment in the motion picture industry that could be costing the studios millions of dollars at the bottom line: family comedies and dramas that are rated 'PG' by the MPAA. Based on an analysis of 1,187 films released from 1984 through 1991 that played on at least one hundred screens during their peak, the most successful group of films were rated 'PG'. . . . Ironically, while 'R'-rated films are less likely to score big at the box office and are less profitable than films with other ratings . . . the percentage of 'R' raters in the mix has increased from 50.3 percent in 1989 to 58.2 percent in 1991. At the same time, the percentage of 'PG's fell from 22.4 percent in 1989 to 18.6 percent."

The Kagan report—precisely echoing data presented in Chapter 18 of this book—provides dramatic statistical support for a conclusion that tens of millions of moviegoers have reached on their own: Hollywood is out of touch with major portions of its potential audience. An industry that steadily increases the percentage of 'R'-rated films—despite their consistently weaker prospects at the box office—may not be malicious, but is most certainly dysfunctional.

"A Change of Heart"

In recent months, a number of the industry's more enlightened executives have begun to confront the deep-seated problems of their business and to launch attempts to reconnect with alienated elements of the mass audience.

In July 1992, Jeffrey Katzenberg, chairman of Walt Disney studios, addressed a national convention of video dealers in Las Vegas and told them: "When our critics charge that we show violence that is too graphic, depict sex that is too gratuitous, or feature lyrics that are too inflammatory, we're all too quick to offer the defense that it's only a movie, or piously invoke the First Amendment. The sad result is that more and more movies get made that are uninspiring or formulaic movies that are seemingly driven to offer nothing more than the cheap thrill. . . . Responsibility is the issue. We should not be distracted by talk of censorship, the First Amendment, or some cultural elite. Each of us in Hollywood has the opportunity to assume individual responsibility to create films that educate rather than denigrate, that shed light rather than dwell in darkness. . . ."

A month later, Peter Chernin, president of Fox Entertainment Group (and more recently named chairman of Twentieth Century Fox motion picture division), spoke to a cable convention on the "legitimate, genuine concerns millions of Americans have about what we're putting on television. The entertainment industry needs to be sensitive to community and individual values if we're going to be present in virtually every home in America."

Peter Tortorici, senior vice president of programming for CBS, also seemed to catch on to the new respect for heartland values. "We keep getting responses from viewers saying they want family entertainment," he told the *Los Angeles Times* in December 1992. "They want a show they can safely watch with their kids. They want a show that provides a family experience. Shows from the past, like 'The Waltons' and 'Highway to Heaven,' those shows haven't been around for a long time."

In addition to such sympathetic statements, the entertainment industry has begun to take a few concrete steps to recapture the confidence of some of its disillusioned consumers. *The New York Times* ran an encouraging holiday season article (November 12, 1992) under the headline "Hollywood Testing the Financial Value of Family Values," in which it listed an impressive array of new projects that the writer characterized as a "feel-good flood."

Four weeks later, at the other end of the continent, the *Los Angeles Times* filed its own report on the changing attitudes of the entertainment elite. "Hollywood is taking note of two recent studies," wrote Jane Galbraith, "one by film critic Michael Medved and the other by entertainment industry consulting firm Paul Kagan Associates, Inc.— positing that PG-13 and lower-rated features are more likely to turn a profit than those rated R." Galbraith reported the amazing news that even Arnold Schwarzenegger, the undisputed king of "R"-rated bloodbaths, had decided to tone down his new movie *The Last Action Hero* to qualify for a "PG-13" rating. Even more surprising, Paramount Pictures announced that Eddie Murphy agreed to restrain his dialogue in the upcoming *Beverly Hills Cop III* to avoid the "R" rating—which means that the irreverent star may have to master a whole new vocabulary.

On the television front, advocates for more responsible standards witnessed even more epochal developments: the three major networks sent an unprecedented letter to Senator Paul Simon promising to "limit the depiction of violence" in entertainment programs and outlined broad standards to avoid glamorizing excessive gore and suffering. The cable television industry quickly followed suit, issuing a statement that declared: "We believe that the gratuitous use of violence depicted as an easy and convenient solution to human problems is harmful to our industry and society. We therefore discourage and will strive to reduce the frequency of such exploitative uses of violence. . . ."

The early weeks of 1993 brought new and unmistakable evidence that the climate of Hollywood opinion has shifted decisively and conventional wisdom has changed. On March 9th, Mark Canton, Chairman of Columbia Pictures, told the leading convention of movie exhibitors, "Together, I think we can make the needed changes. If we

don't, this decade will be noted in the history books as the embarrassing legacy of what began as a great art form. We will be labeled 'the
decline of the empire' . . . any smart business person can see what we
must do—make more 'PG'-rated films."

Speaking at the same industry gathering, Jack Valenti, longtime
president of the Motion Picture Association of America, conceded,
"We have to increase the theater audience—we just have to do it"
while acknowledging that the best way to achieve that purpose would
be to "start pictures with less violence, less sensuality, and less raunchy
language."

The most perplexing question about this refreshing new attitude is
why the Hollywood establishment took so long to readjust its thinking
and to reach these painfully obvious conclusions.

In the months and years to come we will see whether these good
intentions actually pay off with discernible improvement in the content
of our popular culture. Of course, all the sympathetic statements by
Hollywood honchos could be written off as so many pious but meaningless platitudes, calculated attempts to appease the industry's critics
without making meaningful changes. Nevertheless, even the most cynical observers must agree that the new willingness to confront these
questions, and to discuss the entertainment industry's responsibilities
to the rest of us, represents a most welcome development.

Despite the intemperate anger and the personal abuse that this
book provoked in some quarters—most particularly from my fellow
film critics—I am grateful for whatever contribution my arguments
have made to facilitating this discussion. Contrary to dramatic over-
statement in some superheated press accounts of my role in the industry, I never planned to make my work the focus for some organized
crusade, but I will confess to considerable satisfaction that, in my own
small way, I seem to have been able to rattle the cage. Perhaps in the
years ahead we may yet witness the fulfillment of the hope W. H.
Auden expressed in his 1930 poem *Petition*, to—

Harrow the house of the dead; look shining at
New styles of architecture, a change of heart.

PART I

THE

POISON

FACTORY

1

A Sickness
in the Soul

Alienating the Audience

America's long-running romance with Hollywood is over.

As a nation, we no longer believe that popular culture enriches our lives. Few of us view the show business capital as a magical source of uplifting entertainment, romantic inspiration, or even harmless fun. Instead, tens of millions of Americans now see the entertainment industry as an all-powerful enemy, an alien force that assaults our most cherished values and corrupts our children. The dream factory has become the poison factory.

The leaders of the industry refuse to acknowledge this rising tide of alienation and hostility. They dismiss anyone who dares to question the impact of the entertainment they produce as a "right-wing extremist" or a "religious fanatic." They self-righteously assert their own right to unfettered free expression while condemning as "fringe groups" all organizations that plead for some sense of restraint or responsibility. In the process, Hollywood ignores the concerns of the overwhelming majority of the American people who worry over the destructive messages so frequently featured in today's movies, television, and popular music.

Dozens of recent studies demonstrate the public's deep disenchantment. In 1989, for instance, an Associated Press/Media General poll showed that 82 percent of a scientifically selected sample felt that movies contained too much violence; 80 percent found too much profanity; and 72 percent complained of too much nudity. By a ratio of more than three to one, the respondents believed that "overall quality" of movies had been "getting worse" as opposed to "getting better."

In 1990, a *Parents* magazine poll revealed similar attitudes toward television. Seventy-one percent of those surveyed rated today's TV as "fair, poor, or terrible." Seventy-two percent of this sample supported strict prohibitions against "ridiculing or making fun of religion" on the air, while 64 percent backed restrictions on "ridiculing or making fun of traditional values, such as marriage and motherhood." A Gallup Poll in 1991 turned up additional evidence of the public's suspicious and resentful attitude toward televised entertainment. Fifty-eight percent of Americans said that they are "offended frequently or occasionally" by prime-time programming; only three percent believed that TV portrayed "very positive" values.

This widespread concern over the messages of the popular culture stems from an increasingly common conviction that mass entertainment exacerbates our most serious social problems. A *Time*/CNN survey in 1989 showed that 67 percent believe that violent images in movies are "*mainly* to blame" for the national epidemic of teenage violence; 70 percent endorse "greater restraints on the showing of sex and violence" in feature films. A *Los Angeles Times* survey of the same year reported 63 percent who assert that television "encourages crime," while a 1991 *Newsweek*/Gallup Poll showed 68 percent who hold that today's movies have a "considerable" or "very great" effect in causing real-life violence.

"This Simply Cannot Go On"

The Hollywood establishment chooses to ignore these public attitudes, or else to downplay their significance. Surveying the severe financial problems that currently plague every component of the entertainment industry, the top decision-makers see nothing more than a temporary slump in business. In one typical comment, John Neal, senior vice president for marketing for United Artists Entertainment, optimistically declared: "All it takes is one big hit movie and suddenly the whole picture changes."

That "one big hit movie," however, will do nothing to end the alienation of an increasingly significant segment of the mainstream audience. The public's growing disillusionment with the content of the popular culture represents a long-term trend that won't suddenly disappear with the end of a recession, or the release of a new batch of lucky box-office blockbusters. The depth and breadth of the current crisis suggests fundamental flaws in the sort of entertainment that Hollywood, in all of its many manifestations, seeks to sell to the American people. That is why ventures as varied as home video and rock 'n' roll radio, feature films and prime-time television, are all suffering similar and simultaneous setbacks.

Consider, for example, the baleful situation with the three major television networks. In the last fifteen years they have lost a third of their nightly audience—some 30 million viewers. As a result, their cumulative profits have sunk from $800 million in 1984 to $400 million by 1988, to less than zero in 1991. Business analysts advance many theories for this disastrous falloff, but even television insiders consider that much of the public's disenchantment relates directly to the quality of the programs. "The networks have lost audiences because they've lost touch with the American viewer," according to Gene DeWitt, head of a prestigious New York media consulting firm interviewed by *Time* in November 1990. "They haven't delivered programs that viewers want to watch."

Syndicated columnist Mike Royko spoke for many Americans when he recently declared, "I enjoy TV trash as much as the next slob. But the quality of truly trashy trash has declined." He went on to explain that of the top seventy-one shows in the Nielsen Ratings, "there isn't even one that I now watch regularly." His fellow columnist Cal Thomas announced his resolution at the end of 1990 to give up watching the networks altogether. "They have not only abandoned my values," he wrote, "they now have sunk to the sewer level, dispensing the foulest of smells that resemble the garbage I take to the curb twice a week."

Many of the major networks' lost viewers have fled to the new Fox Network, or to the abundance of alternatives on cable TV, but these additional options have done nothing to increase the public's approval of what it is watching. A survey commissioned by the National Association of Broadcasters found that a growing number of households with TV sets "feel increasing dissatisfaction" and that "the majority of viewers believe television is a negative influence."

One reflection of viewer restlessness is the tendency toward "grazing" in their nightly viewing—using remote controls to switch stations in the middle of a program. According to a major survey for *Channels* magazine in 1988, 48.5 percent of all viewers regularly change programs during a show—and nearly 60 percent of viewers in the crucial eighteen-to-thirty-four age group. "Grazing is by definition a sign of dissatisfaction," explained James Webster, professor of communications at Northwestern University. "Viewers know what is going to happen, and they wonder what they're missing on some other channel." According to the Gallup Poll, in 1974, 46 percent of Americans rated watching television as their favorite way of spending an evening; by 1990, that number had fallen to 24 percent.

This diminished enthusiasm for the popular culture and its products has even infected the huge teenage audience for popular music—an audience never before noted for its finicky taste or searching discernment. Overall sales of records, cassettes, and CDs plummeted a disastrous 11 percent in the first six months of 1991, and signs of restlessness and frustration turned up everywhere in the music business. Bob Krasnow, chairman of Elektra Entertainment, told *Billboard* magazine: "In 1991, the record business finds itself dangerously close to creative stagnation. All the formulas have been played out." Meanwhile, numerous articles asked "Is rock dead?" while all measures of public response suggested that this once robust art form was, at best, on life-support systems.

For instance, rock 'n' roll's share of the music industry's total take slipped from 46.2 percent in 1988 to 37.4 percent in 1990. Just weeks before his death in October 1991, the legendary concert promoter Bill Graham observed that "until now, rock was recession proof . . . but we have just gone through the worst six months ever in the rock concert industry." Attendance at rock concerts across the nation plunged by more than 30 percent compared to the previous year.

At the same time, the "Top 40" radio format continued its long-term slide in the Arbitron radio ratings, abandoned by even those teenagers who have always provided its core of support. In 1991 an unprecedented 56 percent of the teenage radio audience preferred listening to other formats; as a result, country and western for the first time passed Top 40 in overall popularity. In fact, the steady growth in the audience for country music, with its earthy and unpretentious attempts to connect with the everyday concerns of Middle America, provided one of the few bright spots in the general gloom of the music business. Country star Garth Brooks confounded all expectations by creating 1991's top-selling album, *Ropin' the Wind,* which is expected to reach sales of more than 7 million units. Music industry analyst Bob Lefsetz, publisher of *The Lefsetz Letter,* declares, "Country music, unlike the rest of popular music, is talking about real lives. About real people. These artists are telling you what they feel. They're making honest records, and that's why their music is connecting with the public."

Feature films, by contrast, are connecting with a shrinking percentage of the American people. Sharply increased ticket prices and the controversial content of recent films have combined to make moviegoing a form of entertainment that appeals primarily to an elite audience. According to 1991 figures from the Motion Picture Association of America, 27 percent of those who have attended college describe themselves as "frequent" moviegoers, but only 11 percent of those who failed to complete high school place themselves in that category. More significantly, 45 percent of *all* Americans are identified as "infrequent" moviegoers (less than twice a year), and a full 33 percent declared that they *never* go to the movies. Several other recent studies (Gallup, Gordon Black Corporation, Barna Research Group, Media General) show similar percentages (ranging from 35 up to 45 percent) who stay away from motion pictures altogether.

The absence of these potential patrons has devastated the movie business. At the height of the usually prosperous summer season, ticket sales plunged more than 31 percent in 1991, bringing the feature film business its worst August in twenty-three years. Even video rentals, whose seemingly inexorable rise has played such a significant role in keeping struggling studios afloat, declined 6 percent during the year. Industry analysts reported that poor audience response to the new feature films had begun to rub off on the home video business, producing a new wariness on the part of prospective renters.

An upsurge in ticket sales during the holiday season generated some reassuring headlines about the movie business, but year-end reckonings offered no real grounds for joy. According to figures from *Variety*, 1991 brought only 960 million motion picture admissions—the lowest total in fifteen years. The first months of 1992 confirmed the disastrous long-term trend: according to Exhibitor Relations Co., a widely used box-office data tracking firm, movie grosses between January 1 and April 15, 1992, fell an additional 9 percent from their already dismal performance of the previous year. This meant reduced income for the major studios of some $200 million. During the usually busy Presidents' Day weekend, *Variety* reported that movie admissions fell a spectacular 30 percent from 1991.

As a result of the shrinking movie audience, the precarious economic situation of the major studios began attracting headlines of its own. Two of the industry's most important and respected production companies, Orion and MGM, have recently frozen their release and production schedules as they teeter on the verge of financial collapse. Cannon Films and Weintraub Entertainment Group, both of them well-financed and high-flying independents as recently as a few years ago, have now closed down altogether. Even Carolco Pictures, producer of the year's top hit, *Terminator 2,* found itself forced to cut production and to lay off one-fourth of its employees as part of its December 1991 retrenchment plan.

Peter Dekom, the universally respected entertainment lawyer and show business analyst, describes the current condition of the movie industry as "a catastrophe." In a widely circulated September 1991 memo entitled "Chicken Little Was Right," he concludes that "We in the industry are all wondering how we keep our life-styles together, because each and every one of us knows this simply cannot go on."

Sleaze and Self-Indulgence

Even without the pronouncements of experts, ordinary Americans understand that Hollywood is in serious trouble. As a point of reference, ask yourself a simple question: when was the last time that you heard someone that you know say that movies—or TV, or popular music, for that matter—were better than ever? On the other hand, how recently have you listened to complaints about the dismal quality of the movies at the multiplex, the shows on the tube, or the songs on the radio?

In recent years, not even Jack Valenti, the well-paid cheerleader for the Motion Picture Association, can claim with a straight face that the movie business is scaling new artistic heights. David Puttnam, Oscar-winning producer of *Chariots of Fire* and former chairman of Columbia Pictures, reports, "As you move around Hollywood in any reasonably sophisticated group, you'll find it quite difficult to come across people who are proud of the movies that are being made." In December 1991, industry journalist Grover Lewis went even further when he declared in the pages of the *Los Angeles Times:* "The movies, which many of us grew up regarding as the co-literature of the age, have sunk to an abysmal low unimaginable only a few years ago."

In fact, nearly everyone associated with the industry acknowledges the obvious collapse in the caliber of today's films, and at the same time manages to blame someone else for the disastrous situation.

Jeffrey Katzenberg, production chief at the beleaguered Walt Disney Studios, shrugs his shoulders and cites inscrutable Higher Powers. "We're in the hands of the movie gods," he told the *Los Angeles Times,* "who will either shine down and give us good fortune or not. . . . That's part of what keeps people going in this business—the magical and mysterious nature of it."

Producer Gene Kirkwood (*Rocky*) offers a less "magical and mysterious" explanation for Hollywood's troubles, pointing his finger at the writers. "When you look at the writing that's around today, most of which is not very good, it makes you want to go back to the old films," he explains. One of the writers of those old films, Oscar-winner I. A. L. Diamond (*The Apartment*) in turn cites "the lawyers and agents who run the studios, and the subliterate subteenagers who form the bulk of the audience" for creating the present problems. Julia Phillips, the outspoken outcast who produced *The Sting,* specifically accuses Mike Ovitz, head of the Creative Artists Agency, who "first ruined movies, then sold out to the Japanese."

Film critic Michael Sragow manages to identify an even more nefarious and omnipotent culprit, blaming the industry's whole sorry mess on an over-the-hill Warner Brothers star who actually abandoned the movie business more than twenty years ago. Asserting that "American movies are still reaping the harvest of Ronald Reagan's reign of mediocrity and escapism," Sragow concluded in 1990 that it was actually the former President who "ate Hollywood's brain."

While searching for scapegoats, the entertainment industry ignores the obvious: that Hollywood's crisis is, at its very core, a crisis of values. It's not "mediocrity and escapism" that leave audiences cold, but sleaze and self-indulgence. What troubles people about the popular culture isn't the competence with which it's shaped, but the messages it sends, the view of the world it transmits.

Hollywood no longer reflects—or even respects—the values of most American families. On many of the important issues in contemporary life, popular entertainment seems to go out of its way to challenge conventional notions of decency. For example:

• Our fellow citizens cherish the institution of marriage and consider religion an important priority in life; but the entertainment industry promotes every form of sexual adventurism and regularly ridicules religious believers as crooks or crazies.

• In our private lives, most of us deplore violence and feel little sympathy for the criminals who perpetrate it; but movies, TV, and popular music all revel in graphic brutality, glorifying vicious and sadistic characters who treat killing as a joke.

• Americans are passionately patriotic, and consider themselves enormously lucky to live here; but Hollywood conveys a view of the nation's history, future, and major institutions that is dark, cynical, and often nightmarish.

• Nearly all parents want to convey to their children the importance of self-discipline, hard work, and decent manners; but the entertainment media celebrate vulgar behavior, contempt for all authority, and obscene language—which is inserted even in "family fare" where it is least expected.

As a working film critic, I've watched this assault on traditional values for more than a decade. Not only have I endured six or seven movies every week, year after year, but I've also received a steady stream of letters from moviegoers who are upset by one or another of Hollywood's excesses. At times, they blame me for failing to warn them ardently enough about avoiding a particular film; in other cases they are writing to express their pent-up frustration with an industry that seems increasingly out of control and out of touch. My correspondents frequently use words such as "disgusting" or "pathetic" to describe the sorry state of today's films. In 1989 a young woman from Westport, Connecticut, expressed these sentiments with memorable clarity. "The problem is that whenever I take a chance and go against my better judgment and venture back into a movie theater," she wrote, "I always feel like a worse person when I come out. I'm embarrassed for the people who made this trash, and I'm embarrassed for myself. It's like watching the stuff that I've just watched has made me a smaller human being. Isn't that sad?"

It *is* terribly sad, especially in view of the technical brilliance that turns up in so many of Hollywood's most recent productions. When people express their disappointment at the generally low level of contemporary films, they seldom indict the camera work, the editing, the set design, or even the acting. In fact, these components of moviemaking have reached a level of consistent competence—even artistry—that would be the envy of of Hollywood's vaunted Golden Age. I regularly marvel at gorgeous and glowing visual images, captured on screen in the service of some pointless and heartless waste of celluloid, or sympathize with an ensemble of superby talented performers, acting their hearts out, and trying to make the most of empty material that is in no way worthy of them. If Robert De Niro and Dustin Hoffman have failed to inspire the sort of devoted and consistent following once enjoyed by Jimmy Stewart or John Wayne, it is not because they are less capable as actors. What ails today's films has nothing to do with the prowess or professionalism of the filmmakers. The true sickness is in the soul.

"A Performance Piece by Michael Jackson"

This heartbreaking combination of dazzling technique wedded to a puerile and degrading purpose recently shocked the country in one of the most heavily hyped entertainment "events" in history: the world premiere of the music video "Black or White," from Michael Jackson's album *Dangerous*.

On November 14, 1991, Fox Network, MTV, and Black Entertainment Television simultaneously broadcast the first showing of this eleven-minute extravaganza, which had been created by director John Landis at an unprecedented cost of $7.2 million. To prepare the public for the momentous occasion of the televised premiere, Epic Records released the song (without the accompanying images) to radio stations just two days in advance. Within twenty-four hours, "Black or White," described by the record company as "a rock 'n' roll dance song about racial harmony," had been added to the playlists of 96 percent of America's 237 Top 40 radio stations. This broke the previous record for a first-day release—94 percent—which had been set by Madonna's "Like a Prayer" in 1989.

On the fateful Thursday night of the televised premiere, an estimated 40 million individuals tuned in—helping Fox Network score the highest ratings of any night in its five-year history. To insure maximum exposure to the children and preteens who make up such an important part of Michael Jackson's core audience, the video featured well-advertised cameo appearances by both TV favorite Bart Simpson and diminutive movie star Macaulay (*Home Alone*) Culkin.

The video begins, in fact, with a tender domestic scene between Culkin and George Wendt (of TV's "Cheers"), playing his irritable dad. Macaulay is upstairs in his room, happily listening to music, when his father orders him to turn it down, threatening the child with a wagging finger. In response, the adorable boy hauls some huge amplifiers and speakers downstairs, tells Dad to "Eat this!" and proceeds to blast the music at such an ear-shattering level that he literally blows his parent through the roof.

The video proceeds to a display of a dizzying succession of more or less random images, including dancing Cossacks in the Kremlin, whooping Native Americans in feathers and paint, and Michael and a partner hoofing their way through hundreds of speeding cars on a busy freeway. The most memorable sequence involves a series of fifteen magical transformations in the course of little more than a minute, using the costly computer-generated special effect called "morphing" and made popular by *Terminator 2*.

The most troublesome transformation comes near the end of this incoherent epic, as the song concludes and the soundtrack falls silent except for a selection of jungle growls, screeches, and roars. A stalking black panther turns miraculously into Michael Jackson as we've never seen him before—attempting a feeble impersonation of a sulky, menacing, inner-city tough guy, tap-dancing down a wet, deserted street. As if to prove his manliness, Michael grabs repeatedly at his crotch, with close-ups showing our hero pulling the zipper of his pants suggestively up and down. *Entertainment Weekly* magazine later counted thirteen instances in which the superstar touched his "private parts," and at one point he performs an exaggerated simulation of masturbation. Finally, this inane episode reaches its creepy climax, as Jackson picks up a garbage can to shatter a store window, and uses a crowbar to savagely bust up a parked car, for no apparent reason whatever. As director John Landis helpfully explained in an interview prior to the premiere broadcast: "The epilogue is really a performance piece by Michael Jackson that can stand totally on its own. It's essentially an improvisation of Michael's."

The national television audience failed to appreciate that improvisation. Immediately following the telecast, switchboards at MTV, Fox Network, and all the network affiliates lit up with outraged complaints. One Fox official commented: "In all my years of television, I never saw anything like it. We couldn't believe the volume, and we couldn't believe the intensity. It was like a tidal wave." A spokesman for Jackson's production company confirmed that negative feedback was coming at them "from all directions."

Within twenty-four hours, the chagrined superstar agreed to delete the controversial four-minute epilogue from all future versions of his video and issued an elaborate apology to his fans. "It upsets me to think that 'Black or White' could influence any child or adult to destructive behavior, either sexual or violent," his statement read. "I've always tried to be a good role model and therefore have made these changes to avoid any possibility of affecting any individual's behavior. I deeply regret any pain or hurt that the final segment of 'Black or White' has caused children, their parents, or any other viewers."

Fox Network issued a lame apology of its own, admitting that "based on calls we've received, the strong symbolism used in one sequence overshadowed the film's message about racial harmony. We apologize to anyone who interpreted that sequence as sexually suggestive or violent and was offended."

It is impossible to imagine how anyone could possibly interpret the sequence as anything *other* than "sexually suggestive or violent"—after all, toying with your fly in intense close-up and using a crowbar to shatter a parked car amount to the sort of "symbolism" that is hardly ambiguous.

The unanswerable question about this entire affair is how the experienced executives at the network, the record company, and Jackson's PR agency could seem to be so sincerely surprised by the public's outraged response. Did it never occur to them that people might find it more than a bit distasteful to use Macaulay Culkin and Bart Simpson to promote a video freak show that unequivocally encouraged vandalism and crotch-grabbing as forms of self-expression? With so many tens of millions of dollars riding on the outcome, with Michael's album setting all-time records for both its production and promotional costs, how could they afford to be so blind?

The lessons of this astonishing affair mirror three of the major arguments that I am advancing in this book.

First, the Michael Jackson fiasco shows that some of the most powerful, highly paid, and widely respected titans in Hollywood are hopelessly out of touch with the public they are trying to reach. They don't begin to understand the values of the average American family, or the special concerns of the typical parents who worry about unwholesome influences on their children.

Second, the Jackson affair clearly demonstrates that the American people understand that media images influence real-life behavior. The entertainment industry may deny its own impact, but ordinary citizens know better. They know perfectly well that if tens of millions of kids watch repeatedly as Michael Jackson gleefully smashes a car with a crowbar, then their own car is that much more likely to get smashed someday—and their own kids are that much more likely to try some smashing. The logic of this assumption is so obvious and inescapable that only the most shameless entertainment executives and their hired academic experts would even attempt to argue against it.

Third, the outcome of the "Black or White" controversy proves that an outraged audience can force changes on even the most powerful figures in show business. As a result of the spontaneous public outcry, Michael Jackson and his associates agreed to the uncomfortable and expensive expedient of cutting four questionable minutes from their eleven-minute video. Similar pressure, applied in a sustained and coordinated manner on a range of issues in American entertainment, could alter the entire direction of the popular culture.

Common Interests and Common Attitudes

Unfortunately, the prevailing attitude toward Hollywood recalls Mark Twain's celebrated comment about the weather: everybody talks about it, but nobody does anything about it. In the case of the entertainment industry, most people recognize its powerful influence on their lives, but they assume that there is nothing they can do to change its course or reduce its impact.

That is not true, because the popular culture is hardly a force of nature, or an immutable aspect of the atmosphere around us. It is a man-made product, generated by a surprisingly small community of vulnerable and insecure human beings. That community has reconsidered its values and modified its priorities several times in the past, and future changes are not only possible, they are inevitable.

In that context, it's important to remember that the term "Hollywood" most often describes an industry, not a place. Of the ten major movie production companies, only one of them, Paramount, is actually located within the geographic boundaries of the sadly seedy district of Los Angeles that is officially designated "Hollywood." The rest of them are scattered throughout Southern California, while maintaining important "branch offices" in New York.

Their business is by no means limited to making motion pictures: all of the "majors" are connected to massive entertainment conglomerates that own everything from television networks to theme parks, from book publishers to gigantic record companies. Partially as a result of this concentration of show business resources, the dividing lines that once separated the various entertainment endeavors have never been so easily blurred. Distinguished movie directors regularly devote their talents to creating "music videos"; these productions in turn are featured on a round-the-clock television network devoted to promoting new hit records. In past years, major motion picture stars tried to avoid appearing on television, except for occasional high-profile specials; today, even the most critically acclaimed figures in the movie business will attempt serious and ambitious projects for TV. While some distinctions in emphasis and style still apply to the different branches of the business, it is now more appropriate than ever before to discuss "Hollywood" as one all-encompassing industry, united by common interests and common attitudes.

Feature film production remains the key to understanding those attitudes because it is still the most prestigious expression of the popular culture. Established TV stars and popular singers regularly dream of making the transition to motion pictures not because they can earn more money that way (they usually can't), but because they are far more likely to be taken seriously as creative artists if they develop movie careers. Garry Marshall reached a much larger audience with his television series "Happy Days" than with all his feature films combined, but it is those films (including *Nothing in Common* and *Pretty Woman*) that won him deeper respect from the critics and his peers. By common consent, the movies represent Hollywood's·cutting edge, and provide the best perspective for understanding the industry's prospects and problems.

A *Traitor to the Industry*

In examining those prospects and problems, this book addresses some crucial questions concerning the current crisis in the popular culture:

- What are the values which today's movies, TV, and popular music transmit to America and to the world?
- How are Hollywood's messages affecting our society and our children?
- What are the underlying motivations of the moguls and creative artists who control the media culture?
- What can be done to make the entertainment industry more responsible and responsive to the public it is supposed to serve?

By asking these questions, and providing honest answers to the best of my abilities, this book will undoubtedly outrage a heavy majority of show business professionals. I am painfully aware that one of the consequences of its·publication will be my potentially permanent estrangement from some of the thoughtful and well-intentioned people in Hollywood I have been proud to call my friends. In their view, I am a traitor to an industry that has always been good to me, and the criticisms that I raise here are misguided, offensive, even dangerous.

A few months ago, I showed an outline for this book to a close friend who works for one of the major studios. He strongly urged me to drop the project and warned of the outcome if I refused to do so. "I hope you realize," he told me, "that if you insist on going forward with something like this, you're going to become the most hated man in Hollywood."

That is a designation I am willing to accept, if the ensuing controversy will serve to open minds, and to encourage both producers and consumers of popular entertainment to examine its content with fresh eyes.

In any event, I could no longer ignore destructive trends that seemed increasingly obvious to me, or continue to focus exclusively on reviews of individual films while pretending not to notice that Hollywood's "big picture" had grown so much darker and more ominous. No matter how elegant and diverting the passing parade, it's time to step forward to suggest that the Entertainment Emperors are wearing no clothes.

Whatever my doubts about the industry, I continue to cherish occasional new films and to feel a sense of vicarious exultation whenever a filmmaker, in defiance of all odds and expectations, manages to create something of value and beauty. Whenever I go to a screening, I surrender myself to that thrilling and pregnant moment when the lights go down, leading to that on-screen enchantment that novelist Theodore Roszak writes about so well: "I see it as a softly focused square of light, and see myself dazzled and aroused, seated in the embracing darkness, savoring the enticement."

Like all moviegoers, I still savor the enticement, and hope that this appalling but amazing industry will regain its bearings and once again merit the affection of its audience.

A Bias
for the Bizarre

One Small Skirmish

The publicist promised me I would love the "very special" film with the odd and complicated title.

"We showed it to some of the critics in New York, and they just went nuts over it!" she crowed over the phone. "I'm ready to make you a bet that this one will make it to your Best of the Year list!"

Publicists are paid to wax enthusiastic over their movies, but this sort of praise went above and beyond the call of duty. I felt intrigued enough by her descriptions of the new release to ask whether I should consider bringing my wife, Diane, along with me to the screening.

This isn't a simple question, since Diane is notoriously squeamish about movie violence. As a clinical psychologist, she happens to believe it's bad for anyone to watch graphic gore on screen. More importantly, she feels an intense personal revulsion whenever guts are splattered, or limbs are severed, in vivid images ten feet high, backed up by jaw-rattling THX sound. This allergy to brutality means that Diane seldom accompanies me to press screenings, since nearly all the films I have to review contain elements that she would prefer to miss.

This time, however, the publicist promised me I had nothing to worry about. "It *is* a very dark comedy," she admitted, "but it's lots of fun—terribly witty and terribly sexy. I really think your wife will enjoy it."

With this assurance in mind, I managed to persuade my skeptical spouse to come along to the screening of Peter Greenaway's much-heralded epic, *The Cook, the Thief, His Wife and Her Lover,* in the spring of 1990. Almost immediately after the lights went down, I knew we were in trouble.

The opening scene takes place in the parking lot of an imposing restaurant, lit by ghostly neon, where a pack of stray dogs snarl over bloody hunks of rotten meat. Two refrigerator trucks pull up, loaded with dead fish and hanging pig carcasses, respectively. Attention then focuses on a group of foppishly dressed thugs who tear the clothes off a struggling, terrified victim in order to smear his naked body with excrement. They force filth into his mouth and rub it in his eyes, then pin him to the ground while the leader of the band proceeds to urinate, gleefully, all over him.

The "fun" proceeds in much the same spirit, for two all-but-unbearable hours. We see sex in a toilet stall, deep kisses and tender embraces administered to a bloody and mutilated cadaver, a woman whose cheek is pierced with a fork, a shrieking and weeping nine-year-old boy whose navel is hideously carved from his body, a restaurant patron whose face is scalded by a tureen of vomit-colored soup, and an edifying vision of two naked, middle-aged lovers writhing ecstatically in the back of a truck filled with rotting, maggot-infested garbage. The grand finale of the film shows the main character slicing off—and swallowing—a piece of carefully seasoned, elegantly braised human corpse in the most graphic scene of cannibalism ever portrayed in motion pictures. There is, in short, unrelieved ugliness, horror, and depravity at every turn.

Naturally, the critics loved it.

I could hardly blame the film's publicist for misleading me (and my long-suffering wife), since so many of my critical colleagues enthusiastically applauded this unspeakable film.

For instance, Caryn James of *The New York Times* declared that *The Cook, the Thief, His Wife and Her Lover* was "something profound and extremely rare: a work so intelligent and powerful that it evokes our best emotions." She went on to urge her readers to ignore the controversy over the "X" rating originally attached to this worthy work, since "*The Cook* has nothing sensational, pornographic or disreputable about it."

The two best-known critics on national television called the picture "provocative," and awarded their coveted "Two Thumbs Up" endorsement. Richard Corliss of *Time* magazine went even further, piling on the adjectives and hailing the film as "exemplary, exciting, extraordinary" as well as "splendid, meticulous, extravagant." He concluded his rapturous review by declaring "this movie rates an X as in excellent."

For me, this sort of critical praise proved even more disturbing than the movie itself. The film just made me sick, but the reviews made me angry. The glowing notices for *The Cook* gave prospective moviegoers no honest indication of the intensity of the horrors they would experience if they went to see the film. My partner and I had initially thought that we'd ignore the picture on "Sneak Previews," the weekly show we host on PBS, because we felt that discussing it on the air would only provide additional publicity. Jeffrey Lyons and I frequently disagree on the movies we review, but we certainly saw eye-to-eye on *The Cook, the Thief, His Wife and Her Lover*, and we wanted to avoid contributing in any way to the movie's success.

Two weeks after the picture's release, however, we changed our plans. When some of our esteemed colleagues actually began using words like "splendid" and "profound" to describe this putrid, pointless, and pretentious piece of filth, we decided that we had to respond in public.

The result was a special segment on our show in the course of which I violated one of the great unwritten rules of the so-called critical community: I not only attacked the film, but I also spoke harshly of my fellow critics. I objected in particular to the tendency to characterize this picture as a "raunchy black comedy," or a "searing social commentary," while downplaying, or ignoring altogether, the brutal and nightmarish content that director Greenaway served up with such sadistic abandon. I clearly displayed my irritation when I declared: "When you look at the great reviews for a loathesome little picture like this one, you can understand why so many people don't trust film critics anymore. Sometimes I think that they're absolutely right not to trust us, and I actually feel ashamed to be part of this profession."

After breaking ranks in this way on national TV, I encountered a minor—and entirely predictable—firestorm concerning my comments. The day after our broadcast, one of my colleagues called me at home and berated me for acting like an "arrogant and irresponsible demagogue." Other friends agreed that I had gone too far, while our show received several letters of complaint. One note from a viewer in Oregon eloquently summarized these protests: "I was angered and disgusted by your unfair and savage attack on *The Cook, the Thief, His Wife and Her Lover*," she wrote, and then went on, revealingly: "Though I have not seen the film, I certainly plan to do so and your review was way out of line. The one thing we don't need is a Jesse Helms clone on PBS. . . . If you are so full of old-fashioned, judgmental, right-winged bigotry, then that is your problem but you have no right to pollute the airwaves with your narrow-minded stupidity. . . . Your job is to tell us if a movie is skillful or not, but please stay off your moralistic high horse and keep to the business of reviewing movies."

This letter represents just one very small skirmish in the "culture wars" currently raging in our society, but it forcefully reveals what those wars are all about. My correspondent is saying that it's fine for me to speak about a film being in or out of focus, about sloppy or competent editing, about a convincing or unconvincing performance, but heaven forbid that I should ever, under any circumstances, address its moral or intellectual content. According to this line of reasoning, I must never attempt to evaluate the messages that a film is sending to the moviegoing public. In other words, the one aspect of a work of art that is always off-limits for a critic to consider is the one aspect that matters most.

This is the very nature of the cultural battle before us. It is, in its essence, a war against standards. It is a war against judgment. In fact, its proponents insist that the worst insult you can offer someone today is to suggest that he or she is judgmental.

One of the symptoms of the corruption and collapse of our popular culture is the insistence that we examine only the surface of any piece of art or entertainment. The politically correct, properly liberal notion is that we should never dig deeper—to consider whether a given work is true, or good, or spiritually nourishing—or to evaluate its impact on society at large. We routinely focus on superficial skill and slick salesmanship, while ignoring the more important issues of soul and substance. In the process, we have abandoned traditional measures of beauty and worth, accepting the ability to shock as a replacement for the old ability to inspire.

"Incompatible Worldviews"

Our ability even to address these questions has disappeared, along with all consensus on the purposes and boundaries of mass entertainment. The only area in which today's cultural combatants seem able to agree is in acknowledging the severity and significance of the current conflict.

"We are in the midst of a culture war," declared Michael Hudson, executive vice president of the liberal (and Hollywood-funded) lobbying group People for the American Way. "The extremist right-wing political movement no longer has the evil of communism to fight. So they look to other fields, including putting on economic pressure to boycott television programming." Jack Valenti, longtime president of the Motion Picture Association of America, similarly characterized criticism of Hollywood's product as a dire threat to our most precious liberties. "What we cannot do is allow zealots or self-anointed special groups who claim divine vision to intimidate us or coerce us or frighten us," he proclaimed in his podium-pounding 1991 "State of the Industry" speech to four thousand movie exhibitors. "Too many brave young men have died on battlefields, and are dying now, to protect, defend and preserve our right of choice." (In other words, the blood of heroes has consecrated Hollywood's inalienable right to continue producing films like A Nightmare on Elm Street, Part VI.) Mary Schmidt Campbell, New York City's commissioner of cultural affairs, agrees that basic issues are at stake. "This is no longer a fight about obscenity," she told a cheering Washington crowd that gathered in 1990 for "Cultural Advocacy Day." "This is about the very principles of democracy and the fundamental values of this country."

The other side of the political spectrum views the struggle over cultural issues with similarly ferocious intensity. According to conservative congressman Henry Hyde (R.-Illinois), America is already "involved in a Kulturkampf . . . a war between cultures and a war about the meaning of culture." Columnist (and erstwhile presidential candidate) Pat Buchanan, never noted for his gentle or understated rhetorical style, announced that "the arts crowd . . . is engaged in a cultural struggle to root out the old America of family, faith and flag, and re-create society in a pagan image." Dr. James C. Dobson, the popular Christian psychologist whose "Focus on the Family" radio show airs on twelve hundred stations, concluded: "Nothing short of a great Civil War of Values rages today throughout North America. Two sides with vastly differing and incompatible worldviews are locked in a bitter conflict that permeates every level of society. Bloody battles are being fought on a thousand fronts, both inside and outside of government."

In the face of such apocalyptic pronouncements, it's important to keep the ongoing warfare in proper perspective. This means acknowledging at the outset that the shape of the battle is not symmetrical. While one side indeed claims to represent a coherent worldview, derived from several millennia of Judeo-Christian civilization, the other insists that it is fighting only for "freedom of expression," with no other ideological agenda. In these terms, the struggle in Hollywood is not so much a fight between two competing sets of values as it is a dispute over whether it is appropriate to impose values at all on the creation or evaluation of entertainment.

For instance, those who defend contemporary rap music, with its extravagantly brutal and obscene lyrics, do not generally condone the conduct described in the songs; they suggest, rather, that it is inappropriate to judge such material on a moral basis. By the same token, producers of movies or TV shows that seem to glorify violent or promiscuous behavior do not assert that watching these entertainments is actually good for you. Instead, they maintain that the images they create amount to a "value-neutral" experience, with no real impact on the viewer and no underlying influence on society. The apologists for the entertainment industry seldom claim that Hollywood's messages are beneficial; they argue, rather, that those messages don't matter.

As producer David Puttnam observes: "What I find fascinating is that the colleagues in my industry whom I work with, many of whom are absolutely first-class people, don't want to get into this type of debate. They don't really want to acknowledge the awesome responsibilities that the medium brings."

A Preference for the Perverse

Hollywood's refusal to confront the substance or the consequences of the entertainment it creates has produced a pervasive emphasis on form over content. The prevailing notion is that a piece of work must be judged by some higher standard of excellence, some objective measure of technical brilliance, rather than an evaluation of the attitudes it conveys.

According to this line of reasoning, a hit song that glorifies gang rape and the genital mutilation of women still deserves praise for its "infectious beat" and "vivid imagery." Showing a human head exploding on screen is also considered admirable—so long as the brains are splattered in artful slow motion, and the special effects are chillingly realistic. By the same token, critics wax rhapsodic about *The Cook, the Thief, His Wife and Her Lover,* because its images of necrophilia, cannibalism, and child abuse are presented with such zest and conviction.

The entertainment industry's leading arbiters of taste regularly applaud achievements of stylistic elegance but ghastly content. In the remake of *Cape Fear,* America's most acclaimed director (Martin Scorsese) created an utterly gratuitous scene in which one of our most distinguished actors (Robert De Niro) bites off the cheek of his victim while he holds her pinned to a bed, then spits the wedge of flesh contemptuously back toward what remains of the young woman's bloody, mutilated face. In *The Silence of the Lambs,* another lavishly gifted director (Jonathan Demme) devoted his considerable talents to bringing to life two serial killers: one of whom eats, and the other of whom skins, his victims.

Neither of these stylistically brilliant films served any discernible artistic purpose beyond horrifying and titillating the moviegoing audience, and yet both emerged as critical favorites for 1991. These brutal and ultimately exploitative motion pictures received innumerable honors as examples of the highest achievements to which today's movie industry can aspire. Months before *The Silence of the Lambs* swept the Oscars, the New York Film Critics Circle awarded this genuinely horrifying film an unprecedented four major prizes (for Best Film, Best Director, Best Actor, and Best Actress). Named as runner-up film in three of those categories (Best Film, Best Director, and Best Actor) was *My Own Private Idaho*—an idiosyncratic (but beautifully photographed) account of two cocaine-snorting, homeless homosexual hustlers who peddle their bodies in order to stay alive on the sordid streets.

Even the Academy of Motion Picture Arts and Sciences, guardian of the most sacred and self-important of all Hollywood traditions, has begun providing encouragement to the industry's peculiar tendency to focus its most intense artistry on the most degraded aspects of human nature. At the Oscar ceremonies of April 1991, the Academy concentrated almost exclusively on sordid and detestable characters when it came to handing out its coveted acting awards. Kathy Bates won the Best Actress Oscar for playing a sadistic psycho who kidnaps and tortures her "favorite writer" (James Caan) and who, in the climactic scene in *Misery,* cripples him for life by shattering his ankles with a sledgehammer. Best Actor went to Jeremy Irons in *Reversal of Fortune,* for his eerily effective portrayal of Klaus von Bulow, the cold-blooded and adulterous aristocrat accused of twice attempting to murder his heiress wife. Joe Pesci in *GoodFellas* won the Oscar for Best Supporting Actor for playing the most loathsome loser of them all—a demented, dangerous, and sadistic Mafioso who kills more for pleasure than for profit.

The Oscar nominations of February 1992 (for movies released in the course of 1991) again displayed the Academy's ferocious fascination with the dark side. Consider the anointed candidates for Best Actor: three of them played murderous psychotics (Anthony Hopkins in *The Silence of the Lambs,* Robert De Niro in *Cape Fear,* and Warren Beatty in *Bugsy*); one of them played a homeless, delusional psychotic (Robin Williams in *The Fisher King*); and one of them played a good, old-fashioned, manic-depressive neurotic (Nick Nolte in *The Prince of Tides*) who is the product of a viciously dysfunctional family background. On the industry's glittering "night of nights," this collection of decidedly downbeat antiheroes is placed before the public as the representatives of the most noble and notable characterizations of which the acting craft is capable.

The pattern of honoring ugliness has become so pervasive that it suggests that such shocking work is honored *because* of its hideous elements, not in spite of them. The message in the movie business seems to be that portrayals of cruelty and dementia deserve more serious consideration, more automatic respect, than any attempts to convey nobility or goodness. In the last few years, the most influential leaders of the entertainment industry have gone beyond an admirable openness to dark and disturbing material: they have demonstrated a powerful (and puzzling) preference for the perverse.

Excretion and Masturbation

This preference reflects the desperate desire of filmmakers, music producers, and even television executives to win acceptance as serious artists, not just entrepreneurs of entertainment. They take their cue from other fields of artistic endeavor, where the most respected work of the moment aims to upset us rather than uplift us, and producing pain is considered a more meaningful achievement than providing pleasure. Anyone who has recently attended a poetry reading, or sat through a "new music" concert, or turned up at a gallery opening for a trendy new sculptor can attest to this tendency. The audience seldom walks away from such experiences with a warming glow of joy or satisfaction. In fact, the arts establishment encourages all-out assaults on our sense of comfort and coherence, while turning a suspicious eye on any efforts that respect convention, including representational painting, rhyming poetry, melodic music—or life-affirming movies.

Irving Kristol defines "postmodern art" as "a politically charged art that is utterly contemptuous of the notion of educating the tastes and refining the aesthetic sensibilities of the citizenry. Its goal, instead, is deliberately to outrage those tastes and to trash the very idea of an 'aesthetic sensibility.'"

The controversial policies of the National Endowment for the Arts provide some of the most striking illustrations of the practical pursuit of these priorities. In 1989 the NEA indignantly denied a modest ($10,000) request from the New York Academy of Art to provide young painters with basic skills in representational drawing. In the words of Susan Lubowsky, director of the NEA Visual Arts Programs, "teaching students to draw the human figure is revisionist . . . and stifles creativity." Less than a year later, the Endowment paid $70,000 of government funds for a gallery show that featured Shawn Eichman's "Alchemy Cabinet," displaying a jar with the bloody fetal remains from her own abortion. The federal arts administrators also found funds to provide grants to performance artists such as John Fleck (whose act includes a sequence in which he publicly urinates on a picture of Christ), and the estimable and outspoken Annie Sprinkle, who masturbates on stage with various sex toys and then invites members of the audience to explore her private parts with a flashlight.

No doubt inspired by such evidence of the Endowment's broad-minded largess, Frederick Hart, the distinguished sculptor who created the celebrated *Three Soldiers* statue at Washington's Vietnam War Memorial, applied for a grant to complete a series of "Creation Sculptures." To his surprise and chagrin, the Endowment turned him down. "The NEA told me what I was doing wasn't art," Hart recalled. At the same time the aesthetic bureaucrats smiled upon a very different sort of public statuary, authorizing $20,000 for a project in a Lewiston, New York, park whose self-proclaimed goal was "to create large, sexually explicit props covered with a generous layer of requisitioned Bibles."

This bias for the bizarre has proven so potent and so persistent that it fatally undermines the argument that the NEA and the rest of the arts community care nothing about the underlying values of the work they honor. When the National Endowment elects to fund public displays of masturbation and excretion, while denying support for classical sculpture or realistic painting, it is making a powerful value judgment. That judgment reflects the conviction that only work that could be described as "daring," "unorthodox," or "experimental" is worthy of official sponsorship, while projects that fall within the traditional mainstream are inherently less valuable to society.

"Life Stinks"

To a surprising extent, the same prejudice has begun taking root in Hollywood. This does not mean that the major studios are currently competing for the rights to film lavishly praised performance artist Karen Finley as she smears her nude body with chocolate, or burns the American flag while chanting "God is dead." However deeply they may be distanced from the values of Middle America, entertainment executives cannot run their corporations in the same way they might run an avant-garde arts center in Seattle. Most projects are designed, however imperfectly, to reach a mass audience—though even such commercial ventures are often marred by shocking or propagandistic elements that have been incongruously imbedded within the material.

Hollywood's predilection for nihilistic content is demonstrated more clearly in those infrequent entertainment endeavors that are known as prestige projects—intended to impress critics and other insiders, rather than to please ordinary moviegoers. Not surprisingly, Hollywood shows its values system most unmistakably when it attempts to make serious statements.

Consider, for example, the 1991 decision by the massive entertainment conglomerate MCA/Universal to produce an incomparably repellent and pretentious little picture called *Closetland*. The film used only two actors (Alan Rickman and Madeline Stowe), and the action, such as it was, played out exclusively on one claustrophobic set, painted entirely in shades of silver and black. The filmmakers apparently intended some sort of searing parable about the universal oppression of women, and therefore showed the male "interrogator" mercilessly and graphically torturing his female victim. He forces her to drink his urine, rips her toenails out with pliers, handcuffs her to a bed, spits a half-chewed clove of garlic into her mouth, administers electric shocks to her genitals, and penetrates her anus with a red-hot metal poker as she howls in agony. Perhaps the most amazing aspect of this "challenging" (and critically acclaimed) drama was the presence of populist filmmaker Ron Howard's name on the credits as co-executive producer. Perhaps he felt a perverse need to demonstrate to the public how far he had traveled from Mayberry, RFD.

Other major studios have followed Universal's lead in releasing incoherent and offensive material as a means of achieving artistic respectability. Twentieth Century Fox took great pride in promoting *Naked Lunch* as one of the studio's candidates for critical acclaim and industry awards, despite the fact that the film bears only the most casual connection to the classic junkie novel by William Burroughs on which it is allegedly based. In the course of the film, director David Cronenberg depicts gigantic talking vaginas, and huge insects with dripping penises dangling from their foreheads. At one point, a German sybarite (who seems to be attempting a bad Peter Lorre imitation) eagerly places his mouth on one of these male insect organs and performs one of the most bizarre sex acts ever portrayed in a mainstream motion picture. Other characters indulge in sweaty but emotionless group gropes and every manner of drug abuse, including injecting bug poison directly into their veins. Eventually, the same long-suffering actress (Judy Davis) is shot twice through the forehead. Many critics reviewed the film as if it were an uproarious, hallucinogenic comedy. Twentieth Century Fox certainly displayed a sense of humor when it elected to release this knee-slapper on Christmas Day, when the industry has traditionally emphasized family fare. It is safe to assume that no one will ever confuse this new holiday treasure with *Miracle on 34th Street*.

Of course, the studios have every right to make such movies, and one could even argue that in doing so they've demonstrated the sort of courage and selflessness rarely associated with Hollywood. No one ever expected that *Naked Lunch* or *Closetland* would become box-office blockbusters; decisions to proceed with these projects could never be explained in purely financial terms. That's why these films are so revealing when it comes to exposing the philosophical underpinnings of today's Hollywood: this is the sort of art that leading filmmakers choose to create when they are freed of all commercial considerations.

The most significant shapers of the entertainment industry, in their quest for artistic legitimacy, have adopted a view of the world that is surprisingly dark, even desperate, highlighting elements of chaos, cruelty, and random violence while emphasizing every possible failing of America and its institutions. It is no accident that the richly gifted funnyman Mel Brooks, when crafting his most ambitious, personal, and "serious" movie comedy, decided to call it *Life Stinks*. (His original title, *Life Sucks*, made the same point in an even more uncompromising fashion.)

It is not within the purview of this book to debate this fundamental proposition; I will make no attempt to determine whether, in point of fact, life either "stinks" or "sucks." I will submit, however, that few Americans (outside of Hollywood) would agree with such sentiments. When an industry attempts to market a Mel Brooks comedy with a title that conveys a grim, pessimistic view of human existence, then it's safe to say that industry has lost touch with its public. Needless to say, *Life Stinks* bombed miserably when it opened in July 1991, then bombed again when MGM attempted a second release in October of the same year. To date, it stands as the least successful of all the director's films. "I assumed that America understood irony, since it's an ironic title," Brooks lamented over the wreckage of his dream. "I was wrong."

Messages Matter

Other industry heavyweights have made similar mistakes by assuming that the public shares Hollywood's increasingly cynical and gloomy take on contemporary reality. The American people may not analyze entertainment from an ideological perspective, but they can surely sense it when some product of the popular culture conveys an outlook that radically differs from their own. Messages matter—not least at the box office. Cultural and political attitudes, even if subtly expressed, even if unconsciously absorbed, can contribute powerfully to a sense of distance or discomfort on the part of the audience. If these attitudes reflect the public's own most heartfelt convictions, they can generate a warm and sympathetic response; when they assault traditional values they often arouse vague feelings of resentment that help to doom a project's commercial prospects.

This appeared to be the case with *Hudson Hawk,* the most notorious flop of 1991—which became known in Hollywood as "Hudson the Duck," in tribute to a previous stinker of comparably bloated proportions. Both *Hudson Hawk* and *Howard the Duck* (1986) were dumb, boring movies loaded with cheesy special effects, but these failings alone cannot account for the surprisingly passionate hatred they engendered among the unlucky few who actually saw them. Moviegoers regularly used words like "revolting" or "slimy" to describe *Hudson Hawk,* setting up some of the most overwhelmingly negative word-of-mouth within memory.

Even allowing for the fact that much of this negativity centered on the sleazy personality of the film's star, Bruce Willis, the picture's ideological underpinnings surely did their part in alienating the audience. After all, this seedy adventure centered on a character who is a career criminal, while many of the bad guys work for the Vatican. Andie Mac-Dowell plays a nun who is employed as a secret agent for the corrupt Church, while a wizened cardinal orders her to use her sexual allure to serve his sinister purposes.

Howard the Duck also seemed to go out of its way to offend the sensibilities of the mainstream audience. In one of its most memorably annoying scenes it offered one of Hollywood's first-ever visions of interspecies sex, as the title character, a cigar-chomping plastic duck from outer space, cuddles in bed beside a sexy rock star played by Lea

Thompson. To make clear Howard's arousal, the filmmakers cause the feathers at the back of his neck to slowly stand erect.

When I recently appeared as a guest on a radio talk show, a housewife from suburbia called in and spoke, I believe, for millions of filmgoers. "I don't know what's wrong with movies today," she said, "but I sure know they're not making them for people like me. It seems like the only people they're trying to please are either kids or perverts."

Choice, Not Repression

In response to such anguished expressions of disgust, the defenders of the Hollywood status quo invariably raise the dreaded specter of censorship. They justify the current propensity for repellent material by intoning solemn platitudes about the need to protect "diversity" and "freedom of expression."

In one typically sweeping statement, the huge Time-Warner conglomerate recently attempted to disguise an example of its own acutely irresponsible corporate behavior in the cloak of constitutional highmindedness. "It is vital that we stand by our commitment to the free expression of ideas for all our authors, journalists, recording artists, screenwriters, actors and directors," the company nobly proclaimed in an official pronouncement of June 11, 1992. Several law-enforcement officials and organizations had bitterly criticized the release of a song called "Cop Killer" in which rap star Ice-T unequivocally encouraged his fans to "bust some shots off" and "dust some cops off." In response, Time-Warner insisted that its decision to move ahead to promote and distribute the song "is not a matter of profits, it is a matter of principle. . . . We believe this commitment is crucial to a democratic society, where the full range of opinion and thought—whether we agree with it or not—must be able to find an outlet."

This line of reasoning is not only unconvincing, it is ultimately insincere. Would Time-Warner have felt the same "commitment" to providing an "outlet" for a Ku Klux Klan sympathizer who glorified the shooting of black children?

The conclusion is inescapable that the corporate commitment to the First Amendment is selectively applied. Imagine that a major filmmaker proposed a movie about a respected organization of feminists who are secretly plotting to castrate all the males in the country, or that a veteran TV producer suggested a "docudrama" exploring the lurid sex life of Dr. Martin Luther King. What if a major box-office star wanted to make an intense drama about the celebrated Hollywood blacklist of the 1950s, in which the accused screenwriters were, in fact, lying Stalinist stooges, and the colleagues who exposed them were portrayed as heroes? What about a big-budget spectacle dramatizing the ideas of "Holocaust revisionists"—showing an implacable international Jewish conspiracy that faked evidence throughout Europe to perpetrate the hoax of Nazi genocide?

Would anyone seriously suggest that "freedom of expression" or "diversity" required that the entertainment industry give these projects the green light?

The advocates of openness are not, in truth, as open as they sound. They would all agree that there are some subjects so sensitive, some themes so offensive, that they should not be explored. In the final analysis, no one questions that boundaries must exist for the entertainment industry; the only real issue is where those boundaries should be drawn.

To urge that Hollywood should display a more mature sense of social responsibility in establishing those boundaries is hardly a call for censorship, or a demand for stifling anyone's creativity. Each year, the major entertainment companies receive literally hundreds of thousands of movie treatments, proposals for TV series, and demo tapes from aspiring rock groups; only the tiniest fraction of this vast assemblage of material is ever selected for commercial development. This means that not all would-be writers will enjoy an equal "right" to express themselves on screen. Does it make sense to suppose that all the myriad of unproduced screenwriters or unrecorded singers have been censored or stifled? Or have they merely experienced the harsh reality of an industry that must be extraordinarily selective about the projects that receive its financial backing? It is a question of choice, not repression.

The process of making these choices remains highly subjective, since no one has yet devised a reliable or scientific method for predicting the commercial success of a particular piece of popular entertainment. In selecting those properties to push forward and those proposals to bury, the industry's leaders may concentrate their attention on prospects for profit, but they will also, and inevitably, inject their personal perspectives. No one expects them to invest heart and soul in projects they find distasteful; they will always be more likely to take their chances on material that communicates messages they can endorse. With every entertainment endeavor involving such a huge element of risk, these considerations become a surprisingly significant—though often unacknowledged—aspect of Hollywood's decision-making. Every commitment to produce a movie, TV show, or popular song involves an element of conscious or unconscious value judgment.

In making those judgments, the industry's leaders have established unmistakable patterns that reflect something more than a random response to the demands of the marketplace. The themes that turn up with such astounding regularity in our television, movies, and popular music have not been included coincidentally, nor are those sentiments drawn haphazardly from all points of the ideological compass.

The perspectives of the loony left, for instance, are robustly represented in Hollywood—as evidenced by the triumphal career of Oliver Stone—while the outlook of the radical right is all but invisible. Several mainstream record labels have released recent albums with songs that glorify the left-wing racist Louis Farrakhan; it is hard to imagine those same music companies sanctioning similar tributes to the right-wing racist David Duke.

"Malign Propaganda"

For all their insistence that they are merely entertainers with no issues to advance or axes to grind, the top people in this business have recently committed themselves to enlightening the public on a number of highly fashionable issues. These industry leaders take great pride in the positive plugs for condom use, or saving the rain forests, that they've been able to insert in even the most incongruous contexts on television, in movies, and in popular songs.

Such efforts highlight the schizophrenic attitude of show business professionals toward the larger significance of what they do. On the one hand, they believe that they can influence the audience on behalf of worthy causes like safe sex and recycling; on the other hand, they continue to insist that the violence, hedonism, and selfishness so often featured in their work will have no real-world consequences whatever.

This glaring internal contradiction leads to the astonishingly illogical conclusion that popular culture's only possible impact is beneficial. Whenever it delivers positive messages, we are asked to believe that people will pay close attention; if the messages are destructive or vicious, we're told that the public automatically tunes them out. If Hollywood creates some noble project that raises a serious issue, we're asked to applaud a significant public service; when the business revels in the ugliest and most degraded aspects of human nature, we're urged to dismiss it as harmless entertainment.

These laughably ludicrous distinctions are regularly imposed on every area of show business. In the world of popular music, both critics and industry executives heap lavish praise on "socially conscious" artists like Tracy Chapman or U2. Their songs are considered meritorious and significant precisely because of their ability to influence the audience and to arouse the masses over issues like homelessness, racism, and U.S. imperialism. At the same time, anyone who attempts a serious examination of the appalling lyrics of violent, woman-hating groups like Guns n' Roses or Geto Boys or Napalm Death is instantly urged to chill out and lighten up. When it comes to music's good guys the words they sing are all-important; with its notorious bad boys, the words are supposed to be totally irrelevant.

"There's no message to heavy metal," says Penelope Spheeris, who directed two acclaimed documentaries about the contemporary metal scene. "It's about being rich and famous and getting laid."

Of course, it never occurs to Ms. Spheeris that an emphasis on "being rich and famous and getting laid" in itself constitutes a powerful message. Much of popular culture may be worthless, but none of it is devoid of impact. For better or worse, the values in every piece of popular entertainment, no matter how mindless, will touch the audience.

Producer David Puttnam, whose courageous statements and thoughtful films have established him as an anomaly in the entertainment industry, makes the point with clarity and force. "Every single movie has within it an element of propaganda," he told Bill Moyers in 1989. "You walk away with either benign or malign propaganda."

The chapters that follow will explore the malign propaganda that has come to dominate Hollywood's product in recent years and will demonstrate its devastating impact on society at large.

PART II

THE
ATTACK
ON RELIGION

A Declaration
of War

"Father, Forgive Them"

On the morning of August 11, 1988, more than 25,000 people gathered at Universal City, California, in the largest protest ever mounted against the release of a motion picture.

The huge crowd assembled from every direction, filling all streets and sidewalks surrounding the legendary "Black Tower" that housed the corporate command center of the vast conglomerate, MCA/Universal. For several hours, long lines of cars and vans disgorged their passengers, clogging traffic and forcing police to close freeway off-ramps within a two-mile radius. All observers commented on the remarkable age range of the protesters, with preschoolers in strollers and senior citizens in wheelchairs well-represented, along with every category in between. The demonstrators carried hand-lettered signs proclaiming "Please Show Respect for My God," "The Lie Costs $6.50; the Truth Is Free," and "Father, Forgive Them."

An acquaintance who worked at Universal at the time recalled the nervousness that prevailed throughout the day inside the company's main office building. "That was one time it was really scary to be in the Black Tower," she said. "There were just so many of them! When you looked down, fifteen stories down, they were everywhere. The crowd seemed to go on for miles. We felt like we were trapped. A guy down the hall said it was like the Russian Revolution, and we were in the Winter Palace. My boss kept expecting them to charge—to break down the doors and to trash the building. He thought they were going to try and kill people. We had extra security all day because everybody was expecting a fight."

The huge throng failed to live up to these dramatic expectations; despite the feelings of hurt and rage that many of the demonstrators expressed to members of the press, the police reported no incidents of either violence or vandalism. The protesters assembled in order to show their passionate opposition to the next day's scheduled release of Martin Scorsese's *The Last Temptation of Christ,* not to exact vengeance from the studio that produced it. They sang a few hymns, cheered lustily for more than a dozen occasionally emotional speakers, and then peaceably dispersed. By midafternoon the terrified honchos in the Black Tower breathed a collective sigh of relief and returned to their business—without making any serious attempt to come to terms with the significance of what had just occurred outside their windows.

The movie moguls, together with many of their supporters in the news media, persisted in dismissing the demonstrators (and all others opposed to the production and release of *The Last Temptation of Christ*) as representatives of a lunatic fringe of religious fanatics and right-wing extremists. In one typical piece of commentary, columnist Mike Duffy of the *Detroit Free Press* decried those who criticized the film as "sour, fun-loathing people" and "the American ignoramus faction that is perpetually geeked up on self-righteous bile. . . .

"They looked for Reds under every bed with Joe McCarthy.

"They cheered police dogs in Selma. . . .

"And now the know-nothing wacky pack has latched onto Martin Scorsese and *The Last Temptation of Christ.* . . ."

In point of fact, the "know-nothing wacky pack" that protested the movie included such "fringe groups" as the National Council of Catholic Bishops, the National Catholic Conference, the Southern Baptist Convention (with 14 million members), the Eastern Orthodox Church of America, the Archbishop of Canterbury (head of the world-wide Anglican Church), the archbishop of Paris, twenty members of the U.S. House of Representatives (who cosponsored a bipartisan resolution condemning the film), the Christian Democratic Party of Italy (that nation's largest political party), and Mother Teresa of Calcutta, the Nobel Prize–winner who invariably turns up on polls as one of the world's most admired human beings. Mother Teresa sent a particularly passionate "message to America" that was read to the demonstrators in which she called on all people of good will to use "prayer as the ultimate weapon to fight this ultimate disgrace."

In fact, all of those who addressed the enormous crowd that gathered at Universal the day before the picture's release spoke in temperate tones that gave scant indication that they had been "geeked up on self-righteous bile."

One of Hollywood's own received an especially warm response— Ken Wales, former vice president at Disney studios and veteran producer of more than twenty feature films. "As a member of this industry I wish that there were hundreds of stars and writers and directors standing here with me," Wales pleaded. "I suppose they are out protesting toxic waste! Let me tell you, there is toxic waste in other areas besides our rivers. That happens in the pollution of our minds, our souls, and our spirits!"

Another speaker on the program was Rabbi Chaim Asa, a Holocaust survivor and leader of a large Reform temple in Fullerton, California. Speaking slowly and deliberately, but with great intensity, Rabbi Asa explained that he had come to "join in protesting the indignity of this particular attempt to defame your God. . . . Millions across the country are saying, 'You are touching something very deep, very sensitive in my soul. Please don't do it, because this is not fair!' I protest vehemently, as many of my Christian friends did when someone tried to burn our temple in Fullerton. . . . I will try to express to my Christian friends—if their pain is deep now, so is my pain for them."

Stonewalling

The executives at Universal remained remarkably insensitive to that pain; their public statements contained not the slightest hint of conciliation or apology. Instead, the studio brass incongruously invoked the First Amendment and struck a series of smug, self-serving poses that seemed to suggest that this for-profit corporation felt a solemn and selfless duty to promote a film that tens of millions of its potential patrons found offensive.

"Though those in power may justify the burning of books at the time, the witness of history teaches the importance of standing up for freedom of conscience . . . ," declared a pompous, full-page "open letter" from Universal Pictures published in newspapers around the country. "In the United States, no one sect or coalition has the power to set boundaries around each person's freedom to explore religious and philosophical questions. . . ."

This tendentious civics lesson made no attempt to explain why the conglomerate's principled defense of the Constitution required it to finance, promote, and distribute certain religious and philosophical explorations, but not others. Hadn't the company somehow breached its commitment to "standing up for freedom of conscience" by passing up the opportunity to produce a film version of Salman Rushdie's best-selling novel *The Satanic Verses*—a book that offered a revisionist view of Mohammed in some ways comparable to Scorsese's revisionist portrayal of Christ?

When it came to the prospect of enraging the Islamic faithful, the instinct for self-preservation took precedence over the commitment to controversial religious explorations, but the Universal bosses felt no corresponding compunctions when it came to offending Christians: time and again during the *Last Temptation* battle, the studio seemed to go out of its way to insult the organized religious community. Dr. Richard G. Lee, pastor of the seven-thousand-member Rehoboth Baptist Church in Atlanta, Georgia, managed to collect more than 135,000 signatures on his petition protesting the film's release. When he and his associates repeatedly called Universal to request that a representative of the company make ten minutes available to formally receive the petitions and the attached list of names, the public relations executives refused to cooperate. "We contacted their offices," Pastor Lee recalled, "and in our last conversation they told us, 'We don't care about your petitions. Leave them with the guards, and we'll put them in the dump.' They were saying, 'We don't care about the opinions and the heartbeat of 135,000 Americans.'"

Ultimately, all the major Hollywood studios offered formal support for this callous attitude and endorsed Universal's position on the film. Jack Valenti, president of the Motion Picture Association of America, issued a statement in which he ringingly declared: "The key issue, the only issue, is whether or not self-appointed groups can prevent a film from being exhibited to the public. . . . The major companies of MPAA support MCA/Universal in its absolute right to offer to the people whatever movie it chooses."

No one ever challenged that "absolute right"; Universal's critics merely questioned the way the studio elected to exercise it. The dispute concerned the movie company's *choices*, not its rights. To assert that a studio has the right to release "whatever movie it chooses" is not to insist that every possible release is equally defensible.

Would Mr. Valenti have spoken out in behalf of a film biography of slain black leader Malcolm X that portrayed him as a paid agent of J. Edgar Hoover's FBI who secretly worked to discredit the civil rights movement? What about a movie version of the life of the assassinated gay hero, San Francisco supervisor Harvey Milk, that suggested that he was actually a closet heterosexual (and inveterate womanizer) who only pretended to be gay in order to seek political advantage? Or a revisionist view of Holocaust victim Anne Frank that portrayed her as an out-of-control teenage nymphomaniac who risked capture by the Nazis night after night to satisfy her raging hormones?

It is difficult to imagine the industry's leaders rallying to the support of any such outrageous and patently offensive projects in the way they rallied to the support of *The Last Temptation*. For Hollywood, in other words, some martyrs are more sacrosanct than others.

In 1984, four years prior to the battle over the Martin Scorsese film, organized protests erupted over the release of a sordid little exploitation picture called *Silent Night, Deadly Night*, which portrayed a department store Santa as a blood-soaked psychotic slasher. Many Hollywood leaders actually supported the protesters, and neither Jack Valenti nor anyone else from the motion picture establishment ever spoke up for the producers' "absolute right" to besmirch the image of Kris Kringle. This may reflect the fact that the people behind *Silent Night, Deadly Night* wielded considerably less clout than the people behind *The Last Temptation;* but it also indicates that Santa Claus is more sacred to the entertainment industry than Jesus.

In fact, the industry's stubborn and purportedly principled defense of Universal's right to offend a significant segment of the public with the Martin Scorsese film stands in striking contrast to the deference displayed to a wide range of "politically correct" special-interest groups, both before and after the *Last Temptation* controversy. For instance:

• In 1990 animal rights activists demanded that Disney studios eliminate what a spokesman for the Humane Society described as "an antiwolf statement" in the film adaptation of Jack London's novella *White Fang*. The producers agreed to remove a dramatic scene in which a wolf attacks a man and even added a disclaimer to the film which stated that "there is no documented case in North America of a healthy wolf or pack of wolves attacking a human."

• In 1991 screenwriter and independent producer Jonathan F. Lawton altered the storyline in his script *Red Sneakers* under pressure from the Gay & Lesbian Alliance Against Discrimination (GLAAD). His original concept involved a heroine who leaves her older female lover for a man—a plot that allegedly affronted lesbian sensibilities. In the revised (and, according to GLAAD, "much improved" version), the main character views the older woman more as a mother figure than as a lover, and that older woman is also provided a happy romance with another lesbian.

• In another well-publicized incident, the religious leaders in one Hopi Indian village reviewed the script for Robert Redford's upcoming film *Dark Wind* and reached the conclusion that the screenplay portrayed their ancient rites in a "sacrilegious" manner. Producer Patrick Markey promptly agreed to make changes.

The sensitivity that Hollywood flaunted during these and many similar episodes makes the industry's stonewalling during *The Last Temptation* controversy even more difficult to understand. Leaders of the motion picture business showed more concern with possible sacrilege against the religious traditions of a single Hopi village than with certain offense to the faith of tens of millions of believing Christians; the prospect of being labeled "antiwolf" produced greater worry than the prospect of being labeled "anti-Christ."

In response to this charge, the industry's defenders might insist that the examples of accommodation cited above involved adjustments that were made *during* the production process, while the bitter fight over *The Last Temptation of Christ* erupted as Universal prepared a finished film for national release. This argument, however, only highlights Universal's surprising unwillingness to receive input from respected Christian theologians or organizations in the scripting of their inevitably sensitive project. Animal rights activists, gay advocacy groups, and ethnic organizations of every description are frequently consulted on questions of content in feature films, but Martin Scorsese and his associates kept their plans for *The Last Temptation* a closely guarded secret from all church leaders.

It is difficult to quarrel with the substance of a press statement released on July 12, 1988, by the broad-based religious coalition opposed to the release of Scorsese's film. At the time, they noted the studio's "presumed unwillingness to release a major film maligning the character and distorting the historical record of any other religious, ethnic, or national hero" and therefore condemned "the highly discriminatory nature of Universal's decision against the Christian community."

Much of the press coverage of the increasingly bitter dispute also seemed highly discriminatory. Television news repeatedly misrepresented the nature of the national movement opposing the movie's release by focusing on one utterly unrepresentative individual as the preeminent symbol of that movement: the Reverend R. L. Hymers, pastor of an obscure church in downtown Los Angeles. With his snarling moon face and explosive temper, his predictions of impending apocalypse (through earthquakes and "killer bees"), his blatantly anti-Semitic ravings against the "Jewish money" behind the movie, and a long history of legal problems stemming from past violent outbursts, Hymers lived up to anyone's worst nightmare of deranged religious fanatic. Naturally, the press couldn't get enough of him.

The mainstream Protestant and Catholic leaders who coordinated the major efforts against *The Last Temptation* not only disowned Hymers, they publicly denounced him. They pointed out that he represented no significant constituency, and spoke only for his own struggling, 250-member Fundamentalist Baptist Tabernacle. Nevertheless, Hymers appeared on literally hundreds of TV interviews and talk shows, as well as gracing the pages of *Time, Newsweek,* and *People,* while respected Christian leaders like Pastor Jack Hayford and the Reverend James Ogilvie (whose congregations each boasted more than twenty times the membership of Hymers's) were virtually ignored. When Hymers and less than one hundred of his followers staged a "mock crucifixion" on the sidewalk in front of the home of Universal president Lew Wasserman, he received more television coverage than the subsequent demonstration at the Black Tower, which drew a crowd that the police estimated at 25,000.

The media not only misled the public about the leaders of the protest, but also distorted the substance of their objections to Scorsese's film. News stories focused again and again on the "dream sequence" at the end of the movie, emphasizing one brief scene in which Jesus makes love to Mary Magdalene and asserting that this image alone had provoked the furor in the religious community. In fact, Christian leaders identified more than twenty elements in the finished film that offended them deeply, ranging from an early scene in which Jesus crouches by the bed and watches with voyeuristic intensity as Mary Magdalene has sex with ten different men, to a later conversation in which the Apostle Paul confesses that he doesn't really believe in the Resurrection and admits that "I've created truth out of what people needed and believed."

By ignoring the issues raised by all other aspects of the film and concentrating exclusively on the sex scene between Magdalene and Christ, the press helped to make the protesters look like narrow-minded prudes. Dr. Larry Poland, whose "Mastermedia" ministry works to bring Christian ideas to leaders in the entertainment industry, saw an especially flagrant example of this tendency in the coverage on the CBS television station in Los Angeles. In filing a report on the film and the protests, entertainment correspondent Steve Kmetko authoritatively (and fatuously) concluded: "As far as the controversy goes, the movie follows Christian doctrine very closely." Kmetko then joined the two news anchors in some spontaneous banter about the movie and its infamous love scene:

ANCHOR #1: "So you mean, Steve, that all of this protest about the film surrounds the equivalent of one page from a two-hundred-and-fifty-page book?"

ANCHOR #2: "Or really just thirty seconds of a two-hour-and-forty-minute movie?"

KMETKO: "That's it."

This sort of one-sided coverage made it easier for everyone in the industry to ignore the uncomfortable questions raised by the controversy—questions about Hollywood's underlying hostility to religious belief and to religious believers. Instead of confronting the situation honestly, show business leaders issued an endless series of smug pronouncements in defense of Mr. Scorsese's First Amendment rights—inconsistently coupled with condemnation of those who chose to exercise *their* First Amendment rights by protesting the film. In all the bitter weeks of charges and countercharges, Hollywood never seemed to understand the demands of those who opposed the picture. What they wanted from the industry wasn't censorship; it was sensitivity.

Solemn Stupidity

As the controversy intensified in the days immediately prior to the film's release, I tried to focus on my job as a movie critic and to stay away from the increasingly hysterical theological and constitutional debates. I wanted to see *The Last Temptation of Christ* with an open mind and to assess its artistic excellence (or inadequacy) as a motion picture, rather than surveying its importance as a battleground in the ongoing culture war. As a practicing Jew, I could sympathize with the sense of violation and outrage that many of my Christian friends felt as soon as they heard about the film, but I never shared their visceral reaction; nor did I experience the similarly passionate (and similarly instinctive) impulse of some industry insiders who rushed to the defense of the film the moment it was attacked by the religious right.

With these intense emotions very much in the air, I gathered with a dozen other critics to see the picture at a weekday afternoon screening two weeks before its release. We sat together in a small screening room at the Universal lot, chatting as we waited for the lights to go down. I think we all felt the electric atmosphere in that room, connected with our knowledge that we were about to witness a significant moment in cinema and social history. Our anticipation arose in part from the expectations surrounding any film by Martin Scorsese, the most acclaimed director of our time. In one well-publicized national poll, a group of the most prominent critics in the country made Scorsese's movie *Raging Bull* their runaway choice for best American film of the 1980s.

Unfortunately, as *The Last Temptation of Christ* unreeled before our astonished eyes, it became clear almost immediately that he might have retitled this new film *Raging Messiah*. Within its first five minutes the picture offers a sequence in which Jesus (Willem Dafoe) inexplicably assists the Romans in crucifying some innocent Jewish victim. As they nail the poor man's feet to the bottom of the cross, blood spurts out and covers Christ's somber cheek.

Such graphic and shocking gore recurs at regular intervals, providing the only relief to long, arid stretches of appalling boredom, laughable dialogue, and unbearably bad acting. Even those who publicly praised the film confessed that its two-hour-and-forty-four minute running time amounted to something of an ordeal for the audience; I found the entire experience as uplifting and rewarding as two hours and forty-four minutes in the dentist's chair.

After the first half hour of this solemn stupidity I began to feel sorry for the actors. Barbara Hershey played Mary Magdalene and for some odd reason, director Scorsese had decided to cover her lovely body from head to toe with intricate and abstract tattoos. Try as I might, I couldn't avoid recalling the lyrics of the Groucho Marx ditty "Lydia, the Tattooed Lady" whenever Miss Hershey appeared on screen. Most other women in the cast had been similarly decorated— as if Scorsese had made a startling archaeological discovery that indicated that ancient Judea boasted tattoo parlors on every corner catering exclusively to females. In reality, however, Jewish and biblical law strictly prohibited tattoos of any and all kinds, for both men and women, making a mockery of all the boasts in the official press kit about Scorsese's "exhaustive research" on Judean customs at the time of Jesus.

Other members of the cast suffered even more intense embarrassment than Miss Hershey. Following the lead of the Nikos Kazantzakis novel that served as the source for the film, the script tries to make Judas Iscariot the most admirable and devoted of Christ's disciples, but in his performance as Judas, the woefully miscast Harvey Keitel inspires unintended hilarity rather than sympathy. With his thick Brooklyn accent firmly intact, braying out his lines like a minor Mafioso trying to impress his elders with his swaggering, tough-guy panache, Keitel looks for all the world as if he has accidentally wandered onto the desert set from a very different Martin Scorsese film. He is also required to wear a flaming orange fright wig that gives him an unmistakable resemblance to a biblical bozo.

The picture is crammed with such idiotic touches—from Jesus reaching into his chest and pulling out his bloody pumping heart to display to his impressed apostles, to the resurrected Lazarus answering a question about the contrast between life and death by mumbling, "I was a little surprised. There isn't that much difference." In response to such memorably miscalculated movie moments, some of my generally restrained colleagues, who attended the same critics' screening I did, began snickering, hooting, and laughing aloud midway through the picture's all-but-insufferable length.

When we finally staggered out into the light of day, blinking our eyes and shaking our heads in disbelief, a TV camera crew from a national entertainment show approached a few of the recognizable reviewers in the crowd and asked for our instantaneous responses. I told them, "It is the height of irony that all this controversy should be generated by a film that turns out to be so breathtakingly bad, so unbearably boring. In my opinion, the controversy about this picture is a lot more interesting than the film itself."

That comment may have forever ended my chances of making Martin Scorsese's Christmas card list, since it was widely and repeatedly quoted in the national media as part of the continuing debate on the motion picture and its significance. I stand by the comment today, not only as an expression of my own opinion, but as an accurate summary of the general reaction of those who sat beside me in that screening room and watched the film for the first time that afternoon.

I was therefore amazed and appalled in the days that followed at the generally respectful—even reverential—tone that so many of my colleagues adopted in their reviews. In particular, I found it impossible to understand the one critic who had snorted the loudest and clucked the most derisively at the afternoon screening we both attended, but whose ultimate report to the public featured glowing praise and only the most minor reservations.

When I called him to ask about the contrast between his privately expressed contempt and his on-the-record admiration, he proved surprisingly candid in explaining his inconsistency. "Look, I know the picture's a dog," he said. "We both know that, and probably Scorsese knows it, too. But with all the Christian crazies shooting at him from every direction, I'm not going to knock him in public. If I slammed the picture too hard, then people would associate me with Falwell—and there's no way I'm ready for that."

I believe that his confidential comments offer the best explanation for the utterly undeserved critical hosannas that the picture provoked in many quarters. Other critics may never acknowledge the antireligious prejudice that helped to produce their positive reviews—and some of them may not even be consciously aware of it. Nevertheless, I remain convinced that many of my colleagues automatically assumed that any film that caused so much upset to the conventional religious community must be brave, significant, and worthy of praise. Critics invariably disagree about the quality of major movies, but the level and intensity of the disagreements on *The Last Temptation* went far beyond expected differences in taste and seemed to suggest ideological agendas at work.

In a sense, the response to the film (including Scorsese's surprise nomination for an Academy Award as Best Director, and official endorsements by the Writers Guild, the Directors Guild, and the Motion Picture Association of America) represented the movie industry's "circle the wagons" mentality at its most hysterical and paranoid. Veteran star Mickey Rooney, one of the few established Hollywood figures to speak up against Scorsese's acclaimed "masterpiece," concluded: *"The Last Temptation of Christ* provides a good example of the film establishment rallying around a bad film to protect its own selfish interest. . . . That film, no matter what its defenders say, was a slap in the face to Christians everywhere, but Hollywood cradled the picture as if it were *Citizen Kane."* When religious figures across the country attacked the picture, the members of the Hollywood community felt called upon to close ranks and to do rhetorical battle with any who dared criticize the industry and its values.

That's why so many of the film's supporters not only praised it as a work of art, but defended it as an act of faith. The noted theologian Joel Siegel of "Good Morning America" insisted it was "deeply felt and ultimately faith-affirming," while Marshall Fine of Gannet News Services called it "a work of immense imagination, one that never betrays its unshakable faith." David Ehrenstein of the *Los Angeles Herald Examiner* declared, "It is without question one of the most serious, literate, complex and deeply religious films ever made, brilliantly directed by Martin Scorsese."

The public wisely ignored such glowing notices and the film quickly developed the deadly word-of-mouth it so richly deserved. Despite saturation coverage in the press—exceeding even the epic hoopla connected with the debut of *Gone With the Wind*—the movie promptly bombed at the box office. Its domestic gross of $7 million scarcely covered the expenses for promotion and distribution, let alone the original cost of the production. The movie's rental and sale on videocassette proved similarly disappointing; Blockbuster Video, the Florida-based corporation that operates the nation's largest chain of video stores, refused to even stock the title for fear of offending its customers. Though precise figures will never be made public, best estimates indicate that Universal's overall loss on the project could hardly have been less than $10 million—an appalling result for a project that had received the most lavish prerelease publicity in modern motion picture history.

4

Comic Book Clergy

Opposite Extremes

Universal's woeful experience with *The Last Temptation of Christ* typifies the pervasive and self-destructive hostility to religion that has taken root in Hollywood.

In the ongoing war on traditional values, the assault on organized faith represents the front to which the entertainment industry has most clearly committed itself. On no other issue do the perspectives of the show business elite and those of the public at large differ more dramatically. Time and again, the producers who shape our movies, television, and popular music have gone out of their way to affront the religious sensibilities of ordinary Americans.

To maintain a sense of perspective, it is important to remember that this represents a relatively recent development in Hollywood history. For the first fifty years of its existence, the movie capital produced numerous entertainments that celebrated—or at least respected—the major religious traditions. Biblical blockbusters like *Samson and Delilah, David and Bathsheba, Quo Vadis?, The Robe, The Ten Commandments,* and *Ben Hur* were specifically designed to appeal to the predilections of the pious, and each of these films became the nation's top box-office hit in the year of its release. Such sandals-and-sandstorm epics may not stand today as examples of deathless works of art, but in their day they won a great deal of critical acclaim at the same time they achieved consistent commercial success. *Ben Hur,* for instance, set a record by sweeping up eleven Academy Awards in 1959—a total that still remains unsurpassed.

By noting this past penchant for religious material, I am not suggesting that Tinseltown could ever have supplanted the Vatican or Jerusalem as a source of spiritual authority and enlightenment; nor am I nominating the moguls who made the movies as candidates for canonization. As religious role models the past leaders of the film colony most certainly fell short, but they understood the importance of honoring the faith of their prospective patrons.

For them, it was not only a matter of good business, but an element of "good citizenship." As Neal Gabler so persuasively points out in his book *An Empire of Their Own,* the Jewish immigrants who founded the film business wanted more than wealth and power: they felt a powerful craving for acceptance as mainstream Americans. Making movies that expressed an affectionate attitude toward the Christian conventions of the nation's dominant culture could help them to achieve the respectability they so passionately desired.

With this goal in mind, the films of Hollywood's Golden Era invariably portrayed clergymen in a sympathetic light. Movie legends such as Bing Crosby (*Going My Way, Bells of St. Mary's, Say One for Me*), Pat O'Brien (*Angels with Dirty Faces, The Fighting 69th*), and Spencer Tracy (*Boys Town, Men of Boys Town*) won public adoration and critical applause by playing earthy, compassionate men of the cloth. Other major stars attempted to duplicate their success in uplifting ecclesiastical roles but achieved far less memorable results—including Clark Gable, who portrayed an idealistic minister in *Polly of the Circus* (1932); Frank Sinatra, who played a saintly parish priest in *The Miracle of the Bells* (1948); and Mickey Rooney, who impersonated a two-fisted frontier preacher in *The Twinkle in God's Eye* (1955). In all of these films, and many more, the members of the clergy gave hope to underprivileged kids, or comforted GIs on the battlefield, or helped decent but down-and-out families to survive hard times. If a character appeared on screen wearing a clerical collar it served as a sure sign that the audience was supposed to like him.

In the last fifteen years, Hollywood has swung to the opposite extreme—presenting a view of the clergy that is every bit as one-sided in its cynicism and hostility as the old treatment may have been idealized and saccharine. Whenever someone turns up in a contemporary film with the title "Reverend," "Father," or "Rabbi" in front of his name you can count on the fact that he will turn out to be corrupt or crazy—or probably both.

Kicking the Catholics

As the world's single most visible and powerful religious institution, the Roman Catholic Church has provided a convenient focus for the anticlerical impulse in Hollywood. Consider, for example:

• *The Runner Stumbles* (1979). This notorious turkey from director Stanley Kramer features Dick Van Dyke hilariously overacting in his deadly serious role as a small-town priest who falls in love with a sensitive young nun (Kathleen Quinlan), and then stands trial for her murder.

• *Monsignor* (1982). Fresh from his success with *Superman,* that distinguished thespian Christopher Reeve apparently craved another role that allowed him to wear a cape, and so played a prince of the Roman Catholic Church. This pernicious prelate engages in every imaginable sin, including the seduction of a glamorous, idealistic nun (Genevieve Bujold) and complicity in her death. His shady dealings with the Mafia to control the Vatican bank eventually bring him to the peak of power under the approving eye of a shriveled, anorexic Pope.

• *Agnes of God* (1985). The movie opens with the uplifting spectacle of disturbed young nun Meg Tilly giving birth in a convent, murdering her baby, and then flushing the tiny, bloody corpse down the toilet. Anne Bancroft, as the stern Mother Superior with appallingly medieval ideas, wants to cover up the crime and protect the culprit, but Jane Fonda plays a probing psychiatrist determined to get to the bottom of the case. Columbia Pictures promoted the duel between Bancroft and Fonda as a dramatization of the "eternal conflict between science and faith," but with the movie so squarely on Fonda's side this is hardly an equal struggle.

• *Heaven Help Us* (1985). This raunchy teen comedy, originally produced under the title *Catholic Boys*, exposes the horrors of a parochial education in Brooklyn in the early 1960's, with the repressed and fascistic stupidity of priests comically contrasted with the lusty high spirits of a band of lovably rebellious students, led by Andrew McCarthy and Kevin Dillon.

• *The Penitent* (1988). Raul Julia plays a farmer in New Mexico who joins a primitive and brutal Catholic cult after his bored wife gets involved in an affair with his boyhood pal (Armand Assante). Every year, the scowling, sadistic sect reenacts the Crucifixion, selecting a lucky nominee (guess who?) for the honor, and performing the service on screen with a maximum of blood, gore, cockeyed camera angles, and wacked-out, quasi-religious visions.

• *Last Rites* (1988). Tom Berenger is a moody priest (and the son of a ranking Mafioso) who falls passionately in love with a mysterious Mexican "hot tamale" (Daphne Zuniga). He abuses his position in the Church in his desperate efforts to protect her, and is ultimately entangled with murder and the mob.

• *We're No Angels* (1989). Robert De Niro and Sean Penn play two lunk-headed petty crooks who escape from prison and pretend to be priests. The two sleazy fugitives are instantly honored as distinguished Church scholars by the stunningly stupid and superstitious members of a religious order who run the monastery where they seek refuge. The movie is supposed to be a remake of a 1955 escaped-cons comedy with Humphrey Bogart, but the earlier (and far superior) film contained none of the anticlerical elements of ecclesiastical masquerade that are central to the plot of the more recent version.

• *Nuns on the Run* (1990). The same plot that worked so poorly in *We're No Angels* receives another workout—this time with the protagonists in drag. Robbie Coltrane and Eric Idle play two small-time gangsters who try to cheat their boss and then are forced to hide out in a convent. The film features a long monologue in which Coltrane attempts to offer a garbled and offensive explanation of the concept of the Trinity before concluding, "It's not supposed to make sense! It's religion!" Twentieth Century Fox released this British bomberino in the United States with great fanfare but no commercial success.

• *The Godfather, Part III* (1990). The first sequence of the film features the murderous Mafioso Michael Corleone (Al Pacino) receiving the highest possible honors a lay Catholic can achieve from the hypocritical honchos of the Church of Rome. The movie rambles on to allege corruption in every corner of the Vatican, including the murder by poison of the one Pope who promised reform. In the end, writer-director Francis Coppola shows far more sympathy to the Mafia than to the Church, and the leaders of organized crime display more scruples and human emotion than the leaders of organized religion.

• *The Pope Must Die* (1991). This putrid comedy trots out every hoary anti-Catholic canard of the last two thousand years, including sultry and seductive nuns who provide the Holy Father with his own private harem, and conniving cardinals who control illicit arms deals, organized crime, and sleazy banking around the world. Robbie Coltrane (again!) portrays a grossly overweight priest who, in a past escapade with sexpot Beverly D'Angelo, has fathered the world's most famous heavy-metal rock star. Through a series of supposedly comical miscues this cuddly cleric is accidentally elevated to the papacy. Once secure on the throne of Saint Peter, he pigs out on Communion wafers in a closet of his private apartment and discovers deeper and deeper levels of corruption in the worldwide activities of the Church. The movie then begins to take itself seriously, as "Pope Dave" invades the Vatican bank and imitates Christ's behavior to the money changers in the Temple while the background score tries to whip up an heroic mood. The official press kit from Miramax Films pretentiously propounds: "*The Pope Must Die* is a film that urges an end to the corruption that threatens the Catholic Church. And its hero is a priest who cares enough about the Church to risk his life to save it."

In addition to such crude and simplistic attacks on Catholicism, Hollywood has deployed some of its most gifted actors in more satisfying stories that show idealistic priests whose good intentions are ultimately undermined by the prevailing hypocrisy of the church hierarchy. Robert De Niro in *True Confessions* (1981), Jack Lemmon in *Mass Appeal* (1984), and Jeremy Irons and Robert De Niro in *The Mission* (1986) all lend their considerable talents to dramas that contrast the sincerity of specific prelates with the cynicism of the Church itself. In these relatively rare films, individual believers may be sympathetically portrayed but the corrupt religious structures that they serve are ultimately unworthy of their sincerity.

In *Black Robe* (1991), another film with manifestly serious intentions, director Bruce Beresford offered a beautifully photographed tale of an enigmatic, cold-hearted, half-mad French Jesuit who attempts to bring Catholicism to the Indians of the Canadian wilderness in 1634. Ultimately, the antihero's efforts prove not only pointless, but tragic and destructive.

The most important point to keep in mind about all these movies and their grim and skeptical view of the Church of Rome is that their negativity is never answered by simultaneous releases that offer a sympathetic treatment of Catholicism. If, for instance, Twentieth Century Fox had chosen to balance *Nuns on the Run* with *The Mother Teresa Story*, it would be far more difficult to accuse the studio of anti-Catholic prejudice; as it is, the charge of underlying bias seems hard to rebut.

In fact, when pressed to think of a *single* film of the last fifteen years that presented a sympathetic view of the Church and its role in the world, one of the industry's most outspoken defenders could come up with only one: 1989's *Romero,* starring Raul Julia. This film biography of the murdered Archbishop of San Salvador most certainly makes a hero of a man of the cloth, but the Romero of the movie is celebrated more for his politics than for his piety; the film concentrates on his principled opposition to the American-backed government of his country and his ultimate martyrdom at the hands of unidentified right-wing forces. Moreover, despite heavy-handed and propagandistic messages that are totally in line with "politically correct" thinking in the film capital, *Romero* actually originated outside of the movie mainstream. The producer happened to be Father Ellwood "Bud" Kaiser, a Paulist priest, who enlisted private Catholic support for the low-budget production rather than relying on established producers or studios.

Bashing the Born-Agains

While the Catholic Church provides one prime focus for Hollywood's antireligious animus, it is by no means the only faith to feel the wrath of the entertainment industry. In recent films, Protestant clergymen have fared no better than their Catholic counterparts:

• *Crimes of Passion* (1984). As a sweaty, Bible-toting Skid Row evangelist, Anthony Perkins generates the same warmth and charm he brought to his famous role as Norman Bates in *Psycho*. He grits his teeth and twitches constantly, and in some scenes even drools, quoting biblical verses at the same time he amuses (and abuses) himself at sleazy peep shows. Obsessed with a part-time hooker (Kathleen Turner), this preacher pervert plans to "save her soul" by murdering her through the sexual insertion of a huge stainless steel cylinder with a lethally sharpened tip.

• *Children of the Corn* (1984). Kiddie Christians form a Kookie Killer Cult! In this laughable adaptation of a dreadful Stephen King short story, a group of religion-drenched adolescents go off the deep end, slaughtering their impious parents and taking over an Iowa town. From their headquarters in the local church, they follow a power-mad pubescent preacher called Malachi and spice up the style and language of Pentecostal Christianity with occasional indulgence in bloody human sacrifice.

• *Poltergeist II* (1986). This sorry sequel to the successful horror film of 1982 featured a hymn-singing preacher from beyond the grave (Julian Beck) who leads a band of demonic Bible-belters in trying to drag a hip suburban family down to hell. This other-worldly clergyman mouths Christian platitudes in breathy, soothing tones and, when he smiles, he bears an eerie resemblance to that celebrated born-again, Jimmy Carter. *Poltergeist II* stands as a striking example of the way that mainstream moviemakers have turned traditional thinking on its head—the only force that can save the likable secular family from these crazed Christians is an American Indian medicine man (Will Sampson), who mobilizes the protective power of ancient paganism.

• *The Vision* (1987). An impressive cast (Dirk Bogarde, Lee Remick, Helena Bonham-Carter) is utterly wasted on an insipid sci-fi fantasy about conspiring Christians who use hypnotic TV technology in a ruthless plot to take over the world. The advertising layout promoting the film could hardly be more candid about its antireligious agenda: "THE THREAT: Right-wing evangelists with an arsenal of riches and a hunger for power. THE CONSPIRACY: To reach across Europe via satellite television with the word of God. THE MISSION: To control *your* mind. WHEN THIS NETWORK GOES ON THE AIR, START PRAYING."

• *Light of Day* (1987). This somber stinker, written and directed by *Last Temptation* screenwriter Paul Schrader, portrays a prominent midwestern minister (Tom Irwin) as a pious, pompous fraud. His evil influence shatters the happiness of a likeable blue collar family, when the mother (Gena Rowlands) becomes a religious fanatic and bitterly rejects her two children, aspiring rock 'n' rollers played by Michael J. Fox and real-life rock star Joan Jett. Ultimately, the pastor's guilty secret is exposed: this mendacious man of God had secretly seduced Joan Jett when she was still a teenager, fathered her illegitimate son, and then denounced the girl for her immoral and irresponsible life-style.

• *Salvation!* (1987). Another holy hypocrite hides his private pruri-ence behind a mask of public piety—with Stephen McHattie trying his best to breathe life into his role as a delusional televangelist who is blackmailed after a sizzling sex incident.

• *Pass the Ammo* (1988). For those who just couldn't get enough of Jim and Tammy Fay Bakker on "Nightline," there was this soggy spoof about a smarmy TV preacher (Tim Curry) and his warbling wife (Annie Potts). Not content to depict their well-deserved public disgrace and the collapse of their ministry, this merciless movie refuses to let go until it has also blown their studios and TV transmitter to kingdom come in a series of noisy (and poorly staged) special-effects explosions.

• *The Handmaid's Tale* (1990). Some of the industry's most presti-gious performers (Robert Duvall, Faye Dunaway, Natasha Richardson, Elizabeth McGovern, Aidan Quinn) appeared in this pointedly political polemic about what life might be like if Christian fundamentalists came to power in America. As portrayed in the film, these religious zealots are considerably less lovable than Nazis, who at least had stylish uniforms to recommend them. In the course of the movie, the vicious theocratic government enslaves and degrades all women, pursues genocidal policies against ethnic minorities, burns books with "non-scriptural" messages, oppresses working people, assembles huge crowds to watch public hanging and torture, and uses brute force to enforce even the most arcane regulations from the Bible. In the movie's nightmarish vision, the evil evangelists who run the country aren't even sincere in their fanaticism: they emphasize modesty and purity and sobriety in all their rules and pronouncements, but secretly operate decadent bordellos for their private pleasure. Canadian author

Margaret Atwood, who wrote the novel that provided the basis for the film, describes *The Handmaid's Tale* as "my take on American Puritanism." When she first came up with the idea of doing the book, she says that she told herself, "I think I'm going to write about how religious fanatics would run the world if they got their druthers."

• *The Rapture* (1991). Mimi Rogers plays a buxom swinger, addicted to group sex with strangers, who sacrifices these satisfactions when she makes a sudden commitment to Christ. At first, her religious transformation appears to have positive consequences, but before the end of the film her "faith" causes her to take her six-year-old daughter out to the desert where they wait for days in the burning sun for the Rapture that is supposed to precede Christ's second coming. When nothing happens, the heroine takes a revolver, holds it to her daughter's head, and, while mumbling invocations of the Almighty, blows the child's brains out.

Throughout the film, Christian believers are portrayed as twitching zombies, with an obvious edge of madness behind their fervent beliefs. The only church you ever see in the film is a cultish congregation of about a dozen leisure-suited losers who worship an eleven-year-old African-American "prophet" who barks out weird metaphysical commands like a pint-sized Jim Jones. Naturally, those who belittle religious thinking deliver all the best lines. For instance, when the main character first displays her interest in Christianity, her boyfriend tells her, "It's like a drug. You feel pain. So instead of doing heroin, you do God." At the end of the film, after murdering her daughter, this tormented woman at last discovers the "courage" to blame God (who else?) for her own mad act. "You're supposed to love God no matter what," she declares. "But I *don't* love Him anymore. He has too many rules."

In an interview after the film's release, writer-director Michael Tolkin explained that he had altered the ending of the picture to make the antireligious message even more unequivocal. In the original version of the picture, the heroine "realized she made a mistake and she wants to go to heaven." Filmmaker Tolkin believes that final version features a character who is "stronger" because "she's rejecting God for creating a universe that put her to the test in the first place."

In another interview, Jim Svejda of CBS Radio asked Tolkin about charges that his film unfairly attacked religious believers. "It's not antireligion," he answered. "It's anti-God."

• *At Play in the Fields of the Lord* (1991). Peter Matthiessen's 1965 novel about crazed and arrogant missionaries in the Amazon rain forest had been considered an intriguing but unfilmable property in Hollywood for more than two decades before Universal Pictures, already well-known for its sympathy to the Christian community, courageously committed close to $30 million to bring it to the screen. The result, with a running time of more than three hours, an all-star cast, a two-time Oscar-winning producer (Saul Zaentz), and spectacular rain forest locations, represents the most ambitious all-out attack Hollywood has ever launched on organized religion. No faith is spared: in addition to the psychotic, repressed, relentlessly obnoxious and mean-spirited Protestant missionaries, the cast of characters also includes a foul-smelling, cynical Catholic priest and an alcoholic, whore-mongering, heavily-tattooed Jewish mercenary who offers contemptuous recollections of his own Bar Mitzvah. The script could hardly be more straightforward in laying out its antireligious agenda in one incident after another:

—A particularly heavy-handed episode involves the adorable nine-year-old son of one of the missionaries (Aidan Quinn) contracting jungle fever after he's bitten by a mosquito. As the child lies dying, he pathetically asks his father, "Why did God create mosquitoes?" When the little boy finally expires, the senior missionary (John Lithgow) briskly announces, "Well, the Lord has taken him," to which the child's father angrily responds, "The Lord hasn't taken him! Death has taken him! I don't want to worship a God who would do something like this!"

—Daryl Hannah, as the disillusioned wife of the shrill and fanatical John Lithgow, goes to visit the seedy Catholic priest her husband has labeled "the opposition" and who presides over a tiny church in a remote Brazilian village. "Do you really *believe*, Padre?" she asks him. In response, the man of the cloth merely shrugs. "I love the Church," he answers. "For a man like me, I need it. I need it!"

—Just before he dies in the jungle, missionary Aidan Quinn discovers that the primitive tribesmen he has been teaching have confused his talk of Jesus with their own traditions of "Kisu," a local god of demonic force. "I taught them that Jesus was an evil spirit!" he moans to Tom Berenger, an

American mercenary who has gone native and joined the jungle tribe. "Jesus, Kisu, what's the difference?" Berenger responds. "It's all hocus pocus anyway, isn't it, Martin?"

Though this line equates Christianity with the superstitions of the naked and painted jungle dwellers, the rest of the movie treats the native religions with far more respect than it accords any Western faith. Taking note of this preferential treatment, *Movieguide,* a publication of the Christian Film and Television Commission, makes an important point. "Filmed on location in the remote Amazon, the producers attempt to portray the fictitious Niaruna tribe as realistically as possible," writes Dr. Paul Reisser. "Ex-tribes-people were used in the cast, and were consulted extensively regarding costumes, body paint, and rituals. However, no one appears to have spent more than five minutes researching the lives and activities of contemporary missionaries."

• *Guilty as Charged* (1992). Described by its producers as "a stylish, witty, and macabre black comedy," this pathetic little picture stars Rod Steiger as a murderous maniac who just happens to be a Christian fanatic. He operates an inner-city slaughterhouse by day, but by night picks up convicted or accused murderers after they've been released by the authorities. He imprisons these poor souls in a home-made dungeon he's constructed in the basement of his meat factory, and one by one he executes them in a huge electric chair, decorated with religious motifs, that he's designed for the purpose. As the victims fry, howling in fear and pain, Steiger exults at the top of his lungs: "We praise the Lord for the Department of Water and Power! The Holy Spirit is electricity, and the chair is God's instrument of Justice and Salvation!" In this sadistic work, the hero is assisted by a slimy, Bible-toting sidekick described in the press materials as "a creepily pious minister," played by Isaac Hayes. In one touching scene, Hayes comforts a frightened boy who's just been incarcerated in the basement death row. "You don't even have to smell yourself!" he proudly declaims, concerning the virtues of electrocution. "That's the best part, 'cause there ain't nuthin' that smells worse than a man's body cookin' in the chair!" Crosses abound in this nightmarish world—prominently displayed in every cell and on the walls of the electrocution chamber, and formed from two strips of surgical tape fastened over the eyes of each victim before he dies. "Another lamb, on his way back to God!" Steiger enthuses, as they strap one more terrified customer to the chair. "Hallelujah!!"

Jabbing the Jews

In addition to the obvious antipathy to various forms of Christianity displayed in so many recent movies, Hollywood has also attempted some significant jabs at Judaism. For several reasons, however, the ridicule of the rabbis has been less intense than the negativity that is injected into the caricatures of Christian clergy.

This has less to do with the high concentration of Jews in the movie industry than with the prevailing perception that Judaism is all but irrelevant as a religious system. According to the most recent statistics, only 2.4 percent of the U.S. population identifies as Jewish, and the level of religious commitment and practice within that tiny group is significantly lower than that within *any* Christian denomination. The secularists who run the entertainment business can look upon the powerful Catholic Church, or the burgeoning born-again movement, as a threat or a challenge; Judaism, on the other hand, seems so statistically insignificant that it threatens no one, and offers a much less attractive target.

Nevertheless, on those relatively rare occasions when rabbis have appeared on screen they have hardly been treated with respect or reverence. A notorious example involved one of the skits included in Woody Allen's 1972 comedy, *Everything You Always Wanted to Know About Sex (But Were Afraid to Ask)*. As part of a fictitious TV quiz show called "What's My Perversion?", an elderly rabbi with a thick Yiddish accent wins the right to enact his private fantasy on live television. At his direction, a statuesque, scantily clad blonde whips him and declaims "You naughty rabbi!" while the Talmudic scholar writhes with pleasure and watches his elderly wife fall to her knees in front of him to eat a plate of greasy pork chops.

In a much later Woody Allen film, *Radio Days* (1987), the writer-director weaves a wonderful tapestry of dozens of colorful 1930s characters, and nearly all of them—burglars, Mafia hit men, philandering husbands—are portrayed with loving attention to detail that emphasizes their endearing human qualities. The only exception to this rule, and the least attractive character in the entire film, is "The Rabbi," played by Kenneth Mars with an accent so overdone and bogus it sounds more Martian than Yiddish. This sneering, self-important authoritarian forces the boys in his Hebrew school to go begging for contributions "to benefit Jews in Palestine" and after he discovers that one of his charges (Woody Allen's alter ego) has stolen from the *pushke* (collection box), he viciously smacks the boy in front of the child's embarrassed parents. Later in the same movie, another superficially pious figure (the boy's grossly overweight Uncle Abe, played by Josh Mostel) condemns the family's neighbors for listening to the radio on the holiest day of the year, Yom Kippur. He goes off indignantly to try to silence the noise, but returns an hour later, suddenly singing the praises of the enlightened people next door who have persuaded him to abandon his solemn fast by joining them in a delicious plate of pork chops.

The most recent graduate of the Woody Allen Rabbinic Seminary appeared in *Crimes and Misdemeanors* (1989). Unlike his predecessors, this clergyman (played by Sam Waterston) is Reform rather than Orthodox, and is described by his friends in the movie as a warm, decent, even saintly human being. Nevertheless, at the end of the film this good man suffers the loss of his eyesight, which most critics have understood as the filmmaker's commentary on the rabbi's "moral blindness" in insisting that God controls the world.

Far less sympathetic rabbis appear in *Enemies, a Love Story* (1989), in which Alan King plays a smug, pompous faker whose windy sermons are ghostwritten for him by the movie's main character; *The Outside Chance of Maximilian Glick* (1989), in which Saul Rubinek plays a fervently devout Hasidic rabbi who becomes so frustrated with his Canadian congregation that he runs away, shaves his beard, and transforms himself into a stand-up comedian; and *Homicide* (1991), in which a collection of religious figures with skullcaps and the traditional fringes (*tzitzis*) dangling at their belts participate in a dark conspiracy with Israeli agents to undermine the American authorities and manipulate the divided loyalties of a Jewish cop (Joe Mantegna).

Even less likable were the conspirators in *Naked Tango* (1991), which showed superficially devout Jews engaging in white slavery and prostitution in 1920s Buenos Aires. As written and directed by Leonard Schrader, brother of Paul Schrader (of *The Last Temptation* and *Light of Day*), this lurid and decadent film makes a point of showing that the hypocritical Hebrews have set up a kosher slaughterhouse and even a synagogue immediately adjacent to the bordello in which they practice monstrous cruelty; they even discuss their criminal plans while wearing skullcaps and apparently gathered for some unidentified religious occasion.

As the charismatic leader of another fanatically pious Hasidic sect in *The Chosen* (1981), Rod Steiger wasn't involved in illegal or immoral activities, but the entire arc of the story involves the need for the rabbi's son (Robby Benson) to escape his father's domination and to liberate himself from the restrictive bonds of a nostalgically portrayed but utterly outmoded religious tradition. Similarly, Barbra Streisand's *Yentl* (1983) paints an essentially affectionate portrait of its long-bearded Eastern European rabbis, but the system they serve is depicted with far less sympathy. The premise of the movie is that traditional Judaism is so irredeemably sexist that it forces the intellectually ambitious heroine (Ms. Streisand, of course) to disguise her gender in order to satisfy her desire for Jewish learning. Ultimately, she abandons the masquerade and flees to America, leaving behind both the social restrictions and the superstitious religiosity that have stood in her way. The underlying message echoes one of the most common complaints against organized faith, suggesting that religious convention is at best a crutch or a relic, and is, in any case, an obstacle to personal fulfillment.

A Perverse Idealism

In looking over the varied list of antireligious message movies compiled above, the average filmgoer will see many titles that he doesn't even recognize. This is no accident, since the overwhelming majority of these pictures performed abysmally at the box office. Even many projects with big-name stars and substantial budgets failed to connect with the public; in fact, some of them never even achieved national release.

The very fact that so many of these films flopped so resoundingly says volumes about the depth of Hollywood's hostility to religion: it definitively demolishes the argument that the industry only turns out such tendentious tedium in order to give the public what it wants. The American people most emphatically do *not* want movies like *Monsignor* or *The Pope Must Die* or *Pass the Ammo* or *The Handmaid's Tale* or *Naked Tango*—in fact, their rejection of such material has been so consistent that even the most obtuse movie producer should have begun to get the idea. If a formula is frequently successful, it's easy to understand why producers keep repeating it and reworking it in the hopes of further profit, but it's difficult to explain why the industry should continue to favor and finance the same anticlerical characterizations and messages that have failed in the past with such stunning predictability. Taken together, the cinematic assaults on religion have lost hundreds of millions for the people who made them, but the major studios (as well as the independent production companies) persist in throwing good money after bad.

This tendency represents a perverse sort of idealism. For many of the most powerful people in the entertainment business, hostility to organized religion goes so deep and burns so intensely that they insist on expressing that hostility, even at the risk of financial disaster. When otherwise savvy producers are willing to defy logic, past experience, and commercial self-interest in order to create movies that promote antireligious stereotypes and messages, then it is clear that a powerful prejudice is at work.

Gratuitous Insults

Evidence of that prejudice turns up not only in those films that focus specifically on religious issues and individuals, but also appears in the form of gratuitous insults inserted in movies that have nothing at all to do with spiritual themes. The negative attitude toward Judeo-Christian believers is so pervasive and so passionately held in Hollywood that some producers will use every opportunity to express their contempt, even if it means inserting derisive comments or characterizations in wildly incongruous settings.

The costly 1988 remake of *The Blob*, for instance, is not generally recognized as a work of profound theological substance, but it does contain its own oblique indictment of religion. The plot focuses on a gob of killer Jell-O from outer space that menaces a small town, and one of the minor characters in the threatened village is the soft-spoken, bespectacled pastor (Del Close). This superficially saintly man turns out to be a secret drunk and a lunatic, with fevered delusions of Armageddon. The last scene in the movie shows his crazed, sweaty sermon about the impending end of the world, while he fiendishly contrives to revive the title monster and unleash it once again as a threat to humanity.

Another sci-fi fantasy film with gratuitous antireligious overtones is *Edward Scissorhands* (1990), about a man-made mechanical boy (Johnny Depp) whose unfinished fingers have been fashioned by his mad-scientist creator out of scissor blades. He is misunderstood by most people in the suburban neighborhood where he seeks refuge, but the most hysterically hostile response comes from the only religious figure in town—a shrieking, hymn-singing harpie with stained-glass windows in her home and a rotating neon cross in her living room.

The one committed Christian in Spike Lee's *Jungle Fever* (1991) is painted in similarly lurid tones. As part of a significant subplot, Ossie Davis provides a smoldering, powerhouse performance as "The Good Reverend Doctor," a retired minister of the Gospel who is the father of the main character (Wesley Snipes). His religious fanaticism makes the old man bitter, intolerant, explosive, and ultimately homicidal: in one of the film's climactic scenes he brutally murders his older son (Samuel L. Jackson) and then proudly sets down the smoking gun on top of his opened Bible.

The wretched relationship between a clergyman and his child also figured prominently in *Footloose* (1984). John Lithgow plays a key supporting role as a mean-spirited fire-and-brimstone preacher who tyrannizes a small town in the Bible Belt and imposes strict local rules against all public dancing. This cinematic exposé fearlessly confronts this tragically common national problem, dramatizing the familiar dilemma of repressed and regimented teenagers who are prevented by their all-powerful parents from ever enjoying themselves. Liberation finally arrives in the person of the new boy in town (Kevin Bacon) who arrives from the big city and attempts to organize a dance for the bitterly oppressed local teens. In the face of this enlightened challenge, the sick and insecure pastor lashes out viciously at his own lovely (and previously loving) daughter (Lori Singer).

His cruelty is trivial, however, when compared to the vicious extremes displayed by the devout villain in *Misery* (1990). Kathy Bates won the Best Actress Oscar for playing a sadistic and psychotic slob who tortures and cripples her favorite novelist (James Caan) while holding him prisoner for weeks in her remote cabin in the mountains. When her victim looks through her proudly maintained scrapbook, he discovers that she had tuned up for this orgy of cruelty by murdering a series of patients while working as a nurse in a hospital years earlier. Perhaps in the hope of giving this slick and empty horror picture some deeper significance as a piece of social commentary, director Rob Reiner focuses repeatedly on the tiny gold cross that Ms. Bates wears around her neck; it often catches the light and flashes out at the camera, particularly on those occasions when her behavior is most menacing and bizarre. The character also makes several references to God, Jesus, church, and the Bible that are clearly meant to make her all the more terrifying to the audience.

A similar approach is employed in Martin Scorsese's acclaimed *Cape Fear* (1991), though in this instance there is nothing subtle or demure about the cross that is attached to the crazed killer: it appears as a gigantic tattoo covering every available inch of Robert De Niro's muscular back. This brutal ex-con, a convicted rapist who has graphically mutilated one of his victims, murdered a family's beloved dog, and threatened the head of the household (Nick Nolte) with bloody retribution for a past affront, also sports biblical quotations tattooed on each arm, complete with specific citations for chapter and verse. Other religious references abound, as De Niro discusses his membership in a Pentecostal church, carries a Bible under his arm in several scenes, and smugly assures the family whose life he has so horribly disrupted that he is only interested in "saving souls." In the movie's protracted and blood-soaked climax, this religious role model licks his lips as he prepares to rape Jessica Lange, shouting out to her, "Are you ready to be born again? After one hour with me, you'll be talkin' in tongues." Eventually, he speaks in tongues himself, during a brief break between his savage assaults on the husband, the wife, and their teenage daughter.

The most astonishing aspect of all the religious references that director Scorsese chose to inject into his story is that none of these elements appeared in the source material that inspired the film. The new *Cape Fear* is a remake of a 1962 thriller that starred Gregory Peck and Robert Mitchum (both of whom make cameo appearances in Scorsese's version), and Mitchum, who played the De Niro role in the original, somehow managed to project plenty of menace and cruelty without employing a single religious symbol. Scorsese's decision to alter the first film by turning the bad guy into a Pentecostal Christian can only be interpreted as a powerful statement—though perhaps an unconscious one—of his underlying sense that there is something twisted, threatening, and scary in fervent religiosity. It had been only three years since the same director had done battle with the Christian community over the release of *The Last Temptation of Christ;* the emphasis on the religious dimension of the villain in *Cape Fear* might well be described as Scorsese's revenge on the born-again believers who had so passionately protested his previous picture. The fact that Universal Pictures, still licking its own wounds from the *Last Temptation* fiasco, happened to be the company that financed and enthusiastically promoted *Cape Fear,* only strengthened the impression that De Niro's characterization amounted to a deliberate slap at some old enemies.

What surprised me most about the wildly enthusiastic critical response to the film at the time of its release was that so few of my colleagues took note of this connection, or joined me in pointing out the movie's defamatory treatment of committed Christians. Imagine that the picture had portrayed the vengeful psychotic as a member of some other group known for its abiding faith and passionate commitment—say the ACLU, or Greenpeace, or the National Abortion Rights Action League, or the AIDS Coalition to Unleash Power, or the American Indian Movement. Wouldn't his identification with one of these causes or life-styles seem an absolutely unnecessary affront to all others who shared such values? Why, then, should industry insiders so cheerfully accept the decision to make the evil maniac an evangelical Christian?

Just a few months before Universal released *Cape Fear,* the entertainment press and the studio establishment gave respectful treatment to representatives of GLAAD (The Gay and Lesbian Alliance Against Discrimination) who protested the movie *The Silence of the Lambs.* They complained that in portraying a brutal serial killer (Ted Levine) with effeminate mannerisms (and a poodle named Precious), the movie perpetuated hateful stereotypes and slandered all gay people. Why is it offensive to portray a creep and a murderer as a homosexual, but totally acceptable to present him as a religious Christian? The contrast between the serious discussion of the potentially offensive content in *The Silence of the Lambs* and the total silence concerning the possibility of antireligious bigotry in *Cape Fear,* or *Misery,* or so many other films highlights the irrational double standard that afflicts nearly all industry insiders.

That same double standard applies to lines of dialogue that sometimes arrive out of left field to question God or to blast religion. In contrast to Hollywood's Golden Age, no self-respecting filmmaker today would ever insert a speech in which the hero of a movie suddenly insisted that all his friends must believe in God or go to church; this sort of message would be considered too heavy-handed, too embarrassing, too preachy. Preaching *against* religion is, however, entirely accepted, and used as a means of helping a film to achieve a veneer of seriousness and "class." In a key scene in *Born on the Fourth of July* (1989), the paralyzed hero (Tom Cruise) passionately rejects God and denounces his Roman Catholic upbringing on the same night that he finally confronts his doubts about the Vietnam War. "There is no God!" he shrieks to his horrified parents. "God is as dead as my legs!"

Star Trek V: The Final Frontier (1989) provides a more exotic setting for its antireligious messages. The *Enterprise* is hijacked by the members of a strange cult, who dress themselves in sackcloth and sandals like the Apostles in an old-time biblical movie. Following a dangerous and exhausting voyage, the crew reverently confronts a misty, white-bearded power identified as "God" (and played by one George Murdock), only to discover that this potent force is actually an evil demon that must be destroyed. After an orgy of incoherent special effects, and the demise of the malevolent "God," the members of the crew spend a few pensive moments on the bridge of the *Enterprise* trying to decide "what it all means," and the following exchange ensues:

CAPTAIN KIRK (William Shatner): Cosmic thoughts, gentlemen?

"BONES" McCOY (DeForest Kelley): We were speculating. Is God *really* out there?

CAPTAIN KIRK: Maybe he's not out there, Bones. Maybe he's right here. [*He points to his chest.*] The human heart.

Delivering such secular humanist sermons may have brought a glow of satisfaction to William Shatner, who directed the film based on his original story, but they hardly helped to win the support of the moviegoing public. The God-bashing theme combined with the picture's innumerable artistic shortcomings to produce a major commercial disappointment; of all the six *Star Trek* movies, this fifth entrant in the series drew by far the smallest audience.

5

Forgetting
the Faithful

The People's Religion

The apparent eagerness of some of Hollywood's most powerful personalities to belittle religious believers is a puzzling predilection for people whose professional survival depends entirely on pleasing the public; it stems from a fundamental failure to recognize the heartfelt commitment to traditional faith that characterizes a significant—and growing—percentage of the American population.

In 1988 pollster George Gallup delivered a speech concerning the evolution of public opinion in which he predicted that the 1990s would become known as the "Decade of the People's Religion." In the course of his address, Gallup reported that his latest surveys showed that "levels of religious belief and practice in the U.S. are extraordinarily high. For example, the large majority of Americans believe in a personal God . . . believe their prayers are answered and say that religion is either 'very' or 'fairly' important in their lives. In fact, only 4 percent of Americans are totally 'nonreligious'—that is, say religion is not at all important in their lives, do not belong to a church or attend a church, and have no religious affiliation."

These figures contrast dramatically with the results of a 1983 *Pub-*

lic Opinion survey of 104 of the most influential leaders of TV's creative community that showed a full "45 percent who claim no religious affiliation whatsoever" and an astounding "93 percent who say they seldom or never attend religious services." In an October 1991 interview with a Catholic newspaper in New York, veteran television producer John Prizer conceded, "The lack of religious commitment on the part of people in Hollywood is quite astonishing. I can't think of a director or actor or writer under forty-five who goes to church or synagogue."

This appallingly unrepresentative personal perspective has helped to blind Hollywood's leaders to the intense involvement of most Americans with organized faith. As *Newsweek* magazine reported in January 1992: "This week, if you believe at all in opinion surveys, more of us will pray than will go to work, or exercise, or have sexual relations." According to *Newsweek*'s research, 78 percent of Americans pray at least once a week, and more than 40 percent attend worship services on a weekly basis. *This means that the number of people who go to church in a given week is more than five times larger than the number of people who go to the movies.*

In December 1991, a *Time*/CNN poll offered similarly striking figures concerning the depth of religious feeling on the part of the American people: 78 percent support prayer in the public schools, 89 percent back a moment of silence at the start of the school day, and 63 percent say they could not vote for a presidential candidate who didn't believe in God. By a ratio of five to one (55 percent to 11 percent), the public believes that there is "too little" religious influence in America rather than "too much."

Perhaps most astonishing of all, a poll reported in *U.S. News and World Report* (December 1991) asked American voters to describe "their greatest objective in life"; fully 56 percent listed "a closer relationship to God" as their top personal priority.

In the light of such figures, Hollywood's persistent hostility to religious values is not just peculiar, it is positively pathological. Rather than readjusting their view of reality in order to come to terms with the religious revival in America—and the widely reported resurgence in church attendance and affiliation—most people in the movie capital simply choose to ignore what the surveys tell them. They retreat ever deeper into their precious and hermetically sealed little world of Malibu "enlightenment," and continue to write off all religious believers as so many slope-browed bumpkins who get their clothes from K mart and their ideas from the *National Enquirer.* A few of the best-informed moguls may be vaguely aware of research results that challenge these stereotypes, but even those who know the studies stubbornly refuse to believe them.

I've seen public demonstrations of this denial behavior at literally dozens of Hollywood parties and receptions. On these social occasions I make it a point to ask movie professionals about their impressions of the public that supports their careers. In particular, I find it fascinating to watch them guess at the percentage of Americans who attend church or synagogue every week.

In more than five years of playing this little game with scores of acquaintances in the entertainment industry, no one has ever guessed weekly attendance at worship services as higher than 20 percent; the most common response is "5 percent or less." When I then tip my hand and cite all the surveys that show that the actual number is 40 percent or more, their response is not so much embarrassed as it is disbeliev-ing. I remember one producer in particular who steadfastly refused to credit the idea that nearly half the American people participated in religious services every week. "If all those people really go to church," he snorted, "then how come I don't know a single one of them?"

The answer, of course, is that his range of acquaintance is radically unrepresentative of the American mainstream. The only committed Christians that he sees regularly are the evangelists he occasionally watches on TV. No wonder that the entertainment industry so often paints a flamboyant and bizarre portrait of religious life: Hollywood's writers and directors are far more familiar with Jimmy Swaggart than they are with any of the working clergy in their local communities. Writer-director Michael Tolkin, for example, freely admits that he became addicted to an odd assortment of religious programs on cable as part of the "research" for his film *The Rapture.*

The industry's blind spot toward religion also reflects the fact that so many of the people who shape our popular culture have personally rejected the established institutions of organized faith. The previously cited survey of 104 key television executives indicates that even though 93 percent say they received a "religious upbringing," only 7 percent currently describe themselves as "regular" participants in church or synagogue services. If they have "outgrown" the religious conventions of their own childhood, they naturally expect that the rest of the country will follow their admirable example. In terms of its religious dimension, as in so many others, the vision of reality that appears on our movie and television screens is a world that Hollywood has created in its own image.

The View from Mars

Imagine what conclusions a perceptive Martian might draw about the way we live and worship in these United States if his only source of information were an interplanetary rent-by-mail service that provided him with video versions of all the latest Hollywood releases.

This outer-space observer would never guess that religion played a powerful role in the daily lives of tens of millions of Americans. How many times in recent films would he have seen contemporary urbanites entering a church—except for an occasional funeral or wedding? Based on his movie viewing, our Martian would surely assume that the Judeo-Christian tradition had shrunk to the status of a seedy sideshow in today's society, exclusively engaging the energies of deranged or devious individuals.

The summer of 1991 provided several appalling examples of the movie industry's insistence on erasing even the most rudimentary religious feelings from the characters it creates. In that single desultory season, Hollywood unleashed three big-budget medical melodramas— *Dying Young* (with Julia Roberts), *The Doctor* (with William Hurt), and *Regarding Henry* (with Harrison Ford). In all three films, the protagonists faced dire illnesses and long hospitalizations, with life and death hanging dramatically in the balance. At no point in these proceedings, however, did the main characters, or any of their friends or family members, turn for even one moment to the power of prayer, or ask to see a member of the clergy, or in any way invoke the name of God.

While *Newsweek* reports that 78 percent of the country prays *at least* once a week under ordinary circumstances, it seems safe to assume that the propensity toward prayer only increases as an individual deals with death. The old saw suggests that "there are no atheists in foxholes"; by the same token you will find precious few atheists on operating tables. Hollywood's refusal to show religious reflection on the

part of vulnerable people in this situation is not only a waste of an obvious dramatic opportunity, it is fundamentally unrealistic.

Equally unrealistic was the portrayal of the fictional village of
Grady, South Carolina, in yet another release in the summer of '91:
Doc Hollywood. The plot of this inoffensive and intermittently entertaining comedy is intended as a paean to "small-town values": after a
highway mishap forces him to spend some time in a rural hamlet that
desperately needs a doctor, yuppie physician Michael J. Fox decides to
give up his dreams of glitz and glory in L.A. and to throw in his lot with
the quaint and lovable locals.

In one sense, he has indeed found a new home that is remarkable:
the village in the movie must be the only town of any size in the entire
state of South Carolina with no church to serve its citizens. We see
dozens of these colorful characters fishing on the lake, tending their
farms, staging the annual Squash Festival, working in an auto shop,
feasting at a barbecue in the mayor's backyard, and hanging out endlessly at the greasy spoon on Main Street, but not one of them—
regardless of race or age—ever attends church or participates in religious services. This may represent Hollywood's dearest dream of small-
town nirvana: a village with all the homey virtues of the Deep South
but none of that embarrassing and unwelcome religiosity you normally
associate with the Bible Belt.

Doc Hollywood notwithstanding, the movie industry has generally
acknowledged that backwoods boroughs in the American heartland
are somewhat more hospitable to religious values than, say, the
municipality of Beverly Hills. Two of 1991's better films, for example,
Paradise and *The Man in the Moon,* drew much of their strength
from loving recreations of rural villages of the 1950s where nearly all
the townspeople attend church. Yet even in such rustic and long-ago
settings, Hollywood's persistent prejudice still prevails: in both films,
the leading men (Don Johnson and Sam Waterston, respectively) are
noble providers and protectors who also happen to be identified as
the village atheists. Despite the pleading of their frustrated wives
(Melanie Griffith and Tess Harper), they steadfastly refuse to set foot
in church; coincidentally, each of these enormously admirable figures
makes it a point to go fishing (and to commune with nature) on Sunday mornings. Whatever the virtues of these two fine films, they provide one more indication of Hollywood's irresistible impulse to iden-

tify rejection of organized religion with personal heroism and integrity.

The Museum-Piece Approach

This antireligious bias has been stifled only in exceedingly rare instances in recent years, allowing for a few films that have portrayed organized faith in a favorable and affectionate light; not surprisingly, these exceptions invariably involve some exotic setting, far removed in space or time (or both) from today's big-city realities. The museum-piece approach in each of these films presents organized religion as a fascinating—even beautiful—relic of the past that may continue to exist in some isolated pockets in the boondocks, but that is no more meaning-ful to mainstream America than the artifacts of the ancient Aztecs. In these nostalgic affirmations of that "old-time religion," the church is suf-ficiently distant from the daily life that most of us lead that it represents no threat to the militant secularism that Hollywood embraces so enthu-siastically; religion remains at all times reassuringly irrelevant.

• *Chariots of Fire* (1981), for instance, takes place entirely in the vanished, aristocratic England of the 1920s. Within that context, this inspiring film makes a hero of a handsome Scottish missionary (Ian Charleson) who is so devout that he refuses to run in the Olympics if it would force him to violate the Sabbath.

• *Tender Mercies* (1983) focuses on a dusty, lonely Texas cross-roads, and shows the power of religious faith to transform the life of a washed-up, alcoholic country-and-western singer (Robert Duvall). The moving and understated baptism scene takes place in a tiny country church.

• Horton Foote, the same great screenwriter who created *Tender Mercies*, also wrote *The Trip to Bountiful* (1985)—about a sweet and profoundly religious old lady (Geraldine Page) who wants to escape from the Houston home of her materialistic son and daughter-in-law in order to visit her tiny hometown once more before she dies. The set-ting again is rural Texas—this time in the 1950s.

• Small-town Texas in the 1930s is the locale for *Places in the Heart* (1984), with Sally Field fighting to save the family farm, and an astonishing concluding scene that shows all the characters in the film, including several who died earlier in the story, taking Communion together in a humble country church.

• *Witness* became one of the top-grossing movies of 1985, with Harrison Ford as a fugitive Philadelphia cop who is sheltered in a secluded Amish community in the farming country of central Pennsylvania. The portrayal of the Amish and their uncompromising rejection of modernity is not only sympathetic—it is idealized.

• *Driving Miss Daisy* (1989) tenderly presented two elderly believers, one white and Jewish (Jessica Tandy) and one black and Christian (Morgan Freeman), who develop a mutually dependent and loving relationship in Atlanta in the 1940s and 1950s.

• *Ramblin' Rose* (1991) centers on a churchgoing, warmhearted, intelligent couple (Robert Duvall and Diane Ladd) in rural Georgia in the 1930s, and their consistent kindness to a homeless wench (Laura Dern), whose need for male attention causes considerable trouble in their tiny town.

In addition to their sympathy to religious characters, and their remote settings, the extraordinary films mentioned above shared another common element: an impressive level of both commercial and critical success. These seven pictures won two Oscars for Best Picture of the year, three for Best Actress, and one for Best Actor. The religious overtones in these movies most certainly contributed to their prestige, adding a sense of depth and timelessness to otherwise simple stories. The public also responded extraordinarily well to the respectful and affirmative views of faith featured in these films: all of these titles exceeded expectations at the box office and *Chariots of Fire, Witness*, and *Driving Miss Daisy* became huge international hits.

Considering the traditionalist leanings of so many Americans, the success of such films can hardly come as a surprise; far more difficult to explain is Hollywood's failure to follow these triumphant examples and to introduce similarly sympathetic attitudes toward religion in movies set in modern metropolitan areas. In feature films, contemporary cities and suburbs remain religion-free zones. The movie industry has ignored the success of films that look favorably on faith with the same sort of self-destructive stubbornness that has led to its continued sponsorship of antireligious-message movies.

Reinforcement from Rock

In outlining Hollywood's assault on religion I have concentrated on motion pictures, where the antifaith messages have been particularly overt and insistent, but the same values receive regular reinforcement through all other channels of the popular culture.

Rock 'n' roll music, for instance, has come a long way since the days when John Lennon could spark angry protests throughout the United States by making an offhand comment to a rock journalist that suggested that the Beatles were more popular than Jesus. In 1966 the resulting uproar forced even Lennon, at the peak of his popularity and his influence, to issue a public apology. "I'm sorry I said it, really," the chastened star told a crowded press conference. "I'm not anti-God, anti-Christ, or antireligion."

Today, comments like Lennon's could never cause controversy; a contemptuous attitude toward religion is all but expected from mainstream pop performers. In 1991 Irish singer Sinead O'Connor, the unsmiling bald banshee who has inexplicably attracted a worldwide following, told *Spin* magazine: "I think organized religion is a crutch. . . . It's a huge abuse to teach children that God is not within themselves. . . . That God is bigger than them. That God is outside them. That's a lie. . . . Nobody has the right to tell anyone else what to think or believe. Especially the Catholic Church, with the amount of murdering or pillaging that it's done." In contrast to the angry reaction that greeted O'Connor's similarly provocative comments about the American national anthem, her theological musings attracted little attention; we are no longer in any sense surprised at rock 'n' roll philosophers who go out of their way to express antireligious sentiments.

Madonna, the consummate superstar of the MTV age, has abused Christian symbols from the beginning of her career: her performing name is itself an ironic commentary on the strict Catholic upbringing that she has "transcended." Her controversial "Like a Prayer" video (1989) takes place almost entirely inside a small church, where she comes to worship the weeping carved image of an African-American saint. In an ecstasy of piety and erotic attraction, she kisses the feet of the icon, then falls to the ground, reaching for her crotch and simulating masturbation. This minidrama also shows the scantily clad star magically developing stigmata—displaying wounds on her palms like the suffering Jesus—and dancing in front of three burning crosses.

Following her lead, innumerable performers attempt to attract attention by injecting religious elements into their outrageous acts, appealing to the public with names like "Jesus Jones," "Faith No More," "The Jesus and Mary Chain," and "MC 900 FT JESUS," who croons a charming ditty called "Killer Inside Me." Along similar lines, the critically acclaimed New Wave band Dead Kennedys released a 1985 album entitled *Franckenchrist*. In addition to providing the group's teenage fans with the usual shrieking solos by lead singer Jello Biafra, this elegant work of art came packaged with a free pornographic poster entitled "Penis Landscape" that showed a dozen graphic close-ups of male-female copulation.

Another provocative title, "Losing My Religion" by R.E.M., sounded a note that the entire industry enthusiastically endorsed, nominating the song for all of 1991's major music awards. In the same year, the popular heavy-metal group Metallica sang of "The God That Failed":

> I see faith in your eyes, never you hear the discouraging lies . . .
> The healing hand held back by the deepened nail, follow the God that
> failed.

Such muddled material pales in comparison to the far more emphatic spiritual statements from satanic posers like Venom in their 1985 song "Possessed":

> I am possessed by all that is evil, the death of your God I demand,
> I spit at the virgin you worship and sit at Lord Satan's left hand.

With groups like Black Sabbath and Judas Priest achieving vast popularity, it's easy to exaggerate the significance of satanic influences in contemporary music. Despite the prominence of pentagrams and severed goat's heads on countless album covers, describing publicity-hungry musicians as devoted followers of the Prince of Darkness is to give them more credit than they deserve. Ever since Mick Jagger titillated the public with "Sympathy for the Devil," popular performers have cultivated diabolical pretensions, but this hardly means they are sincere in their satanism. When *Rolling Stone* describes Peter Criss of Kiss leaping on stage and declaring to the audience, "I find myself evil! I believe in the devil as much as God!" it should be taken no more seriously than his producer's solemn boast that the boys are "symbols of unfettered evil and sensuality." Nevertheless, the frequent emphasis on the dark side and its symbols, no matter how shallow and self-serving, bears witness to the estrangement of the mainstream music business from conventional religious values.

God on "The Tonight Show"

In the world of television, that estrangement is more subtle, involving an overriding allergy to religious content more than the insertion of openly offensive material. It certainly says something about the state of the medium that the single best-known believer on network TV is the prim, sanctimonious (and schizophrenic) "Church Lady" on "Saturday Night Live." As portrayed by the versatile Dana Carvey, "she" begins each of her "Church Talk" skits with an air of artificial and saccharine enthusiasm ("Isn't that special!"), but is gradually transformed to a raving lunatic who sees Satan's influence everywhere.

God's influence, on the other hand, is all but invisible on American television. As TV screenwriter Lloyd Billingsley observed in a powerful 1985 article for *Christianity Today:* "I cannot remember any episode of any show in which a character was religiously motivated to do or not to do some important act. . . . In the unwritten constitution of television, the separation of church and screen is strictly adhered to, even in family programs such as 'The Cosby Show.' God is effectively written out of existence (except in repeated ejaculatons like 'Oh, my God!') and Judeo-Christian values on such things as adultery and divorce are disregarded."

Billingsley is hardly alone in noting the striking absence of religious elements in the portrayal of American reality that appears night after night on the small screen. Dan Wakefield, creator of the acclaimed NBC series "James at 15," wrote a 1989 article for *TV Guide* entitled "We Need More Religion in Prime Time". He noted that "religion is rarely mentioned in current prime-time dramas or sitcoms that supposedly reflect the way we live now. Yet religion and spirituality are increasingly a prime (if not yet prime-*time*) factor in contemporary life."

Along similar lines, feminist social critic Barbara Grizzuti Harrison asked, "Did you ever hear the word *God* on 'The Tonight Show'? Wouldn't it seem likely that some of the ethnic characters in, say, 'Hill Street Blues' might express their anguish or their hopes in the form of prayer? In spite of the show's claim to verisimilitude, they don't. Ever."

These impressions have been powerfully confirmed by statistical analysis. In a 1992 study, professors from Northwestern University, the University of Dayton, and Duke University Medical Center evaluated more than one hundred productions on the four major networks for their religious content and images. They concluded that only 5.4 percent of the characters had an identifiable religious affiliation—although 89 percent of Americans claim affiliation with an organized faith. In summing up their report, the researchers concluded: "Television's treatment of religion tends to be best characterized as abuse through neglect."

S. Robert Lichter, Linda Licther, and Stanley Rothman observed similar patterns in their invaluable 1991 study, *Watching America,* for which they researched some 620 prime-time shows dating back to 1955, and evaluated the background, occupation, and motivation of 7,365 major characters. Concerning the depiction of religious leaders and ideas, their conclusions proved unequivocal. "Clergy are a rarity on prime time," they wrote, "and religious themes are rarer still. Just over one in every hundred census-coded characters have had religious vocations, and their number has dipped *below* the 1 percent mark since 1975. . . . On television religion is relegated mostly to Sunday mornings and televangelists."

The rare exceptions to this rule often involve religious individuals and institutions that are shown in the most unflattering imaginable light. Television movies like *Glory! Glory!* (1989) or *Pray TV* (1982) concentrate on hypocritical media ministers and their manipulation of the public, while *Judgment* (1990) focused on a popular parish priest who molested his male students. Another movie of the week, *Flight of Black Angel* (1991), centered on an air force officer and born-again Christian whose apocalyptic visions lead him to a mad mission to nuke Las Vegas, while the lavish miniseries *The Thorn Birds* built its whole elaborate plot around one tormented priest (Richard Chamberlain) who violates his vows.

In addition to these television "events," regular weekly episodes of prime-time series have demonstrated an increasing eagerness to rely on religious figures as convenient and colorful villains. In one memorable adventure of "T. J. Hooker," William Shatner finally manages to track down a ruthless, Scripture-spouting crook who leaves Bibles as calling cards at the scene of his crimes. During the first four months of 1989 alone, the American Family Association identified several instances of network series that showed members of the clergy in despicable behavior, including ABC's "The Women of Brewster Place," showing a preacher propositioning a woman after his sermon and eventually luring her to his bed; NBC's "UNSUB," in which "Bishop Grace" murders two teenage girls in his congregation; and NBC's "In the Heat of the Night," in which a "Reverend Haskell" dies after enjoying an adulterous affair with one of his parishioners. More recently (9/27/90), "Knots Landing" features a crazed born-again character who attempts to murder his ex-wife's fiancé, and "Shannon's Deal" (5/7/90) shows two more fundamentalist kidnappers (denounced in the script as "Bible-thumpin' hayseeds"), together with a devout Christian who murders his wife and then justifies the killing as "an act of God . . . unstoppable as a flood." A figure of faith also fares poorly on "The Golden Girls," in an episode (9/29/90) presenting an adopted woman who discovers her natural father was a superficially pious monk who enjoyed a brief fling with a monastery cook. Two recent episodes of "Law and Order" (12/11/90 and 1/8/91) have taken aim at religious fanatics who happen to be active in the pro-life movement: one of them is exposed as a vicious wife-beater, while another attempts to kill one of her Christian colleagues who has hypocritically visited a clinic to seek her own abortion.

Though TV producers have seldom gone as far as moviemakers in attempting to advance an antireligious agenda, their corrosive contempt for conventional Judeo-Christian practices will occasionally turn up in unexpected contexts. In 1990 the Fox Television Network chose to promote its most popular show with a satirical scene that mocked a family saying grace. With all of the Simpsons gathered around their dinner table, Bart solemnly intones, "Dear God, we pay for all this stuff ourselves, so thanks for nothing."

It apparently never occurred to the mighty moguls at Fox that by featuring this witty line in an ad for their cherished program they risked offending a portion of the potential audience in a nation where tens of millions of families say grace themselves on a regular basis. Similarly, Amanda Donahoe, who plays one of the glamorous attorneys on the hit NBC series "L.A. Law," felt no trepidation whatever in venting her extreme anti-Christian views in a 1991 profile in *Interview* magazine. "I'm an atheist, so it was actually a joy. Spitting on Christ was a great deal of fun," she gaily observed concerning her role in the Ken Russell horror spoof, *The Lair of the White Worm*. "I can't embrace a male god who has persecuted female sexuality throughout the ages. And that persecution still goes on today all over the world."

"Sunday Dinner"

The same sort of distaste for the conventional convictions of mainstream Americans helped to undermine an otherwise intriguing attempt to transcend TV's traditional taboo concerning religious content. In 1991, Norman Lear, the legendary creator of "All in the Family," "Sanford and Son," and many other topical and influential shows of the 1970s, returned to prime time after an absence of thirteen years in order to bring the public a new CBS series that would forthrightly confront issues of faith. With unusual intensity, he involved himself in every detail of his new "spiritual sitcom," "Sunday Dinner," and even wrote the first episode himself. As he reviewed television history for *The New York Times* just before his new show's debut, Lear declared: "With all these thousands of hours and half hours, nobody's really talked much about God and faith and the inner life. 'Sunday Dinner' intends to evoke that conversation."

Whatever its intentions, the show presented a cockeyed, superficial, and strangely slanted view of religion in America. The main source of spiritual enlightenment in the show is a gorgeous young environmental lawyer (Teri Hatcher) whose personal faith is a ditzy and unstructured combination of New Age mysticism, feel-good psychology, primitive nature worship, ecological activism, and what she calls "cosmic piety." To show her special connection to a "Supreme Being," she regularly turns her moist eyes heavenward and speaks aloud to a Higher Power who is variously addressed as "She," "He," "It," or "The Chief." She also offers occasional pearls of timeless wisdom, as when she explains that "the natural world is the largest sacred community to which we all belong."

Not surprisingly, the other characters in the show are at first unimpressed by the spiritual depths plumbed by this pious pilgrim. They include her new husband, a much-older widower (Robert Loggia) who is comfortable with his cheerful agnosticism, and his three quarreling children: one of them a microbiologist and militant atheist, another a dabbler in faddish Eastern religions, and the third a thoroughly secularized "Reagan-era yuppie who worships only wealth and power." In other words, this major network "breakthrough" concerning religious issues concentrates on five major characters—*not one of whom regularly attends church or synagogue of any kind.*

The only representative of conventional religiosity in the show is the aging Aunt Martha (Marian Mercer), a character who seems to have been inspired at least in part by "Saturday Night Live"'s "Church Lady." She is narrow-minded, judgmental, and disapproving when it comes to the heroine's "new alternatives" in spirituality, and spends much of her time muttering in the kitchen about how sad it is that her own church is empty every Sunday. This is particularly surprising since all available figures indicate continued gains in church participation across the country; in October 1991, the National Council of Churches reported that church membership was growing at nearly twice the rate of overall population growth, and that evangelical Protestants and Roman Catholics showed much larger increases than the liberal Protestant denominations.

Regardless of the actual attendance at Aunt Martha's congregation, the public participation in the First Church of Norman Lear proved predictably pathetic, and his heavily hyped new show disappeared into the Great Beyond of failed TV series within two months of its debut.

Nevertheless, it is worth remembering the way that the show's mistakes reflected the personal values and prejudices of its producer. "The framework of 'Sunday Dinner' comes directly out of my own experience," Norman Lear proudly declared. "I've always scraped the barrel of my own experiences. . . . In this case, I remarried, to a younger woman with enormous spirituality, who has a doctorate in religion and philosophy, who was raised in a churchgoing fundamentalist family but has gone another way."

Had the new Mrs. Lear not "gone another way," it is hard to imagine that she and the veteran producer ever could have found common ground; he has invested a great deal of his money over the years in the establishment of People for the American Way—the liberal lobbying organization specifically designed to counteract the influence of conservative Christians.

As to his current spiritual focus, Lear admits that he has come a long way from his conventional Jewish background. He has studied the teachings of the Chinese philosopher Lao-tzu and keeps a copy of his *Tao Te Ching* in his office; he is also deeply immersed in the pantheistic teachings of a Passionist priest named Thomas Berry and has bought the TV rights to Berry's book *Dream of the Earth*. "I don't support a particular church, or synagogue in my case," he explains, "and I think one's relationship with a higher being or a higher meaning, two terms that are interchangeable with me, is terribly personal." In short, Lear endorses the same sort of eclectic and unfocused spirituality that his main character espoused on his failed show. It is a religious approach that is unquestionably popular in Hollywood but it has demonstrated little appeal to the mass of everyday Americans who participate in established Judeo-Christian institutions.

Spirits and Spirituality

Norman Lear has plenty of company among major producers who have misunderstood the nature of America's religious revival. Many of his counterparts in the motion picture business have recognized the hunger for transcendent meaning that has taken hold in every corner of the country and they have tried, in their own insipid way, to satisfy it. No one should be surprised that the result of these efforts has been so uninspiring: while America yearns for spirituality, Hollywood has provided only spirits.

In so doing, the movie industry has cranked out a seemingly endless series of reincarnation romances. On one level, these fantasies seem calculated to appeal to a generation of aging baby boomers who are suddenly worried about their own mortality. The underlying message is shallow but reassuring: don't think that all your fun must suddenly stop simply because you are dead. In line with the one enduring interest of the '60s generation, these are not merely life-after-death movies; they are also, for the most part, sex-after-death movies. Eerie love scenes between normal flesh-and-blood characters and some spirit or other from beyond the grave provide a common dramatic focus for such films. Perhaps it seems too easy today for passion to overcome all the old barriers between rich and poor, young and old, Catholic and Jew, or even white and black; crossing the line between the living and the dead offers moviemakers a more formidable challenge:

In *Made in Heaven* (1987) the reincarnated Timothy Hutton comes back to earth to pursue erstwhile angel Kelly McGillis.

Beetlejuice (1988) features the ghosts of Alec Baldwin and Geena Davis continuing their romantic yuppie life despite the inconvenience of their demise.

Chances Are (1989) shows the reincarnated Robert Downey, Jr., returning for Cybill Shepherd.

Ghost (1990) allows the spirit of Patrick Swayze to protect (and to romance) his earthly girlfriend, Demi Moore.

Ghosts Can't Do It (1990) depicts the soul of the dead Anthony Quinn taking over the body of a hunky young male for hot sex with his bereaved widow, Bo Derek.

Almost an Angel (1990) follows dead thief Paul Hogan as he's transformed into an angelic do-gooder and falls in love with Linda Kozlowski.

Eternity (1990) stars Jon Voight as a medieval prince who is reincarnated in present-day California where he rediscovers his sexy, long-lost princess.

Jacob's Ladder (1990) assigns a dead GI from Vietnam (Tim Robbins) to a hallucinatory afterlife in New York City that he shares with his hot-blooded girlfriend, Elizabeth Peña.

Truly Madly Deeply (1991) enables the ghost of dead cellist Alan Rickman to return to share the apartment and bed of his grieving lover, Juliet Stevenson.

Switch (1991) punishes a hopeless male chauvinist first by killing him, and then by reincarnating him in the body of the sexy Ellen Barkin, in which form he/she finds ecstasy with his onetime best buddy, Jimmy Smits.

Defending Your Life (1991) sends Albert Brooks to "Judgment City" for processing after his death, where he falls halo over heels for a fellow spirit, Meryl Streep.

Dead Again (1991) centers on L.A. detective Kenneth Branagh, who is actually a reincarnated spirit trying to solve a forty-year-old murder, and finding love with another shade from his past life, Emma Thompson.

Last, and certainly least, *And You Thought Your Parents Were Weird!* (1991) features Allen Thicke as a dead scientist who comes back to earth as the guiding spirit of a robot that's been assembled by his teenage son and who, in that form, provides an erotic (if mechanical) massage for his beloved widow.

As if this weren't enough (and it most certainly is), life-after-death elements figure prominently in numerous other recent films including *Angel Heart* (1987), *The Believers* (1987), *The Serpent and the Rainbow* (1988), *Field of Dreams* (1989), *Ghostbusters II* (1989), *Ghost Dad* (1990), *In The Spirit* (1990), and that metaphysical masterpiece, *Bill and Ted's Bogus Journey* (1991).

This parade of afterlife excursions produced one enormous international hit (*Ghost*), a few pictures that achieved respectable box-office success (*Field of Dreams, Beetlejuice, Dead Again*), and an abundance of expensive and embarrassing flops (*Made in Heaven, Chances Are, Almost an Angel, Jacob's Ladder, Switch, Ghost Dad*, and so forth). In terms of the religious implications, it's significant to note that the one film of this batch that connected most notably with the public (*Ghost*) is the one that came closest to endorsing traditional Christian concepts of reward and punishment after death. Though its theology is hardly orthodox in every detail, *Ghost* does show its hero spirit moving on to a higher plane after hovering briefly on earth, while its bad guys are dragged down by hideous demons the very moment they die and are escorted, we must assume, to an extremely unpleasant permanent destination.

The other products in this assemblage bear far less connection with mainstream Western concepts of eternity. They follow the Tibetan Book of the Dead and the spiritual guidebooks of L. Ron Hubbard far more closely than they follow the Bible; they reflect Hollywood's interest in the occult rather than the public's passion for religion.

This is hardly surprising, given the spiritual inclinations of the members of the entertainment industry. This is a group that seldom questions the magical healing power of crystals, where stars pay handsome fees to learn esoteric systems of Eastern meditation or to liberate their own "inner child," and the ability of certain enlightened guides to "channel" for long-dead souls is accepted without embarrassment. It is, in short, a community in which Shirley MacLaine has more followers than either Jesus or Moses.

I vividly recall a private conversation with the chief creative force behind *Eternity* immediately after I had watched this painfully earnest film for the first time. The filmmaker apologized for the movie's manifold shortcomings—including a palpably preachy courtroom scene in which Jon Voight makes a passionate case for reincarnation—but he assured me that his film's enduring messages mattered far more than its commercial prospects. "I think it's really important to open up people's minds to the idea of past lives. That was my passion when I was doing this film! I know it's a tough sell, probably, but if I can get just a few people to look more seriously at the reality of reincarnation, then I think I've done something that's really worthwhile."

An All but Irresistible Target

This is the sort of sincere stupidity that stands behind Hollywood's exceedingly ill-considered approach to religious material over the last ten years. I would never suggest that offensive movies like *The Last Temptation of Christ* and *The Pope Must Die* and *At Play in the Fields of the Lord* are the products of some self-conscious cabal, nor can I imagine a group of conspirators getting together in some sealed room to figure out how they can insert antireligious messages in the latest *Star Trek* movie, or Madonna's new music video, or an upcoming episode of "Knots Landing." The religion bashing that occurs in the popular culture is spontaneous and instinctive rather than calculated; it arises out of the personal prejudices and preferences of the people who create that culture.

Everyone understands that movie, TV, and music moguls are motivated mightily by the pursuit of profit, but the public remains largely unaware of the passion with which these people pursue the respect of their peers. The desire to be taken seriously—to be acknowledged as an artist and not just an entertainer—is so powerful that at times it overwhelms even economic self-interest.

That desire makes religion an all-but-irresistible target: it is the one subject in the world that everyone acknowledges as fundamentally serious. If writers and directors take a swipe at religion in one of their films, no matter how clumsy or contrived that attack may be, they can feel as if they've made some sort of important and courageous statement. When a degenerate pop star appears on stage and rubs her crotch with a crucifix instead of her hand, it lends the act an aura of deeper significance—a significance that will be duly and pretentiously pondered by the most prestigious rock critics.

Insults to religion of even the most childish variety provide the perpetrators with a unique charge of psychic satisfaction; they allow pampered, powerful, and hopelessly shallow members of the Hollywood establishment to picture themselves as daring young rebels who are fearlessly challenging The Ultimate Authority. Outraged responses by religious organizations or individuals only encourage this sort of posing, as sleazy producers happily pretend that their insensitivity serves some higher cause. Hence the makers of *The Blob* can take pride in the idea that they've created something more than a slick monster movie about a huge strawberry Jell-O that eats a town. By portraying a demented and hypocritical minister as a key character in that town, they've also delivered a "worthwhile" blow against religious fanaticism.

Such messages win applause in Hollywood, even when they're hopelessly simplistic and one-sided. By sneering at zealots and deriding conventional religious beliefs, a filmmaker can win the respect of his colleagues, even if his work is rejected by the larger public.

In this context, I will never forget an astonishing private conversation concerning the motivations behind the notorious 1985 fiasco, *King David*. This Godzilla-sized turkey cost nearly $30 million to make and attracted less than $5 million in ticket sales. It featured Richard Gere in the title role—a bizarre casting choice that led some industry wags to refer to the project as "An Israelite and a Gentleman." Like *The Last Temptation of Christ*—Hollywood's only other attempt of recent years to dramatize a biblical story—*King David* took extreme liberties with its source material. The film advances the radical and totally unsupported notion that David became thoroughly embittered and disillusioned at the end of his life, freeing himself from his previously held primitive beliefs and abandoning his faith in God. One of the concluding scenes shows the angry and aged monarch violently rejecting his past faith as he smashes the scale model of the temple in Jerusalem he had intended to build.

A few weeks before the film's release, one of its producers spoke to me proudly about the chances he and his colleagues had taken in this revisionist view of their hero. "We could have gone the easy way and played to the Bible Belt," he said. "But we wanted to make a film with guts. We wanted to do it with integrity. We don't see David as some Holy Joe, praise-the-Lord kind of guy. We wanted to make him a richer, deeper character."

In his mind, in other words, secure religious faith is incompatible with depth of character. The real-life King David authored the Book of Psalms, but Hollywood, in its wisdom, chose not to portray him as a "praise-the-Lord kind of guy."

Making Distinctions

The distortions and insults about organized religion will continue unabated as long as our popular culture continues its overall campaign against judgment and values. A war against standards leads logically and inevitably to hostility to religion because it is religious faith that provides the ultimate basis for all standards.

The God of the Bible is not a moral relativist, and He is most definitely judgmental. The very nature of the Judeo-Christian God is a Lord who makes distinctions. In the Book of Genesis, God creates the world by dividing the light from the darkness, dividing the waters above from the waters beneath, dividing the water from the dry land, and so on. In traditional Jewish homes, when we say farewell to the Sabbath every Saturday night, we divide the holy day just passed from the more ordinary week ahead, reciting a blessing that praises God for separating various aspects of reality, one from the other—for making distinctions. To the extent that we as human beings feel that we are created in God's image, and that we are fundamentally different from the animals, we make distinctions, too—and we have standards.

That is a position that is honored by millions upon millions of our fellow citizens but it is regularly ridiculed in the mass media. No one expects a radical reversal of this situation, with Hollywood emerging overnight as an effective advocate for religious values, but a greater sense of neutrality and balance ought to be possible when it comes to portrayals of organized faith.

That is a case I have been making since 1986—two years prior to public outcry over *The Last Temptation of Christ*—when we broadcast a special edition of our PBS show "Sneak Previews," called "Hollywood vs. Religion." That particular show generated a great deal of healthy public controversy, and I've continued to address the subject through articles, lectures, and TV appearances.

As one might expect, I've received my share of knocks for this high-profile position, and my basic plea for fairness has occasionally been distorted and misunderstood. In July 1991, for example, the *Boston Globe* ran a lead editorial in which it assailed a speech I had given on the subject as "a reactionary ragout of paranoia, false history, and internal contradictions." The editorial went on to paraphrase an element of my presentation, in order to rebut it with ridicule, claiming that I had stated that "Hollywood once made movies to instill the values of morality, family, and religion. Was he thinking of *Birth of a Nation,* of *Duck Soup,* or *Citizen Kane*?"

The editorial writer scored his point against an assertion I never made. In fact, I never claimed that Hollywood had once made movies to *instill* these values; but I do believe that the film industry used to make movies that *respected* them. The distinction is a crucial one, because it is the essence of my argument that the products of the popular culture should become *less* propagandistic, not more so.

Asking Hollywood to begin to show some restraint and balance in its antireligious fury is not the same as suggesting that the industry must transform itself into an agency for advancing the Word of God.

In that regard it is worth recalling that for more than forty years the industry followed an *explicit* standard when it came to movie portrayals of organized religion and the clergy. That official standard stated:

No film or episode may throw ridicule on any religious faith;
    Ministers of religion in their character as ministers of religion should not be used as comic characters or as villains;
    Ceremonies of any definite religion should be carefully and respectfully handled.

These eminently reasonable guidelines, violated so repeatedly and so gratuitously in recent years, appeared as Article VIII of the notorious Production Code of 1930. All of the industry's various attempts to impose restrictions on itself in terms of movie content, from "The Formula" of 1924 to the "Standards for Production" of 1968, included similar prohibitions on the ridicule of organized religion.

The Production Code is today generally reviled as a misguided attempt at repression and censorship, and recent attempts by the Catholic Archdiocese of Los Angeles to revive the code have provoked an outraged response from the industry. Regardless of the obvious problems in enforcing such a system, it would be difficult to improve on the statements of Article VIII as an informal and unofficial basis for handling religious material.

This approach recognizes the special delicacy of religious feelings within a pluralistic society; civic peace requires that public attacks on anyone's religious beliefs should be deemed unacceptable as a form of popular entertainment. Far from discouraging the presentation of religious themes and figures in motion pictures, this special respect toward an inherently sensitive subject led historically to a wealth of satisfying and successful films, many of which we recall today with a special (and poignant) fondness. The studios' unanimous acceptance of the guidelines in the old Production Code not only assured that the industry would avoid unnecessary offense to the Christian majority, but guaranteed that religious minorities would not suffer from the sort of vicious caricature to which German filmmakers subjected that nation's Jewish community throughout the 1930s.

To suggest that the major entertainment corporations might exercise greater discretion and sensitivity before investing their millions in projects that assault someone else's religious faith is not to call for an end to free expression in Hollywood. If we recognize the fundamental dignity of our fellow citizens, then it means that we should go to great lengths to keep from trampling on something so personal as religious belief. It was not so long ago that all civilized people avoided attacking another man's religion as a matter of common decency; the popular culture—and the nation at large—could only benefit if Hollywood learned to display that same level of respect.

PART III

THE ASSAULT ON THE FAMILY

6

Promoting
Promiscuity

A Curious Inconsistency

Recent public opinion polls reveal a curious inconsistency in American attitudes toward the family.

Most people in this country believe that the family as an institution is in serious trouble; at the same time, they're certain that their own families are doing fine.

A November 1991 survey for Massachusetts Mutual Life Insurance Company produced typically contradictory results. When asked to assess the strength of "family values" in the society at large, survey respondents painted a gloomy portrait: 65 percent felt that those values were "declining," with heavy majorities agreeing with the statement "It's harder to be a parent than it used to be."

On the other hand, the same people radiated optimism and satisfaction when commenting on their personal experience. In the Massachusetts Mutual study, 67 percent described themselves as "very" or "extremely satisfied" with their own family life; identical percentages rated relationships with their children as "good" or "excellent." A 1991 Gallup Poll found 93 percent who consider family life "very important," with a similarly hefty percentage saying that spending time with family members provided them with the greatest sense of fulfillment in their lives.

Why do these conflicting concepts coexist? How can the overall condition of the American family possibly be so bad when the huge majority of our fellow citizens feel so richly satisfied in their relationships with their closest kin? Columnist Ellen Goodman described the perplexing attitude that prevails today as the "I'm okay, but you're not" syndrome. Hundreds of millions of Americans apparently believe that their pleasant domestic arrangements represent a blessed exception, a rare island of sanity in an ocean of insecurity and unhappiness. Why should so many people assume that the family is falling apart—when their own firsthand experience tells them that all is well?

The answer, of course, involves the influence of the popular culture, with its clearly demonstrated and uncompromising contempt for conventional family values. The music industry shamelessly promotes promiscuity, motion pictures focus relentlessly on family dysfunction and divorce, while television programs broadcast the deadly message that kids know better than their doltish and irrelevant parents.

In other words, the contrast between private contentment and public pessimism that shows up in major polls mirrors the huge chasm between our own view of the world and Hollywood's—between the relatively happy real-life experience of most American families and the grim and poisonous visions that regularly emerge from the entertainment industry. Those antifamily images have become so deeply ingrained in our national consciousness that few Americans can summon the courage or the strength to dismiss them as the destructive distortions that they are.

Popular Music: As Nasty as It Wants to Be

Perhaps the most damaging of all those distortions involves the glorification of sexual adventurism and the focus on physical pleasure as an end in itself.

This is a theme that is exploited by every element in the popular culture, but it is nowhere more powerfully expressed than in the music business—a mighty industry of staggering global impact that devotes nearly all of its energies to the endless celebration of the raw power of lust.

At this point I must offer a candid warning to sensitive readers: if you are easily offended by gutter language and graphic images then you are strongly advised to avoid this section of the book. Unfortunately, there is simply no way to write honestly about contemporary popular music without violating traditional standards of decency. Discreet references to "raunchy lyrics" or "obscene material" cannot suffice; they amount to a polite cover-up that effectively conceals the extent and the intensity of the degradation.

If you are unfamiliar with the messages in today's music, prepare to be appalled. Even if you feel that you know something about the songs and videos that our children consume with such notable gusto, the specific lyrics that follow will demonstrate that the situation of the moment is worse than you assumed. In any event, there is no excuse for trying to protect the reader from material that is readily and regularly available to every teenager in America.

Consider, for example, the extravagantly popular and influential rock group Guns n' Roses. By many measures of success, they reign today as the most prominent and idolized musicians in the world. Their 1987 album *Appetite for Destruction* sold an astonishing total of more than 12 million copies in America alone, enough for nearly half the teenagers in the country to own one.

Given the natural tendency of kids to listen together to music that they enjoy or to share their tapes and CDs with friends, this means that the overwhelming majority of American adolescents have now been exposed to the following poetry:

> Panties round your knees, with your ass in debris . . .
> Tied up, tied down, up against the wall
> —from "Anything Goes"

or, as a tender alternative:

> Turn around bitch I got a use for you
> Besides you ain't got nothin' better to do—and I'm bored.
> —from "It's So Easy"

Guns n' Roses' most recent albums, *Use Your Illusion I* and *Use Your Illusion II*, dominated the rock 'n' roll charts as the top sellers of

1991, and offered more of the same. "Pretty Tied Up" described a "bitch" who craved whipping and abuse from all the band members:

> She ain't satisfied without some pain
> Friday night is goin' up inside her—again

Another popular heavy metal band, Motley Crüe, carried these sadistic impulses to their logical conclusion in their song "You're All I Need":

> Laid out cold, now we're both alone
> But killing you helped me keep you home.

The *Girls, Girls, Girls* album which contained this couplet rose to number two on the *Billboard* pop charts and sold over two million copies.

Defenders of this material insist that it is a form of raunchy, irreverent humor rather than a serious incitement to sadism. Terry Higgins, however, a Milwaukee rock reviewer who specializes in the heavy-metal scene, recently told the *Chicago Tribune:* "I think the kids take the lyrics a lot more seriously than some of the death metal bands, who almost take a comic book, slasher-movie approach to their music. But if I had a fourteen- or fifteen-year-old listening to some of this stuff, I might not trust him to have the proper perspective."

Whether considered from the point of view of their creators or of the audience, these songs have nothing to do with romance of even the most fleeting variety, and everything to do with violent hostility toward women. This theme is made even more explicit in the contributions of another top-selling group: the rap musicians known as NWA—Niggers with Attitude. Their album *Niggas4life* zoomed to the number-one position on the *Billboard* chart just two weeks after its release in June 1991. In all probability, few American parents realized that the top-selling pop album in the country included songs like "She Swallowed It," describing a "preacher's daughter" who "did the whole crew" and will "even take a broomstick up the butt." This young lady receives the highest praise,

> Because the dumb bitch licks out their asshole . . . .
> And if ya got a gang of niggers the bitch'll let ya rape her.

Along similar lines, the Houston rappers known as the Geto Boys provided their adolescent audience with additional encouragement for violent and sadistic fantasies. In 1989 their album *Grip It! On That Other Level* cracked the *Billboard* Top 30 and was certified gold when its sales passed 500,000 copies. The most popular rap on the record, "Gangster of Love," could hardly be more explicit in its misogyny, describing an eager sex partner who "opened my butt cheeks and started lickin' on my asshole." The lead rapper knows how to reward such attentions, since

> I'm a motherfuckin' heart-breaker, I have 'em cryin' for months
> 'Cause I would fuck their best friends and put a whippin' on their cunts.

With their first album, the Geto Boys managed to seize the public's attention without radio air play or the support of a major record label; for their equally violent and pornographic follow-up, the prestigious Warner-Elektra-Atlantic Corporation (part of the huge Time-Warner conglomerate) enthusiastically agreed to distribute their work.

In light of the outrageously offensive excesses of groups like the Geto Boys and NWA, it is difficult to understand why their fellow rappers, the notorious Florida group 2 Live Crew, should be singled out as the focus for the sort of bitter public controversy that the others avoided.

The contents of their much-discussed album *As Nasty as They Wanna Be* (which has sold an impressive total of more than 1.7 million copies) generally parallel the themes of many other rap musicians. The only distinctive element in 2 Live Crew's approach involves their consistent emphasis on mutilating the genitals of their female partners:

> A big stinkin' pussy can't do it all
> So we try real hard just to bust the walls.
> —from "Put Her in the Buck"

> He'll tear the pussy open 'cause it's satisfaction
> The bitch won't leave, it's fatal attraction.
> —from "Dick Almighty"

Let me fill you up with somethin' milky and white
'Cause I'm gonna slay you rough and painful . . .
I wanna see you bleed!
—from "The Fuck Shop"

I won't tell your momma if you don't tell your dad
I know he'll be disgusted when he sees your pussy busted.
—from "Me So Horny"

These quotations from *As Nasty as They Wanna Be* will give some indication of why Judge Jose A. Gonzalez of the federal district court in Fort Lauderdale ruled that the album was legally obscene. No brief excerpts, however, can properly convey the enormously depressing experience of listening to all of the songs in their entirety: the cumulative impact is mind-numbing and overwhelming. Bob DeMoss, who heroically holds down the unenviable job of monitoring rock lyrics for the Christian ministry Focus on the Family, meticululously analyzed the contents of this album. In less than sixty minutes of "entertainment," DeMoss counted 226 uses of the word "fuck," 81 uses of the word "shit," 163 uses of the word "bitch," 87 descriptions of oral sex, and 117 explicit terms for male or female genitalia. Using the conservative estimate that each of the album's 1.7 million owners will listen to it at least ten times, this means that an average teenager who has purchased *As Nasty As They Wanna Be* will hear 1,170 references to genitals and 870 descriptions of oral sex. As R&B singer Nona Hendryx observes, "What concerns me is what children get out of it, who don't have the wisdom to discern. We have lost a generation. If you just eat potatoes all the time, you're going to turn into a potato head."

Charges of Racism

Unfortunately, any condemnation of rap music leads inevitbly to charges of racism—to the accusation that those who question the messages in these records do not understand the African-American experience and are attacking one of its authentic expressions only because of their hatred of all things black. Luther Campbell, the lead singer of 2 Live Crew, has been particularly outspoken in portraying himself as the victim of racial bias. "Why condemn me—a black artist and entrepreneur—for my particular brand of adult entertainment?" he pleads.

His position has received suprising support from some academic experts. Professor Henry Louis Gates, who currently heads the department of African-American Studies at Harvard, testified at the 2 Live Crew obscenity trial that the group actually exemplified a long and honorable ghetto tradition. He called their body of work "refreshing" and "astonishing" and compared its use of bawdy language to the works of Chaucer, Shakespeare, and Joyce. Gates insisted to the jury that lines such as "Suck this dick, bitch, and make it puke" actually amounted to an imaginative use of metaphor. "It's like Shakespeare's 'My love is like a red, red rose,'" the good professor helpfully explained, while misattributing Robert Burns's most famous line to Shakespeare. "That doesn't mean your love is red and has petals. No, it means your love is beautiful." This invocation of The Bard of Avon (or, as it happens, Robert Burns) to defend the content of rap music brings to mind George Orwell's comment, "There are some ideas so proposterous that only an intellectual could believe them."

Fortunately, some of America's most prominent African-American leaders stepped forward to disassociate themselves from 2 Live Crew's attempts to portray themselves as the representatives of a tradition of passionate protest. "We are particularly offended by their efforts to wrap the mantle of the black cultural experience around their performances by saying this is the way it is in the black community, and that they are authentic purveyors of our heritage," declared Dr. Benjamin Hooks of the National Association for the Advancement of Colored People (NAACP). "Our cultural experience does not include debasing our women, the glorification of violence, the promotion of deviant sexual behavior, or the tearing into shreds of our cherished mores and standards of behavior."

Other black thinkers took a similarly dismissive view toward claims that rap performers who boasted so endlessly of their sexual exploits gave valuable voice to the gritty reality of the streets. Clarence Page wrote that "it is interesting to note how many of rap's supposedly authentic ghetto voices are, in reality, offspring of the black middle class dressing down and acting out behavioral stereotypes associated with young low-income blacks, mostly for the consumption of young middle-class whites."

In the summer of 1991, improved computer technology enabled *Billboard* magazine to confirm Page's assertion, showing that the bulk of record sales for the "cutting edge" rappers came from suburban shopping malls, not inner-city music shops. Jon Shecter, the Harvard-educated editor of *The Source*, the respected journal of "Hip-Hop Culture," noted that while "it's a cool status symbol among white kids to like and identify with N.W.A., most of the black community doesn't like them." In an analysis for *The New Republic*, Princeton's David Samuels concludes: "The more rappers were packaged as violent black criminals, the bigger their white audiences became."

"Rotten to the Core"

The most degrading messages in contemporary music not only transcend all racial boundaries; they also erase all gender distinctions when it comes to appalling content. Female performers (and female audiences) have struggled to keep up with adolescent males when it comes to purveying graphic boasts about sexual conquest and performance. Christina Amphlett, the seductive lead singer of the Divinyls, released a surprise hit called "Lay Your Body Down":

> I'm the mistress of the night, no stranger to your fantasy
> Lashings of a recipe, I'm whipping something up.

Her song "I Touch Myself," with its dreamily erotic video played repeatedly on MTV, was described by *Rolling Stone* as "one of the catchiest songs ever written about masturbation."

Meanwhile, a "girl group" called Hole offered considerably darker material in their 1992 album *Pretty on the Inside*, with shrieking lead singer Courtney Love howling endlessly about her experience turning tricks as a teenage whore.

Another all-female group, BWP (Bitches With Problems), released a best-selling album Columbia Records called *The Bytches*, which featured a feminine reflection of the sadistic boasts of male rappers:

> See how much of a bitch that loves to be fucked . . .
> Up in my ass, deep down in my throat . . . But my cunt's so horny I
> don't give a shit.

Somewhere between the macho posing of performers like Guns n' Roses and NWA and the "slut rock" of girl groups like Hole and the Divinyls stands the androgynous omnisexuality of the priapic Prince— described by prestigious rock critic Robert Hilburn as "the man who was at the absolute creative center of pop in the '80s." His 1980 song "Sister" featured teasing references to incest ("My sister never made love to anyone else but me/She's the reason for my sexuality") and by 1991, this fading superstar offered an explicit endorsement of orgiastic indulgence in "Gett Off." He urged his listeners:

> Everybody grab a body, pump it like u want somebody . . .
> Gett off—23 positions in a one-night stand.

He goes on to describe some of those twenty-three positions, including sex on the kitchen floor, in the bathroom "standing on the tub and holding on the rod," in the closet "under the clothes," on the dresser "with your feet in the drawers," in the pantry "on the shelf," and on the pool table where he promises "to put the eight-ball where it's sure to stick."

The lavish video that accompanies this erotic apartment tour features two spectacularly beautiful, blindfolded young women who are led into the orgy by oiled bodybuilders in loin cloths, while quick images flash before the viewer of literally dozens of semi-nude bodies writhing in ecstasy. On another number featured on the same five-song videocassette (released by Time-Warner) Prince leers into the camera and croons:

> I am Violet the organ grinder . . .
> I live for the organ that I am grinding.

This one piece of poetry could stand as a summary for everything that is most destructive in today's popular music: nearly all prominent performers could echo the statement that "I live for the organ that I am grinding." At least in terms of the personalities they project to the public, these are remarkably one-dimensional characters, ruled entirely by their all-powerful genitalia. Seldom do they entertain the notion that a human being might be more than a collection of body parts and hormones. Life is nothing more than an endless series of conquests and seductions, occasionally interrupted by naked rage at the opposite sex. Consider what our children learn from contemporary music about what it means to be a man, or what it means to be a woman. Feminists have rightly complained that contemporary rock is deeply demeaning to women, but it is worse than that: it is insulting to the most basic notions of humanity.

Some leading pop ensembles may use language that is more polite than the graphic lyrics cited above, but the messages they send are no less lascivious. One of the top-selling singles for 1991 was a number called "I Wanna Sex You Up" by the group Color Me Badd—a quartet with the audacity to boast that their music actually affirms "wholesome Christian values." In the music video for her song "Open Your Heart," Madonna pretends to be a cynical, black-corseted performer at a sleazy X-rated peep show, and encourages a frightened but fascinated eleven-year-old boy to join the middle-aged patrons in watching her strip.

The sweaty and slimy single-mindedness of so much of contemporary pop has begun to trouble even some veteran observers inside the industry. Rock critic Steve Simels of *Stereo Review* writes of Madonna's retrospective assemblage of music videos: "*The Immaculate Collection* still makes me want to take a shower when it's over, and I think I know why—it's so nakedly, so honestly scummy. . . . I'm hardly advocating some sort of ethical litmus test for pop music. But we shouldn't pretend this stuff is value-neutral, either."

Joni Mitchell, the singer and composer who created some of the most memorable and poetic popular music of the 1970s, has also become disillusioned with the direction of her industry. In 1991 she told *Rolling Stone:* "Music has become a burlesque over the last few years—video's done that. Every generation has to be more shocking than the last. But at a certain point you've got to reel it in because decadence ultimately isn't hip. Our country is going down the tubes from it. It's rotten to the core."

"Nonstop Masturbational Fantasies"

Mitchell's comments acknowledge the enormous distance between the sexual messages in today's songs and the content of popular music of the past. Previous pop idols—including Frank Sinatra, Elvis Presley, and the Beatles—may have alarmed parents with their rebellious poses and the erotic edge to their performances, but they were tender, wholesome romantics when compared to contemporary paragons like Guns n' Roses and Madonna. The differences are fundamental, qualitative as well as quantitative—representing not only the extent of the titillation but the nature of the underlying fantasy it communicates. In the best-selling song of his entire career, Elvis Presley pleaded:

> Love me tender, love me true, all my dreams fulfill
> For, my darling, I love you, and I always will.

The vision of "Love Me Tender" stands light-years removed from the notion of romance conveyed by the recent NWA hit "Findum, Fuckum and Flee":

> When the pussy holes are open, ready to fuck until my dick is raw . . .
> So come here, bitch, and lick up the, lick up the, lick up the dick!

The most successful singers of the past most certainly exploited sexuality as part of their appeal, but the reveries they described in their songs still centered on intense—and usually long-term—emotional relationships between men and women. What is most striking about the popular music of the moment is the cold, bitter, and sadistic edge to the vision of fleeting sex it promotes.

Even the Rolling Stones—the most notorious of all of yesterday's rock 'n' roll bad boys—are sentimental softies by today's standards. Their controversial come-on ballad "Let's Spend the Night Together" offers a lavishly indulgent and considerate proposition when compared to the suggestions regularly made on the radio in the '90s; it's hard to imagine the members of Motley Crüe or Metallica willingly spending an entire *night* with anyone. If the Stones attempted to rewrite their most infamous song in order to conform to more contemporary fantasies, they might have to retitle it "Let's Spend Ten Hostile Minutes Together (So I Can Degrade You and Beat You Up)."

Not surprisingly, kids across the country seem to be getting the message. In 1990, *Time* magazine reported on a San Antonio radio station that offered free concert tickets for the best reply to the question, "What would you do to meet Motley Crüe?" A sixteen-year-old girl responded by providing an elaborate sadomasochistic scenario, offering herself as the bleeding victim. A boy, fourteen, said he would give the band his mother to do with as they pleased. A thirteen-year-old girl wrote simply but eloquently, "I'd leave my tits to Motley Crüe."

Such suggestions amount to something more than attempts at off-color humor: they represent some prevailing adolescent notions of the sort of encounter that might prove most powerfully appealing to an especially admired group of glamorous grown-ups. Younger children also feel the impact of the MTV model of interaction with the opposite sex, parroting the lyrics of salacious songs they can scarcely understand. Music analyst Bob DeMoss describes a college professor of his acquaintace who, while shaving one morning in his bathroom, nearly cut himself when he heard his six-year-old boy walking by the door and singing a rousing chorus of "Do you think I'm sexy—and you want my body." The father discovered that the boy had learned the song from the radio on the school bus he took every day on the way to first grade. A sixth-grade teacher from Sioux Falls, South Dakota, wrote DeMoss about a field trip she took with her kids in May 1990. During the long bus ride, her "good kids from good homes" shocked her when they killed time by taking out portable tape players and listening repeatedly to obscene rap lyrics by NWA.

Such anecdotes reflect the imperial and all-penetrating reach of popular music, as well as the fact that its most irresponsible messages are so seldom balanced by more nourishing notions. The most avid adolescent fan can listen for hours each day without once hearing the suggestion that truly satisfying love between adults might require some elements of consideration, self-discipline, or even sacrifice. Instead, the role model suggested by "Findum, Fuckum and Flee" bestrides the globe, all-conquering and unopposed, as the ideal of resplendent manhood.

No wonder that Professor Allan Bloom concluded that the rock business "has all the moral dignity of drug trafficking." No one, in fact, has written more passionately and persuasively about rock 'n' roll and its impact than Professor Bloom. In *The Closing of the American Mind,* he conjures up an unforgettable image:

> Picture a thirteen-year-old boy sitting in the living room of his family home doing his math assignment while wearing his Walkman headphones or watching MTV. He enjoys the liberties hard won over centuries by the alliance of philosophic genius and political heroism, consecrated by the blood of martyrs; he is provided with comfort and leisure by the most productive economy ever known to mankind; science has penetrated the secrets of nature in order to provide him with the marvelous, lifelike electronic sound and image reproduction that he is enjoying. And in what does progress culminate? A pubescent child whose body throbs with orgasmic rhythms; whose feelings are made articulate in hymns to the joys of onanism or the killing of parents; whose ambition is to win fame and wealth in imitating the drag-queen who makes the music. In short, life is made into a nonstop, commercially prepackaged masturbational fantasy.

Bloom concludes that "rock music has one appeal only, a barbaric appeal, to sexual desire—not love, not *eros,* but sexual desire undeveloped and untutored. . . . The words implicitly and explicitly describe bodily acts that satisfy sexual desire and treat them as its only natural and routine culmination for children who do not yet have the slightest imagination of love, marriage or family. This has a much more powerful effect than does pornography on youngsters, who have no need to watch others do grossly what they can so easily do themselves."

Parents remain appallingly ignorant of the actual content of the songs their own children so avidly consume, and in any event prefer to believe that an obsession with pop performers is only a passing stage, with no lasting impact on the formation of character. Allan Bloom knows better. "As long as they have the Walkman on, they cannot hear what the great tradition has to say," he writes. "And after its prolonged use, when they take it off, they find they are deaf."

Titillation on the Tube

The erotic references on network television are neither as intense nor as omnipresent as those in popular music, but to a surprising extent they convey the same underlying message: that sex should be viewed as an end in itself, a glorious form of recreation that has nothing to do with responsibility or commitment. In fact, television treatments of romantic relationships strongly suggest that sensuality is most satisfying when it is shared outside of marriage, and that long-term alliances only serve to diminish the pleasure of the partners.

Anyone who doubts that commercial TV regularly and powerfully encourages casual sex is someone who hasn't watched "Studs," the voyeuristic game show on Fox Network that became an enormous overnight hit in the fall of 1991. Each week, two muscle-bound and macho contestants go out on steamy blind dates with each of three glamorously coifed and miniskirted young lovelies, and then compete on the air for the title of "King Stud." To earn this singular honor they must accurately match the women they dated with a series of lurid one-line "quotes" that the ladies provided to the show's staff about their reactions to the aspiring studs. On a typical show, these statements included: "I reached down and, oh, my God! He had buns of granite!" and "His body was so firm that even his hair was hard." Other comments, read aloud to the snickering and hooting studio audience, are merely excercises in double entendre. When members of the female panel report that "I was in ecstasy when he gave me his creamy pudding" or "One stroke of his stick and I was all his," they are actually describing nothing more exciting than sharing dessert at a picnic or competing in a game of pool.

Meanwhile, the leering host (Mark DeCarlo) relentlessly probes the contestants and the ladies for every lubricious detail of their interactions. One willowy blonde, with long bare legs and a skintight black dress, declared, "By morning, he had explored every crevice in my body." DeCarlo pressed her shamelessly for specifics as she described their foreplay. "Okay, you were tickling and kissing," the host demanded, "but when did the crevice exploration begin?"

In a significant number of instances, the ladies cheerfully admit that they "went all the way" with one (or both) of the hopeful hunks they have just met. In other cases, the participants may be marginally more discreet but will still describe an abundance of first-date groping, licking, and undressing: after all, the manly contestants are expected to paw and prod every one of the three women they date or else they have no chance of emerging as "King Stud." In an era of AIDS awareness and supposedly heightened consciousness about date rape, the public celebration of such drooling and brutish encounters between complete strangers emits an especially fetid aroma; the values of this network show would embarrass even an adolescent Neanderthal. Nevertheless, within six months of its premiere, "Studs" had emerged as a new national craze and regularly won the ratings race for its time slot in the majority of the sixty cities in which it aired.

"A Potpourri of Tangled Love Affairs"

The attitudinal underpinnings of "Studs" are in no way atypical of television today. In their desperation to compete with cable, with its multitude of "adult entertainment" alternatives, the networks have made increasingly shameless efforts to exploit sexuality and to introduce the same prurient appeal to prime time. In the process, they have created a televised view of erotic activity that is as unrealistic in its overemphasis on lust as was the entertainment of the Eisenhower era in ignoring the subject altogether. After analyzing some 620 prime-time shows covering the last thirty years of television history, S. Robert Lichter, Linda Lichter, and Stanley Rothman concluded: "Beyond simply reflecting our changing sexual mores, television has endorsed the changes, and may have accelerated their acceptance. . . . It has lately played a leading role in questioning traditional moral standards before a vast national audience."

In their 1991 book, *Watching America,* Lichter, Lichter, and Rothman report that "television now offers a little something for the voyeur in every viewer, from the opening credits through the heavy-breathing plot turns to the, well, climax. It invites us to embrace a potpourri of tangled love affairs, kinky vices and erotic experiments utterly unknown in the medium's earlier days." They specifically cite recent TV movies like *The Sex Tapes Scandal,* about a deluxe prostitution ring that specializes in sadomasochism, or *Favorite Son,* in which a glamorous political aide (Linda Kozlowski) disrobes in front of her married lover, handing him a satin ribbon and begging him to "Tie me up. Come on! Tie me up." In the opening credits of "Cagney and Lacey," the two unflappable policewomen walk nonchalantly past a flasher who opens his trenchcoat to reveal himself, while the credits for "Spenser:

For Hire" show the detective and his lover sharing a passionate kiss while taking a shower together. In one particularly memorable episode of "Hill Street Blues," police officers discover a man who's died in his bedroom with only his pet sheep as witness. Eventually, they conclude that the unfortunate victim has suffered a heart attack while making passionate love to the animal.

Other observers find other moments in recent shows that have pushed the envelope of televised titillation. Columnist Cal Thomas felt particularly troubled by the NBC program "Hull High," citing a 1990 episode in which the lucky and lusty male students welcomed a drop-dead gorgeous teacher who aroused them all with a steady stream of sexual innuendo. This eager educator even starred in a jiggling video production number entitled "Soft and Round as a Peach." Responding to criticism of his show, executive producer Gil Grant merely shrugged. "It's a kid's fantasy," he declared, "a boy's fantasy."

Cynthia Crossen, writing in the October 1991 *McCall's* on the subject "Is TV Too Sexy?," mentions the celebrated lesbian kiss on "L.A. Law," and the title character on "The Trials of Rosie O'Neill" wondering aloud whether she "ought to get my tits done." She also remembers Rachel Ward, provocatively clad in soaked clothes (with no underwear), warming up a tropical paradise on the CBS miniseries *And the Sea Will Tell,* as well as Rebecca DeMornay wearing almost nothing to greet Jason Robards in another miniseries, *An Inconvenient Woman.* "These days Americans can hardly turn on their television sets without seeing or hearing something about sex," Crossen concludes.

Content analysis of prime-time programming unequivocally supports such observations. In 1988 the Planned Parenthood Federation of America commissioned an exhaustive study by Louis Harris & Associates which found that in the prime afternoon and evening hours the three largest networks broadcast a total of more than 65,000 sexual references every year. This means hourly averages of twenty-seven instances of sexual content, with between one and two depictions or discussions of intercourse or "deviant and discouraged sexual practices." The study determined that the average American TV watcher now views 14,000 references to sex in the course of a year.

The Lichter, Licther, and Rothman analysis reveals that in addition to a spectacular increase in the amount of erotic activity in prime time, the context in which that behavior occurs has shifted dramatically. Prior to 1969, their tracking studies turned up references to sex outside of marriage in only one out of every thirty shows on TV's nightly bill of fare. More recently, extramarital experiences appeared in one show in six, and they report that the ratio "continues to narrow."

Moreover, the attitude toward such adventures has changed fundamentally. Before 1970, 38 percent of all shows that depicted nonmarital sexuality clearly condemned it as morally unacceptable. More recently, only 7 percent of the shows that portray such affairs present them in a disapproving light, while 41 percent endorse them without qualification.

Such figures clearly reflect the personal values of the people who write and produce prime time. In their landmark 1983 study of 104 of the most powerful and influential creative personnel in television, the Lichter/Rothman team found that only 16 percent "strongly agreed" with the simple statement that "adultery is wrong," while 51 percent declined to condemn cheating in even the mildest terms. In 1987, Terry Louise Fisher, one of the producers of "L.A. Law," forthrightly expressed the unconventional attitude of the industry at large when she told *The New York Times:* "We may be heading for a new repression, a new 'Father Knows Best' era. I hope not. *For television, married or celibate characters aren't as much fun."*

This peculiar notion that marriage and fun cannot comfortably coexist is by now deeply embedded in the television culture: the only sort of steamy sex that seems to be forbidden on the small screen is the kind that might connect two married people to each other. Al and Peg Bundy of the Fox Network's "Married . . . with Children" sitcom represent Hollywood's image of the typical husband and wife, as she complains endlessly—and graphically—about her nonexistent sex life.

Even before that controversial series helped redefine our notions of contemporary family life, TV had all but banished the idea of physical intimacy between married people. In 1981 the *Journal of Communication* published a study called "Physically Intimate and Sexual Behavior on Prime-Time Television." Researchers Joyce Sprafkin and Theresa Silverman monitored one episode of each of the major network series—fifty-eight programs in all. In those shows they found forty-one instances of sexual intercourse outside of marriage, and only six references to intercourse between married people—a ratio of almost seven to one!

Ten years later the emphasis on extramarital sex had dramatically increased. In the "Spring Sweeps" period of 1991 (April 28–May 25), researchers for the American Family Association logged a total of 615 instances of sexual activity depicted or discussed on prime-time shows. By a margin of *thirteen to one* (571 to 44) these references favored sex outside of marriage over intimate relations between life partners.

This disparity sends the powerful message that extramarital erotic activity is inherently more exciting than anything that might happen between husband and wife. In 1988, William A. Henry III, the Pulitzer Prize–winning television critic for *Time* magazine, elegantly summarized the situation in an article in *TV Guide:* "It's not the prevalent sex outside marriage but rather the scarcity of sex inside marriage that makes TV so prurient," he wrote. "Prime time implies there is no fun without sin, no kiss except a stolen one."

"TV Virginity Week"

In the last two television seasons, those stolen kisses have increasingly involved adolescents as well as adults. With considerable fanfare, the networks unleashed a flurry of controversial shows suggesting sexual intercourse between characters who are too young to legally buy liquor—and in some cases even too young to drive. "It's happening all over the dial," the executive producer of Fox's "True Colors" told the *Los Angeles Times.* "I guess this is TV virginity week."

• The 1991 minitrend began in May's season-ending show of the Fox network's "Beverly Hills 90210," in which the dark-haired seventeen-year-old beauty Brenda (played by Shannen Doherty) lost her virginity with her sallow-faced suitor, Dylan. According to the plot, the two trendy teenagers had known each other for three months.

• In September the mood of sexual experimentation reached NBC's "Blossom," in which the fourteen-year-old title character (Mayim Bialik) debated "going to second base" with her ardent boyfriend, and engaged in some heated "action." One of her close friends tells her: "Seems like yesterday we started wearing bras and here we are talking about taking them off."

• The same week, on Fox's "True Colors," eighteen-year-old Terry Freeman (Claude Brooks) is ridiculed by his entire family because he is still a virgin. He is shown reading a book entitled "How to Make Love for the First Time." By show's end, his experienced girlfriend has informed him that she intends to quickly correct his unfortunate condition.

• The new season of the top-rated "Roseanne" series on ABC opened with a show that centered on Becky, the sixteen-year-old daughter of the main character, and her exciting new life as a sexually active teen. Roseanne takes her to her gynecologist so she can get birth control pills in order to be properly prepared for the adventures that lie ahead; later she discovers that the girl is already enjoying intercourse with her boyfriend. Roseanne's sister, Jackie, applauds the main character's willingness to facilitate the girl's sex life: "Isn't it great, Roseanne, that Becky has such a progressive, open-minded mom that she can talk to about that?" When Roseanne moans, "She's all grown up, Jackie, she doesn't need me anymore!" her sister reassures her: "Of course she needs you! She needs you to pay for the pills."

• Intense hype surrounded the nearly simultaneous season premiere of ABC's "Doogie Howser, M.D.," in which the brilliant physician hero (Neil Patrick Harris) celebrates his eighteenth birthday by going to bed with his girlfriend for the first time. "A man is a lot of things, but he's *not* a virgin," the deep-thinking Doogie philosophizes before his big night. "Being a virgin is driving me nuts," he comments later in the same show. "It's beginning to affect my work as a doctor." Fortunately, one of his close friends is willing to help Dr. Howser deal with his embarrassing problem and even provides the show with an edge of political correctness by handing out condoms as the two pals prepare for their nocturnal adventures. "Tonight—we are *men!*" he declares with chest-thumping bravado.

In addition to airing the shows themselves, the networks powerfully magnified their public impact by broadcasting countless ads promoting the racy teen-sex episodes of each of the series. Needless to say, these panting promos involved unabashed exploitation of the "raging hormones" theme; they attempted to lure viewers by making the shows seem far more outrageously erotic than they actually were and by making the teenage characters look more daring and seductive. The whole world knew that Doogie Howser would lose his virginity on the season's premiere long before the show ever aired, thanks to a repeatedly run network promo that showed the bare-chested hero carrying his girlfriend to bed.

As a result of these ubiquitous and obnoxious advertising campaigns, even those viewers who chose *not* to watch the programs still took in their basic message—that all normal and healthy teenagers are sexually active well before they graduate from high school. By the end of September 1991, any American youngster who watched television with even moderate regularity would have received the unequivocal impression that the popular culture expected that he or she should become erotically experienced and cheerfully enter the brave new world of adolescent intercourse.

The producers who create this impression justify their work as part of a noble national crusade to fight AIDS and promote proper birth control precautions. "Beverly Hills 90210," for instance, specifically hired a birth control expert as a consultant for the show, acquiring the services of Marlene Goland of the Center for Population Options. "Because of AIDS, the networks know they have to teach and educate or the consequences can be fatal for teenagers," Ms. Goland declared. Ironically, the show to which she provided her expertise made no discernible effort to "teach and educate" on these issues: when Brenda makes love to her boyfriend they never discuss AIDS or other risks. These youthful role models also appear to ignore all contraceptive precautions, since subsequent shows depict Brenda going throught a pregnancy scare.

Even those shows that do encourage the use of condoms provide a thoroughly one-sided view of the risks of adolescent sexuality, since the alternative of abstinence is never seriously addressed. Hollywood refuses to consider the possibility that teenagers could be urged to avoid intercourse altogether—even though a 1991 *USA Weekend* survey showed that 41 percent of American adults—*and a surprising 35 percent of all teens*—believed that the message of "no sex" would be more effective in fighting AIDS than the message of "safe sex." Despite the apparent eagerness of a large segment of the audience to hear calls for self-control, the entertainment industry refuses to vary its shallow—and ultimately demeaning—view of young people as creatures who cannot possibly restrain their lustful impulses.

A Surprisingly Conservative Streak

Television's portrayal of teenagers in heat typifies its power to set new standards for the society at large. In a nation in which the average citizen watches the tube for close to thirty hours each week, the characters on the small screen serve to define what constitutes normal and desirable behavior. Children and adolescents regularly imitate heroes from television in shaping their styles of speech, dress, and grooming; it is only to be expected that they will similarly try to follow the lead of these fictional role models when it comes to intimate relationships. After many hours of programming and promos showing TV teens shedding their virginity like a shabby, childish garment they have recently outgrown, any adolescent who tried to abstain from sex would get the idea that he or she was "weird" and hopelessly out of step.

In October 1991, one thoughtful high school student expressed his frustration in a plaintive letter to the *Los Angeles Times*. "The producers of these shows are operating under a false premise: that all teenagers today are 'doing it,'" wrote Marcel Omohundro. "That is simply not the case. There is a huge segment of the population of young people who are not having sex. But they are not represented on TV. Where is the balance? Where are the portrayals of young people who have decided to wait until marriage to have sex? Their resolve to wait is being undermined by the unbalanced notion that all young people are having sex."

Similar sentiments emerged from a surprising source: Shannen Doherty, the gifted and alluring young actress who stars as Brenda in "Beverly Hills 90210." Shortly after her character lost her virginity on the show, Doherty told an interviewer: "I wasn't too thrilled about it. I didn't think she should go to bed with someone she's been seeing for three months. . . . There are virgins in this world, girls who can say no. From now on they can look at my character and say, 'Wow, she's doing it, why can't we?' I didn't want teens all over the world thinking it was okay."

Such concerns are echoed by Michael A. Carrerra, professor at

New York's Hunter College and director of the Adolescent Sexuality Program for the Children's Aid Society. "I am disturbed about the day-in, day-out litany of television suggesting what 'real' men are all about," he declared. "What kids learn from this is that sex is all below the waist." In a 1988 interview for *Parade* magazine, Carrerra went on to point out that the sexual attitudes of real-life teenagers are far more complex and conservative than their one-dimensional portrayal in the media. He cited a major survey by Mark Clements Research, Inc., in which a national cross section of teenaged boys showed that 80 percent ranked love as more important than sex. "The findings are consistent with the clinical and practical experience of myself and my staff. I believe that boys are much more sensitive and responsible than they have been given credit for."

A wealth of data from other sources supports this more balanced view of American adolescents and undermines the contention of leading TV producers that their prurient programming merely reflects reality, or gives teenagers what they want. In November 1991, a poll for *USA Weekend* by ICR Survey Research turned up some startling results concerning the attitudes of contemporary young people. When asked the question, "Do today's teenagers hear too much, too little or just about enough about saying *no* to sex?," 54 percent of the teens said they heard "too little," as opposed to 12 percent who felt they heard "too much." In other words, by a ratio of nearly five to one, a representative group of American adolescents believed that they should hear more—rather than less—about sexual abstinence. In the same survey, the youthful respondents confronted the question: "Does the safe-sex message trouble you, because it might condone casual sex?" An amazing 63 percent said, "Yes, it troubles me"—an even higher percentage than the 54 percent of the adult population who expressed that opinion.

Contrary to the view of the world that is so potently promoted on prime-time TV, in which "everybody's doing it," the most recent study (September 1990) from the Public Health Service of the Department of Health and Human Services shows that nearly 65 percent of all American females under age eighteen are still virgins. Even in the age cohort fifteen to nineteen—the group regularly associated with raging hormones and unbridled erotic indulgence—nearly 50 percent of the girls have *never* had sex. Of the remainder—misleadingly labeled "sexually active"—almost one in seven had engaged in intercourse *only once in their lives*. Less than one-third of the total sample had experienced intercourse at all within the last month.

TV's thoroughly unrepresentative emphasis on teenage sexuality reflects the medium's general tendency to overstate erotic activity. The fictional characters who populate prime time are vastly more adventurous in their sexual attitudes and practices than the audience to which they are appealing. All serious studies of American values show a surprisingly conservative streak in public opinion concerning personal relationships. A 1991 *Los Angeles Times* poll of some 2,205 American adults showed the public evenly divided between those who believed that all premarital sex was "wrong" and those who thought it was "all right." Amazingly enough, even 40 percent of the single people in the survey considered premarital sex inappropriate.

Such attitudes are reflected to a considerable extent in patterns of behavior. A 1990 RAND report showed that for nearly all Americans, monogamy was not only an ideal, but a reality. "The vast majority of sexually active adults in the general population said they were involved with a single partner," the report concluded. "Only 4 percent had more than one sex partner." The study's principal author, David Kanouse, concluded that Americans "lead rather conservative sex lives." Other surveys showing substantial percentages of married people who confessed that they had been unfaithful to their spouses failed to make clear that for many—if not most—of these respondents, an episode of infidelity represented a single indiscretion over many years of marriage, rather than a consistent pattern of behavior. In any event, more traditional values prevail today throughout the country, even in the city that gives birth to most of our popular culture. Survey author Kanouse concluded: "This study belies the image of Los Angeles as the land of highly active sexual adventurers. The local findings are in line with national data that shows a low number of people with simultaneous sexual partners."

In light of such findings, television's radical distortion of contemporary reality seems especially irresponsible: remember that this is a medium that refers to sex outside of marriage *thirteen times* more frequently than it mentions intimacy between husband and wife. No won-

der that a 1991 Gallup Poll showed that 58 percent of the American
public said they are offended frequently or occasionally by current
television programming. Only 3 percent believed that TV portrayed
"very positive values."

"Double-Entendre City"

Had the survey been taken a few months later, after the network
series premieres in the fall of 1991, the number of television enthusiasts might have dropped even lower than the 3 percent measured by
Gallup, since the new season plumbed new lows in smutty and witless
dialogue. In October, Jay Martel, the intrepid television critic for
Rolling Stone, reviewed twenty-six new network series and found that
the debut show for *every one of them* included an example of "that current staple of American humor, the dick joke." For instance:

• On the first show of the prep school comedy, "Teech," on CBS,
the sexy assistant headmaster goes to the boys' dorm wearing a skimpy
and highly provocative outfit. One of her incredulous colleagues asks,
"You walked past two hundred adolescent boys dressed like that?" Her
response: "I love the sound of expanding khaki in the evening."

• Another new series, "Palace Guard" (also on CBS), stars Hollywood hunk D. W. Moffett. On the first show, as he is arrested in bed,
he stands up naked while the arresting officers stare at his crotch. "I
know, I know," he says, putting on his pants. "Hold your applause."

• On "Good and Evil" (ABC), a blind character who is a regular on
the show attempts to identify someone by touching his face. He first
guesses that he's a woman, but then feels below the belt. "A man!" he
shouts. "Oh! And quite a man, may I add!"

Amazingly enough, some of the industry's most respected producers
take pride in such locker-room humor as a sign of the medium's new
maturity. NBC executive Perry Simon argues that off-color dialogue "is a
reflection of the quality of the programs. I think it makes the audience
feel it is witty and clever. . . . Certain of these adult lines can be . . . the

most memorable or character-revealing moments in the whole show."

The talented writer-producer Glen Gordon Caron, creator of "Moon-lighting," happily informed USA Today: "We're double-entendre city. And you have to be of a certain age to get them, and a certain sophistication." To make sure that the reporter understood "Moon-lighting"'s true position as part of a noble tradition, Caron added that, "Shakespeare used them all the time."

Television's juvenile addiction to off-color material emerged most clearly of all on the forty-third Emmy Awards telecast in August 1991. On the occasion theoretically dedicated to honoring the most uplifting and worthy of all of the medium's achievements, the Television Academy instead presented an evening that Pulitzer Prize–winning critic Howard Rosenberg described as "raunchy," "appalling," "taste-less," and "a sneak attack on unsuspecting Americans who might have been watching this with their families."

The sexual references commenced in the first few minutes of the show, when presenters Jane Seymour and John Goodman discussed forty-three years of past Emmy winners. Seymour began: "If you laid every one of them end to end . . .," and then Goodman interrupted, ". . . you'd be exhausted."

Later, comedian Gilbert Gottfried got up to present an award and offered a full five-minute monologue on masturbation, including spe-cific references to the peculiarities of his penis. His material seemed so offensive that the Fox Network deleted it from its delayed broadcast of the live show for the Pacific time zone.

Nevertheless, even in that edited version, the show contained an abundance of questionable material, including at least a half dozen additional references to male sex organs. Shortly after the broadcast, Claudio Letelier wrote in the Los Angeles Times:

I am a visitor from Chile, and this is my first trip to your country. I find many things to admire. . . . However, I am more than puzzled by the incredibly low intellectual and cultural standards of the American people, which, in many ways, translate themselves into a kind of television pro-gramming that frankly is not in keeping with the tastes and requirements of an educated nation.

The Aug. 25 Emmy show seemed to define for me the extreme lack of "class" of this industry. If you called it "raunchy," it is in no way descriptive enough to describe the type of toilet humor that was expressed by men and women alike in this program.

It is regrettable that artists who tend to become role models for youth behave in such a fashion. I do not say that this type of humor does not exist in my country, but it is restricted to the privacy of homes where good friends can resort to a few minutes of obscenity and off-color jokes. However, we would never dream of exposing our children to it.

"A Love Crash"

Tens of millions of Americans surely sympathize with Letelier's point of view. Disillusionment with television is all but universal in our country today—and is reflected by the drastic reduction in the overall size of the viewing audience for the major networks. Concern over the sexual messages our children receive is in no way limited to the "religious right" or to conservatives in general; it is shared by observers of every political and social perspective.

For example, Faye Wattleton, then president of the Planned Parenthood Federation, told *The New York Times* in 1988: "Clearly, the American television networks are doing us—their viewers—a tremendous disservice. They obviously see no need to balance their overly romanticized and unrealistic portrayal of sex with messages about responsibility." Along similar lines, Peggy Charen, longtime president of the Boston-based advocacy group Action for Children's Television, worries that our prime-time programming is "giving teenagers a terrible message." Despite her "fierce First Amendment sympathies," Charen believes that citizens should make a concerted effort to influence the content of the popular culture for the better. "We have to teach children about caring," she says. "Sex on television so often has nothing to do with love, and so much of it happens with violence."

Many other commentators have made similar observations, but none of them more poignantly than the brilliant director and screenwriter (and four-time Oscar winner) Joseph Mankiewicz. In a May 1991 interview, the creator of films such as *All About Eve* and *A Letter to Three Wives* discussed the simpleminded and loveless approach to sexuality that has come to dominate all of the popular culture:

I couldn't do films today. . . . I'm just a little bit sad about the kinds of movies they're making now. . . .

Today's films don't seem to exist without the destruction of property, the destruction of human beings, the actual stripping of any kind of mystery or individuality, really, from sex, by putting as much as possible on the screen. . . .

Sex for the most part on the screen is physically engendered. Rarely do you see two people come together lovingly and tenderly. Or tentatively. It's like two cars hitting each other. It's not an auto crash. It's a love crash.

7

Maligning Marriage

Another key element in the entertainment industry's attack on the family involves its relentlessly negative portrayal of marital relationships. In Hollywood's view of the world, marriage is an institution that is outmoded, oppressive, and frequently dangerous.

The last few years have brought us an astonishing array of matrimonial horror stories, altogether unbalanced by movie alternatives that offer a more optimistic view of the conjugal connection. At times, the antimarriage agenda of such films is unmistakably apparent.

Deadly Delusions

The 1991 hit *Sleeping with the Enemy* is especially emphatic in its indictment of conventional wedlock as a cruel and unhealthy arrangement. Patrick Bergin plays a domineering yuppie husband who is so abusive that his "perfect" and superficially submissive wife (Julia Roberts) must fake her own death and assume a new identity in order to escape his brutality. When he discovers her discarded wedding ring, he realizes she is still alive and he ruthlessly tracks her down to another state, insisting that she must return to their horrific home to honor her marriage vows. A bloody and climactic confrontation ensues in which the wife murders this nightmarish mate in order to protect her hard-won freedom. The last shot of the movie shows a close-up of her wedding ring, glinting in the light as it rolls onto the floor, released from her husband's dead hand: he's clutched the token, along with his deadly delusions about the unbreakable bonds of matrimony, until the bitter end.

The same director (Joseph Ruben) previously created another vicious creep whose obsession with unattainable images of marital perfection leads to murderous results. *The Stepfather* (1987) generated only modest business at the box office, but earned surprisingly positive reviews with its tale of a mild-mannered psycho (Terry O'Quinn) who marries a succession of widows and divorcees and then slaughters them (along with their children) when they fall short of his vision of an ideal, "old-fashioned" American family. This demented defender of "family values" continued to display his homicidal habits in *Stepfather II* (1987) and *Stepfather III* (1992).

Similarly abusive husbands met gruesome fates in a spate of other recent films: in *Mortal Thoughts* (1991), the loutish, wife-beating Bruce Willis dies a well-deserved death at the hands of his wife and her best friend; in *Fried Green Tomatoes* (also 1991), two more best friends (Mary Stuart Masterson and Mary Louise Parker) conspire to conceal the murder of another battering bad guy (Parker's husband) and ultimately serve his cooked corpse to the suspicious sheriff. The wife (Mary Beth Hurt) acts alone in *Defenseless* (1991) to dispatch her monstrous mate, a prominent businessman who's been conducting a steamy, exploitative affair with their teenage daughter.

Another favorite theme in recent films involves the impeccably handsome husband who presents himself to the outside world as the ideal spouse, but who, in the privacy of marriage, turns out to be a cold-hearted and often bloody beast. Jeremy Irons won the Best Actor Oscar in 1990 for playing such a character in *Reversal of Fortune:* he delivered a memorably chilling and enigmatic performance as the elegant, adulterous socialite physician Klaus Von Bulow who stands accused of placing his wife in a permanent coma. In the chilling true story *Not Without My Daughter* (1991), Alfred Molina is also a prominent physician who seems, at first, to fill every need for his adoring wife, Sally Field: he is a doting father, a tender, loving husband, and a good provider. All it takes, however, is a brief visit to his family in Iran before he is transformed into an abusive, brutal, religious fanatic and male chauvinist madman, forcing his poor wife to attempt a harrowing escape.

Sean Young faces a similarly terrifying escape from another "perfect husband" (Matt Dillon) in *A Kiss Before Dying* (1991). This cold-blooded con man manipulates visions of marital bliss to victimize twin sisters, murdering the first one on the day of their engagement, and planning to perform a similar job on the surviving sister shortly after their lavish society wedding. In *Naked Tango* (1991), terror again follows within moments after a wedding ceremony: shortly after their Orthodox Jewish nuptials, Esai Morales pressures his new wife to have sex with another man and when she refuses he tries to stab her to death. Lorraine Braco, a struggling single mom in *Radio Flyer* (1991), also sees her dreams for happiness shattered immediately after her marriage to a virile hunk (Adam Baldwin) who has seemed the answer to all her prayers. It takes her many months to discover that this seemingly likeable blue-collar guy is secretly and sadistically battering her seven-year-old son. As if this weren't enough, he even attempts to kill the family's loyal German shepherd.

"She thought her life was perfect," proclaimed one of the ad lines for the 1991 Goldie Hawn thriller *Deceived*—offering an ominous warning to all those misguided souls in the moviegoing audience who may have felt satisfied and secure in their own marriages. In that particular movie, our girl Goldie appears to "have it all"—a glamorous career, a bright, beautiful daughter, and a devoted and brilliant husband (John Heard). As the picture progresses, she discovers that her partner is actually leading a double life and a triple life, with several false identities and faked deaths, another wife in another city, and participation in a murderous international art theft conspiracy. Eventually, inevitably, the heinous brute attempts to kill her, and she fights for her life in a bloody and protracted confrontation. Reflecting on her situation as she gradually awakens to the horrid reality of her marriage, Goldie tearfully delivers the movie's punch line: "It turned out that everything I believed was a lie."

This is a theme that surfaces in film after film showing couples who enjoy superficially sound relationships: in the world of today's feature films, "marital bliss" is most often a trap and a deception in which your spouse may become your deadly enemy virtually overnight. Husbands are most often characterized as the betraying and dangerous partner, but wives also do their share of homicidal double-dealing. In *Total Recall* (1990), Arnold Schwarzenegger learns that his blond and gorgeous consort (Sharon Stone) has been working undercover for an evil secret agency that is trying to control and manipulate him. When he confronts her with this information, she begs him to recall the sacred bonds of matrimony. "Sweetheart, be reasonable!" she pleads. "After all, we're married!"

"Consider that a divorce," the hero deadpans as he calmly shoots her through the forehead.

Kevin Kline is notably more forgiving toward his wife (Tracey Ullman) in *I Love You To Death* (1990)—even after she tries to murder him with poisoned spaghetti sauce and bloody gunshot wounds to punish his chronic infidelity. Roseanne Barr achieves far greater success in her vengeful schemes against her cheating husband (Ed Begley, Jr.) in *She-Devil* (1989), while Kathleen Turner is more than a match for her estranged hubby, Michael Douglas, battling him with astonishing and sadistic ferocity in *The War of the Roses* (1989). "The decade in family cinema ended not with a heartwarming salute to home's cozy comforts but with an explosion of hateful marital fireworks," wrote Susan Faludi in her controversial 1991 best-seller, *Backlash: The Undeclared War Against American Women.* "In both *The War of the Roses* and *She-Devil,* the wives are virtual witches, controlling and conquering their husbands with a supernatural and deadly precision."

Many other films highlight the emptiness and cruelty of married life. In director Paul Mazursky's unwatchable embarrassment *Scenes from a Mall* (1991), a long-wedded couple played by Woody Allen and Bette Midler spend the entire movie hurling food and insults at each other in a crowded shopping plaza while they tediously discuss their various infidelities and betrayals. The ironically titled *Marrying Man* (1991) offers Alec Baldwin and Kim Basinger as a mismatched pair who marry—and then divorce—three times in succession, alternating moments of burning lust with explosions of violent rage. *Thelma and Louise* (1991) portrays a marriage so cold and oppressive that Geena Davis quite literally becomes a fugitive in the process of escaping it; *Leaving Normal* (1992) provides a strikingly similar setup, with Meg Tilly abandoning her abusive second husband and teaming up with a cynical waitress (Christine Lahti) to forge a challenging new (and marriage-free) life in the wilds of Alaska.

Though these two may have escaped from the woes of wedlock, other characters in recent films find no refuge from marital misery in the comforting environment of a small town. In *Falling from Grace* (1992), John Mellencamp returns to his rural Indiana home only to begin a heavy-breathing affair with his brother's insatiable wife (Kay Lenz). It turns out that this same hot property is simultaneously sleeping with the father of both boys (Claude Akins), while the incorrigible old man still finds time to make a heavy-handed pass at Mellencamp's mate, Mariel Hemingway.

Barbra Streisand's much-praised *The Prince of Tides* (1991) similarly focused on the contrast between life in a picturesque small town (this time in South Carolina) and the sophisticated world of New York City, while presenting itself to the public as a warm and fuzzy, feel-good, pro-family treasure. In point of fact, this handsomely shot and well-acted picture lavished virtually all its attention on three radically dysfunctional marriages: the doomed union of Nick Nolte's ambitious mother (Kate Nelligan) and his violent, abusive father; the Nolte character's own frayed relationship with his physician wife (Blythe Danner), in which both spouses become involved in passionate outside affairs; and psychiatrist Streisand's cold, loveless relationship with her sneering husband, a philandering violinist played by Jeroen Krabbe. In the course of its various flashbacks and plot detours, this allegedly life-affirming piece of sentiment presents no less than four adulterous relationships: Blythe Danner with a fellow doctor; Kate Nelligan with a wealthy Carolina aristocrat (whom she later marries); Jeroen Krabbe with a glamorous fellow musician; and Nolte and Streisand.

"Happy Marriages Don't Sell"

The most striking aspect of this avalanche of major Hollywood projects that portray troubled and nightmarish marriages is that their impact is so seldom counteracted by pictures that portray relationships between husband and wife in more positive terms.

No sane observer would ever suggest that moviemakers should limit themselves to making films that glorify the institution of marriage, or to portraying married life as an uninterrupted panorama of sweetness and light. The problems that real people encounter in intimate relations are too dramatic and too absorbing to be ignored on the big screen: they provide an irresistibly compelling subject for serious movie artists. As Tolstoy so famously observed in the opening line of *Anna Karenina:* "All happy families are alike; every unhappy family is unhappy in its own way." To some extent, a tendency to focus on troubled relationships is natural and inevitable.

Nevertheless, Hollywood's current fascination with the most disastrous, bizarre, and destructive family situations goes well beyond the normal tendency to focus on dramatic, real-life difficulties, and amounts to a stacked deck against the very institution of marriage. This emphasis on the most extreme sorts of intimate ugliness is not only irresponsible, it is self-defeating for the industry. Anyone can relate to a film that honestly portrays the ordinary ups and downs of family life, but fevered fantasies about handsome husbands who are actually killer con men, or wives who turn out to be vicious and vengeful shrews, seem irrelevant and implausible to most Americans. A film like *Kramer vs. Kramer* (1979) could connect with a mass audience through its sensitive and realistic portrayal of fundamentally decent people caught in the grip of a painful divorce; on the other hand, lurid, cartoonish horror stories like *Deceived, Mortal Thoughts, A Kiss Before Dying, She-Devil,* or *Scenes from a Mall* left filmgoers absolutely cold—despite the participation of some of the industry's biggest stars.

The dismal commercial performance of nearly all of the antimarriage message movies of recent years (with rare exceptions like *Sleeping with the Enemy*) rebuts the suggestion that Hollywood is merely responding to some odd and insatiable public appetite for films that show matrimony to be murderous and menacing. In fact, to the extent that the American public has been able to vote on the issue with its box-office dollars, the people have expressed a clear preference for movies that provide a kinder, gentler view of matrimony.

The overwhelming popularity of a handful of such films indicates the existence of a huge moviegoing audience that is eager, at least on occasion, to spend its ninety minutes in the dark with characters who are happily married. In the last few years, industry observers found themselves largely puzzled by the unexpected box-office drawing power of two bittersweet Steve Martin comedies (*Parenthood* [1989] and *Father of the Bride* [1991]), kiddie adventures about loving parents and endangered offspring (*Home Alone* [1990] and *Honey, I Shrunk the Kids* [1989]), and even a model-mommy-vs.-nasty-nanny thriller (*The Hand That Rocks the Cradle* [1992]).

Whatever their artistic shortcomings, each of these hugely profitable movies showed devoted husbands and loyal wives who face adversity together. Perhaps one explanation for their stunning success is that they had so little competition in appealing to that substantial segment of the public hungry for motion pictures that display a more affectionate attitude toward the family. In any event, even the most cursory review of recent box-office returns definitively discredits the endlessly repeated mantra mouthed by so many Hollywood powerbrokers who continue to insist that "happy marriages don't sell." It wasn't true in Hollywood's Golden Age, and it's certainly not true today. Commercial considerations can in no way account for the industry's seemingly irresistible impulse to malign marriage.

Husbands and Wives in Short Supply

Nor can those concerns in any way explain Hollywood's all-but-exclusive focus on heroes and heroines who are single or divorced. According to Census Bureau statistics, two-thirds of all Americans above the age of eighteen are currently married. Among the remaining one-third (including all those who are widowed or divorced, or were never married), recent surveys show that some 80 percent plan on wedlock for the future. This means that more than 90 percent of the nation's adults are either married at the moment, or expecting marriage at some point in the years ahead. Viewed another way, less than 9 percent *of singles* (according to a landmark 1982 study by Jacqueline Simenauer and David Carroll) agree with the statement "I prefer the singles life-style."

These simple but unassailable demographic facts make it difficult to understand why Hollywood should tilt so heavily toward projects centered on single heroes; in view of the makeup of the potential moviegoing audience, it makes no sense at all that husbands and wives should be in such short supply as the leading characters of contemporary motion pictures. If you want to test the premise that married people are seriously underrepresented, all you have to do is to pick up a copy of your local newspaper and turn to the entertainment section to see what's playing at your local theaters. On any given weekend, you will see that movies with unattached protagonists will outnumber those titles with married main characters by a ratio of four or five to one. On some weeks of the year, movies about married people will be altogether unavailable.

This shortage of material about normal married couples makes the emphasis on dysfunctional families even more worrisome: the embittered and murderous couples portrayed in movies like *The War of the Roses* and *I Love You to Death* may be the only marital role models that a typical moviegoer will encounter in the course of a year. The emphasis on disastrous relationships, and the paucity of positive alternatives, contribute powerfully to the prevailing sense that marriage is an institution under siege; that happy couples are an endangered species; that misery and cruelty are inevitable by-products of the traditional family structure.

Innocent Illusions and Grim Realities

Television broadcasts the same messages with ever-increasing frequency and intensity—marking a radical departure for an entertainment medium once known for its affectionate and idealized view of family life in these United States. In its infancy, television encouraged wary Americans to invite the amazing (and frightening) new machine into their living rooms by offering endless images of adoring and endearing couples who were blessed with squeaky-clean kids. These model families dominated network programming for more than two decades, from "I Love Lucy" to "Dick Van Dyke," from "Lassie" to "Make Room for Daddy," "The Adventures of Ozzie and Harriet," "Donna Reed," "Father Knows Best," "Leave It to Beaver," "The Real McCoys," and endless others. Those of us in the baby-boom generation who grew up on such fare inevitably recall such shows with fond nostalgia, not because of their artistic excellence (which, if truth be known, was never especially impressive) but for their innocence, their sunny simplicity, and their underlying decency.

Innocence and decency are precisely those elements most notably absent from TV today as the networks offer a radically altered view of the American family. "Married . . . with Children," the popular series whose very title proclaims its intention to survey the overall state of matrimony in this country, portrays the nuclear family as a comically outmoded and beleaguered structure that creates endless difficulties for those enslaved to it. Other top-rated shows like "The Simpsons" offer a view of marriage and parenting that is scarcely more uplifting, while many Americans object to the earthy imperfections of the Connor family in ABC's "Roseanne." "If you watch Roseanne Barr on television, you don't get a very good role model," warned future presidential candidate H. Ross Perot in a Washington interview on September 26, 1991. ". . . You and I didn't see that kind of stuff growing up." Nor did we see the steamy plot twists of prime-time melodramas, from "Dallas" and "Dynasty" through "L.A. Law" and "Falcon Crest," to new series like "The Palace Guard" and "The Powers That Be," which all show families wracked with intrigue and adultery, divorce and disillusionment.

"The Cosby Show" defies the trend toward "more realistic" (read "more troubled") portrayals of upper-middle-class life at least in part because it seems so refreshingly unconventional to present a black family in this context: because of their ethnicity, the Huxtables can be "disgustingly wholesome" and politically correct at the same time. "Brooklyn Bridge" tries for a similar sort of reassuring appeal by placing its own warmhearted ethnic clan in a nostalgic immigrant neighborhood some forty years in the past. TV's recent tendency to set its most loving and exemplary families in previous decades, or in cute and quaint small-town enclaves, says volumes about the medium's underlying skepticism about the state of family life in today's big-city America. That skepticism informs the dark humor of the weekly comedy "Civil Wars" on ABC, with Mariel Hemingway and Peter Onorati starring as a pair of glamorous but constantly bickering divorce lawyers. A divorce attorney also figures prominently in the pilot for Shelley Long's new CBS sitcom "Good Advice," in which the star plays a marriage counselor with a flagrantly unfaithful husband.

While weekly series offer a far harsher view of family life than ever before, it is made-for-TV movies that remain the most significant source of antimarriage messages on the small screen. As television critic Harry Waters wrote in *Newsweek* in 1991: "Since nobody knows how to create a hit series anymore, everybody's cranking out those high-rated, two-hour 'made-fors': their number has tripled in the last five years. And of the approximately 250 set for this season, nearly half show women undergoing—and overcoming—some form of physical or psychological mistreatment." This single season's worth of televised "entertainments" includes cheerful tales that show:

—a dental hygienist who's beaten to death by her dentist husband, who then tells the police she had been sexually molesting their baby (*In a Child's Name*, CBS);

—an overweight socialite who vengefully guns down her ex-husband and his new wife after he has jilted her (*A Woman Scorned*, CBS)

—an innocent wife (Donna Mills) who is imprisoned for the misdeeds of her manipulative and homicidal husband (*False Arrest*, ABC)

—a mother of four (Susan Dey) who is savagely beaten by her lawyer husband until she stops him with a bullet through the chest (*Bed of Lies*, ABC)

—an adulterous housewife who is wrongly accused of knocking off her best friend, and is finally chased around her house by the real killer (*The Woman Who Sinned*, NBC)

—a manic-depressive mother (Sarah Jessica Parker) whose illness creates a nightmarish situation for her five children (*In the Best Interest of the Children*, NBC)

—a fast-talking con man (Treat Williams) who persuades his married lover to murder her husband, while he pulls the trigger on his own long-suffering wife (*Till Death Do Us Part*, NBC)

—a gifted commercial artist (Blair Brown) with two perfect daughters and a seemingly rock-solid marriage who suddenly learns of her husband's infidelity, then reveals her own dark past . . . as a prostitute (*Those Secrets*, ABC)

—an unsuspecting single mom (Cheryl Ladd) who's framed by her drug-dealing boyfriend and whose imprisonment causes her three children to fall apart (*Locked Up: A Mother's Rage*, CBS)

—a superficially happy wife and mother (Pamela Reed) whose family is destroyed when her husband and neighbors discover she is actually an escaped con (*Woman with a Past*, NBC)

There are also many other TV movies about alcoholic fathers (*Keeping Secrets*, ABC); sadistic sons (*My Son Johnny*, CBS), and violent, avenging moms (*A Mother's Justice*, NBC).

In the increasingly gloomy view of family relationships purveyed week after week in made-for-TV films, even the sweet and unsullied life of young Theodore "Beaver" Cleaver must inevitably turn sour. A 1983 TV movie called *Still the Beaver* reunited most of the cast of the original "Leave It to Beaver" show, for a plot that portrayed the aging Beav as unemployed, pathetic, and facing divorce. The producers could hardly send a more obvious message that the innocent illusions of the previous generation must give way to grim new realities.

Defenders of the entertainment industry insist that television actually performs a public service by adjusting its images of family life to suit the bleak domestic landscape that currently prevails across the country. They point out that most of the innumerable TV movies that dramatize murderous couples or oppressive parents are actually based on true stories, and that these tales reflect the larger reality of a nation in which the institution of the family is disintegrating before our eyes. According to this line of reasoning, dark visions of matrimony are inevitable and appropriate in a society in which half of all marriages are doomed to end in divorce.

The Myth of the Fifty-Percent Divorce Rate

The problem with this argument (aside from the inherent dangers of self-fulfilling prophecies) is that it is based on incorrect assumptions and ignores all available data—including straightforward statistics that show that the commonly accepted figure about the divorce rate is profoundly misleading.

The notion that every marriage has a 50-percent chance of failure is so deeply ingrained in our national consciousness that even well-informed and thoughtful observers seldom bother to question it. The media have repeated this conclusion so frequently that it has taken on a life of its own, encouraging—and justifying—the emphasis on marital dysfunction that turns up so frequently in television and motion pictures.

According to responsible statisticians, however, the claim that half of all marriages are bound to fail has never been justified, and stems from a simplistic misreading of the numbers. Veteran pollster Louis Harris, for instance, cites the rock-solid figures compiled by the U.S. Center for Health Statistics and declares that these facts "are directly contrary to the media's loud proclamation that one out of every two marriages now will end in divorce." In his 1987 book, *Inside America,* Harris reports the shocking news that our best numbers show that only 10 percent of all ever-married men, and 13 percent of all ever-married women have *ever* been divorced. As he concludes, *"This in turn means that almost 90 percent of all marriages survive."*

The difference between this 90-percent survival rate for marriage and the conventional wisdom claiming a 50-percent divorce rate is so enormous—and so enormously significant—that the contradiction requires some detailed explanation. This book can offer no more important contribution to the reader's understanding of the huge gap between Hollywood's vision and America's reality than helping to clear away the confusion on this critically important matter. This means explaining how so many pundits can proclaim that half of all marriages fail—and how they can be so horribly wrong.

In 1981 the number of divorces in the United States hit an all-time record of 1,213,000. Marriages in that year totaled 2,422,000, so commentators eagerly jumped to the conclusion that half the marriages were bound to fail.

The logic in this leap is utterly lacking. Imagine that the number of divorces had risen even higher—that there had been 2,422,000 divorces and 2,422,000 marriages. Would this mean that 100 percent of marriages were doomed to failure?

Of course not. Calculating the divorce rate by comparing the number of marriages to the number of divorces in a single year is like computing the likelihood of dying by contrasting yearly births with yearly deaths. Let's say that the number of deaths in a given year is twice the number of births. Does this mean that your chances of dying are twice your chances of being born? If the situation is reversed, and the number of yearly births is twice as large as the number of yearly deaths, does that indicate that only half of all people will ever die?

Such calculations are meaningless because they ignore the fact that the huge majority of people neither die nor are born in a single twelve-month period. By the same token, more than 98 percent of all Americans go through a year without getting married, *and* without getting divorced. Their reality is in no way reflected in the facile comparisons of *annual* marriage/divorce statistics. As it happens, the overwhelming percentage of this 98 percent who are untouched by the annualized numbers are *already* married. And statistics show that most of them will remain married for the rest of their lives.[°]

The most simple questions provide the most direct answers. In a major 1991 survey for the Massachusetts Mutual Life Insurance Company, the Washington, D.C., polling firm of Mellman and Lazarus concluded that *only 15 percent of all American adults had ever been divorced*—meaning that only 20 percent of those who had married had ever been divorced—numbers which coincide precisely with the raw data available from the 1990 census. Such figures are by now so well-known to experts that they have even made it to the pages of *Cosmopolitan* magazine (March 1992)—a journal not normally noted for its fervent defense of hearth and home. In the course of an article on AIDS, Daniel Lynch supported the surprising news that American marriages actually stand a 90-percent chance of survival.

This arcane detour into the world of statistical analysis is necessary to understand the way that the numbers have been distorted by Hollywood and leading journalists to make divorce look like a far more prevalent practice than it really is.

In fact, the news on the marriage front is even better than this brief discussion reveals. Between 1981 and 1987, the number of marriages went up 3 percent nationwide while the number of divorces *declined* by 5 percent—the first time this has happened in modern times. On May 21, 1991, the National Center for Health Statistics of the U.S. Department of Health and Human Services published a summary of recent data on divorce and concluded: "The divorce rate per 1,000

[°]The fact that most adults are already married rather than single further undermines the "50-percent divorce rate" myth. Because two-thirds of all adults are currently married, *the pool available for divorce is much larger than the pool available for marriage.* In other words, even if the number of marriages and divorces *were* equal in a given year (which has never happened), it would mean that a much higher percentage of those eligible for marriage were, in fact, marrying than the percentage of those eligible for divorce who were, in fact, divorcing. This is especially true because such a significant percentage of those counted as single are actually elderly widows and widowers who are unlikely candidates for marriage. This means that even when the number of yearly divorces approaches 50 percent of the number of yearly marriages, a single individual is more than *four times more likely to marry* in the course of a given year than a married couple is to divorce.

Another problem in the statistics involves the common reality of one individual who divorces more than once. Those rare individuals who experience multiple divorces produce a huge and disproportionate impact on the overall numbers. Imagine, for example, that Elizabeth Taylor comes to a dinner party with six other individuals, all of whom have been married to the same partners all their lives. How do you calculate the divorce rate at that table? If you simply compare the number of marriages to the number of divorces the divorce rate is 50%—a total of fourteen marriages and seven divorces. The fact is, however, that more than 85 percent of the people in the room have never been divorced. In other words it takes six families like the folks down the block to balance one Liz Taylor in the raw divorce numbers.

population and the divorce rate per 1,000 married women eighteen years of age and over both dropped for the third consecutive year. Both rates increased sharply in the 1970s, peaked in the late '70s and early 1980s, and *have generally declined throughout the remainder of the 1980s"* (italics added).

Louis Harris concludes: "The evidence strongly suggests that marriage just might be making a strong comeback and divorce might be on the wane. Such a conclusion, of course, flies wildly in the face of all conventional wisdom."

"The Last Married Couple in America"

The entertainment industry ignores and distorts these changing realities of marriage and divorce, contributing to the public's prevailing ignorance concerning hopeful trends in family stability. Hollywood expressed its own jaded view of the situation with a 1980 release called *The Last Married Couple in America*—a witless George Segal–Natalie Wood comedy about the irresistible appeal of divorce and erotic adventure. In view of the passionate commitment to marriage and family of the overwhelming majority of Americans, it's hardly surprising that this heavily hyped picture proved to be a dismal flop at the box office.

A decade later, despite steadily declining divorce rates, an action comedy starring the nation's number-one box-office draw indicated that the industry maintained its inaccurate vision of the universality and inevitability of marital breakup. In *Kindergarten Cop* (1990), Arnold Schwarzenegger plays a divorced police officer who goes undercover as a kindergarten teacher in a small Oregon town. It turns out that all the cute and well-scrubbed children in his class are the products of parents who are divorced—except for one pathetic child who, along with his mother, is savagely beaten by a brutal dad. While it's perhaps possible that some elite kindergartens in Beverly Hills might boast a parent roster predominantly comprised of divorced single parents, the idea of transplanting this unusual situation to a sleepy rural village in Oregon is nonsensical.

Hollywood not only misrepresents the prevalence of divorce, but also distorts the public's current attitudes toward the institution of marriage.

Outside the entertainment industry, only tiny percentages of Americans view the traditional family as some outmoded structure. In terms of their reverence for the institution of marriage, adolescents express much the same attitudes as their parents: In a 1990 survey for the University of Michigan, 78 percent of high school seniors listed the goal of a good marriage as *"extremely* important" to them. In fact, even those people who have gone through divorce express a clear preference for the married state. In their ground-breaking survey of three thousand single men and women across the country, Simenauer and Carroll discovered that nearly two-thirds of those who had been divorced said they preferred married life to single life—and would marry again if given the opportunity. Amazingly enough, even among those who had been divorced twice or more, a majority preferred marriage.

This corresponds with survery results from Louis Harris: by a whopping margin of 65 percent to 18 percent, his respondents expressed their opinion that married people are happier than singles.

Moreover, when asked if they would remarry their spouse if they had to do it all over again, an amazing 85 percent of all husbands and wives responded that they would. According to the 1991 Massachusetts Mutual survey, 67 percent of married Americans said they were *"very* satisfied" with their own family lives.

These numbers hardly suggest an institution that is on its last legs, or an outmoded living arrangement that is producing seething discontent in the heartland. The portrait of hopeful and contented families that emerges in every responsible study of the American public stands in striking contrast to the horrific view of family decay and dysfunction so relentlessly emphasized on television and in motion pictures.

In its approach to the family, as in its previously discussed outlook on religious practice, Hollywood is profoundly out of touch with America. The themes that turn up on movie and television screens express the current quirks and fads of the utterly unrepresentative—and unresponsive—entertainment community rather than the broad-based values of the public at large.

To make this observation is not to say that America is a nation composed exclusively of happily married couples—nor to suggest that Hollywood should ignore the severe family problems that are an undeniable and tragic feature of contemporary life. No one would complain about the presence of a few TV movies about abusive husbands or worried moms with guilty secrets; the problem is the absence of alternative visions of married life to balance these nightmares. It's the wildly disproportionate emphasis on the darkest, most downbeat aspects of marriage that betrays Hollywood's antifamily agenda.

Underlying Attitudes

At times, entertainment companies have been remarkably candid—even arrogant—in publicly acknowledging that agenda. In September 1991, for instance, MGM released a dreary little picture called *Crooked Hearts*, about a disturbed and disintegrating clan with an especially troubled oldest son (Vincent D'Onofrio) who becomes so enraged by his parents' hypocrisy that he quite literally burns their house to the ground. In the press materials distributed by the studio, writer-director Michael Bortman solemnly declared: "*Crooked Hearts* is a story about the dream of family and one boy's awakening from it." The implication, of course, is that someday we may all be lucky and mature enough to "awaken" from "the dream of family" in the manner of this enlightened youth. At a key moment in the film, the D'Onofrio character informs his siblings: "This family is a drug. And we're all junkies." In case we missed it the first time, this crucial insight is repeated—word for word—fifteen minutes later, warning us once again of the dire dangers of "family addiction."

The most amazing aspect of this particular film fiasco is that its underlying attitudes actually crept into MGM's national ad campaign designed to boost public interest in the picture. The newspaper layouts that appeared in every city in which the picture opened used the same promotional line:

> THEY SMOTHER YOU WITH LOVE
> DRIVE YOU TO INSANITY
> SHIELD YOU FROM THE TRUTH . . .
> WHAT ARE FAMILIES FOR?

Try to imagine the thought process behind this particular ad. Somewhere, lurking in the bowels of one of our major studios, is a public relations genius who concluded that this sneering indictment of family life would actually help to draw millions of people to the theaters; we are dealing with some poor benighted soul so sadly out of synch with his fellow citizens that he (or she) concluded that the public would warm to a movie that described "families" (in the most general sense) as smothering institutions that drive us insane and shield us from the truth. Needless to say, moviegoers stayed home in droves; in spite of its intriguing and attractive cast (D'Onofrio, Peter Coyote, Jennifer Jason Leigh, Juliette Lewis), *Crooked Hearts* earned pathetic receipts at the box office and sank without a trace.

The same antifamily assumptions, however, also helped to shape a much more successful movie: Martin Scorsese's brilliantly executed 1991 remake of *Cape Fear.* The previous section of this book noted the manner in which director Scorsese and screenwriter Wesley Strick altered the substance of the original 1962 film to give their picture an all-new, antireligious twist: they took the murderous psycho (Robert De Niro) who menaces a Carolina family and turned him into a killer Christian who carries a Bible in several scenes. The marriage-bashing message that Scorsese and Strick simultaneously added to the film required even more substantive changes. In the original *Cape Fear,* the hero, Gregory Peck, is a devoted husband and father determined to protect his precious family from a demented ex-con. In the Scorsese version, by contrast, "hero" Nick Nolte is hardly heroic: he is a chronically unfaithful husband who threatens his wife with physical violence when she confronts him with his history of infidelity. He also raises his hand to his pot-smoking fifteen-year-old daughter when he finds it difficult to communicate with her.

The official production notes released by Universal Studios to promote the movie indicate that such changes are highly purposeful, and reflect a deep-seated cynicism about family life on the part of the filmmakers. "At the opening of the film, the Bowden family appears to be a happy one," reads this handout to the press. "That's deceptive," says Scorsese, who wanted to portray "*a more realistic family.*"

It says volumes about Hollywood's jaded and myopic view of American marriage that the industry's most revered director considers a dysfunctional family inherently "more realistic" than a happy one.

Encouraging Illegitimacy

In addition to its increasingly unflattering portrayal of traditional families, the entertainment industry actively promotes alternative arrangements for raising children. In particular, Hollywood disregards the conventional notion that kids fare best in a situation where they live together with a father and a mother who happen to be married to each other.

Challenging Family Pieties

For many of the leaders of the show business community, promoting single parenthood and out-of-wedlock birth is a matter of conviction, not just convenience. An impressive array of the most prominent entertainers proudly bear children without benefit of matrimony. Goldie Hawn and Kurt Russell, Woody Allen and Mia Farrow, Susan Sarandon and Tim Robbins, Jessica Lange and Sam Shepard, Jessica Lange and Mikhail Baryshnikov, Sean Penn and Robin Wright, Farrah Fawcett and Ryan O'Neal, Jack Nicholson and Rebecca Broussard, Eddie Murphy, Glenn Close, Christopher Reeve, Mick Jagger, Al Pacino, Rod Stewart, Ed Asner, Sting, William Hurt, Ice Cube, and many others all seem to make a deliberate point of avoiding marriage, even after they bring children into the world.

"Illegitimacy chic" is as much a part of the contemporary Hollywood scene as a passion for distributing condoms or saving the rain forests. As Jessica Lange, mother of three out-of-wedlock children, told *Glamour* magazine in 1988: "My family doesn't think marriage is all that important." In fact, the fearless pioneers of this brave new world of "postmarital" modernity at times take serious offense at the mere suggestion that they may have made hypocritical concessions to outmoded conventions.

I encountered this sensitivity under surprising circumstances in December 1991, during an appearance as a guest on a call-in radio show on station KABC in Los Angeles. In the course of discussing recently released films, I happened to recommend the touching and amusing Steve Martin comedy *Father of the Bride* as a rare example of a major Hollywood film that took an unreservedly affectionate view of middle-class family life. In that context, I praised the talented team that had worked together to create the film, noting that director Charles Shyer and cowriter/coproducer Nancy Meyers had themselves been married for many years and had doubtless drawn on their own emotions and experiences as parents.

A few minutes later in the program I was surprised when a caller came on the air to correct me. Describing himself as a friend of Shyer and Meyers, he explained that even though they had "been a couple" for more than fifteen years and had raised two children together, they were *not* married—and would have been offended to hear their relationship described inaccurately. In other words, Hollywood may be the only community in the world in which the assumption that a long-term couple might actually be married could be construed as some sort of insult.

After this conversation on the radio, I checked the public record and discovered that the caller had been entirely correct in describing his friends' living arrangement and their attitude toward marriage. In a 1985 interview with the *Los Angeles Herald Examiner,* Ms. Meyers emphatically declared: "I'm not very fond of what a lot of wives go through in their marriages. Especially when you're a mother. You seem to establish these patterns. I'm adamant about being separate. . . . we were very comfortable not being married." She went on to describe the cautionary message in *Private Benjamin,* which she and Shyer cowrote: "It's about what marriage does to women."

Private Peccadillos, Public Pieties

The movie colony's private contempt for middle-class morality is, in fairness, nothing new; in terms of the personal lives of its leading celebrities, Hollywood has never served as a beacon of family values. Kenneth Anger's *Hollywood Babylon* and numerous other volumes document the chaotic and unconventional intimate experiences of some of America's most adored movie idols, even in the industry's fondly remembered Golden Age. In past decades, however, these personal peccadillos would be carefully concealed, not flaunted in the pages of *People* magazine or trumpeted triumphantly in interviews for "Lifestyles of the Rich and Famous." In their heyday, the studios employed armies of publicists to try to put the most wholesome face on the sometimes erratic behavior of the major stars.

Needless to say, the strict standards of the past led to a great deal of hypocrisy, cruelty, and intolerance—such as Ingrid Bergman's forced exile from Hollywood after her divorce and remarriage in 1950. The moguls treated their stars like wayward children, and top performers built their careers as much on their misleading off-screen images as their thespian abilities. Whatever their passions and predilections behind closed doors, Hollywood's major stars protected their popularity by paying public tribute to mainstream mores.

To a surprising extent, that situation has been reversed: today, a conventional marriage might cause more embarrassment to an aspiring sex symbol than casually conceiving a baby with a boyfriend. Susan Sarandon welcomes more publicity for her out-of-wedlock pregnancy at age forty-five than Mel Gibson allows to his notoriously old-fashioned (and devoutly Catholic) home life with a wife and six children. Contemporary entertainers win the admiration of their peers and the Hollywood press by challenging, rather than respecting, the old-fashioned family pieties.

"Baby Boom"

These challenges play a role in their on-screen work as well as in their private lives.

Before their success with *Father of the Bride,* the very emphatically

unmarried Shyer-Meyers team helped lead Hollywood's late '80s redis-
covery of the indestructible appeal of adorable toddlers. Their film
Baby Boom (1987) joined *Three Men and a Baby* (1987) and *Look
Who's Talking* (1990) as box-office leaders among this new wave of dia-
pers-and-formula comedies. Despite their apparent intent of celebrating the joys of child-rearing, these films displayed a dismissive or contemptuous attitude toward marriage: in each of them, single characters
performed the parental roles with the cute and cuddly kids. The underlying message could hardly be more clear: babies may be rewarding
and irresistible, but they are best enjoyed without the inconvenient
entanglements of marriage.

Similar signals emerged from the mega-hit *Ghost* (1990), billed by
Paramount as one of the Great Love Stories of our time. This crafty
tear-jerker featured Demi Moore and Patrick Swayze as the perfect
yuppie couple of the '90s: they share a trendy and elegant apartment,
and a passion for pottery, but their athletic appetite for each other
remains utterly unencumbered by formal commitments. After an
unfortunate mishap, this love is so potent and powerful that it manages
to conquer death itself, but in life it never proved quite strong enough
to overcome the characters' reluctance to marry. It is surely significant
that in its most prominent recent exploitation of the ideal of eternal
love, Hollywood chose to focus on an unmarried cohabiting couple,
rather than a pair of newlyweds.

This emphasis on deathless love unfettered by formal commitment
can only encourage the tragic epidemic of out-of-wedlock births that is
currently sweeping the country. Nowhere has that trend produced
more destructive results than in the African-American community, and
high-profile black-theme movies have been especially notable in glamorizing illegitimacy. *Do the Right Thing* (1989), *Boyz N The Hood*
(1991), *Juice* (1992), and *Gladiator* (1992) all feature handsome,
charismatic, and admirable young black males who have proudly
fathered babies out of wedlock.

Of course, single parenthood is a fact of inner-city life, but not all
aspects of that reality are presented on screen with the same easygoing
acceptance. Crack addiction is also tragically common among young
black males, but it plays no significant role in these films. The
moviemakers understand that it would be profoundly irresponsible to
create films that seemed to sanction drug abuse, but they fail to make

the same association with out-of-wedlock births—despite eloquent warnings by Jesse Jackson and other African-American leaders about the sad cycle of "babies having babies" and its devastating impact on prospects for progress. In short, glamorizing illegitimacy is about as helpful to black America as glamorizing crack, but Hollywood's hostility to marital conventions overrides any sense of social concern.

"Pregnancy Has Replaced Weddings"

Surprisingly, television has played an even more prominent role than feature films in promoting child-bearing outside of marriage. In October 1991, Caryn James noted in *The New York Times* a "TV epidemic of older single mothers. . . . Obviously, the boom in single parenthood means that pregnancy has replaced weddings as that special event used to perk up ratings." She identified seven presumed pregnancies in prime time for the new TV season; six of those expectant mothers happened to be unmarried. James cited a successful artificial insemination on "Designing Women" (with a sperm bank specimen affectionately called "Bongo") and a proposed insemination for the heroine of "The Trials of Rosie O'Neill"; and dramatic home pregnancy tests for single characters on "Sisters" and "Anything But Love." On "Cheers," Sam and Rebecca decide to have a baby even though they're not in love and have no plans to marry, and Rebecca is sorely disappointed when *her* pregnancy test turns out to be negative. Most famously, of course, Candice Bergen conceived an out-of-wedlock child during a brief encounter with her idealistic ex-husband on the hugely popular show "Murphy Brown."

As columnist Mona Charen aptly notes, "In a thousand ways, the *Murphy Brown* show snidely implies that only middle-American dunderheads believe you ought to be married before getting pregnant." The network executive who berates Murphy over the possibility that her out-of-wedlock pregnancy may hurt ratings is portrayed as insensitive, shortsighted, and hopelessly narrow-minded. As Charen writes: "Note the sly insinuation. The emphasis on marriage is just another prejudice—like racism or sexism—held by the unenlightened."

Perhaps the most straightforward endorsement of single parenthood came on the 1991 season premiere of "Empty Nest." Barbara, the

ditzy daughter, decides that she wants to conceive a baby through a
sperm bank. Her benighted father is opposed to the idea, but his daughters patiently explain to him that marriage is by no means a prerequisite
for a "modern woman" who wants to become a mother. As Barbara eloquently inquires, "Why should I obligate a guy for the rest of his life
when I only need him for an hour?" Such powerful logic eventually persuades the old man to endorse his daughter's plan, but she changes her
mind at the last moment when a promotion comes through at work.

In previous seasons, Blanche's daughter on "Golden Girls"
(9/22/90) used artificial insemination to conceive a child and ultimately
won her mother's support, while Susannah on "thirtysomething" celebrated Valentine's Day of 1989 by becoming accidentally pregnant and
planning for the baby with no intention of marriage—though later in
the series she weakened and stepped up to the altar.

Television's innovative twist to the new baby boom even included
one affirmative-action delivery: a male extraterrestrial gave birth amid
much fanfare on "Alien Nation." Meanwhile, *Time* magazine observed
in November 1991 that "traditional child-bearing has virtually disappeared from the airwaves."

A Trap That Lasts a Lifetime

This disappearance can hardly be explained as a reflection of society at large. In recent years, all the women's magazines have run major
articles on the "new traditionalism" and the revived interest in large,
old-fashioned weddings. Among real-life Americans artificial insemination is so rare as to remain statistically insignificant, but characters on
TV go to the sperm bank as casually as they visit an automatic teller.
"There is a distinctly 'Hollywoodian' perspective layered on top of the
'Californian' one on television," says David Stewart, a market-research
psychologist at the University of Southern California. "It's novelty-
seeking, eccentric, and nonconformist, as artists tend to be. It wants to
reject traditional values." Roslyn Heller, coproducer of a new movie
called *American Heart* (about a troubled thirteen-year-old who tries to
build a connection with his hostile ex-con father), frankly declares,
"We're reevaluating the family in the '90s."

Across the country, however, traditional patterns of family life remain surprisingly intact. According to 1990 figures from the Census Bureau, 72.5 percent of all children in the country under eighteen *currently live with both parents*. Among the white Anglo majority in the United States, 79.0 percent of all children live in two-parent homes; in the African-American community, the figure is 37.7 percent—contributing to a host of social problems. The welfare of Americans of every ethnic background depends upon defending and enlarging the percentage of these intact, traditional, two-parent families, and Hollywood can play an important part in that effort.

Despite the fact that experimentation in out-of-wedlock childrearing is temporarily trendy, the evidence is overwhelming that such arrangements are disastrous for the children involved. In 1985 a major research project by Stanford University's Center for the Study of Youth Development showed conclusively that children in single-parent families have higher arrest rates, more disciplinary problems in school, and a greater tendency to smoke and run away from home than do their peers who live with both parents—*no matter what their income, race, or ethnicity.*

More recent data, gathered by *U.S. News and World Report* (June 1992) from the National Center for Children in Poverty, the American Enterprise Institute and the National Center for Criminal Justice, demonstrate some of the devastating handicaps faced by the offspring of unwed mothers. These children are more than twice as likely to repeat a grade in school (33 percent to 13 percent) than children living with both parents; more than three times more likely (17 percent to 5 percent) to be suspended or expelled from school; and more than four times more likely to be assigned to a juvenile correctional facility. Amazingly enough, children raised by never-married mothers were nearly three times more likely (39 percent to 14 percent) to spend more than ten years on welfare *than children raised by divorced single mothers.*

Furthermore, despite Hollywood's emphasis on "courageous" and well-heeled role models like Murphy Brown, the economic status of the vast majority of unwed mothers is unequivocally appalling. Finding yourself suddenly saddled with a baby and no husband is one of the worst disasters that can befall an ordinary young woman, and often represents a trap that lasts a lifetime.

Mona Charen persuasively summarizes the destructive implica-

tions of the entertainment industry's obsession with promoting unconventional alternatives in child-rearing:

> Surely even sun-dazed Southern Californians can look beyond their hot
> tubs every now and then and see the wreckage that family breakdown is
> creating in American life. There is only one way to stop the epidemic of
> illegitimacy and the resulting poverty among children—and that is to
> bring back the stigma of unwed motherhood. The TV writers are moving
> in the opposite direction. They may congratulate themselves for being
> brave—but what they really are is pernicious.

Kids Know Best

In addition to its relentless antimarriage messages that undermine the connection between husbands and wives, the popular culture also helps to poison relationships between parents and children. No notion has been more aggressively and ubiquitously promoted in films, popular music, and television than the idea that children know best—that parents are corrupt, hypocritical clowns who must learn decency and integrity from their enlightened offspring.

The Ultimate Source of Wisdom

Teenagers in particular are portrayed as the ultimate source of all wisdom, sanity, and sensitivity and our one hope for redeeming the world from the terrible mistakes of the benighted generations that preceded them. With Bart Simpson regularly turning up on lists of the most admired Americans, we've come a long way from the model of the hugely popular Andy Hardy movies of the 1930s, with young Mickey Rooney learning life lessons from his father (Lewis Stone), a stern but kindly small-town judge. If they remade those films today, it would be Andy who taught the old man a thing or two—about tolerance, or environmentalism, or the joy of spontaneous sexuality, or new styles in hair or clothes, or the horrors of sexism or homophobia. The

movies would end with the newly sensitized judge smiling with gratitude as he claps his hands, kicks up his feet underneath his robe, and
boogies energetically along with the high-stepping local kids in a huge
production number choreographed to an infectious rap beat.

In today's climate, a television series called "Father Knows Best"
would be absolutely unthinkable—it would be deemed too judgmental,
authoritarian, patriarchal, and perhaps even sexist. A program entitled
"Father Knows Nothing" would stand a far better chance.

Even those who praise contemporary shows like "The Simpsons"
acknowledge that they encourage a cynical attitude toward parents,
deriding their irrelevant ideas and outmoded values. In a surprisingly
appreciative piece in *Christian Century* magazine, Victoria Rebeck
wrote: "The Simpsons are a typical American family—in a way most
family-based shows never acknowledge. The Simpson children wrestle
with problems . . . while getting sincere but useless, perhaps even damaging, advice from their parents." In other words, all those six- and
seven-year-olds in their Bart Simpson T-shirts, proudly dragging their
Bart Simpson lunchboxes off to school, will feel appropriately encouraged to disregard any "useless" and potentially "damaging" advice their
own parents have to offer.

"Ineffectual or Downright Evil Adults"

In addition to their common comical roles as bumblers and bozos,
Mom and Dad are also frequently portrayed in a far darker, more disturbing light. The current emphasis on cases of child abuse and instances
of nightmarishly dysfunctional families provides a new focus for Hollywood's increasingly favored formula of evil parents vs. enlightened kids.
Consider the example of *Radio Flyer* (1992)—a big-budget, big-studio
bomb unconscionably promoted as an *E.T.*-style adventure fantasy for
children. The film actually focused on a vicious stepfather who repeatedly and sadistically beats his seven-year-old stepson (and even tries to
kill the family dog), while the child's mother is too busy with her job as a
waitress to notice that anything's wrong. As Kenneth Turan of the *Los
Angeles Times* eloquently explained: "One of the problems with the PG-
13 *Radio Flyer* is that it relentlessly sanctifies childhood as the most special time on earth and turns its two protagonists into pint-sized saints

who do as much silent suffering at the hands of either ineffectual or downright evil adults as any medieval martyr you can think of."

Disgusting and destructive parents have become such a fixture in the minds of Hollywood's screenwriters and directors that they turn up in every sort of picture, from slapstick comedies to musical romances to probing melodramas. In *Dead Poets Society* (1989, with an Oscar-winning screenplay by Tom Schulman), a cruel and emotionally abusive father drives his sensitive son to suicide—despite the best efforts of prep school English teacher Robin Williams. Cameron Crowe's *Say Anything* (also 1989) is a superb film that will stand as one of the finer teenage romances ever to emerge from Hollywood, but it throws in a subplot involving a typically corrupt and embarrassing parent. John Mahoney plays the hard-working single father of high school valedictorian Ione Skye, and through the first half of the movie he appears to be an ideal dad—loving, warm, supportive, and decent. Eventually, however, his daughter discovers that he has been secretly stealing hundreds of thousands of dollars through a truly despicable nursing homes scam; this putatively perfect parent winds up behind bars, leaving his brilliant daughter to fend for herself with the help of her devoted new boyfriend.

Made-for-television movies similarly and insistently cite the sins and shortcomings of "toxic parents," showing their tragic impact on unfortunate children who fall victim to suicide, drug addiction, and other horrors. Surveying a crop of mid-1980s TV movies, Richard Zoglin wrote in *Time* magazine:

> One message is distressingly familiar: Mom and Dad, more often than not, are at fault. If parents have not overtly caused the problem (like the molesting father in *Something About Amelia*), they are, at the very least, insensitive or inattentive to the gathering storm clouds. In *Not My Kid,* the fact that the parents are completely surprised to learn of their daughter's drug problem is seen as proof they have fallen down on the job. . . . *Surviving* is even more damning in its indictment of the suicidal teenagers' parents. Lonnie's folks (Marsha Mason and Paul Sorvino) offer little understanding or support for their daughter after an earlier attempt to kill herself.

Some of our leading pop culture philosophers have gone so far as to suggest that parental mistreatment of the younger generation is part of an organized campaign of enslavement and oppression. Axl Rose, the deep-thinking lead singer of the hugely popular Guns n' Roses rock group, angrily decried the "forces"—including parents and school—that "rob young people of their individuality and aspirations." As part of his "homecoming" concert in Indianapolis in the summer of 1991, Rose went on stage and delivered an angry, incoherent harangue in which he told his cheering fans that "kids in Indiana today are just like prisoners in Auschwitz!" When he later defended these appalling remarks in conversation with reporters, no one thought to ask Rose the obvious question: if he really believes that parents are like guards at a Nazi death camp, wouldn't teenagers be perfectly justified in killing them in order to achieve their freedom?

"And a Little Child Shall Lead Them"

Though few pieces of popular entertainment recommend murder as a solution to our national parent problem, the notion of mandatory reeducation camps for recalcitrant grown-ups might actually be in line with Hollywood's thinking. In film after film, children assume the task of improving the character and correcting the defects in their often pathetic progenitors. In a witty and perceptive article in the *Washington Monthly,* Beth Austin observed: "Children who put their parents back on track show up throughout these family-oriented movies. . . . The calm, dependable, unbelievably wise and loving parents who once populated Hollywood have been replaced by a passel of unstable neurotics who need a good twelve-step program—or a good twelve-year-old—to bring them back onto solid family ground."

On occasion the all-knowing offspring who patiently improve their parents are considerably younger than twelve. *Little Man Tate* (1991) features a gentle, sweet-spirited seven-year-old with a genius IQ who is adored both by his earthy, working-class, unwed mother (Jodie Foster) and a brilliant psychologist (Dianne Wiest) who wants to develop his phenomenal intellect. Eventually, the adorable little tyke helps both women recognize their limitations. As Peter Rainer commented in the *Los Angeles Times:* "By the end of the film, the prodigy has awakened both women to a fuller appreciation of what life has to offer. And a little child shall lead them. . . ."

An even littler child leads the way in *Look Who's Talking* (1990), where an infant is equipped with Bruce Willis's wisecracking voice to comment on the foibles of *his* unwed mother (Kirstie Alley) and her blundering relationship with her new beau (John Travolta). Eventually, the all-knowing baby must take matters into his own pudgy hands to help the adult dunderheads find happiness in each other's arms. In a similar vein, the watchable holiday comedy *All I Want For Christmas* (1991) shows two charismatic kids who hatch an elaborate and ingenious plot to force their foolish, divorced parents to get back together: the children (and the audience) know that despite their silly arguments these two emotionally blocked adults truly belong together.

In the huge hit *Back to the Future* (1985), a likeable and sophisticated kid also manages to save his pathetic parents from failure and frustration: Marty McFly (Michael J. Fox) travels thirty years back in time and meets his own father as a laughably unpopular high school nerd. Needless to say, the all-knowing child of the '80s gives his incompetent old man of the '50s the courage and gumption he needs to turn his life around at a decisive moment, thereby altering the entire course of his father's existence for the better.

Steven Spielberg (who produced the *Back to the Future* films) also used fantasy in *Hook* (1991) to advance his kids-good, adults-bad theme. In order to restore his family's fading happiness, workaholic lawyer Robin Williams must not only listen to his children, he must become a child himself—returning to his previous incarnation as the perpetually immature Peter Pan. In the peculiar universe of this motion picture, adults have everything to learn from childhood, but kids can gain nothing of value from their parents. A familiar formula is turned upside down: in traditional coming-of-age stories, an adolescent faces a climactic test in which he must learn to act like a man, but in this new dumbing-of-age saga, the adult can overcome a crisis only if he learns to act like a kid.

The Principle of Puerile Power

The underlying lesson of *Hook*—that the grown-up hero is totally helpless against the bad guy, but when he becomes a child again he can easily defeat him—reflects the frequently advanced Hollywood idea that kids are more powerful than parents. This notion found its most extreme (and distasteful) expression in *Problem Child* (1990), and its sorry sequel, *Problem Child 2* (1991). In both films, John Ritter and Amy Yasbeck play a well-intentioned middle-class couple who end up adopting two demonically destructive children; those new additions then proceed to wreak havoc on everything and everyone in their vicinity. The feeble humor of the two pictures centers largely on the ineffectual efforts of the parents at controlling the omnipotent members of the younger generation.

The even more obnoxious Warner Brothers comedy *Don't Tell Mom the Babysitter's Dead* (1991) portrays adults as similarly outclassed when it comes to confrontations with their youngers and betters. A single mom takes off for an Australian vacation with her boyfriend, leaving her five children in the care of a stern, elderly babysitter. Within hours of their mother's departure, her foul-mouthed, pot-smoking rebellious brood succeeds in providing so many shocks to the old lady's system that she obligingly drops dead, leaving the high-spirited kids to bury her corpse in the front yard and to enjoy all the charms of an unsupervised summer. The sixteen-year-old daughter (Christina Applegate, the teenage sexpot of "Married . . . with Children") proceeds to get a job at a major corporation by lying about her age; she instantly ascends the corporate ladder and begins to bring in the big bucks. The other kids also blossom in their mother's absence—including the dope-addled oldest son, who discovers God-given talents as a world-class gourmet cook; a ten-year-old boy, who makes out with his girlfriend in the back seat of a car; and even younger and more enterprising children who teach the audience that it's perfectly appropriate to steal from the purses of unsuspecting adults when you really need the money.

A critic's favorite called *Pump Up the Volume* (1990) offered additional support for the notion that the unfettered instincts of teenagers provide the most reliable guide to decent behavior and the restructuring of society. Christian Slater plays a bright high school kid who secretly operates a pirate radio station from the basement of his parents' home. On the air, he assumes the identity of "Happy Harry Hard On," delivering a series of brooding, masturbatory monologues that transfix the other adolescents in his suburban community. His broadcasts not only liberate the young people in town from the oppressive conventions of their parents, but ultimately expose the horrid hypocrisy of the administrators of his "model" high school.

In the ponderous musical *Newsies* (1992), the principle of puerile power is elevated to the status of a political program. The year is 1899, and New York's unstoppably singing, dancing paperboys launch a strike against the city's press lords in a lighthearted "Hey, kids, let's-put-on-a-show!" spirit. Needless to say, they triumph over all obstacles (including historical accuracy), and bring the city's entire power structure to its knees. The rousing conclusion involves a seemingly endless production number that explicitly celebrates the inevitable victory of good-hearted youngsters against insensitive and mean-spirited adults.

Family Films, Destructive Messages

Hollywood's emphasis on super kids and superfluous adults has become so pervasive that it turns up even in some of our era's most beloved and beautifully crafted family films. The top-grossing feature in movie history offers a classic expression of the kids-know-best theme: in *E.T. The Extra-Terrestrial* (1982), adults are all insensitive or cruel to the visitor from outer space, and the children must band together to rescue the peaceful emissary from the Great Beyond. *Honey, I Shrunk the Kids* (1989) presents Dad (Rick Moranis) as a terminally klutzy mad scientist who inadvertently reduces his own offspring (and two of the neighbor brats) to the size of termites. Freed from their unwholesome dependence on their feeble and foolishly feuding parents, the kids must learn to fend for themselves and work together during their heroic trek through newly gigantic obstacles in the backyard. *The Little Mermaid* (1990) won well-deserved praise for its glorious animation and irresistible music, but the story line effectively encouraged children to disregard the values and opinions of their parents. The blustery, tempestuous King Triton of the watery deep tries to stop his pubescent mermaid daughter, Ariel, from pursuing the earthbound Prince Eric. The heroic lass stubbornly defies his commands in order to follow her heart, and in the end, of course, pure, powerful adolescent love triumphs over all stuffy parental reservations about human-mermaid intermarriage.

These prominent and popular examples indicate that fine family films do not always convey fitting family messages. In selecting appropriate movie fare for their children, parents may count the number of curse words or worry over the incidents of violence, but they rarely consider the underlying images and values that the stories convey. If they did, they could hardly be so enthusiastic over entertaining but adult-bashing fare like *Honey, I Shrunk the Kids* or *The Little Mermaid*—or that other recent blockbuster, *Home Alone* (1990).

The phenomonal popularity of this mildly diverting comedy (it is now third on the list of the all-time top-grossing motion pictures) testifies to the public's powerful hunger for movies that portray reasonably well-adjusted, happy middle-class families. Despite their embarrassing ineptitude in departing for a Paris vacation while accidentally leaving behind their eight-year-old son, these preoccupied parents (John Heard and Catherine O'Hara) clearly love their children. The mother overcomes numerous difficulties to fly back to Chicago to rescue the stranded Kevin (Macaulay Culkin), but the irony is that he's doing far better without his parents around than he ever did in their disapproving presence. After their departure, he courageously comes into his own, brilliantly defending his home from two bumbling, slap-happy, middle-aged burglars and helping an old man from the neighborhood reconcile with his estranged children and grandchildren. The young moviegoers who so eagerly consumed this appealingly packaged concoction inevitably admired Kevin and learned from his self-reliant example that contemporary kids need adults for only one purpose: comic relief.

A *Legacy of the '60s*

The portrayal of parents as irrelevant—or outright evil—has become so pervasive in every corner of our popular culture that we have begun to take it for granted as a harmless convention of mass entertainment. We blithely assume that our children can absorb innumerable images of inept and idiotic parents in movies, television, and popular songs, while remembering at all times that their own mother and father are completely different. We dangerously underestimate the impact of an omnipresent popular culture that repeatedly reassures our kids that they instinctively know better than the tired losers of the older generation.

This ruinous attitude is a legacy of the much-heralded youth movement of the 1960s. With slogans like "Never trust anyone over thirty" and "Question authority," adolescents of that era emerged as the first generation in human history to declare that nineteen- and twenty-year-olds around the world would teach their admiring elders how to live and love. To a remarkable extent, the nation's opinion leaders accepted that assumption, inexplicably assigning earth-shattering significance to an overcrowded rock festival in upstate New York and to improvised, incoherent motion pictures like *Easy Rider*. A surprising number of middle-aged, middle-class Americans began imitating the young in their hairstyles, political passions, clothing, musical preferences, and psychedelic or sexual explorations.

This notion of young people leading the way proved particularly congenial to Hollywood, with its long-standing emphasis on youth and beauty. The movie industry had always understood that kids could work magic, from the eighteen-year-old Lillian Gish, to the twenty-eight-year-old Irving Thalberg, to the twenty-six-year-old Orson Welles. The youth culture of the '60s provided a valuable ideological underpinning for the notion that young people possessed some secret, mysterious power denied to older and less fortunate members of humanity. Before long, the industry placed a self-conscious premium on executives, writers, and directors—as well as stars—who fell somewhere on the sunny side of thirty.

However unfair this emphasis might prove to graying veterans of the movie wars, on one level it made sound demographic sense: the emergence of the famous baby-boom generation introduced a disproportionate percentage of the population that could serve as a ready-made market for Hollywood's new youth fare. Curiously enough, the antiadult messages that characterized that era have remained a fixed and prominent feature of the industry's product for more than twenty years, long outliving the temporary population bulge that initially encouraged them. Though Hollywood now faces the dramatic and historic "graying of America," it continues to emphasize the kids' point of view. By 1990, one-third of the nation—including some 80 million baby boomers—had begun to approach the half-century mark. Between

1990 and the year 2000, the number of Americans eighteen to thirty-four will decrease 3 percent, while the age group between forty-five and fifty-four will increase by 47 percent. *TV Guide* reported in 1990 that the median age of the prime-time TV watcher had risen to forty-four—an all-time high—and that would increase to forty-nine by the end of the century. In view of these trends, the continued tendency to glorify kids and to denigrate grown-ups is not only destructive to the social order, but it is also surely bad for business.

Harder Than It Has to Be

Ultimately, the idea that children will teach their parents, that adolescents will show the way for all the rest of us, is unfair to those on both sides of the generation gap. Young people, however, are its chief victims, since the very idea that kids know best forces them to accept an intolerable burden. They are expected to reinvent the wheel for a weary humanity, and denied the chance to benefit from the experience of all those who have gone before. In the past, the process of growing up has been considered difficult enough in its own right, without taking on the additional responsibility of saving unforunate adults.

The respected neoconservative thinker Irving Kristol writes: "One accepts a moral code on faith—not on blind faith but on the faith that one's ancestors, over the generations, were not fools and that we have much to learn from them and their experience."

The popular culture regularly discourages such acceptance, telling the young people who are its most avid consumers that they have little to gain from the examples of the past. As Kristol writes: "The consequence of such moral disarray is confusion about the single most important question that adults face. 'How shall we raise our children? What kind of moral example should we set? What moral instruction should we convey?' A society that is impotent before such questions will breed restless, turbulent generations. . . ."

The evidence of that restlessness and turbulence is everywhere around us, seriously exacerbated by the entertainment industry's contemptuous attitude toward the institution of the family. "Many now react to the word *family* as if it were just another noun like *roller skates* or *television*," writes Steve Allen, himself a Hollywood insider with impeccable liberal credentials.

> Humans can do without roller skates or TV but they literally cannot long survive, as a rational, emotionally healthy species, without a secure family structure.
>
> The reason, to belabor the obvious, is that the family is the soil in which each year's new crop of humans grow. It is mostly the failed family, therefore, which has produced our present millions of prison inmates, rapists, drug addicts, burglars, muggers, sexual psychopaths, nonprofessional whores of both sexes and general goofolas.

The "general goofolas" who shape much of the popular culture are by no means single-handedly responsible for this sad situation, but they do make a significant contribution to the ongoing confusion. Their antifamily messages—promoting promiscuity, maligning marriage, encouraging illegitimacy, and undermining parental authority—may not make it impossible to maintain a solid marriage or to raise decent kids, but they certainly make it harder than it has to be.

PART IV

THE GLORIFICATION OF UGLINESS

The Urge to Offend

This Lurid Freak Show

On March 30, 1992, before a worldwide television audience of more than a billion people, the Hollywood establishment offered a dramatic demonstration of its enthusiastic embrace of ugliness.

On that night, the Academy of Motion Picture Arts and Sciences presented every one of its most prestigious awards to *The Silence of the Lambs*—a movie politely described as a "thriller" or a "psychological murder mystery." These respectful Oscar night designations, however, hardly did justice to the gruesome contents of a motion picture that had previously been honored by the newsletter for slasher film fans, *The Gore Gazette*, as its "Movie of the Year."

After all, the plot of *Silence of the Lambs* centers on a transvestite serial killer who stuffs the larvae of a rare moth down the throats of his victims—after he has skinned them. He selects overweight women as the preferred targets of his wrath, holding them prisoner and starving them for a time before slaughtering them so that their skin will hang loose on their frames, facilitating his work. The FBI's only hope for catching this murderous, maniacal monster rests with yet another murderous, maniacal monster—this one a former psychiatrist who lives for

the thrill of consuming human flesh. He fondly recalls the incomparable pleasures of a delicacy prepared by cooking human liver together
with fava beans, then elegantly served with "a nice Chianti." During his
escape from prison, he bites off the tongue of one of his guards before
he dispatches him—all the while enjoying the delicate strains of Bach's
Goldberg Variations.

To be sure, every detail of this lurid freak show is artfully executed,
and the acting is most certainly brilliant and intense. The incongruous
use of classical music, the clipped British accent of the cannibalistic
leading man, and the appropriately moody lighting and camera work
helped lend the picture an aura of high-toned artistry that made it a
critic's favorite. The ecstatic reviews that greeted the film invariably
focused on its dazzling style, while paying scant attention to its bizarre
substance. Those of us who dared to question the horrific contents of
this motion picture exposed ourselves to charges of prudery, faintheart-
edness, and philistinism.

One of the few journalists willing to take that risk and to examine
The Silence of the Lambs in a more meaningful perspective was
Stephen Farber, former film critic of *California* magazine. "Yes, the
picture is tactfully made," he wrote in a courageous article in the *Los
Angeles Times,* "but the question remains, why make it at all? The
skilled craftmanship and the directorial restraint can't change what the
film is—a thoroughly morbid and meaningless depiction of the modus
operandi of a couple of sadists. . . . We know that these kinds of mad-
men exist, but the film offers no insight into what makes them tick. . . .
The criminals are so bizarre and extreme in their sadistic pleasures that
they are more ridiculous than frightening. . . ."

Twelve months after Farber's piece appeared in print, his on-target
complaints about the film, along with all other reservations as to its
excellence and importance, disappeared beneath an avalanche of acco-
lades from the entertainment elite. On Oscar night, the Motion Picture
Academy made *The Silence of the Lambs* only the third film in movie
history (after *It Happened One Night* [1934] and *One Flew Over the
Cuckoo's Nest* [1975]) to win all the major awards, including Best Picture, Best Actor (Anthony Hopkins), Best Actress (Jodie Foster), Best
Director (Jonathan Demme), and Best Adapted Screenplay (Ted
Tally). The Academy voters could hardly have been more emphatic in
endorsing *The Silence of the Lambs* before the entire world as an illus-

tration of the artistic distinction to which all filmmakers should aspire, and a shining example of the finest achievements that their industry has to offer.

In the aftermath of this historic Oscar sweep, many critics congratulated the Academy for its unexpected and fearless open-mindedness in saluting *The Silence of the Lambs,* despite its unsettling elements. These observers missed the underlying importance of what had occurred: the horrifying aspects of this film cannot be written off as some small portion of the whole, some brief and nightmarish detour in an otherwise uplifting experience. The ghoulish and shocking contents of *The Silence of the Lambs* are not incidental to its essence; they are, in fact, its very blood and bone. When the Academy chooses to anoint this particular picture, it is therefore not offering its applause in spite of its grotesque themes; it is doing so because of them.

This penchant for praising the most startling and disturbing forms of entertainment now pervades the entire entertainment industry. It is an increasingly obvious tendency that involves more than the acceptance of ugliness as one aspect of our reality; it amounts to its glorification as the highest aesthetic ideal.

As Stephen Farber writes: "It has become chic to praise a movie for being nihilistic, macabre, unsentimental. . . . When did critics get the lunatic idea that the greatest movies were the cold-blooded dissections of human venality and depravity?"

David Puttnam, the distinguished producer of *Chariots of Fire, Memphis Belle,* and other fine films, recently lamented: "Movies now have an underlying nastiness in them. The thing I loathe more than anything has become fashionable—cynicism."

The Cannibalism Compulsion

That cynicism is clearly displayed in Hollywood's current insistence on pushing the edge of the envelope—shamelessly searching for new subject matter so appalling that it can still shock an audience that is increasingly benumbed by years of prior assaults.

Consider the industry's outrageous and inane obsession with cannibalism; Dr. Hannibal ("The Cannibal") Lecter in *The Silence of the Lambs* is only the best-known among many characters in recent films who enjoy feasting on human flesh. In another performance nominated for a Best Actor Oscar in 1991, Robert De Niro in *Cape Fear* takes a bloody and substantial bite from a young lady's cheek as he's preparing to make love to her, leaving his victim with a mutilated face and requiring hospitalization. *Fried Green Tomatoes* (also nominated for two prestigious 1991 Oscars) introduced cannibalism as a key comedic element: when an abusive, sadistic husband meets the fate he deserves, the movie's main characters dispose of his body by butchering it together with hog meat and cooking pieces of the corpse in barbecue sauce. Eventually, they serve this taste treat to the sheriff investigating the case, who unwittingly relishes his nutritious and tangy repast. "THE SECRET IS IN THE SAUCE!" proclaimed the ads for this "sweet, nostalgic" picture—specifically alluding to its surprise recipe for mystery meat.

By contrast, *The Cook, the Thief, His Wife and Her Lover* (1990) made no attempt to hide a body in heavy sauce; director Peter Greenaway presented *his* cooked corpse in complete and recognizable form, like a pig at a luau, braised to a golden brown with arms folded over the chest, and nicely garnished with vegetables. This critically acclaimed "black comedy" even featured a scene showing knife and fork slicing off a tender piece of roasted male genitals. *Parents* (1988) also drew some shockingly enthusiastic reviews for its portrayal of a smug, conformist, Republican couple of the 1950s (played by Randy Quaid and Mary Beth Hurt) who bring home stiffs from the local morgue, run the severed body parts through a meat grinder, then serve the resulting patties to their unsuspecting son. Randy Quaid turned up again in *Out Cold* (also 1988), costarring John Lithgow, who played the lead part of a shy butcher who helps his partner's wife (Teri Garr) store her late husband's body in the meat locker. Eventually, they devise a means to dispose of the cadaver to their eager customers that guarantees them both fun and profit—though this wretched movie delivered neither.

Auntie Lee's Meat Pies (1990) starred two former Oscar nominees, Karen Black (as Auntie Lee) and Pat Morita. The promotional materials billed the picture as "A black comedy about cannibalism . . . done tastefully" and featured a smiling, buxom blonde holding up a half-eaten pie with bloody body parts and a staring eyeball clearly visible within the crust. *Lucky Stiff* (1988), haphazardly directed by Tony (*Psycho*) Perkins, also tried to find the comic elements in the man-as-meat theme, with gorgeous Donna Dixon luring a fat, lonely loser to her family's home for the holidays where he will become their freshly butchered main course as "Mr. Christmas Dinner." In *Consuming Passions* (1988), yet another cannibal comedy, the main characters are motivated by financial gain rather than blood lust. These enterprising businessmen use human flesh to produce irresistible candy confections—a recipe they have discovered after three workmen accidentally perished in a vat of chocolate. The U.S.-British coproduction boasted a prestigious cast headed by Vanessa Redgrave, Sammi Davis, and Jonathan Pryce.

Society (1992) constituted a pathetic and all-but-unwatchable attempt to mix cannibalism and social criticism. "The rich have always fed off the poor," declared the ads. "This time it's for real." Praised by critic Michael Wilmington of the *Los Angeles Times* for its "gruesome gusto and raunchy good humor," the picture portrays a conspiracy of wealthy snobs who paralyze the less fortunate and then devour their bodies like howling, ravenous wolves. *Eat the Rich* (1987) offered a mirror image of this formula, with impoverished revolutionaries taking over an ultra-trendy restaurant and offering selected pieces of freshly butchered exploiters as popular delicacies on the menu. The hard-driving heavy metal score and cameo appearances by rock 'n' roll royalty like Paul McCartney and Bill Wyman gave the putrid picture an aura of hip irreverence. Wes Craven's *The People Under the Stairs* (1991) projected no such pretensions and no discernible political messages: the cannibalistic clan who inhabit a seemingly abandoned house slaughter, dismember, slice open, and gobble up their victims out of sheer, uncontrollable lust for the joy of consuming human flesh.

Most recently, the Touchstone Pictures division of Disney studios announced plans for a big budget cannibalism contribution of its own. *Alive,* slated for 1993 release, tells the story of a 1972 plane crash in the Andes in which members of a stranded South American rugby team kept themselves going for weeks by eating their colleagues. The same story served as the basis for Allan Carr's failed 1976 exploitation film *Survive,* but Disney's representatives promised that this time around the flesh feast would serve an uplifting purpose. "We're not stressing this as a movie about cannibalism," producer Robert Watts proudly proclaimed. "We're making a movie that celebrates the triumph of the human spirit."

Hollywood obviously feels a much stronger interest in such triumphs than does the general public: the baleful box-office performance of the bulk of these pictures, despite their well-advertised artistic aspects and the presence of some well-known stars, indicates that there is hardly an overwhelming popular demand for movies about the consumption of corpses. The industry's cannibalism compulsion reflects its ongoing (and idiotic) efforts to shock its audience and to obliterate all remaining taboos, rather than a commercially motivated attempt to exploit some hot new trend.

Incestuous Excesses

If cannibalism is the current rage, can incest be far behind?

In fact, the early months of 1992 offered two major releases that took motion pictures into this final frontier. In *Voyager,* Sam Shepard engages in lush, romantic, erotically charged, and beautifully photographed sex scenes with his teenage daughter (Julie Delpy). The shock value of these sequences is somewhat diminished by the conventions of the plot: Shepard doesn't discover that the girl is his child until he is already involved in the affair, and when he finally learns the truth he tries to extricate himself from romantic involvement.

Sleepwalkers provides no such figleaf for its incestuous excesses. This major studio offering (from Sony/Columbia Pictures), aimed obviously at teenagers, features several minutes of graphic, heavy-breathing, partially nude, deep-kissing, sweaty, and orgasmic intercourse between mother and son. The fact that both stars (the lovely and aristocratic Alice Krige and pouting teen heartthrob Brian Krause) are so sensationally attractive only makes their scenes together more difficult to watch. For the first time in Hollywood history, the youthful hero of a film breathlessly addresses his panting, insatiable partner as "Mother" in the midst of making out.

Worst of all, these interludes are altogether irrelevant to the plot of the picture. As concocted by horror master Stephen King, the original screenplay involves strange, feline, vampire-like creatures from ancient Egypt who arrive in an Indiana small town and who must (surprise!) feed constantly on human flesh. The incestuous sex theme could have been totally eliminated from the film without altering the picture's limp story line in any way.

To do so, however, might have undermined the deeper goals of director Mick Garris—the same fearless artist who previously displayed his consummate craftmanship on epic achievements such as *Critters 2: The Main Course* (1988) and *Psycho IV: The Beginning* (1990). As Garris proudly declared in his new movie's press kit: "Our theme on this project was to take Norman Rockwell and send him straight to hell." He wants us to understand that *Sleepwalkers* is something more than the sloppy and sleazy little exploitation picture that it appears to be; it is actually intended as a searing indictment of Middle America's hypocritical pieties, in the tradition of the absurdly overpraised (and equally incoherent) *Blue Velvet*. In this context, the deliberately shocking incestuous elements only work to support the director's preening pretensions of artistry.

The filmmakers may well have been encouraged in this endeavor by the fulsome chorus of praise that welcomed a film that explored similar themes in 1990. *The Grifters* won several important Oscar nominations, including Best Actress and Best Supporting Actress, for its account of the sexual tension between a mother and son who both work as con artists. In the impeccably well-acted climax, Anjelica Huston makes a determined attempt to seduce her boy John Cusack in order to steal his money, but this heartwarming family reunion ends with blood spurting lavishly from his severed jugular vein.

Interspecies Intercourse

Cannibalistic and incestuous elements have become common enough in contemporary motion pictures that they have begun to lose their ability to startle jaded moviegoers, forcing enterprising producers to search for new taboos to shatter.

At MGM, at least, they may have found one: the ailing studio recently paid $500,000 for a script that features a graphic scene in which the President of the United States has sex with a cow.

MGM chairman Alan Ladd, Jr., is so high on this ground-breaking project that he committed an *additional* $250,000 to be paid to screenwriter Joe Eszterhas (who previously wrote *The Jagged Edge, Basic Instinct,* and other successful thrillers) as soon as production begins.

The plot for *Sacred Cows* is set in the midst of a heated presidential campaign, in which the Chief Executive makes a political visit to his brother's farm in Nebraska. During a nostalgic stroll through the family barn, the Leader of the Free World is overcome with passion and forces an unsuspecting bovine to submit to arduous, interspecies intercourse. Unfortunately, a snooping photographer captures the tender moment on film, and the resulting snapshot falls into the hands of the political opposition.

To those of us who fail to appreciate the glamour and charm of barnyard bestiality, this preposterous plot would hardly seem to constitute an appealing premise for a big-budget feature film, but the powers-that-be in Hollywood seem to know better. In February 1992 the *Los Angeles Times* received a copy of the completed script along with unofficial word that "MGM is about to make this movie." The newspaper reported that Paul Newman and Lloyd Bridges are the two front-runners for the coveted role of the priapic President.

Vomit and Urine

Movies that focus on cannibalism, incest, bestiality, or other inherently startling subjects represent only one aspect of Hollywood's current emphasis on ugliness. In addition to cranking out a great many films that concentrate candidly on human depravity, the motion picture industry has also begun inserting ghastly moments and disturbing themes in bland, incongruous contexts where one would never expect to find them. Lush romances, light comedies, serious dramas, political message pictures, even movies intended primarily for kids all contain their share of harsh surprises intended to shock or unsettle the viewer. Most films that are rated PG-13—or even PG—feature potentially offensive elements that are only marginally less intense than their R-rated counterparts. Those sensitive souls, like my dear wife, who would prefer to forgo all such scenes of degradation, graphic violence, or tasteless excess, are generally out of luck when it comes to contemporary motion pictures.

In one powerful and peculiar illustration of its urge to offend, the Hollywood creative community has recently begun drenching even mainstream, general audience movies in a veritable flood of vomit and urine.

Reading this last sentence you may suspect me of irresponsible exaggeration or rhetorical overkill; in this instance, at least, I plead not guilty. Waste fluids do indeed turn up with remarkable regularity in every manner of recent release. If the specifics of these odious inclusions are likely to unsettle you, then you will be well-advised to skip the paragraphs that follow.

Ken Russell's 1991 film *Whore,* for instance, won praise from Roger Ebert and a few other prominent critics for its courageous examination of the beastly behavior of men toward women. The movie's opening scene shows a homeless drunk lying by the side of the road near an urban overpass, making obscene comments to the title character (Theresa Russell), and then depositing a brightly colored explosion of vomit onto the pavement beside him. Moments later, he collapses, rolling his face into the pool of his own filth. The same picture features even more memorable images of regurgitation when it offers flashbacks dramatizing the nightmarish married life of the heroine, before she has liberated herself from that conjugal hell for the harsh life of a hooker. One night, she lovingly prepares a romantic dinner for her loutish husband, who arrives late and drunk. He stands for a moment at the edge of the table, looking down at the neatly arranged platter she has set before him, and then proceeds to throw up all over it, noisily disgorging a huge volume of orange and brown barf.

Whore may offer an especially gritty view of life on the streets, but it is hardly unique in its full-color, Dolby Sound re-creation of scenes of realistic retching. *Kuffs,* a 1992 cop comedy from Universal Pictures that starred Christian Slater, rivaled *Whore* by offering its viewers an impressive doubleheader of cookie tossing. First, straight-arrow police officer Tony Goldwyn unloads onto his own lap while riding in his patrol car—the result of a clutch of sleeping pills that his resentful partner (Slater) has slipped into his coffee. Minutes later, the father of the hero's gorgeous girlfriend (Mila Jovovich) doubles over and hurls onto his own shoes when he stumbles over a bullet-riddled body on the floor of Slater's kitchen.

"Since when did this become a movie staple?" asked *Premiere* magazine in 1988 as this troubling trend first began to gather steam. "We counted more than a dozen films in which people toss their cookies. . . . We're talking about 1987 alone. Hard to believe? Then watch: *Angel Heart, Barfly, The Big Easy, Fatal Attraction, Less Than Zero, Lost*

Boys, Maurice, Near Dark, No Way Out, The Sicilian, Siesta, Tough Guys Don't Dance, and *The Witches of Eastwick."*

In the last-named film, of course, the barfing is deliberately exaggerated—with numerous characters, subjected to spells, heaving out geyser-like eruptions of dark red goo. This supposedly hilarious sequence followed the lead of *Stand By Me* (1986), in which waterfalls of waste emerged from many open mouths in a fantasy sequence based on the gross-out stories that preteen boys tell one another around a campfire. At least Rob Reiner's picture provided an appropriate context for this upchuck extravaganza: vicarious vomiting on screen may be suitable for naughty twelve-year-olds, but it is embarrassing and unnecessary for adults.

"Is it possible that there are emotions and meanings that actors can express only by vomiting?" asked Henry Allen in a lengthy, tongue-in-cheek analysis in the *Washington Post.* "Is it really possible that moviemakers use it to appeal to a more mature, sophisticated audience? . . . Maybe it all means something, the way that thunderstorms used to mean sex and train wheels meant the passing of time in the movies. But what? Someday, someone will explain it, and it will all be very serious, like French explanations of the genius of Jerry Lewis."

Meanwhile, in the four years since Allen's article appeared, Hollywood has provided a wealth of additional examples calling out for such explanation. Films as various as *Roxanne* (1987), *The Serpent and the Rainbow* (1988), *License to Drive* (1988), *The Adventures of Ford Fairlane* (1990), *Dying Young* (1991), *Regarding Henry* (1991), *At Play in the Fields of the Lord* (1991), *Rush* (1991), *Exposure* (1991), *Eating* (1991), *The Cutting Edge* (1992), *Wayne's World* (1992), and *Where the Day Takes You* (1992) all feature dramatic re-creations of regurgitation.

Many of our most gifted and glamorous actresses have recently displayed their versatility by vomiting vividly on screen, including Meryl Streep (*Ironweed,* 1988), Sissy Spacek (*Hard Promises,* 1992), Faye Dunaway (*Barfly,* 1987), and the French beauty Julie Delpy (*Voyager,* 1991).

In *All I Want for Christmas* (1991), the adorable seven-year-old star, Thora Birch, convincingly simulates the sounds of retching while bent over the toilet and hiding from her parents in the bathroom. *Memoirs of an Invisible Man* (1992) used dazzling special effects to achieve an important motion picture milestone: the first vomit scene that actually traces the liquid to its source. Director John Carpenter first shows the digestive juices bubbling deep in Chevy Chase's stomach, then shooting up through his esophagus and throat, before bursting out of his mouth, while our transparent hero watches the entire process in the mirror.

Shakes the Clown (1992), hailed by the film critic for the *Boston Globe* as "the *Citizen Kane* of alcoholic clown movies," also deserves special recognition for its remarkable achievements in this area. Within the first two minutes of his film, writer/director/star Bobcat Goldthwait manages the considerable feat of immersing his title character in *both* vomit and urine. Passed out in the bathroom of a middle-aged floozy (Florence Henderson) he has just met, Shakes awakens with a start when the woman's son accidentally urinates on him. Moments later he drags himself to the toilet and heaves into the bowl, with especially impressive sound effects.

Other urination scenes, while not yet as common as the ubiquitous upchuck incidents in today's films, have appeared with increasing frequency in recent years. In *The Power of One* and *Deep Cover* (both 1992), and *The Cook, the Thief, His Wife and Her Lover* (1990), macho characters assert their manhood by contemptuously directing their flow onto unfortunate victims. In *Closet Land* (1991, coproduced by Ron Howard!), the villainous torturer Alan Rickman forces Madeleine Stowe to drink from a jar of his urine. A few weeks after its release, the L.A. Film Teachers Association honored the movie's writer-director, Radha Bharadwaj, with its "Courage in Filmmaking Award."

Occasionally, female stars get their own turn to relieve themselves on camera. In *Twenty-One* (1991), the luminous Patsy Kensit stares directly into the camera and addresses her narration to the audience as she unself-consciously lifts her skirt, takes a seat on the commode, releases a musical little tinkle, and then ceremoniously wipes herself. Julie Warner, Michael J. Fox's magnetic costar in the romantic comedy *Doc Hollywood* (also 1991) pees with purpose: she wants to throw hunting dogs off the scent of the deer they are tracking. To accomplish this noble goal, she interrupts a walk in the woods with her love interest to drop her pants and to squat down, leaving little deposits in a random pattern at various locations. The camera provides a loving, ground-level shot of the leaves of a bush that is dripping with moisture to show us how effectively she has performed her task.

Prospero's Books (1991), a stomach-turning travesty allegedly based on Shakespeare's *Tempest,* opens with the most protracted and graphic urination scene in motion picture history. As Prospero (a naked John Gielgud) invokes mystical powers in order to produce a storm at sea, director Peter Greenaway shows a nude three-year-old boy peeing from a great height down onto a toy boat in a swimming pool. Thanks to a unique application of movie magic, this copious yellow flow continues unabated for fully four minutes, accompanied by Michael Nyman's otherworldly music and Gielgud's droning rendition of Shakespeare's lines. Minutes later, the same chubby cherub who has so prodigiously relieved himself is attached by his penis to a trapeze, and dangled head down before the camera. At the time of its release, critics for *The New York Times, Rolling Stone, Newsday,* and *Playboy* lauded the film as "stunning," "dazzling," "visually beautiful," and "a landmark."

Though most urination scenes could hardly aspire to this "landmark" status, such sequences turned up in numerous other films from the last few years, including *My Own Private Idaho, True Identity, Look Who's Talking Too, At Play in the Fields of the Lord, Grand Canyon, Ted and Venus, Medicine Man, Far and Away, A League of Their Own, Unforgiven,* and many others.

The most striking aspect of all the graphic sequences noted above is their totally gratuitous nature: no audience ever left a theater feeling cheated because it had been denied the opportunity of seeing its favorite stars vomiting or relieving themselves. Of course, today's film-makers enjoy an absolute right to include such sequences if they choose to do so, but it is still difficult to understand why they excercise that right so frequently and so pointlessly.

This fascination with filth goes to the heart of the current crisis in the popular culture. Reading over the list of motion pictures that feature these bodily functions, you will notice few slasher films or exploitation titles and will find, instead, a preponderance of projects with serious artistic aspirations—many of them critical favorites. The proclivity to portray vomit and urine on screen reflects the increasingly influential notion that the most important form of aesthetic expression is that which will shock the public and challenge outmoded standards of decency. According to this point of view, it is the responsibility of the cinema artist to rub the viewer's face in reality—in all of its smelly, bloody awfulness. With this goal in mind, the bodily wastes that wash ashore in so many recent movies play an important role in allowing the moviemakers to take themselves seriously, and to enhance their self-image as daring rebels refusing to bow to the squeamishness of the great unwashed. In an era in which artist Andres Serrano wins expansive acclaim (and governmental support) for creating a photographic image of a crucifix immersed in his own gold and glowing urine, ambitious filmmakers can hardly be blamed for their desire to incorporate some of the same elixir in their efforts.

Roaches and Maggots

Those efforts at times become almost laughable in their tendency to tart up even the most sleazy and insipid material in the garb of inspired artistry, treating it with a reverence normally reserved for portentous statements of cosmic significance. *Exposure* (1991), for example, goes to graphic and sadistic extremes to tell its hopelessly hackneyed story of a mild-mannered American photographer (Peter Coyote) in South America who must transform himself into a ruthless killing machine. After he's wounded by arrogant drug dealers who also rape his unfortunate girlfriend (Amanda Pays), he spends much of the movie learning how to wield a knife with expert precision in preparation for the inevitable confrontation. Since this training process is depicted in elegantly choreographed slow motion, accompanied by a mellow, jazzy, synthesizer score, some commentators found themselves impressed. "Should be considered for an Oscar," proclaimed Gary Franklin of L.A.'s KABC-TV, while one of his colleagues on another network pronounced the picture "One of the most intriguing films I've seen in ages!"

This "intriguing" gem featured an especially noteworthy barf scene, when one of the thugs who's employed by the drug cartel is forced, at gunpoint, to chew and swallow several cockroaches. He responds to this insect repast with a gulping release of thick yellow vomit, which then forms a puddle on the floor in which he conveniently hides his face.

This scene may help to point the way to innovative outrages for those filmmakers who are already bored with the ordinary mechanics of regurgitation: the prospect of artful on-camera bug swallowing opens up a brave new world of cinematic indulgence. Actor Nicholas Cage actually pioneered this courageous form of self-expression (two years before it turned up in *Exposure*) with his controversial role in *Vampire's Kiss*. Playing a selfish Wall Street yuppie who is transformed into a rampaging bloodsucker, Cage faced a formidable thespian challenge with a scene that called for an extreme close-up of his lip-smacking consumption of a wiggling cockroach. In numerous interviews with the press after the picture's release, Cage boasted of the fact that he chose to swallow a real cockroach to lend the proper conviction to his role. In fact, several sources on the set confirmed that he actually devoured a half dozen of the critters in a series of painstaking retakes designed to capture this magical moment in all its glory.

In another corner of the popular culture, a rising rock star recently duplicated his dedication. Inger Lorre, a willowy, twenty-five-year-old former fashion model and lead singer of the hot new punk-metal group The Nymphs, appeared in a recent music video with a mouthful of maggots. For the song "Sad and Damned," she is shown drinking from a cup, then displaying the white, wiggling creatures on her lips, teeth, and tongue. "They were clean, grown in a lab," Lorre told the *Los Angeles Times* in January 1992. "They didn't come from rotting meat or anything like that."

In another near-legendary incident, Lorre protested the reassignment of her one-time producer by walking into the office of Geffen Records executive Tom Zutaut and urinating on his desk. "I did it because I was angry," she helpfully explains. "I'd do it again."

Lorre's use of maggot imagery is by no means unique in the world of contemporary rock 'n' roll. An acclaimed British group called Carcass frequently refers to the creepy crawlers with felicitous phrases like "purulent torso is a perfect maggots' meal" from their hit song "Swarming Vulgar Mass of Infected Virulency"—released on the same album as their similarly themed ditty, "Cadaveric Incubator of Endo-Parasites." Described in their press materials as a "trio of hard-core vegetarian Liverpudlians," Carcass performs at concerts in front of slide shows of morgue slabs and butcher shops.

Brave innovators like Inger Lorre and Carcass challenge their colleagues to seek out new and previously unexplored arenas for offensiveness. In Milwaukee, Wisconsin, in August 1991, a thirty-four-year-old rock singer named Kevin Michael Allin rose to the challenge. In fact, he helped to take popular music to the next logical level of self-expression as lead singer of a group called Toilet Rockers. In the midst of his concert, Allin delighted his devoted fans by defecating on stage and then throwing his feces out to the cheering audience. When this impressive performance resulted in his arrest on charges of disorderly conduct, Allin's defense at trial centered on the contention that he was "exercising artistic freedom."

A similar exercise intrigues Shane Embury, bassist for the leading "Grindcore" rock group, Napalm Death. "I'm still toying with the idea of making people release their bowels through music," he told the *Los Angeles Times*. "A certain tone you can reach where people lose muscular control. You can't hear it—it's a low frequency—but it really churns your guts."

The Infatuation
with Foul Language

For many members of America's mass audience, a low-frequency tone is hardly necessary to produce gut-churning results: they are already ill over the foul language that pervades our popular culture.

It may seem anticlimactic to discuss the excessive use of four-letter words after covering the current fascination with vomit and urine, roaches and maggots. Audiences are so energetically assaulted with every manner of maiming and mutilation, every imaginable approach to sexual exploitation and debasement of the human spirit, that one might well expect them to overlook the nasty language that usually accompanies the ugliness.

The public, however, remains surprisingly sensitive to the verbal obscenities that have become such a commonplace aspect of our movies, popular music, and even prime-time TV. All public opinion surveys measuring attitudes toward the media report a remarkable unanimity behind the idea that Hollywood should clean up the language in the products it offers to the people.

A well-publicized 1989 poll by Associated Press/Media General asked its respondents: "Overall, do most movies that come out nowadays have too much profanity in them, or not?" An astonishing 80 percent cited "too much" profanity; *not one* of the 1,084 survey participants endorsed the idea that movies today contained "not enough" harsh language.

This sort of statistical response conforms to the strong impressions I've received during more than seven years of communicating with the public as a nationally televised film critic. Among thousands of letters complaining about one or another new movie release—or about the sad state of films in general—foul language is *by far* the most commonly mentioned offensive element, well ahead of excessive violence, graphic sexuality, racial and gender stereotyping, or any other grounds for objection.

Anyone who bothers to listen to the public must come to understand that the explosion of verbal obscenities on screen has contributed powerfully to the sense of many moviegoers that a visit to their local theater has become a demeaning experience.

Ann Landers, whose nationally syndicated column provides a popular forum for the sentiments and values of Middle America, reports a huge volume of mail expressing outrage on this issue. On May 15, 1989, she ran a sampling of these letters under the headline "FILTHY TALK TARNISHING THE SILVER SCREEN." Among the comments she included:

—from Oxnard, California: "I'm sick to death of crude and vulgar language. How much more explicit can it get? . . . Why must decent people be embarrassed in front of their children by obscene words . . .?"

—from Vancouver, British Columbia: "My wife and I have walked out of so many movies because of the dirty language . . ."

—from Panama City, Florida: "Amen to your comments about gutter talk in movies. . . . Rock bottom, I call it."

—from Palo Alto, California: "I'm a sixty-four-year-old male who has been around. Nothing shocks me, but some things offend me. I'm talking about the F-word in the presence of my fifteen-year-old grandson. I'm afraid to take the boy to the movies again."

—from Kansas City, Missouri: "You said it wouldn't hurt Hollywood to clean up its mouth. I agree. In fact, I'll go further and say it would help the box office. My husband and I go to very few movies these days because of the dirty talk. I'll bet millions of Americans feel the same way."

Hollywood's refusal to face the sincere hurt and disappointment behind such statements represents an especially appalling illustration of the industry's underlying contempt for its audience.

Even if one insists that all survey results are overstated, and that letter writers are unrepresentative, it still makes little sense to give needless offense to any significant segment of the moviegoing public. I've heard industry defenders make the argument that among that 80 percent of all Americans who tell pollsters of their annoyance at the street language in films, only a minority are *seriously* alienated by the obscenities. Even so, what producer in his right mind would unnecessarily and knowingly write off 30 percent, or 20 percent, or 10 percent of potential patrons for his movie?

What makes Hollywood's self-destructive obsession with the language of the sewer even more difficult to understand is the total lack of countervailing pressure on this particular issue. Where are the advocacy groups, or even individual members of the audience, who clamor for the industry to maintain its impressive quota of F-words, S-words, and other expletives in film after film? Richard Pine, one of the most savvy and respected literary agents in the business, addresses the situation with common-sense clarity: "Nobody ever walked out of a movie and said, 'Gee, that was a great picture, but the only problem was they didn't say "Fuck" enough.' Who thinks like that?"

Who indeed? Who dictates the idiotic overrepresentation of a few crude Anglo-Saxonisms in today's movie dialogue—especially in the absence of any discernible audience demand for the inclusion of such words?

As with the gratuitous vomit and urine scenes, the utterly gratuitous use of obscene language stems in part from the filmmakers' adolescent insistence on thumbing their noses at all conventional notions of propriety. Many of the major decision-makers in Hollywood can recall a time when even the use of "hell" and "damn" was strictly limited; their current opportunity to pepper their pictures with literally hundreds of far harsher words represents a recently won and deeply cherished freedom. At times, they seem determined to use that freedom simply because it is *there*.

This attitude appears at every level of the production process, from producers to screenwriters to directors to the actors themselves. Certain performers are notorious for their insistence on inserting their favorite words in every film in which they are cast, even when those expletives never appeared in the script. According to veteran observers, Oscar winners Robert De Niro and Joe Pesci are among those who are especially apt to increase the intensity of their characterizations with an abundance of unscripted, improvisatory obscenities.

Significantly, both men appeared in *GoodFellas* (1990), one of Hollywood's all-time champions when it comes to expletives per minute. The Entertainment Research Group of Boca Raton, Florida, which devotes itself to the unenviable (and exhausting) task of counting the obscene words in new movie releases, certified this film's remarkable achievement. With a total running time of 146 minutes, director Martin Scorsese and his cast managed to pack in some 246 F-words, fourteen S-words, seven A-words ("asshole"), and five "slang terms for parts of the male anatomy." This means that viewers of *GoodFellas* heard a major obscenity nearly twice every minute; or, to be more precise, once every 32.2 seconds of the picture's running time.

Brilliantly well-acted, emotionally gripping, and critically over-praised, Scorsese's stylish triumph gave bad language a good name. When this veritable festival of foul speech won an Oscar nomination for Best Picture of the year and swept the leading awards from all the major critics' organizations, it only served to reinforce the idea that the finest in cinematic artistry requires a wealth of obscene dialogue. According to this reasoning, Scorsese needed every one of his hundreds of expletives in order to treat his subject with uncompromising integrity. After all, how can he be expected to shape a convincing film about murderous Mafia hoods without reproducing the filthy language such thugs would surely use in real life?

This argument displays not only a childish literalism but also an ignorance of cinema history.

The mere existence of some unpleasant aspect of reality—say, the morning constipation and hemorrhoidal pain that afflict a significant percentage of our fellow citizens—does not create an obligation to portray that situation on screen. The failure to focus on the moments that a character spends grunting on the commode does not necessarily betray the truth of his existence, nor imply a lack of integrity on the part of the filmmaker. Despite the professed enthusiasm for the subject matter from bands like the Toilet Rockers and performers like Shane Embury of Napalm Death (mentioned above), mainstream filmmakers have—so far—chosen to ignore defecation as a major focus for their artistry. Every movie is inevitably selective in those elements of an individual, or a story, it chooses to convey. Artistic restraint—and consideration for the sensitivities of the audience—do not always amount to dishonesty.

Anyone who remembers *White Heat,* the great Jimmy Cagney film from 1949, knows that the potrayal of a psychopathic gangster can be just as convincing, and just as terrifying, without obscene language. Somehow, director Raoul Walsh managed to bring to life the cruel realities of his main character's world, both inside and outside of prison, while using 246 fewer F-words than Martin Scorsese employed in *GoodFellas.* Can any fair-minded observer watch *White Heat* and honestly declare that its effectiveness has been compromised by the restraint of its language?

In this regard, as in so many others, the classics of Hollywood's Golden Age could provide an education for many of today's filmmakers. Consider John Ford's *The Grapes of Wrath* (1940), with its harrowing tale of embittered farmers (one of them an ex-con) fleeing the horrors of the Dust Bowl in Oklahoma for exploitation in the fruit orchards of California. While real-life "Okies" may well have employed extremely salty language in their moments of rage or pain, the impact of this noble film is hardly reduced by its characters' failure to reproduce those curses.

The same point might be made for the masterful *Paths of Glory* (1957), with its grim, nightmarish account of the fate of three ordinary French soldiers in World War I who are sacrificed by vainglorious higher-ups. The battlefield, and the military prison, as rendered by director Stanley Kubrick, are no less horrifying for their absence of expletives. When viewing this stunning film alongside Kubrick's more recent antiwar epic *Full Metal Jacket* (1987), it is hard to see how the bountiful use of abusive language in the latter project makes it in any way a better film.

While arguments may reasonably rage over the appropriateness of including verbal obscenities in movies about the mob, or migrant farm workers, or long-suffering soldiers in the heat of battle, no one can make a convincing case that those words are essential in lighthearted comedies, or sentimental romances, or adventure movies for kids.

Nevertheless, the Hollywood establishment inserts vile speech in nearly all such projects, without rhyme, reason, or proper warning to the public.

A simple word count on 282 major movie releases from 1991—performed by the aforementioned Entertainment Research Group—proves that the public is correct in its assumption that it is virtually impossible to escape street language in today's films.

A breakdown of 1991 releases according to their MPAA ratings shows that the *average* R-rated movie contains twenty-two F-words, fourteen S-words, and five A-words—providing its viewers with a major obscenity every two and a half minutes. Keep in mind that these figures represent an average—indicating that half the films in this category provide even heftier doses of foul talk.

Far more surprising is the ubiquity of harsh language in films deemed more appropriate for youthful audiences. I am always amazed at how many parents still cling to the notion that a PG or PG-13 rating for a film means that their children will be spared the most intense obscenities. This supposition hardly squares with the fact that 39 percent of 1991 PG-13 films used the F-word, 66 percent used the A-word, and an amazing 73 percent used the S-word!

Even among PG movies—films to which parents eagerly bring their six- and seven-year-old children—58 percent use the A-word, and 46 percent use the S-word. Insisting on this sort of language in so many films for kids is not only unnecessary; it is insane.

Similarly insane is the dramatic drift toward dirty words on prime-time TV; increasingly, Americans find themselves assaulted by crude language in their own living rooms. Bill Bruns and Mary Murphy lamented this trend in a November 1990 article in *TV Guide:*

> Try explaining to your six-year-old, for example, what six-year-old Maizy on CBS's "Uncle Buck" means when she tells her brother, "You suck." Or what fourteen-year-old Darlene Conner on ABC's "Roseanne" is talking about when she brags to her sister that she was "felt up" by her boyfriend . . . . Other words on other shows are coming across loud and clear. Sharon Gless, in the title role on CBS's "The Trials of Rosie O'Neill," candidly tells how "I'm thinking about maybe having my tits done" to cope with her divorce. . . . NBC's "L.A. Law," meanwhile, has attorney Grace Van Owen upset because her former boss, the DA, is "pissed at me." On ABC's "Cop Rock," a judge calls a defendant a "scumbag"—a vulgarism for a condom.

One 1990 scene in "The Trials of Rosie O'Neill" helped to define the new freedom for prime-time producers to use harsh language. In the midst of an argument with her office mate Hank Mitchell (Dorian

Harewood), Rosie blows her stack. "I've had it with the Beverly Hills *crap*. You elitest *son of a bitch!* You're worse than any snob in my mother's club," she snaps.

"I couldn't get into your mother's club," he shoots back. "So *kiss . . . my . . . ass!*"

Producer Barney Rosenzweig fought passionately to keep this scene as written, and considered it a major victory for creative freedom when, after an extended battle, CBS gave him his way.

As a result of his triumph, millions of American kids had the opportunity to hear role models on television engage in precisely the sort of crude and abusive exchange that most parents try hard to discourage in their children.

Not everyone in the television industry is convinced that the medium's new tolerance for explicit language represents progress. Delbert Mann is one of the great directors in TV history, with credits including the original, televised version of *Marty, The Bachelor Party, The Man Without a Country,* and *Playing for Time.* As he reflected on the current dilemma of the networks he has served so well, Mann told the *Los Angeles Times* in 1991: "I get a real sense of America being turned off by the network television we see, and that the language is one reason for the lost network audience. The language is still important to people in this country."

Other television veterans agree with him. "I wish we could go back to the innocent days of television," says distinguished producer David Gerber, chairman of the MGM/UA Television Production Group. "Looking at some of the current shows, I wonder: how far can we go before the audience is offended and turns off? The pendulum always swings back. People in the industry just forget that."

The Addiction to Violence

"Definitely A Causal Connection"

While a fascination with foul language may be the most obvious example of the popular culture's emphasis on ugliness, the addiction to graphic violence is surely the most destructive. While the ubiquitous inclusion of dirty words disturbs millions of people as unnecessary and insulting, the addiction to brutality encourages far more serious sorts of antisocial behavior, with devastating consequences for our civilization.

A wealth of scientific studies in recent years have removed most of the remaining doubts about the link between make believe brutality and real world aggression. "The consensus among social scientists is that very definitely there's a causal connection between exposure to violence in the media and violent behavior," says Daniel Linz, Professor of Psychology at the University of California, Santa Barbara, who has spent much of his career researching the subject. At New York's Syracuse University, Professor of Communications George Comstock reached identical conclusions by going back more than thirty years to analyze the 190 most important research projects that attempted to gauge the impact of television violence on children and young adults. Summarizing his conclusions in 1991, Comstock found "a very solid relationship between viewing antisocial portrayals or violent episodes and behaving antisocially. It holds up regardless of sex."

Two psychologists at the University of Illinois made the same observations after a landmark study of one set of 400 children over the course of more than twenty years. Drs. L. Rowell Huesman and Leonard Eron found that those kids who watched significant amounts of TV violence at age eight were consistently more likely to commit violent crimes or engage in child or spouse abuse at age thirty. When publishing their findings in 1984, they wrote that "we believe . . . that heavy exposure to televised violence is one of the causes of aggressive behavior, crime and violence in society. Television violence affects youngsters of all ages, of both genders, at all socioeconomic levels and all levels of intelligence. . . . It cannot be denied or explained away."

Shocking and Dangerous in Their Time

Unable to dismiss the increasingly unequivocal evidence of the negative impact of brutal media images, apologists for the entertainment industry resort to shrugs of the shoulders, knowing smiles, and the accurate but irrelevant argument that complaints about bloodshed on screen represent nothing new.

It is easy to cite past examples of movie violence condemned as shocking and dangerous in their time, but which look mild and tasteful from today's perspective. When *The Great Train Robbery* became the first smash hit in movie history in 1903, audiences reportedly ran in terror from the screen during the sequence in which a badman with a ridiculously drooping moustache pointed his prop pistol directly at the camera. Twenty-eight years later, the powerful Jimmy Cagney film *Public Enemy* appalled many moviegoers with its dark story of the rise and fall of a minor gangster; the anonymous reviewer for *The New York Times* denounced the picture for its "sensational and sometimes sensationally incoherent murders" ending in "general slaughter." In fact, this "general slaughter" amounted to a grand total of eight deaths in the course of the entire picture—and each of these killings takes place off screen.

Despite the concerns of critics and clergymen, American society somehow managed to survive this celluloid shock to its system and, according to the arguments of the defenders of the Hollywood status quo, it will have no trouble at all surviving the current epidemic of body count movies. By implication, they suggest that those of us who worry over the violent messages in so many of today's films will one day sound as foolish as the critic from sixty years ago who fretted over the contents of *Public Enemy.*

This is in many ways a reassuring line of reasoning; it's only too bad that it makes no logical sense.

Even if one accepts the assumption that *Public Enemy,* with its 8 murders, caused no demonstrable damage to its viewers, it is hard to understand how that is supposed to prove that *Die Hard 2* or *Rambo III* (with bodycounts of 264 and 106 killings, respectively) are similarly innocuous in terms of their audience impact. Not only are the death-counts vastly higher in the latter films, but each of those many moments of mayhem is portrayed in a graphic and horrifying style that would have been unthinkable for any mainstream movie of sixty years ago—or of ten years ago, for that matter. As Tim Appelo reported in a 1990 essay in *Entertainment Weekly:* "Big budget pictures now feature the kind of nonstop gore that used to play only at the midnight show." Comparing the vivid violence in one of today's splatter extrvaganzas with even the darkest gangster movies of the 1930s is no more mean-ingful than comparing the sex scenes in *Basic Instinct* to the sex scenes in *Gone With the Wind;* the distinctions are so obvious and so funda-mental that they serve to define two very different forms of entertain-ment.

Moreover, the reservations raised over the level of brutality in films today seldom center on a single shocker, or even a cluster of cutting-edge releases that test prevailing boundaries of good taste. They focus instead on an industry-wide epidemic that has infected an appalling percentage of contemporary motion pictures, as well as prime time television and popular music, and inserted brutal imagery in every cor-ner of the popular culture. Violent messages are no longer limited to a few feature films per year: they assault the average American in the course of the twenty-six hours of TV and the ten hours of music he consumes each week (if he's a typical teenager), not to mention the powerful and omnipresent promotional campaigns for the several hun-dred intensely violent films released every year by the major studios and production companies. Can anyone doubt that this sort of steady exposure exerts a more profound influence on the mass audience than those isolated instances of brutal and controversial films that have turned up from time to time in Hollywood's past?

Evidence already abounds as to the results of that influence. For one thing, the public has been dramatically desensitized by the overwhelming accumulation of violent images; it is far more difficult to frighten or disgust an audience than ever before.

In this regard, those who try to justify the industry's current excesses by pointing to long-ago releases that once shocked moviegoers are actually undermining their own case. The fact that movies formerly viewed as horrifying are now considered almost laughably tame, in no way demonstrates the innocuous or inconsequential impact of cinematic gore; if anything, it argues for the opposite conclusion, proving that decades of violent entertainment have succeeded in altering the public's perceptions and values.

Only the most jaded nihilist could take comfort from a situation in which bloody scenes deemed unbearably disturbing by past generations are now accepted as an integral element of the popular culture. This higher level of tolerance for media violence may even promote acceptance of the blood-curdling cruelty we experience with increasing frequency in our own homes and communities. It is hardly a positive development for a society when it loses its ability to feel shock.

"An Insatiability for Raw Sensation"

The Hollywood creative community most certainly understands the numbing effects of the blood-soaked diversions it deploys. As with any other addiction, chronic consumers of today's ultraviolent excursions require ever-increased dosages of their drug of choice in order to experience the thrills they crave. One of the industry's more skillful and sensitive directors, Alan J. Pakula (*All The President's Men; Presumed Innocent*) recently declared: "Movie violence is like eating salt. The more you eat, the more you need to eat to taste it at all. People are becoming immune to effects: the death counts have quadrupled, the blast power is increasing by the megaton, and they're becoming deaf to it. They've developed an insatiability for raw sensation."

On a more practical basis, one of Hollywood's most resourceful gore-meisters described the thought processes behind some of his most unsettling innovations. Rob Bottin, who designed the bloody special effects for *Total Recall* and both *Robocop* movies, told *Entertainment Weekly*: "Anything I make has to be something moviegoers haven't seen before. That means new tricks, which means more money, which means the audience is getting their—what is it now?—seven dollars worth. That's the thinking behind bigger and bigger and bigger. The question we always ask is, 'How do we top ourselves?'"

In the summer of 1990, critic Vincent Canby of *The New York Times* set out to quantify the apparently exponential increases in cinematic carnage. Armed with a "handy pocket-sized counter, the sort used to count the heads (still attached to bodies) in a crowd," Canby screened several recent releases and compared the number of killings they contained with the totals in a few earlier films. He discovered, for instance, that "*Dick Tracy*, which will probably be one of the most benign movies of the 1990s, has a higher body count than the original *Death Wish* (1974), which remains one of the sickest movies ever made." This is especially noteworthy since the PG-rated *Dick Tracy*, with its fourteen slayings, aimed unmistakably at an audience of children and teenagers.

In summarizing the results of his investigation, Canby concluded: "If you have the impression that movies today are bloodier and more brutal than ever in the past, and that their body counts are skyrocketing, you are absolutely right. Inflation has hit the action-adventure movie with a big slimy splat."

The influence of that inflation is by no means limited to action-adventure movies. The Entertainment Research Group recently reported that among *all* major releases in 1991—including PG- and G-rated "family films"—62 percent featured violent fight scenes, and 39 percent showed "graphic deaths."

Irrelevant Ratings

Such figures demonstrate the limited utility of the current rating system at a time when Hollywood finds it necessary to soak the majority of its creations in gratuitous gore. Even among those relatively rare releases that draw the purportedly wholesome "PG" rating (less than 18 percent of Hollywood's overall product), an appalling 60 percent show violent confrontations and fight scenes—while 58 percent use the word "asshole," 48 percent use the word "shit," and 44 percent depict the consumption of alcohol. It is small wonder that so many sensitive parents have given up on the MPAA ratings altogether as any sort of reliable guide to appropriate entertainment for their children.

I recently took part in a seminar in the nation's capital on the global impact of American popular culture in which one of my fellow participants, Professor Walter Berns of Georgetown University, made an exceptionally incisive point about the dubious thinking behind the rating system. He pointed out that we now label the most offensive films as "not fit for persons under a certain age. We designate them, and advertise them, as 'adult' films, thereby indicating that they *are* fit for persons *above* a certain age. In this way we say to the schoolboy that he need only wait a few years until he can enjoy what his father already enjoys, or at least is entitled to enjoy. Like a driving or marriage license, it is one of the privileges that comes with growing up."

The irony, of course, is that films rated "R" or "NC-17" are especially unlikely to convey a grown-up point of view. The notion that such movies are intended for "mature audiences" is very simply a lie. What mature characteristics could one possibly associate with the audience for the lavishly violent, simple-minded (and R-rated) *Nightmare on Elm Street* series? In what way does the R-rated *Friday the 13th Part VIII: Jason Takes Manhattan* (1989) represent a more sophisticated, more adult piece of popular entertainment than the PG-rated *Driving Miss Daisy* (also 1989)?

The current rating system not only fails to provide essential information about the contents of motion pictures, but it also advances horribly distorted ideas of what constitutes maturity.

Sadistic Laughter

No aspect of the entertainment industry's exploitation of violence shows greater immaturity—or irresponsibility—than its current tendency to make mayhem a subject of mirth. As the on-screen mutilation and dismemberment become progressively more grotesque and horrible, filmmakers make light of their characters' pain by introducing sadistic humor as an indispensable element of entertainment.

Anyone who has watched Arnold Schwarzenegger in action, dispassionately dispatching dozens of opponents in one of his major film roles, has been exposed to this cruel new notion of comedy. Even on those occasions when he isn't *supposed* to be playing killer robots, the Big Guy deals death with mechanical, deadpan precision; in many instances, the only twinges of humanity allowed to creep into his characterizations are those murderous *bon mots* with which he rids the world of the human rubbish arrayed against him. In *Predator* (1987), the hero impales an extra against a tree with a machete, then urges the bleeding victim to "Stick around." In a defining moment in *Total Recall* (1990), he makes use of an ascending elevator to separate the villainous Michael Ironside from both of his forearms; as he is left holding the bloody stumps that are all that remains of his opponent he quips, "See you at the party."

Other leading action stars have followed Schwarzenegger's lead in trying to milk laughs from lacerations.

• In *Lethal Weapon 2* (1989) Danny Glover eliminates two South African thugs by holding a nail gun to their temples and puncturing their skulls. "I nailed 'em both," he glibly reports.

• In *Hudson Hawk* (1991) Bruce Willis neatly decapitates one of the badguys with his own rapier blades, then tells the headless corpse: "I guess you won't be attending that hat convention in July."

• In *Another 48 Hours* (1990) Eddie Murphy stops a fight in a cowboy bar by shooting one of the troublemakers in the leg. As the man collapses on the floor, shrieking in pain, Murphy smiles sweetly. "Sorry about the kneecap," he says. "I got a little . . . excited."

No one would confuse such dialogue with the verbal thrusts of Noel Coward or Oscar Wilde, but any criticism of the witlessness of these comments misses the point entirely: it's the violence itself that's supposed to be hilarious, and that leaves audiences howling with laughter. A twelve-year-old girl named Betsy, interviewed after a matinee of *Total Recall,* told a reporter for *Entertainment Weekly:* "I can't say that it's violent, really. It's pretty funny to see people getting shot in the head."

The nightmarish mix of comedy and carnage demonstrates more clearly than anything else that the brutality in today's films is different in kind, not just extent, from the screen violence of the past.

Many movie makers refuse to acknowledge this difference, and instead see themselves as heirs to a noble tradition. At a social gathering, I recently listened to a successful producer of cinematic bloodbaths comparing himself to Shakespeare. "You know, four hundred years ago people felt shocked by the violence in *Hamlet*. Just look at how it ends up—dead bodies all over the stage! What we're doing today is just more of the same."

Unfortunately, the proud producer neglected to point out that the Bard never attempted to make cheap jokes out of murder or mutilation; Shakespeare understood that in order to move an audience when depicting a character's death the playwright (or the filmmaker) must affirm, rather than deny, the humanity of the victim.

Today's films, of course, do precisely the opposite: they turn their corpses into cartoons. Though every manner of physical wound or gory disfigurement will be depicted in clinical and convincing detail, the emotional suffering of the casualties (or their loved ones) is altogether ignored. Pity is never invoked: it would be as inappropriate to feel empathy for the brutalized bad guys in one of today's ultraviolent extravaganzas as it would be to show concern for the chronically abused Wile E. Coyote in the "Roadrunner" cartoons. That fondly remembered character only existed on screen for one purpose: to endure the sadistic and comical horrors the animators designed for him. The countless (and largely anonymous) targets of today's macho stars are conceived in similarly one-dimensional terms.

Todd Gitlin, professor of sociology at the University of California, Berkeley, observes that "the viewer who doesn't close his eyes is not drawn to identify with the victims—they are barely on the screen long enough to warrant second thoughts. . . . The secret of the global box office success of these films is that they evoke a forbidden pleasure in the victim's pain. There is a delirium of delight in the perpetrator's ability to get away with murder. The sheer volume and magnitude of mayhem is utterly severed from any conceivably rational objectives."

Mark Crispin Miller made a similar point in *Atlantic Monthly* (April, 1990), comparing the function of screen violence today and in the past: "In *Bullitt* (1968) and *The French Connection* (1971), in *The*

Searchers (1956), and in the movies of Sam Peckinpah, the violence, however graphic, was muted by a deep ambivalence that shadowed even the most righteous-seeming acts of vengeance, and that therefore suppressed the viewer's urge to join in kicking. In contrast, screen violence now is used primarily to invite the viewer to enjoy the *feel* of killing, beating, mutilating."

Even so manifestly gifted and serious a filmmaker as Martin Scorsese seems to have succumbed to the idea that violence on screen can be viewed as light-hearted diversion. His 1991 remake of *Cape Fear* featured several vicious beatings, murders, attempted murders, facial mutilations, attempted rapes, drowning, burning, blinding, strangling, sliding in pools of blood, and even the poisoning of a family dog. When describing the picture to the *Los Angeles Times* prior to its release, Scorsese declared simply: "It's a picture about a man who wants revenge. *And it's a lot of fun.*"

The raucous laughter that echoes through theatres showing similarly sadistic fare suggests that millions of Americans have been influenced by this hideous new concept of *fun*.

Some observers, at least, detect a note of discomfort beneath the howls of glee. In October 1989, Robert H. Knight, a media fellow at Stanford's Hoover Institution, addressed the phenomenon of carnage comedies in a piece in the *Wall Street Journal*. He particularly objected to *A Fish Called Wanda* (1988), the bank robbery farce for which Kevin Kline won the Oscar as best supporting actor. Knight notes that in the course of the film "we are not supposed to be disturbed when an inept killer is crushing a woman's pet dogs to death; we are supposed to laugh at his inability to kill the woman herself, which he finally does when she has a heart attack over the carnage. Are you laughing yet? The people at the theater I went to were howling. A couple of viewers cocked their heads as if they sensed something out of balance, but then succumbed to the good humor around them. Who wants to be a wet blanket?"

Knight also found himself dismayed at the reaction to *Batman* (1989), in which "innocent people die grotesque, agonizing deaths while 'Joker' Jack Nicholson cracks one-liners. The result is an audience uneasily laughing at ghoulish depictions of human suffering. But laugh they do. . . . What is new is that violence and comedy are woven into the same scenes in quality, mainstream films."

This strange wedding of gore and good humor brings a chilling new dimension to the destructive messages that viewers derive from big screen brutality.

Not only do these films suggest that brute force is a prerequisite for manliness, that physical intimidation is irresistibly sexy, and that violence offers an effective solution for all human problems, today's movies advance the additional appalling idea that the most appropriate response to the suffering of others is sadistic laughter.

Music and Mayhem

The cruel and callous exploitation of violence is by no means confined to the motion picture business; the same savage attitudes turn up in every component of contemporary popular culture and, to a startling extent, they've come to dominate the world of popular music.

Brutal imagery plays an increasingly important role in the music videos released by major recording artists, even when the lyrics to their songs include no specific references to violence. A November 1991 research study by the National Coalition on Television Violence examined 750 music videos featured on cable and broadcast television, and found an astonishing average of *twenty acts of violence per hour.* On MTV, the most popular and influential of the major music networks, the situation proved even worse: the researchers for NCTV counted twenty-nine instances of violent imagery in an average hour of programming.

Most of these musical minidramas advance the same violence-is-fun theme conveyed in so many recent motion pictures. For example:

• The video for "What It Takes" by Aerosmith shows the lead singer entering a nightclub where he is due to perform, and provoking a fierce, free-swinging barroom brawl when he sees his ex-girlfriend with another man.

• The "Legs" video by ZZ Top centers on a meek salesgirl who is physically abused by a gang of sadistic bikers. She gets her revenge by changing into some provocative clothes, and returning to the scene of the crime with three other scantily clad beauties who lure a group of brawny construction workers into beating up the bikers.

• "Poundcake" by Van Halen shows a curious young lady staring through a keyhole into a woman's locker room. When the models inside, clad in lingerie and fishnet stockings, discover the snooping intruder, they attempt to put out her eye with a power drill that they use to punch holes in the door.

• Guns n' Roses' "You Could Be Mine" video features a series of ultraviolent scenes from *Terminator 2*. The movie sequences are edited to make it appear that Arnold Schwarzenegger is trying to kill the members of the band—shooting machine guns, hurling grenades, punching through glass, setting off fiery explosions. The tender lyrics feature lead singer Axl Rose joyously exclaiming, "I'll rip your heart in two and leave you lying on the bed."

• Skid Row's "18 and Life" features an angry young man who is thrown out of his parents' home and then expresses his rage in criminal activity. He sets fires, gets drunk, steals a gun, then uses it to shoot his best friend.

• The group appropriately known as Poison contributed the video "Flesh and Blood Sacrifice," which portrays the lead singer caressing a gorgeous and excited young woman who lies on her back beneath him. A huge snake is draped across the woman's seminude body; she slowly licks the animal while the singer squeezes her head in his vice-like grip. "Give me an inch and I'll take it," he croons. "There's no more to think about . . . are you ready to sacrifice?"

Such lavishly degrading and decadent images would be distasteful in any context, but they are particularly objectionable in relation to the target audience to which they are addressed: the average viewer of music videos on TV is somewhere between fourteen and sixteen years of age. In analyzing the content of the videos that appeal so powerfully to these adolescents, and featured round-the-clock on MTV, the National Coalition on Television Violence found that 68 percent of them contained at least one of the following elements: explicit violence, suggestions of violence, sexually suggestive themes, profanity, smoking, and/or alcohol consumption.

Expressing the emotional reaction of many parents and grandparents toward this form of entertainment, Senator Robert Byrd (D-W.Va.) delivered an impassioned speech on the Senate floor on September 18, 1991. "The central message of most of these music videos is clear: human happiness and fulfillment are experienced by becoming a sociopath and rejecting all responsibility," he thundered. "If we in this nation continue to sow the images of murder, violence, drug abuse, sadism, arrogance, irreverence, blasphemy, perversion, pornography and aberration before the eyes of millions of children, year after year and day after day, we should not be surprised if the foundations of our society rot away as if from leprosy."

Senator Byrd's sense of alarm derived from a review of mainstream material, available to all American teenagers on commercial TV; he might have been considerably more upset had he looked over the grotesquely violent lyrics of some "rebel" groups on the fringes of the rock world whose music nonetheless reaches millions of fans.

For instance, try to imagine the Senator's reaction to a song like "I Saw Your Mommy and Your Mommy's Dead" from the popular (and Grammy-nominated) L.A. band Suicidal Tendencies, whose first album became the best-selling American punk-rock record of all time: "I think it's the greatest thing I'll ever see/Your dead mommy lying in front of me." The song also describes her "chopped off toes on her chopped off feet" and the "rodents using her hair as a nest," while concluding with the wish that "I hope she dies twenty times more."

When asked in a 1991 interview about the word "Suicidal" in the name of the group, the band's philosophical lead singer, Mike Muir, declared: "To us, it's a very positive word, a lot of emotion, a lot of hatred, a lot of belief, a lot of things thrown together."

More recently, groups like The Geto Boys have helped to popularize a widely discussed new art form known as "Gangsta Rap," with musical numbers that invariably include grotesquely violent elements. Their 1990 album *The Geto Boys*, distributed by a division of Time-Warner Communications, features elegant numbers like "Assassins," with its inventive rhyme scheme. After a girl is "ready" and starts getting "sweaty," the leader of that group resolves to "Kill that bitch like Freddy!", and then:

"I dug between the chair and whipped out the machete/She screamed, I sliced her up until her guts were like spaghetti."

Later, the poet suggests that the only way to stop her nerves from "jumpin" is to "stab the girl in the tits" and "just cut her to bits."

It is hard to conceive of a less responsible exercise of corporate power than for a major communications conglomerate like Time-Warner to elect to manufacture and distribute such material.

Some of the strongest voices condemning the outrageous brutality in contemporary rap music have come from within the black community. Writing in the *Miami Herald*, Leonard Pitts, Jr., asked his readers, "Maybe I'm crazy, but am I the only one thinks it obscene that this popular new genre was born out of the exploitation of a sick violence that has wrecked thousands of lives? . . . I'm not saying gangsta rap causes this tragedy but that it legitimizes it."

Despite his fears of isolation, Pitts is by no means alone in acknowledging the alarming consequences of the violent messages in popular music. Antiobscenity activist Tipper Gore (denounced by rock legend Frank Zappa as a "cultural terrorist") long ago pointed out the connection between brutal themes in today's music and the increasingly unstable and menacing atmosphere at major concerts. Destruction of property has become commonplace, with damages totalling millions of dollars, while the risk of riots has never been higher. The music's most devoted fans have begun to internalize and act out its aggressive messages. In 1988, Steve Hochman wrote in the *Los Angeles Times*: "Remember when the biggest problem with rock concerts was ticket scalpers? . . . There's now another, sadly inescapable concern facing rock fans: personal safety."

Since the mid-'80's, at least two dozen rock or rap enthusiasts have died in concert-related violence; more than a hundred others have suffered serious injuries.

Life and limb could hardly have been sacrificed for a less noble cause.

Vastly More Violent Than the Streets

The ultimate justification for those who try to excuse Hollywood's addiction to brutality is the by now familiar contention that the violence in our popular culture is only an inevitable reflection of the violence in our streets. This argument absolves the entertainment industry from all responsibility for encouraging destructive behavior, suggesting that the media are merely reporting on a sad situation that already prevails in our deeply troubled society.

Those of us who dare to criticize Hollywood's dark obsessions are regularly charged with "blaming the messenger"—unfairly attacking the industry for truthfully conveying the bad news about social breakdown and bloodlust among our fellow citizens. Many industry insiders stubbornly insist that their work does nothing at all to shape values; it simply mirrors the values of the public at large. In their view, Hollywood is only an effect—and never a cause—of the major problems of our time.

This reasoning runs into trouble on several counts.

First, it can scarcely explain the umistakably sadistic glee displayed in some of Hollywood's big budget, big screen gore fests; the cruel humor and the spectacular special effects with which our technical wizards bring to life the most bizarre murders and mutilations, go far beyond any underlying desire to drive home to us the true horror of current conditions. Anyone who watches movies or TV with any regularity at all knows that there is very little realism in the way they portray violence. Stuart Gordon, who directed the diabolically diverting horror movie *Re-Animator* in 1985, recently made that discovery when he researched a project in the emergency room of a Chicago hospital. He learned, for instance, that most fistfights last only one punch. "The person who throws the punch breaks his hand, and the other person's jaw is broken. And that's the end," Gordon recently told *USA Weekend*. "You break a chair over somebody's head, and that person's got a concussion and is probably unconscious for a couple of weeks. But it's something you see all the time on TV and you assume, you know, it's a fun thing to do."

Hollywood, in other words, does more than recreate real-world brutality; it glorifies violence as an enjoyable adventure and a manly ideal.

Moreover, the notion that the industry's bloody excesses faithfully and responsibly reproduce the grim realities around us can't stand up to the fact that crime and mayhem are so outrageously overrepresented on television. Though the tube still offers less graphic and less disturbing carnage than you can find in any given week at your local multiplex, content analysis makes clear that our TV screens are *vastly* more violent than our streets.

In their indispensable research project *Watching America* (1991), Stanley Rothmann, Robert Lichter, and Linda Lichter reviewed more than 600 prime-time television shows, analyzing TV's portrayal of the society it serves. When it comes to televised presentations of crime and violence, their conclusions are unequivocal: "Our studies show that an evening of prime time puts to shame a night at the station house. Violent crime is far more pervasive on television than in real life, and the disparity widens as the danger increases. For the most serious crime of all, the difference is most dramatic. *Since 1955 television characters have been murdered at a rate 1,000 times higher than real-world victims*" (italics added).

Other antisocial activities are similarly popular with television producers—whose prime-time shows feature an average of 3.6 crimes per episode. This means that the major networks portray at least fifty crimes on a typical night of broadcasting—or 350 crimes in an average week. Rothmann, Lichter, and Lichter report that the normal *nightly* total "would include about a dozen murders and fifteen to twenty assorted robberies, rapes, assaults, and other acts of mayhem. So television is not just more crime ridden than real life. It also highlights the most violent and serious crimes. A majority of crimes portrayed involve violence, and nearly one in four (23 percent) are murders. In real life, according to the FBI, violent crimes account for about 5 percent of all arrests. On television they make up 56 percent of all illegal acts."

Seen another way, since 1975 a major character on prime-time TV stands an 8.6 percent chance of falling victim to violent crime in any given season. His real-world counterpart faced only a 0.5 percent yearly chance of similar victimization during the same period. This means that the make-believe people who inhabit the fantasy world of the tube are seventeen times more likely to go through a personal confrontation with criminal violence than are the flesh-and-blood citizens who watch them every week.

The point of citing these statisics is not to suggest that television—or the music business or the movies, for that matter—must precisely recreate the national crime rate that applies at any given moment. Criminal activity is inherently dramatic; it has always been overrepresented in popular entertainment, and it always will be.

The extent of the overrepresentation on today's prime-time shows, however, destroys the argument that TV producers are merely responding to larger trends in the society when they emphasize violence and criminality. In fact, the evidence suggests that they have pointedly ignored those trends. Throughout the decade of the 1980s, FBI statistics showed slight but consistent drops in the national rate of violent crime, but in the same period the television crime rate increased sharply. The televised brutality which bursts into American living rooms every night expresses the ugly obsessions of the Hollywood creative community, not the shifting statistics of urban reality.

Howard Rosenberg, Pulitzer prize winning critic for the *Los Angeles Times,* lamented "Television's Criminal Tendencies" as he reviewed the 1991–92 network season: "TV's reliance on action and conflict leads it down the criminal path," he wrote. "Series with crime themes consume about 20 percent of the new prime-time schedules on ABC, CBS, NBC and Fox. Moreover, that total excludes such series as CBS' late-night 'Crime Time' strip and '60 Minutes', ABC's '20/20' and NBC's 'Exposé' that regularly feature crime stories. And it also ignores seven network movie blocs that gorge on both real and fictional sensational crime in an attempt to titillate or capture the attention of viewers. . . . Add to this the crime emphasis of predatory newscasts, tabloid programs and talk shows . . . and the picture becomes clear."

This consistent overemphasis on the most menacing forms of human interaction amounts to something more than the harmless pursuit of ratings success. The ominous view of the world conveyed by the popular culture contributes powerfully to the insecurity and paranoia that in turn faciliate increased levels of criminal activity. A fearful attitude makes it far more likely that average Americans will huddle protectively in their own homes, taking no responsibility for the state of their neighborhoods and their communities. As UCLA criminologist James Q. Wilson persuasively argues, "excessive fear of crime contributes to crime"; this isolationism and intimidation help to drive up the level of unopposed antisocial behavior and cede the streets to violent criminals.

"Untying the Fabric of Our Society"

Concern over the violent messages in the popular culture is by no means limited to one side of the political spectrum; progressives are every bit as likely to worry over their impact as committed conservatives. On May 21, 1992, Democratic presidential candidate Bill Clinton told a Cleveland audience, "Of course there's a values crisis in America. . . . Like any parent, I'm troubled by the gratuitous violence and sex and mixed moral signals on television." Marian Wright Edelman, a colleague of Hillary Clinton's as founder and president of the militantly liberal Children's Defense Fund, recognizes that "parents are afraid, and they need help" in counteracting the destructive values advanced by the media. "We're pumping violence as a way to solve disputes. We see guns in too many messages on TV and in movies."

University of Illinois psychologist Leonard Eron worries over television's tendency to portray the specifics of violence in ever more vivid terms. "The more realistic the violence is, the more effect it has, because the youngster thinks that everybody acts this way and that it is an appropriate way to go about solving problems," he says. "Children model their behavior after these characters, particularly if they're seen in a positive light."

Eron's colleague, Dr. L. Rowell Huesmann, told *Newsweek* in 1991 that "serious aggression never occurs unless there is a convergence of large numbers of causes, but one of the very important factors we have identified is exposure to media violence. . . . If we don't do something, we are contributing to a society that will be more and more violent."

The leading lights of Hollywood choose to ignore such warnings and stubbornly, though implausibly, deny that their work plays any role at all in the national epidemic of brutality and lawlessness. Some of them even insist that their blood-soaked entertainments serve a constructive social function. "Maybe we need the catharsis of bloodletting and decapitation," suggests director Martin Scorsese, "like the ancient Romans needed it, as ritual but not real like the Roman circus."

Producer David Puttnam addressed the same analogy from a vastly different perspective shortly after his resignation as president of Columbia Pictures. "What we think of now as the excess of the Roman circuses, where in the end hundreds of thousands of people died, didn't start that way," he reminded Bill Moyers in an eloquent interview for PBS. "They started legitimately as circuses, extremely mild entertainment. But the audience demand for more and more resulted over a period of several hundred years in that form of entertainment becoming more and more bloody, more and more grotesque.

"What might have been a woman raped publicly by a centurion, a year later was a woman raped publicly by an ass, and ten years later was ten women raped publicly by a hundred asses. The audience's desire for that goes way back, deep into history. Someone has to say, 'Enough'—because this is disaster, we are destroying ourselves. Successive societies have destroyed themselves by the failure of their leadership to say, 'I know in many respects that's what you'd like to see, but you know what? It's bad for us, we're damaging ourselves. We are untying the fabric of our society.'"

Hostility to Heroes

Smaller Than Life

Hollywood's ongoing obsession with ugliness manifests itself not only in its urge to offend, its infatuation with foul language, and its addiction to violence, but in a surprising and self-destructive hostility to heroes.

This development marks a drastic and devastating change of focus for the popular culture. In years past, in the heyday of Gary Cooper and Greta Garbo, Jimmy Stewart and Katharine Hepburn, the movie business drew considerable criticism for manufacturing personalities who were larger than life, impossibly noble and appealing individuals who could never exist in the real world. Today, the industry consistently comes up with characters who are *smaller* than life—less decent, less intelligent, and less likeable than our own friends and neighbors. Instead of creating elegant and exemplary figures of fantasy, Hollywood increasingly invests its most serious artistic aspirations on loathsome losers, disturbed and irresponsible misfits who give us little to care about and nothing to admire.

As noted in an earlier chapter of this book, the actors nominated for Oscars for 1991 provided an odd illustration of this trend, reflecting those characterizations that the Academy considered most worthy of its highest honor. Of the five men nominated for Best Actor, three played deranged and sadistic killers (Anthony Hopkins in *Silence of the Lambs,* Warren Beatty in *Bugsy,* and Robert De Niro in *Cape Fear*); one played a homeless and delusional psychotic (Robin Williams in *The Fisher King*); and one played a rejected, depressed, unemployed, and ultimately adulterous husband (Nick Nolte in *The Prince of Tides*).

The nominations for Best Supporting Actor hardly highlighted a more lovable crew: Ben Kingsley and Harvey Keitel played ruthless gangsters (both in *Bugsy*); Tommy Lee Jones portrayed a decadent and devious conspirator in the Kennedy assassination (in *JFK*); and Michael Lerner brought to life a crude, insensitive, and power-mad studio boss from Hollywood's Golden Age (in *Barton Fink*). Of the ten actors considered for the entertainment world's most esteemed awards, in both the Best Actor and Best Supporting Actor categories, only one (Jack Palance in *City Slickers*) portrayed a character who bore even a passing resemblance to a traditional Hollywood hero. In fact, his performance as a wise and weather-beaten trail boss may well have appealed to Academy voters (and won him the award) precisely because it amounted to a nostalgic and self-conscious nod to the glories of Hollywood's past.

On Oscar night, two militant gay rights organizations angrily protested the Academy's favorable attention to *JFK* and *Silence of the Lambs*—both of which featured highly unflattering portrayals of homosexual characters. No fair-minded person could disagree with their contention that some of the year's most eagerly applauded pictures featured insulting images of gay people, but those same movies also included demeaning depictions of heterosexuals, of women and men, of young and old, and of every manner of humanity. Hollywood degrades not only a minority sexual orientation; it degrades the human spirit.

This Peculiar Preference for Punks

In recent months, the emphasis on appalling characters has become so obvious and unbalanced that it has even attracted the attention of that elite journal of opinion, *US* magazine, in its annual summary of what's "in" and what's "out" in the American mainstream. In attempting to fathom the latest fashions in January 1992, the editors declared that "Evil" is now officially "In" and "Good" is definitely "Out." "Ever since the Joker walked off with a movie called *Batman*," they wrote, "Evil, not Love, is what the movies are all about." Noting that all the most prestigious actors now pined to play "the devil incarnate," the magazine concluded that "movie heroes who generate the same kind of heat simply don't exist, leading us to believe that in Hollywood there may be no God, but there certainly is a hell."

Responding to this peculiar preference for punks, even so charming and charismatic a performer as Armand Assante confessed that his ultimate dream as an actor is to "play losers." While promoting his performance as a hot-blooded Latin Lothario in *The Mambo Kings*, he told reporter Anemona Hartocollis of *Newsday:* "I want to do roles that are frail. I think life's a tragic situation. It's hopeless. . . . To me, that's life."

Assante could find plenty of company from other likeable stars who feel similarly compelled to "stretch their acting muscles" by playing dislikeable characters. Billy Crystal, for instance, has earned enormous affection from his fans around the world for his gentle and unfailingly affable comic persona, but for his debut as a director he chose to create a character his own manager candidly describes as "unlikeable." In *Mr. Saturday Night* (for which Crystal is also producer and cowriter of the screenplay), the popular star plays Buddy Young, a frustrated and mediocre comedian of the 1950s; after visiting the set, Kirk Honeycutt of the *Los Angeles Times* reported that the story focuses on an individual who is "not only self-destructive, but also a thoroughly unpleasant person."

"I love playing this guy," Crystal confessed. "Usually movies show self-destructive behavior in terms of drugs or booze. . . . But Buddy's self destructiveness is very interesting because it's about fear. . . . That feeds into a kind of fury that makes people not behave as they should." He went on to describe his directorial labor of love as "*Raging Bull* with laughs."

Crystal's description of his own work reflects an attitude that has become increasingly common among members of the entertainment establishment: the notion that building a project around a central character who is obnoxious and unhappy represents a more worthy artistic ambition than making a likeable, touching (and wildly successful) piece of popular entertainment like, say, *City Slickers*. Today's trend-setters in Hollywood reveal their underlying values in the frequency with which they boast about the dark and daring nature of the projects they undertake, as if everyone agreed that creating demonic and destructive antiheroes constituted the highest level of cinematic achievement.

Shortly before the release of *Bugsy*, screenwriter James Toback bragged about the picture to *Movieline*'s Stephen Rebello. "It is a portrait of a tremendously charming, sex-and-violence obsessed quasi-madman who is infatuated with creation and death," he exulted. "People are going to be astounded by Beatty in this movie. He's a complete psycho."

Beatty's bravura impersonation of this deranged, bloodthirsty, and altogether hateful hood by no means exhausted Hollywood's fascination for this all-but-forgotten footnote figure from history. For reasons that lie buried deep within some dark region well beyond the range of rational calculation, the major studios decided to immortalize Mr. Benjamin ("Bugsy") Siegel not just once but *three* times in 1991: a trio of big-budget films released within six months of one another featured our boy as a prominent character. In *Mobsters*, teen heartthrob Richard Grieco offered a portrait of the gangster as a young man; in *Marrying Man*, Armand Assante (apparently indulging his professed desire to play losers) portrayed the sadistic Siegel as a jealous lover, trying to maintain his control over his lounge-singing mistress, played by Kim Basinger.

Both *Marrying Man* and *Mobsters* proved to be costly and notorious box-office fiascoes, while Beatty's *Bugsy*, despite all the critical praise and ten Oscar nominations, earned only disappointing returns on Tri-Star's enormous investment. The public, in other words, never came to share Hollywood's insane—and inane—absorption with this particular criminal killer.

In fact, commercial self-interest has little or nothing to do with the current love affair with despicable characters. From *Miller's Crossing* to *Billy Bathgate*, from *The Hot Spot* to *State of Grace*, from *Two Jakes* to *Bonfire of the Vanities*, Hollywood's recent past is littered with the wreckage of scores of expensive and ambitious projects that failed precisely because they gave the audience no one to care about. Many of the industry's most influential moguls are gripped by a curious compulsion to provide us with protagonists who display all the charm and nobility of poisonous snakes.

"The Slimy Side of the Street"

This suicidal insistence on forcing moviegoers to confront uniquely unappealing examples of the human condition may have reached its logical conclusion with a revolting little road picture called *Homer and Eddie* (1990). Directed by the renowned and richly gifted Russian-American filmmaker Andrei Konchalovsky, it featured two major stars—Jim Belushi as a goofy, drooling, and infantile wanderer with severe and permanent brain damage, and Whoopi Goldberg as a wild-eyed murderer, career thief, and escaped mental patient who also happens to be dying of an inoperable tumor. Despite the best efforts of its hardworking cast, spending two hours in a dark theater with this pathetic pair is an ordeal of almost unimaginable unpleasantness. Needless to say, *Homer and Eddie* generated some of the year's most paltry box-office returns, and provided yet another illustration of America's emphatic rejection of Hollywood's newfound commitment to vary the lyrics of the old song by walking exclusively on "The Slimy Side of the Street."

Even some of the most critically acclaimed motion pictures of our time, including *GoodFellas, Blue Velvet, Wild at Heart, The Grifters, Ironweed, Bugsy, The River's Edge, Dead Ringers, Naked Lunch, Barton Fink, Salvador, Drugstore Cowboy, My Own Private Idaho, Henry: Portrait of a Serial Killer, The Sheltering Sky, Rush, Last Exit to Brooklyn,* and many others achieved only modest success with the general public and left many moviegoers feeling frustrated. The most common complaint concerning such films involved the numb, cold, empty attitude with which puzzled patrons left the theaters: you could certainly respect the uncompromising intensity and brilliance of the filmmakers, but how was any normal person supposed to warm up to the characters?

The consistently mediocre (or disastrous) audience reception for such difficult films proves absolutely nothing concerning their aesthetic unworthiness, but it does demolish the nonsensical notion that Hollywood's propensity to produce them is driven by a desire to pander to the popular taste. Looking over the grim commercial fate of nearly all of the hero-free films of recent years, no one can suggest with a straight face that this trend arose from the industry's reflex to give the public what it wants: the mass audience has clearly and consistently demonstrated its distaste for such projects. When the major studios and production companies ignore this track record and sign off on disturbing projects about deranged degenerates, they do so because of their distorted ideas as to what constitutes high art—*not* because they believe they're going to make big bucks (or answer some deep-seated national craving) by releasing films like *Naked Lunch* or *Ironweed.*

Presumably, even the most obtuse executives took note of the fact that during the Christmas season of 1991, a rerelease of the thirty-year-old kiddie classic *101 Dalmatians* earned more money in domestic grosses than the heavily hyped, $40 million Oscar contender, *Bugsy.*

Trashing Icons

Despite its ruinous financial consequences, the industry's absorption with the most selfish and destructive forms of behavior remains so powerful and pervasive that it results in harsh accounts of even the most revered American icons. In contrast to bygone days when Hollywood inspired the public with stirring big-screen biographies of American heroes like Abe Lincoln and Lou Gehrig, Sergeant York and General Patton, the movie business now only rarely looks back on fabled figures from our past. When it does so, however, it not only emphasizes their imperfections, but exaggerates them, providing chronically unappealing portraits.

No one is immune from such treatment—not even Babe Ruth, the greatest sports legend of them all and perhaps the most adored public figure of his era. *The Babe,* the much ballyhooed 1992 release starring John Goodman, concentrated almost exclusively on the Bambino's flaws and failures while offering only the briefest and most cursory mention of his astonishing athletic achievements. The movie lavished some fifteen minutes of screen time, for instance, on Ruth's frustrated ambition to work as a major league manager, while dismissing his record-setting sixty-home-run season of 1927 in less than fifteen seconds. Needless to say, this approach resulted in a dreary and depressing (though undeniably well-crafted) film that immediately struck out at the box office.

Other much-admired Americans have received similarly unflattering treatment from the movie industry in recent years. In the aptly named *Insignificance* (1985), Gary Busey played Joe DiMaggio as an abusive, graceless, and dim-witted lout, hypnotized by his own fame. Joseph Pulitzer fared even worse in *Newsies* (1992), in which the script forced the superb actor Robert Duvall to portray the celebrated press baron in utterly one-dimensional terms as a ruthless, cruel, and dishonest exploiter.

Barton Fink (1991) managed to abuse the reputation of Nobel Prize–winner William Faulkner without mentioning his name: John Mahoney, with a makeup job that gave him an eerie and precise resemblance to the real-life Faulkner, played an esteemed (and "fictional") Mississippi novelist who is toiling as a Hollywood screenwriter in 1941. This character is not only a pathetic drunk, given to periodic blackouts, but also a pretentious and incompetent writer whose most recent books actually have been ghostwritten by his secretary/mistress. In a similar vein, Blake Edwards's execrable flop *Sunset* (1988) trashed the memory of the beloved Charlie Chaplin, with Malcolm McDowell in a supporting role as a famous silent-screen comedian who is unmistakably intended to call Chaplin to mind. After all, the McDowell character is said to be famous for his pantomime performances as a "Little Tramp"—though he only uses that gentle persona to mask his true nature as a monstrous serial killer who tortures and murders aspiring actresses.

The urge to assault the cherished recollections of even universally esteemed figures in our culture reached its most infamous expression, of course, in *The Last Temptation of Christ* (1989). Even those many critics who praised the film on aesthetic or theological grounds acknowledged that director Martin Scorsese and his brooding star Willem Dafoe chose to emphasize the shortcomings, confusion, and emotional problems of the most admired personality in human history. Needless to say, this controversial project, like the other cynically revisionist efforts described above, led to disastrous results at the box office.

Popular stars of today, along with worshipped luminaries of the distant past, occasionally fall victim to the antiheroic impulse. No one plays noble or charismatic characters more effortlessly than Robert Redford, but for his most recent starring role he chose to play a heel. In Sydney Pollack's multi-megabuck bomb *Havana* (1990), he takes the part of a two-bit, sleazy, amoral, and carelessly womanizing gambler trying to make a killing in Cuba on the eve of Castro's revolution. He is temporarily transformed when he falls in love with a fiery idealist (Lena Olin) who happens to be married to a leading revolutionary, but Redford spends most of the movie crawling through the city's decadent and grimy underworld, trying to look corrupt and cynical. For the first time in his distinguished career, this popular star selected a part in which his classic hero's face worked against him: audiences found much to hate in *Havana,* including the murky politics, but their displeasure in seeing the adored Redford, of all people, playing a despicable leading man surely contributed to the epic scale of the film's failure.

Only one actor in today's Hollywood seems to understand the public's imperishable hunger for traditional heroes. Kevin Costner has become one of the world's most popular stars by displaying the good sense to choose roles as an honorable and likeable protagonist, in films like *The Untouchables* (1987), *Bull Durham* (1988), *Field of Dreams* (1989), *Dances with Wolves* (1990), and *Robin Hood* (1991). When Costner played controversial New Orleans district attorney Jim Garrison in *JFK,* he worked with director Oliver Stone to eliminate the famous flaws of the flamboyant real-life prosecutor; he reverted to his by-now familiar stance as an ennobled Everyman and provided Stone's ominous, nightmarish film with a moral center that contributed significantly to its success. Costner's ability to establish an image for himself as an old-fashioned, all-American leader—decent, sensitive, and occasionally selfless—helps to explain why this journeyman actor of limited range and ability, lacking the poster-boy good looks of so many of his colleagues, nevertheless reached the peak of international prominence and popularity.

The warm public response to Costner's role in *JFK* contrasts dramatically with the cool reception for the hero of Oliver Stone's previous film, *The Doors* (1990). This costly failure concentrated on the indulgent, irresponsible, and doomed career of rock star Jim Morrison, with loving attention to his drug addiction, epic alcohol consumption, unassailable egotism, violent temper, cruel and exploitative personal relationships, public exposure of his private parts, and wasted poetic talent.

This depressing depiction may have been basically true to the sad facts of Morrison's short life, but it still raises a question as to why a distinguished director and a major studio should choose to lavish a huge budget (some $40 million) on a filmic treatment of such a thoroughly despicable personality. Ian Whitcomb, himself a rock star of the 1960s (and author of the deathless ditty "You Turn Me On") felt particularly offended by the film. "How can people admire Jim Morrison of The Doors, who was no kind of example to anybody—a complete and total failure?" he asked in a 1991 interview with *The Public Perspective*. "It's sickening to me that he's become a cult figure. . . . This destructiveness and suicide, which is what Jim Morrison was about, and what The Grateful Dead are about—the very title spells that—is to me anathema and is to be fought."

Whitcomb, now a Los Angeles radio personality, intriguingly indicts the era of his own greatest fame as the source of the changes he deplores.

> I pinpoint the sixties as being the beginning of that. By destroying the past in the sixties we did the most terrible thing, and rock 'n' roll had a part to play in that. . . . The idols of the past may not have had particularly good private lives, but they kept them private. They stood for positive values, they stood for hearth and home and love. . . . Take a Bing Crosby. Although he was apparently a lush in private life, he never went on the stage with a bottle like Janis Joplin did. Behind the scenes, Crosby bashed up his children, but on stage he sang about "Galway Bay.". . .
>
> The sixties were different . . . they just said, "Do your thing." In our society now, the children of that generation cannot read. . . . I really do feel that we're reaching an age of barbarism, a new Dark Ages, as we had in Britain when Bede and a few monks had to keep the flame alight by sitting in their little cells in the north of England, protecting themselves against the barbarians. Well, those barbarians are around us now. They are the people who are reared on TV and rock 'n' roll.

Creeps and Killing Machines

No figure stands as a more perfectly realized symbol for Whitcomb's new barbarians than the one movie hero of recent years whose image has registered most deeply with the general public. The Terminator could never be construed as a noble or inspiring figure; he is, quite simply, a killing machine, a robot from the future built for mayhem and destruction. He is either a bad guy (*The Terminator,* 1984) or a good guy (*Terminator 2: Judgment Day,* 1991) depending only on the way he is programmed. He has no feelings, no inner struggles, no human relationships, no ideals. Nothing about him is heroic in the traditional sense: he represents deadly and unreflective efficiency as the ultimate standard of manliness.

Arnold Schwarzenegger, the world's number-one box-office attraction, projects this same mechanical machismo in all his major screen roles—whether or not he's supposed to be playing a killer robot. Moreover, his granitic, grunting school of acting has influenced all the other action heroes of our time, helping to make them a singularly sullen and uncommunicative lot.

By and large, these repellent role models can be divided into one of two categories: they are either invulnerable and emotionless martial arts masters (Steven Seagal, Jean-Claude Van Damme, or Chuck Norris) or they are brooding, disturbed, unpredictable head cases (Sylvester Stallone's "Rambo," Mel Gibson's "Lethal Weapon," Michael Keaton's "Batman") whose explosive propensity for violent excess stems from the deep psychic wounds sustained during some traumatic episode of the distant past. "Dirty Harry," Clint Eastwood's twitching, teeth-gritting, trigger-happy, and antiauthoritarian cop, is in many ways the spiritual godfather of the new breed of contemporary action stars. Like Harry Callahan, who made his first appearance in 1971's *Dirty Harry,* these punishing protagonists are capable of only one emotion: raw anger.

In this context, a visit to a typical nursery school can become an alarming experience. There, angelic toddlers play happily with frowning, muscular dolls designed to resemble Rambo or The Terminator, manipulating their movable plastic limbs or speaking affectionately to the scowling faces. A wildly popular new Terminator toy comes fully equipped with its own high-tech arsenal of guns and grenades, various detachable body parts, and the ability to growl out the lines "I'll be back!" and "Hasta la vista, baby!" when you pull a string behind its brawny neck. One can only speculate on the qualities of character our children associate with such effigies as they construct their imaginative worlds around them.

When I spoke with a friend who teaches preschool, she shrugged her shoulders over the presence of such toys in the classroom. "You can't really control it, because they bring the dolls from home," she said. "It's just a fad, really. Last year it was Ninja Turtles, this year it's The Terminator. What really surprises me is that some of these kids have actually seen the movie—their parents take them, even though it's rated R.

"When they start playing Terminator with each other it can get pretty rough, but they'd probably be aggressive anyway. Still, you've got to draw the line somewhere. For me, what I won't tolerate is Freddy Krueger dolls—they have the knives for fingernails, the whole thing. I know some of the kids have them at home, but that's something that definitely doesn't belong in school."

Though this well-intentioned educator may consider Freddy Krueger beyond the pale, the powers-that-be in our popular culture feel no compunction whatever in promoting this fearsome figure as an appropriate hero for our kids. The scarred, cackling, sadistic back-from-the-dead serial killer and child molester of the *Nightmare on Elm Street* series has become one of Hollywood's most important contemporary contributions to our national culture. The National Coalition on Television Violence conducted a 1991 poll of suburban children between the ages of ten to thirteen in which 66 percent of the students correctly identified Freddy Krueger—compared to a mere 36 percent who knew that Abraham Lincoln was a President of the United States.

Some of our current political leaders actually seem to endorse this choice of youthful role models. Tom Bradley, mayor of Los Angeles, issued a public proclamation that designated Friday, September 13, 1991, as official "Freddy Krueger Day" throughout the nation's second-largest city. His honor later defended this ceremonial gesture as an attempt to show civic support for L.A.'s most important industry; "Freddy Krueger Day" had been chosen to coincide with the theatrical release of *Freddy's Dead*, the sixth film installment in the highly profitable *Nightmare on Elm Street* series. Nevertheless, skeptical observers saw a cruel irony in the fact that the leader of violence-plagued Los Angeles should choose to honor a slasher from a cinematic nightmare that bore an increasing resemblance to the nightmarish brutality of the city's streets.

The inclination to turn murderous monsters into popular heroes is no longer an aberration; in the media culture it has become the order of the day. In February 1992, a nationally known novelty publishing company called Eclipse Entertainment acknowledged this development by issuing a highly publicized new set of prize collectibles for kids: serial killer trading cards. The 110 personalities celebrated in the initial "True Crime" offering included Charles Manson, Richard Ramirez, Ted Bundy, John Wayne Gacy, Jeffrey Dahmer, Juan Corona, and all your other favorites. While the front side of each card offered a photo of the criminal in question, the back included a detailed "box score," with information on the number of victims he chalked up, the preferred methods of murder, and the eventual fate of the killer. Valarie Jones, editor of the new series, defended her contribution to our culture as "an educational tool"; it is easy to envision children studying the murder statistics from their killer cards in the same way they memorize batting averages on baseball cards today.

Anyone who doubts that Hollywood actively promotes this fascination with evil should consider the crowd of agents and producers who immediately swarm over any mass murderer the moment he (or she) is apprehended. In January 1991, for instance, Florida police arrested a filthy, overweight, alcoholic prostitute with a bloated and sadly battered face on charges of murdering six male customers. This case of Aileen Carol Wuornos instantly set off what the *Los Angeles Times* described as a "frenzy" among Hollywood writers and producers, with more than a half-dozen production companies (including CBS Entertainment and Carolco Pictures) competing for the rights to her story. For today's ugliness-obsessed entertainment industry, the cruelty of her crimes, combined with the seediness of her circumstances, created an irresistible combination.

Stupidity and Selfishness

The chief alternative to this sort of viciousness is unassailable stupidity, a goofball innocence that Hollywood currently celebrates as a substitute for genuine likeability. The one supposedly endearing attribute of moronic Metalheads like Bill and Ted—and their even more popular counterparts Wayne and Garth—is their obtuse mindlessness, disguised by a laughable pretense of rock 'n' roll sophistica-

tion. In a sense, the addle-brained adolescent protagonists of the *Bill &
Ted* movies (1989 and 1991), *Wayne's World* (1992), and *Encino Man*
(1992) advance the familiar pop culture proposition that kids know
best, but they take the theme one step further: in their movies, *dumb*
kids know best.

White Men Can't Jump (1992) offered similar heroes: two incur-
ably inept basketball hustlers who are too lazy to toil at conventional
jobs, but too erratic and impulsive to make their athletic skills pay off
on a regular basis. Both men (Woody Harrelson and Wesley Snipes) are
overgrown teenagers, taking emotional and financial advantage of the
bright, hard-working, and responsible women who put up with them
for no apparent reason.

"Welcome to the new clod worship, a pop culture deification of the
asinine," writes Jan Stuart in a recent issue of *FanFare.* "Been to the
movies or theater lately? The joint is jumpin' with blowhard anti-role
models who combine Trump-size arrogance with the grace of Al Sharp-
ton . . . turning the ethos of the jerk inside out until jerkiness becomes
a kind of heroism. . . . By and large, that behavior takes as its ideal the
iconoclasm and unformed moral code of adolescent boys."

Stuart sees the same patterns of conduct among the heroes in well-
reviewed 1991 melodramas like *The Doctor* (with William Hurt as a
"sleazo surgeon"), *Regarding Henry* (with Harrison Ford as a "sleazo
attorney"), and *The Fisher King* (with Jeff Bridges as a "sleazo disk
jockey"). To these titles, one might add representatives of the growing
number of "selfish yuppie" comedies, including *Doc Hollywood, The
Super, Taking Care of Business, Other People's Money, Strictly Business,* and many others. In most of these films, the hateful hero ultimately achieves redemption (and raised consciousness) through some
fateful happenstance, like a car crash in a small town, a court sentence
requiring a landlord's residence in one of his own slum buildings, an
incident of throat cancer, or a convenient bullet to the brain. Nevertheless, before the inevitable deliverance, the audience spends its time in
the uncomfortable company of a collection of thoroughly distasteful
creeps.

None of this is in any way novel or revolutionary; honorable Hollywood precedents exist for central characters who exhibit every imaginable form of stupidity or selfishness. Stories about insensitive snobs
who get their comeuppance turned up regularly in the industry's

Golden Age—and long before that, Charles Dickens touched the world with a similar tale called *A Christmas Carol.* While Bill and Ted may not measure up as ideal intellectual role models for the younger generation, they are surely no more brain-damaged than the beloved Three Stooges. And for many years before Robert De Niro was even born, Jimmy Cagney owned the franchise on psychotic gangsters.

In the past, however, projects built around such problematic protagonists represented the exception; today they are very much the rule. The disturbing changes in the popular culture show up not so much in the on-screen presence of a few killers and cretins as in the virtual absence of anyone else. Traditional heroes no longer balance the deranged and pathetic characters who dominate so many contemporary films—particularly those projects that win the most conspicuous critical praise. Hollywood has not only abandoned larger-than-life heroes, but the industry seems to have lost all vision of the heroic elements in daily life—the selflessness and nobility of which ordinary citizens are consistently capable.

"Aiming Far Too Low"

No director in the history of motion pictures has been more attuned to that everyday heroism than the late—and much lamented—Frank Capra. In one statement of his artistic credo, the maker of *It's A Wonderful Life, Mr. Smith Goes to Washington, It Happened One Night,* and so many other great films declared: "Movies should be a positive expression that there is hope, love, mercy, justice, and charity. . . . It is the [filmmaker's] responsibility to emphasize the positive qualities of humanity by showing the triumph of the individual over adversities."

Capra's faith in those "positive qualities of humanity" is perhaps the most significant missing ingredient in today's popular culture.

In the mid-1970s the great director had lunch with *Los Angeles Times* film critic Charles Champlin and told him "that he no longer knew where the audience was or what it wanted, and that he had no heart or skill to make the kind of harsh and pessimistic films the new audience appeared to want."

Nearly twenty years later, at the time of Capra's death in September 1991, Champlin concluded that his old friend had been wrong. "It turned out the audience's real preferences had not changed that radically at all," he wrote. "A comforting number of filmgoers still wanted to escape, be reassured, be uplifted, have a good laugh or a good cry—the kinds of things that made Capra's films Capraesque."

Unfortunately, the industry had largely forgotten how to make such films, and so remained disastrously alienated from a huge potential audience. The new hostility to heroes had nothing to do with the dynamics of the marketplace, and instead reflected the obsessions of ambitious filmmakers who, eager to win respect as serious artists, adopted the embittered attitudes that had already conquered the world of "serious art."

In 1987, Dr. George Roche, president of Hillsdale College, wrote an eloquent and important book about the antiheroic vision that has come to dominate the thinking of the West—a vision that helps to rob both our personal and collective lives of all purpose and meaning. The title of that book, *A World Without Heroes*, precisely describes the cold and empty universe that Hollywood portrays again and again on screen.

Roche writes that "the antihero has nothing to worship but himself and his art, and is inescapably tugged down to the temporal, the mundane and the dark." By contrast, "The hero seeks not happiness but goodness, and his fulfillment lies in achieving it. . . . His example tells us that we fail, not by aiming too high in life, but by aiming far too low."

In the same way, Hollywood fails with its emphasis on ugliness—not by aiming too high, but by aiming far too low.

14

Bashing America

"We Have Become the Enemy"

In one sense, the current hostility to heroes reflects Hollywood's underlying attitude toward American civilization and all its works. According to its defenders, the entertainment industry focuses on violent, corrupt, and demented characters only because it is trying to provide an honest view of a violent, corrupt, and demented society.

Leading members of the entertainment establishment have become remarkably candid in expressing their bitter feelings toward their native land. "The United States is a land that has raped every area of the world," declared *Thelma and Louise* star Susan Sarandon in an interview in May 1991. In the same month, Sean Penn spoke to a press conference at the Cannes Film Festival about the rage expressed in his bloody, brooding directorial debut, *Indian Runner*. "I don't think it scratches the surface of the rage that is felt, if not acted upon, by *most* of the people in the country where I live," the outspoken star solemnly declared. "I was brought up in a country that relished fear-based religion, corrupt government, and an entire white population living on stolen property that they murdered for and that is passed on from generation to generation."

Two-time Oscar-winner Oliver Stone expressed similar sentiments when accepting the "Torch of Liberty Award" from the American Civil Liberties Union in September 1987. "Our own country has become a military-industrial monolith dedicated to the Cold War, in many ways as rigid and as corrupt at the top as our rivals the Soviets," he proclaimed, shortly before the total collapse of Communism in Eastern Europe. "We have become the *enemy*—with a security state now second to none. Today we have come to live in total hatred, fear, and the desire to destroy. Bravo. Fear and conformity have triumphed."

In Stone's view, "this Darth Vadian empire" of the United States must pay for its many sins in the near future. "I think America has to bleed," he told an interviewer for *American Film* in 1987. "I think the corpses have to pile up. I think American boys have to die again. Let the mothers weep and mourn."

While Stone expressed his public hopes for high casualties, other Hollywood heavyweights devised nonverbal means to express their contempt for patriotic conventions. In 1990 television star Roseanne Barr raised a considerable public furor (and risked her show's popularity) with her shrieking, spitting, crotch-grabbing rendition of the "Star-Spangled Banner" prior to a San Diego Padres baseball game.

In the rap music industry the antipatriotic imagery is even more explicit. Ice Cube's best-selling 1991 *Death Certificate* album boasted a cover photo of a flag-draped corpse on a morgue slab with the soles of its bare feet facing the camera; one big toe is prominently tagged with the label "Uncle Sam." Meanwhile, the popular, twenty-three-year-old rapper Paris enjoyed considerable success with his album *The Devil Made Me Do It*, released along with a nightmarish video that shows a jovial, top-hatted Uncle Sam suddenly transformed into a raging, bloodthirsty Satan. The controversial rap star Sister Souljah summed up the judgment of many in the entertainment industry with her 1991 single "The Final Solution": "We should've read the books and understood/That America is no damn good."

Antipathy to the Military

If these attitudes represented only off-screen opinions they would never merit serious discussion. Actors, directors, and popular musicians are unquestionably entitled to their private prejudices, and those ideas become significant only when they are advanced in a consistent and self-conscious manner in the popular culture.

Unfortunately, when it comes to the deep-seated disgust with America and its major institutions, the personal biases of the entertainment establishment show up with increasing regularity in the movies, television, and popular music.

Consider, for example, Hollywood's treatment of the military. In 1990 researchers from Smith College and New York University released the results of painstaking scientific analysis of a representative sample of forty-three years of feature films. "The thematic analysis reveals that since the mid-1960s the United States military has more likely been portrayed negatively than positively," concluded Professors Stanley Rothman, David J. Rothman, and Stephen P. Powers in their paper in *Society/Transaction*. Between 1946 and 1965, only 23 percent of movies portrayed the military in critical terms; between 1965 and 1989, those negative treatments jumped to 40 percent, with another 40 percent classified as "mixed." Concerning Washington's leadership of the armed services, the change in focus was even more pronounced. "In military movies where the government plays a role only 25 percent portrayed the government negatively prior to 1966. Since then 64 percent have done so."

This research project conclusively rebutted the common assumption that the Reagan era witnessed a notable upsurge in reflexively patriotic films that glorified our armed forces. While movies like *Top Gun* (1986), *Iron Eagle* (1986), and *Rambo* (1988) most certainly won huge audiences, they each featured rebellious, nonconformist, individualistic heroes struggling against a military establishment that was portrayed in largely unflattering terms.

In *Top Gun*, the central character, played by Tom Cruise, is known as "Maverick," and he takes great pains to live up to his name: in the course of the film he provokes the wrath of navy brass by breaking the rules of dogfighting, buzzing a control tower, and generally refusing to submit to authority. Rambo (Sylvester Stallone) is even more deeply alienated from a hopelessly corrupt establishment, and his final burst of gunfire in the film is reserved for the gigantic computer at the U.S. command post that's been directing his mission.

Looking over the general portrayal of armed forces personnel in the films of the 1980s, Rothman, Rothman, and Powers concluded that military figures were "variously portrayed as silly, hypocritical, unstable and/or psychotic."

The mediocre Dan Ackroyd/Chevy Chase comedy *Spies Like Us* (1985) demonstrated just how far filmmakers might go in ridiculing Pentagon top brass, even at the height of an era often identified with militant patriotism. The Russian armed services received far more sympathetic treatment from director John Landis than their U.S. counterparts, and at the climax of the picture the Soviets help to foil the evil plans of a loony American general who is willing to blow up the world in order to test the new "Star Wars" missile defense system.

The triumph of U.S. arms in the Gulf War did nothing to alter the entertainment industry's antipathy to the military; in fact, the surprising failure to capitalize on the public's enthusiastic support for Operation Desert Storm demonstrates the way that Hollywood's deeply held biases can interfere with its commercial self-interest.

While the battle raged in the Middle East, many observers speculated on the rash of exploitation films that would inevitably follow America's victory. Radio talk-show host Rush Limbaugh, for example, spoke with his 11 million listeners nearly every day about a fantasy project called *Gulf War Won,* which would star Clint Eastwood as George Bush, Pat Sajak as Dan Quayle, Limbaugh himself as Norman Schwarzkopf, and so forth.

Amazingly enough, none of the expected projects ever materialized: more than a year after cheering crowds welcomed home our triumphant GIs in an endless series of parades and ceremonies, the motion picture business continues to ignore the opportunity to exploit the most popular application of military power in some fifty years. While action director John McTiernan (*Die Hard, The Hunt for Red October*) discusses the possibility of developing some future Desert Storm project with best-selling novelist Tom Clancy, to date only one major studio film contained even a passing reference to the Gulf War. That ten-second visual gag—showing a Saddam Hussein look-alike surprised by a huge unexploded bomb that's dropped on his belly—came in the *Top Gun* spoof *Hot Shots!* (1991), a movie that mocked the supposed ineptitude of air force and navy flyers and made several satiric references to their technically inferior equipment.

Hollywood's lack of interest in exploiting the Gulf War stems, of course, from the industry's own ambivalence toward their nation's victory. Throughout the struggle in the Middle East, the film colony remained a center of antiwar sentiment, and innumerable entertainment industry insiders—led by Woody Harrelson, Kris Kristofferson, and Susan Sarandon—offered outspoken condemnations of administration policy. The talented young actor John Cusack spoke for many of his peers in a May 1991 interview in *Esquire*. "George Bush goes around massacring Iraqis and it's called collateral damage," he declared. "I saw a country so bloodthirsty it began to refer to a war in which real people were dying in football terms. . . . The worst part is that the American people were 100 percent behind it because they have nothing else to believe in."

With this contemptuous dismissal of the patriotic instincts of his fellow countrymen, Mr. Cusack offers one more example of Hollywood's disdainful attitude toward its audience. Show business sophisticates may "have nothing else to believe in," but the majority of Americans maintain their faith and pride in a wide range of national symbols and institutions—emphatically including the armed services of the United States. In its surprisingly unsympathetic attitude to the military, the entertainment establishment is driven more by its own inner demons than by any desire to please the public.

Evil Industrialists

The members of the military by no means stand alone as targets for Hollywood's contempt; the entertainment industry expresses similar cynicism regarding nearly all of our most important institutions.

A previous chapter provided detailed discussion of the popular culture's blatant and pervasive hostility toward organized religion, and in recent years American businessmen have received comparably intense abuse.

In their comprehensive analysis of prime-time programming in *Watching America* (1991), Lichter, Lichter, and Rothman discovered that "big business has become television's favorite villain. Before 1965 there were twice as many good guys as bad guys among corporate executives portrayed on prime time. In the following decade the proportion was reversed—two villains for every hero. *By 1980 a majority of the*

CEO's portrayed on prime time committed felonies" (italics added).

This association of capitalists with criminality represents the most extreme and obvious manifestation of Hollywood's hostility. The businessmen who appear week after week on network series not only engage in *economic* abuses like rent gouging, toxic waste dumping, union busting, and the manufacture of dangerous or shoddy products; they also regularly commit crimes of violence like murder, rape, assault, and robbery. The *Watching America* study found that in contemporary prime time, "although businessmen represented 12 percent of all characters in census-coded occupations, they accounted for 32 percent of the crimes these characters commit. Even this underestimates the venality of TV's businessmen, since their crimes tended to be either violent or sleazy. They committed 40 percent of the murders and 44 percent of the vice crimes like drug trafficking and pimping."

Needless to say, this image of illegal activity bears no resemblance whatever to contemporary reality. In contrast to the harsh facts of the streets, which show the destitute and disadvantaged strikingly overrepresented among violent lawbreakers, on prime time "Wealthy characters are far more likely to commit crimes than those identified as poor or middle class. . . . In particular, a stock criminal type is the businessman whose selfish pursuit of profit leads him into illegal activity. TV businessmen are the largest group of murderers aside from professional gangsters."

The extreme nature of this caricature undermines the argument that television's image of the corporate world merely corresponds to the changed perceptions of the public. Though many Americans may indeed assume that today's business leaders are corrupt and selfish, no one in his right mind actually believes that they are predominantly pimps and murderers.

Unfortunately, the prevailing vision of vicious tycoons has become so deeply embedded in the popular culture that it is now difficult to imagine any alternative presentation of the captains of industry and finance. In this context, it's important to remember that during Hollywood's Golden Age in the 1930s and '40s, businessmen frequently appeared in a highly sympathetic light. In the 1933 George Cukor classic, *Dinner at Eight,* Lionel Barrymore plays a decent and dignified shipping magnate, struggling to keep his company afloat; in the even more cherished family favorite *It's a Wonderful Life,* Jimmy Stewart's character George Bailey is a humane, compassionate, and likeable *banker*. From the perspective of 1990s Hollywood, the very idea of a "likeable banker" has become unthinkable. Another Rothman, Rothman, and Powers study (April 1991) showed that between 1945 and 1965, only 11 percent of feature films portrayed businessmen in negative terms, but in the two decades between 1965 and 1986 the incidence of unsympathetic portrayals soared to 67 percent!

Corrupt Cops

Despite the continued popularity of police officers as protagonists in movies and on television series, their status in the popular culture has also suffered a serious turn for the worse: long before the horrors of the Rodney King incident and its tragic aftermath, Hollywood had begun to reassess its previously supportive attitude toward the police. In the first two postwar decades, only 12 percent of sample movies presented the cops and the criminal justice system in a negative light. In the next two decades the percentage of critical portrayals nearly doubled—to 23 percent.

Moreover, nearly all of the cop heroes in contemporary films are loners and loose cannons who refuse to accept the authority of their ineffectual or corrupt superiors. From *Beverly Hills Cop* (1984) to *Cobra* (1986) to *Basic Instinct* (1992), the determined central character must disregard orders and take matters into his own hands in order to defeat his criminal opponents. The moment when this embattled officer is asked to turn in his badge by his stuffy and intolerant boss has become one of the most predictable plot points in today's police pictures.

Lichter, Lichter, and Rothman reported that television expressed an even more pronounced disillusionment with law-enforcement officials. "These days, TV's police commit crimes as often as everyone else. Moreover, even the good cops today have to contend with a corrupt criminal-justice system. Before 1975, nine out of ten shows affirmed the system's honor. Since then, fully half have portrayed it as corrupt. Today the favored law enforcers are private eyes and private citizens, who work outside the 'system.' More than ever on prime time, insiders break the law and outsiders enforce it."

"America on Trial"

Hollywood's dim view of our religious, military, business, and law-enforcement institutions coincides with its overall vision of America as a society that is cruel, corrupt, and hopelessly unjust.

Elements of intense and embittered social criticism turn up in even the most unlikely contexts, from teen sex comedies to futuristic thrillers, from tender love stories to cartoons for kids. In *An American Tail 2: Fievel Goes West* (1991), a disillusioned immigrant mouse in turn-of-the-century New York tells his family that they have made a terrible mistake to come to the New World. "They said America was the land of opportunity," moans "Poppa Mousekowitz" to his children. "But opportunity for what? To starve? At least in Russia we always had enough to eat."

By contrast, my own grandfather used to say that he thanked God every day of his life for leading him from the misery of Russia to this great and blessed land. Can anyone seriously doubt that his lifelong gratitude was more representative of the immigrant experience than the disillusionment of Steven Spielberg's cartoon mice?

Professor Stanley Rothman of Smith College, who has done more extensive work than any other analyst on the thematic evaluation of motion pictures and television, declared in 1991: "Movies which do not in some way put America on trial for mistakes made in the past and the present have become rarer and rarer."

A typical interchange occurred in Lawrence Kasdan's moving and superbly acted melodrama *Grand Canyon* (1991). As Danny Glover and Kevin Kline ride together through the blighted California community of Inglewood, Glover declares, "This neighborhood has gone to shit," to which Kline emphatically responds, "This whole country has gone to shit."

Without question, many Americans currently agree with that assessment—particularly with the nation still feeling the grip of economic hard times and reeling from the impact of the horrifying riots in Los Angeles. Public opinion polls in 1992 show relatively high percentages of our fellow citizens who take a pessimistic view of the nation's future and question the fundamental fairness of its economic and political system.

This present trend in popular sentiment cannot, however, explain

Hollywood's profoundly cynical view of American society, since that cynicism long predates the nation's sour state of mind. Even at recent moments of superheated patriotism—such as the flag-waving fervor that surrounded the Gulf War—the entertainment business stubbornly maintained its gloomy and critical attitude toward this country and its institutions. Long-term, detailed analyses of movies and television show that this attitude in the industry has prevailed for some twenty years now—despite dramatic ups and downs in the levels of popular optimism.

For instance, shortly after President Reagan swept forty-nine of fifty states with his celebratory "Morning in America" reelection campaign, *American Film* magazine wrote admiringly of the new "bleak chic" that had captured Hollywood. John Powers lavishly praised the crop of thrilling recent films that "paint a world where small towns breed monsters, where the family is limping if not crippled, where the unconscious dances giddy circles around good old horse sense. As they explore the underbelly of psyche and society these films force American viewers to confront the things most likely to offend and frighten our nervous decade: fornication, drugs, profanity, booze, nudity, disfigurement, sadomasochism, casual murder—the blackest whorls of the human mind."

The movie business has consistently focused a great deal of its energy on those dark corners of consciousness, even in years when respondents told pollsters of their strong approval of our national leadership and their boundless confidence in the nation's future. The fact that the grim mood of the moment happens to fall much closer to the industry's abiding alienation is no evidence that the entertainment establishment has suddenly begun responding to the people; it suggests, if anything, that the public may finally be feeling the influence of Hollywood's many years of persistent negativity.

Poisoning the Past

To an outrageous extent, that negativity turns up not only in portrayals of our present situation but in venomous evocations of the American past. The days when Hollywood captured the imagination of the entire world with stirring accounts of our heroic history have given way to an era of self-flagellation and irresponsible revisionism—with a series of preachy, politically correct, propagandistic presentations of our country's many crimes and misdemeanors.

On those relatively rare occasions when a contemporary filmmaker takes us on a journey into the nation's past, the implicit purpose almost always involves a searing indictment of some enormous American misdeed, whether it's our "genocide" against Native Americans (*Dances with Wolves*, 1990), our cruel wartime internment of Japanese-Americans (*Come See the Paradise*, 1990), the ruthless and successful government plot to murder a reformist President (*JFK*, 1991; *Ruby*, 1992), cruel exploitation of immigrant labor (*Far and Away* and *Newsies*, both 1992), the horrors of segregation in the American South (*Mississippi Burning*, 1988; *Heart of Dixie*, 1989; *The Long Walk Home*, 1990); our single-handed and irresponsible launching of the nuclear arms race (*Fat Man and Little Boy*, 1989), our arrogant imperialism in Latin America (*Missing*, 1982; *Under Fire*, 1983; *Salvador*, 1986; *Walker*, 1988; *The Old Gringo*, 1989), or, most notably, the shameful persecution of idealistic dissenters during the McCarthy era (*The Front*, 1976; *Daniel*, 1983; *Insignificance*, 1985; *The House on Carroll Street*, 1988; *Guilty by Suspicion*, 1991).

Most of these films bore only the most casual or careless connection to historical reality, but nevertheless drew warm reviews from a critical community more concerned with a movie's support for "enlightened" anti-American sentiments than with factual accuracy or aesthetic excellence. In a 1991 interview with the Washington newsletter *TV, etc.*, critic Tom Shales of the *Washington Post* acknowledged that *Dances with Wolves* struck him as "not only boring but almost unspeakably pretentious. I thought the film was reviewed for its social message or political message and not on any cinematic standards."

That social and political message, of course, involved a gigantic distortion of the American past and an absurdly idealized view of Indian society. As critic and film scholar Richard Grenier observes:

In the 1860s, the period of *Dances with Wolves*, some of the greatest generals of the Union Army (Sherman, Sheridan, Custer) led American troops against the bloodthirsty Sioux, who erupted in the midst of the Civil War in one of the most savage Indian uprisings in history. Along the western frontier, the Sioux massacred. They pillaged. They raped. They burned. They carried women and children into captivity. They tortured for entertainment. All this was their long-established custom, carried out, indeed, far more frequently against other Indian tribes than against whites. By converting these Sioux Indians into gentle, vaguely pacifist, environmentally responsible bucolics, Kevin Costner, in a state of holy empty-headedness, has falsified history as much as any time-serving Stalinist of the Red Decade.

Grenier makes the persuasive point that *Dances with Wolves* amounts to an ingenious new formula for Hollywood's antipatriotic themes, in which a hero can violently reject "evil America" and its diseased values without appearing patently disloyal. Because the alien culture that he chooses to join happens to be that of our indigenous aborigines, Costner's sensitive Lieutenant Dunbar still seems somehow quintessentially American. Screenwriter Michael Blake openly admitted: "I was afraid that sooner or later someone would say: 'You've got a movie where the hero's a traitor to his country. You can't have a movie like that.' But it never happened."

Even before the critical and commercial success of *Dances with Wolves,* the tendency to portray every imaginable episode in American history as some sort of disgrace had become so pronounced that it extended even to Hollywood's one recent attempt to dramatize the inspiring struggle for American independence.

Only a psychopathologist (or perhaps an exorcist) could possibly explain whatever possessed Warner Brothers to invest more than $35 million in *Revolution* (1985)—an incomparably awful eighteenth-century epic in which the American patriots in the Revolutionary War are actually portrayed as the bad guys!

The hilariously miscast Al Pacino plays a pacifist trapper from the Adirondack frontier who is forced to fight against his will when his teenage son is virtually kidnapped by the Continental Army; later, he and all his comrades are cheated of their promised pay by the corrupt new American government that replaces the British. English director Hugh Hudson seems intent on avenging his nation's battlefield embarrassments of two hundred years ago by presenting the rebellious colonists as an assemblage of crooks and bozos, while their long fight to establish a new nation is shown to be brutal and senseless. The unmistakably anti-American tenor of the entire enterprise helped to seal its doom—and to make *Revolution* one of the most notorious bombs of the entire decade.

The one tragic aspect of this fiasco's entirely predictable failure is that many industry insiders interpreted the public's tepid response as an indication of a general lack of interest in American history. Four years later, the entirely respectable box-office performance of the magnificent and deeply moving Civil War film *Glory* served to contradict this conclusion—as did the record-breaking ratings for the outstanding PBS series "The Civil War." When the entertainment industry offers explorations of the past that touch the passionately patriotic instincts of the people, then the public responds—but such uplifting endeavors remain unhappily infrequent.

Hollywood's Favorite War

The one period of our past to receive the most regular attention in the popular culture is the turbulent decade of the 1960s—the same era that spawned the angry, antiestablishment outlook that still holds sway in Tinseltown. Dramatizations of the issues and events of the '60s allow Hollywood to pursue many of its favorite themes concerning our "sick society," portraying this country as brutal, repressive, and hypocritical, while glorifying those free-spirited revolutionaries who challenged middle-class mores and traditional values. As one of the most divisive and painful episodes in our history, the Vietnam War provides filmmakers with an especially inviting opportunity to portray America at its worst; accordingly, this tragic conflict has recently become Hollywood's favorite war.

During the last ten years, the number of motion pictures about the war in Vietnam has far exceeded the total treatments in that period of all the other wars in our history *combined;* with the arrival of network series like "Tour of Duty" and "China Beach," die-hard fans can even see the Indochina conflict replayed on prime time, week after week. When I asked the producer of one of these shows how he could account for the industry's wildly disproportionate attention to this one conflict, he cited Vietnam's proximity to the present day and the fact that millions of living Americans personally served there. These explanations, however, can hardly suffice: the Gulf War remains a far more immediate and vivid memory and yet, as noted earlier, it has sparked no interest from Hollywood, while the number of surviving veterans of World War II remains considerably larger than those who fought in Vietnam.

The deeper reasons for the special attraction to the Indochina conflict involve its unique status as the only war we ever lost and the unparalleled possibilities it provides to make America—and its military—look bad. As it happens, members of the baby-boom generation who came of age during the Vietnam years increasingly dominate the entertainment industry, and their political consciousness still reflects the antiwar passions of the fondly remembered protests of their youth. With the singular and celebrated exception of Oliver Stone, remarkably few Hollywood figures ever served in the war and their perspective on Vietnam remains that of stateside demonstrators who contemptuously derided our fighting men as "baby killers."

That perspective helps to explain the fact that recent movies about Indochina almost always show American GIs perpetrating ghastly atrocities against innocent civilians—despite the painstakingly plain and well-documented historical record that shows that only a tiny minority of our troops ever engaged in such brutalities.

This smear against the members of our armed forces reached its irresponsible extreme in Norman Jewison's tedious tear-jerker *In Country* (1989), starring Bruce Willis as a shattered, shell-shocked Vietnam vet (is there any other kind in today's movies?) and Emily Lloyd as his teenage niece. The girl wants to learn more about her father, who died in the war shortly before she was born, and she is shocked when she discovers some long-forgotten letters that suggest his guilt in some appalling atrocities. Her mother (Joan Allen) tries to comfort her in a tender scene in which they hug each other on a bed. "Larry has a friend that was in Vietnam and he killed a whole family of people in a hut," the older woman helpfully explains. "A mother, a father, three children, some uncles and aunts and a grandmother. Killed every one of them . . ."

The daughter is naturally horrified. "Did Daddy kill like that?" she asks.

"I don't know," sighs her mother, "but it wouldn't be unusual if he did. *That's what they were sent over there to do.*"

This casual characterization of the American mission in Vietnam is a slander on every one of the more than 3 million men and women who served there.

Vicious Vets, Pristine Protesters

It is, however, entirely typical of Hollywood's invariably insulting treatment of Vietnam veterans, who are unfailingly stereotyped as twitching, crazed, haunted, dangerous, and unpredictable characters who have never recovered from their nightmarish wartime experiences. Many of our most prominent actors crave to play these pathetic specimens—in the same way that their colleagues pine for parts as prostitutes or psychotic killers. Christopher Walken (*The Deerhunter*, 1978), Don Johnson (*Cease Fire*, 1985), John Lithgow (*Distant Thunder*, 1988), Robert De Niro and Ed Harris (*Jacknife*, 1989), and Tim Robbins (*Jacob's Ladder*, 1990) all play emotional cripples permanently warped by the war in supposedly "compassionate" films—not to mention those well-known *physical* casualties, Jon Voight (*Coming Home*, 1978) and Tom Cruise (*Born on the Fourth of July*, 1989). Many people forget that before John Rambo became a grunting, muscle-bound avenger in *Rambo: First Blood Part II* (1985), he was just another nutty Vietnam Vet with a chip on his shoulder who single-handedly destroys an Oregon town.

This original Rambo film (*First Blood*, 1982) helped to advance the assumption that anyone who served in Indochina is a violent explosion waiting to happen—an idea eagerly adopted by lazy screenwriters throughout the industry who, in literally hundreds of TV shows and movies, used a character's background as a Vietnam vet as an easy explanation for every kind of sociopathic behavior. In the action extravaganzas, *Lethal Weapon* (1987) and *Die Hard 2* (1989), for instance, the filmmakers give "depth" to the horribly bloodthirsty bad guys by inserting gratuitous passing references to their service in Vietnam.

On November 10–13, 1989, a group of real-life vets responded to years of negative stereotyping by organizing a Vietnam Veterans Film Festival in Dallas. Under the heading "The Vet Strikes Back!" they protested Hollywood's imposition of "Post Celluloid Stress Disorder" on those who had served their country halfway around the world. "The movies were all produced by persons who had no firsthand exposure to Vietnam," charged the festival's unsigned mission statement, urging the entertainment industry "to let someone else be the villain and give the White Hat back to the veteran who earned it with his service."

In contrast to the disparaging treatment of those who participated personally in the war effort, Hollywood paints only the most glowing portrait of their contemporaries who stayed home and protested American policy. In fact, the years of antiwar activism are viewed as positively paradisiac in films like *The Big Chill* (1983), in which the yuppie characters look back on their radical days at the University of Michigan as a lost Eden of innocent, incomparable idealism. In *Running on Empty* (1988), Judd Hirsch and Christine Lahti play a couple of aging radicals who have been living as fugitives since they blew up a building in the '60s; naturally, they are a passionate, fun-loving couple and model parents to their two terrific kids.

Left-wing crusaders from the '60s are also the heroes in *Rude Awakening* (1989, with Eric Roberts and Cheech Marin), *True Believer* (1989, with James Woods and Robert Downey, Jr.), *Flashback* (1990, with Dennis Hopper and Kiefer Sutherland), *Far Out Man* (1990, with Tommy Chong and Judd Nelson), and *Class Action* (1991, with Gene Hackman and Mary Elizabeth Mastrantonio). All five films contrast the "selfish materialism" of the 1980s with the "commitment," "love," and "activism" of the glorious countercultural past, and show aging idealists who are able to win over younger cynics through the sheer strength of their shining personalities. The fact that each of these pictures bombed abysmally at the box office indicates that the mass audience feels the tug of 1960s nostalgia far less powerfully than do the members of the Hollywood establishment.

Nevertheless, the industry's power structure plows forward with further projects extolling the virtues of the failed and self-indulgent revolutionary posers of twenty-five years ago. Even in its heyday in the late '60s, the Black Panther Party never attracted more than a few hundred active members, but by 1992 it had inspired the development of no less than *five* feature film projects by producers such as Joel Silver, Oliver Stone, and Robert De Niro. This explosion of interest centers on a long-vanished sect that has been conclusively connected to at least a dozen politically motivated murders of its own members or hangers-on, and whose most prominent leaders have all met singularly sordid fates. Nevertheless, producer Matt Tabak, who is developing one of these Panther projects for Warner Brothers, told the *Los Angeles Times* that "we're trying to create a story that's emotional and powerful. We look upon the movement as a very positive one, but one that was repressed by white society."

Hollywood's deep commitment to celebrating radicals and outsiders leads the industry to take some extraordinary commercial risks that are simply inexplicable in terms of financial self-interest. In 1981, Paramount committed a reported $40 million to *Reds,* Warren Beatty's affectionate tribute to the brief, troubled life of John Reed, an early leader of the American Communist Party whose body rests in a place of honor in the Kremlin wall. No one needed a crystal ball to predict that the mass audience would find it difficult to relate to this doomed Bolshevik: despite winning the Best Director Oscar for Beatty, the picture fell an estimated $20 million short of recouping its investment.

For the second half of 1992, the major studios have planned three comparably expensive and ambitious film biographies, with Denzel Washington starring in Spike Lee's *Malcolm X,* Jack Nicholson playing the lead in Danny De Vito's *Hoffa,* and Robert Downey, Jr., impersonating Charlie Chaplin in Sir Richard Attenborough's *Chaplin*—a film that reportedly emphasizes the great comedian's embittered exile from the United States in 1952 at the height of the McCarthy era. Needless to say, all three of the chosen subjects provide the filmmakers abundant opportunities to emphasize injustice, intolerance, corruption, and hypocrisy in the bad old U.S.A. One can only marvel at the fact that major studios have announced no plans to balance such downbeat tales by offering biographical epics with more affirmative potential: despite the unmistakable potential for profit and popularity, patriotic projects are flatly out of fashion in the film industry.

Boyhood Enthusiasms

For me, this sorry situation involves a very personal poignance as I recall the movies that aroused my most passionate enthusiasms as a small boy. At age seven I went three times to see *The Great Locomotive Chase* (1956), starring Fess Parker as a fearless Union officer who leads a daring raid behind enemy lines to steal a key Confederate train. The next year I thrilled to *Johnny Tremain,* which took me to Colonial Boston along with a poor but courageous boy who joins the Sons of Liberty and takes part in the early stages of the struggle for Independence. I also loved *The Buccaneer* (1958), with Andrew Jackson and pirate Jean Lafitte winning the Battle of New Orleans; *The Horse Soldiers* (1959), starring John Wayne and William Holden as Union cavalry officers in the Civil War; *John Paul Jones* (1959), with Robert Stack as the great naval hero of the American Revolution; and, of course, John Wayne's two-hour-and-forty-minute epic, *The Alamo* (1960), with Davy Crockett, Jim Bowie, and Colonel Travis sacrificing their lives with incomparable gallantry for the cause of Texas independence.

During the same era of my boyhood, I savored additional historical adventures on TV, including "The Swamp Fox" (about the dashing Revolutionary War raider Francis Marion), the famous "Davy Crockett" segments from Disney, the sweeping "Victory at Sea" World War II documentary series, and marvelous old movies like *Abe Lincoln in Illinois* (1940), *The Devil and Daniel Webster* (1941), and *Drums Along the Mohawk* (1939), which my parents let me stay up to watch on the Saturday night "Late Show."

I still recall every one of these long-ago entertainments with enormous affection, though I would never go so far as to offer them my blanket critical endorsement. It's easy to spot the artistic and historical shortcomings in such projects, to decry their jingoistic simplicity and to lament the way that America's enemies are callously reduced to two-dimensional bad guys. From a contemporary and politically correct perspective, one might well argue that my endless exposure to such blood-and-guts sagas between the impressionable ages of seven and twelve permanently warped my tender young mind by implanting the dubious proposition that our country's problems could all be solved on the battlefield.

Nevertheless, I miss the energetic, flag-waving films of my boyhood and regret that comparable projects have found no place in today's movie mix. Whatever their flaws, such stories served to fire my imagination with visions of a glorious past that I somehow shared with my classmates and neighbors. It didn't matter that my mother had immigrated from Germany in 1934, or that my father's family arrived here from Russia after World War I; Hollywood's historical spectaculars helped me to identify with Andy Jackson and Abe Lincoln and encouraged the idea that I had every right to claim their legacy as my own. By emphasizing the selflessness of previous generations in the cause of liberty, these stirring sagas fostered both a feeling of pride and a sense of obligation. They also spurred an interest in the more serious study of history—in a way that gloomy guilt-inducers like *Dances with Wolves* or *Come See the Paradise* never could. Even the violent scenes in the old patriotic pictures, with their emphasis on the discipline and sacrifice of the battlefield, conveyed a far less damaging message than the random urban bruality and individualized killing of contemporary kiddie fare like *Kindergarten Cop,* or *Teenage Mutant Ninja Turtles,* or *Die Hard* and *Lethal Weapon*—not to mention the seemingly endless instalments of *Nightmare on Elm Street* or the *Friday the 13th* series.

Exporting Ugliness

The dark visions that Hollywood offers of our present and our past not only influence the attitudes of children and adults in this country, but increasingly shape the image of America in the world at large.

At the same time that the entertainment industry has been losing the support and enthusiasm of domestic consumers, the foreign appetite for American popular culture has dramatically intensified. Inflation-adjusted revenues for U.S. feature films from outside our borders rose 124 percent between 1985 and 1990; as a result, nearly half of all movie income now comes from abroad, compared to only 30 percent in 1980. The trend is expected to become even more pronounced in the years ahead. As James G. Robinson, chairman of Morgan Creek Productions, observed in March 1992: "All of the real growth in the coming years will be overseas."

This significant shift in the source of Hollywood's sustenance means that the industry feels more free than ever before to take risks on movies with messages that are openly anti-American. It no longer matters so much if a picture "plays in Peoria"—so long as it plays in Phnom Penh.

In a sense, the hostile view of American life conveyed by so many recent films, or by worldwide TV hits like "Dallas," connects with the deep resentments felt in many corners of the globe concerning this country's post–Cold War preeminence. If U.S. realities are as harsh and venal as Hollywood suggests, then moviegoers around the world have less reason to feel envy for this society, or dissatisfaction with their own.

Other observers suggest that the astonishing international success of American popular culture occurs *in spite* of the recent critical themes in that culture, and not because of them. "What is it about America, then, that has so captured the world's imagination?" asks Richard Grenier. "Aside from the country's prominence, there seems to have been an irresistible magnetism about a whole assemblage of American attitudes—optimism, hope, belief in progress, profound assumptions of human equality, informality—often more apparent to foreigners than to Americans themselves, that the outside world has found compelling. Over many decades these attitudes became so entrenched in world opinion as 'American' that in recent times, when certain Hollywood films have taken on a distinctly negative tone, America has still retained its dramatic power, Hollywood, as it were, living on its spiritual capital." As Ben Wattenberg suggests, "People everywhere want to share the American experience, to get a bite at the apple of individualism."

Despite enduring aspects of the attraction to American images and ideals, there is reason to question that this infatuation can indefinitely survive the global impact of an entertainment industry whose overriding obsession with ugliness so often involves the public trashing of the very society it represents; it is increasingly unclear how much longer Hollywood can go on "living on its spiritual capital." While the populist products of Hollywood's Golden Age most certainly encouraged the world's love affair with America, today's nihilistic and degrading attempts at entertainment may, in the long run, produce the opposite effect, helping to isolate this country as a symbol of diseased decadence.

The English-born David Puttnam, for one, feels fierce concern for the messages that American popular culture now broadcasts to the world, in contrast to the days of his childhood when

the image that was being projected overseas was of a society of which I *wanted* to be a member.

Now cut to twenty years later—the image that America began projecting in the 1970s, of a self-loathing, very violent society, antagonistic within itself—that patently isn't a society that any thinking person in the

Third World or Western Europe or Eastern Europe would wish to have anything to do with. America has for some years been exporting an extremely negative notion of itself.

So you get into this strange paradox, in which you ask, "Which is more honest?" I've been in this country enough to know that the image America projects now is not an honest one. This is a really wonderful country to a very great extent.

The overwhelming majority of our citizens would, of course, enthusiastically agree with him. With all our faults and unfinished business, Americans of every ethnic origin feel passionately patriotic and display a deep-seated sense of gratitude for the many blessings of the land they love; particularly at moments of international crisis, these underlying emotions are evident and unmistakable. By ignoring—and even insulting—these feelings, the cynical sophisticates who run Hollywood not only separate themselves and their work from the domestic mainstream, but risk the alienation of serious and sympathetic people from around the world.

"A world power, if it is to maintain its position, needs to generate respect for its culture, not only for its miliary prowess . . . ," warned Irving Kristol in 1992. "American popular culture today is less an ornament of American democracy than a threat to this democracy."

Unless the entertainment industry undertakes a comprehensive change in course, that threat can only escalate, with consequences to be considered in the pages that follow.

PART V

AN INESCAPABLE INFLUENCE

Denial Behavior

A Cultural Nuthouse

In the wake of the horrifying riots in Los Angeles, thoughtful observers of every political persuasion began taking a fresh look at the connection between media messages and antisocial behavior.

"Now we live in a cultural nuthouse, a mad world of blood, torture and murder that surrounds us in the movies and follows us home when we turn on TV 'entertainment,'" editorialized A. M. Rosenthal in *The New York Times* (May 5, 1992). ". . . Violence made fashionable in the cause of a buck is unworthy of people of talent. Aren't those who do that becoming ashamed of themselves? Haven't they discovered that ketchup can become blood?"

In their most recent responses to such charges, leaders of the entertainment industry frankly acknowledge the appalling elements in the "cultural nuthouse" they have built, but they refuse to accept the idea that this ominous structure has significantly influenced society.

Instead of defending the content of their work, they simply deny its impact.

This denial generally takes two forms:

First, the industry apologists insist that popular entertainment is by its very nature inconsequential, and that no one is seriously damaged by the fleeting images or subtle themes in a movie, TV show, or popular song. As the Hollywood establishment never tires of pointing out, several decades of research by social scientists have failed to produce conclusive, irrefutable proof that brutality and promiscuity in a product of the mass media can *cause* destructive behavior in the real world.

Second, the princes of the popular culture relentlessly remind us that their dark visions merely reflect the unpleasant realities around us. Their product is more disturbing, violent, and sexually explicit than ever before because they are responding in an honest and artistic way to powerful trends in the society. All those who blame the entertainment industry for our social problems are simplistically confusing cause and effect, and scapegoating the messenger for delivering bad news.

One or the other of these two arguments is solemnly cited whenever anyone dares to question the values that currently prevail in our popular culture. Both lines of reasoning deserve full and frank discussion.

Hollywood 4, Straw Men 0

In March 1992, I took part in a well-publicized panel discussion on the global impact of popular culture sponsored by the American Enterprise Institute in Washington. Seated to my immediate right at the long table of participants was Mr. Jack Valenti, the unfailingly articulate and courtly president of the Motion Picture Association of America, and the most prominent spokesman for the Hollywood establishment. In the course of an occasionally heated exchange of views, Mr. Valenti made an emphatic statement that neatly summed up the industry's first line of defense in all discussions of its impact on society. "I have examined the archives of people who write on socological things in this country and sociologists, and I've found that social scientists are like psychiatrists in a murder trial," Valenti declared. "The prosecution has one . . . and the defense has one. . . . *But I haven't found anybody who has said that movies cause anybody to do anything.*"

Along similar lines, Mike Medavoy, chairman of TriStar Pictures and one of the most thoughtful and respected of all motion picture executives, told a 1991 meeting of Hollywood political activists that even though he personally disliked watching violence on screen, "to make a claim that films are *responsible* for violence in society is ludicrous."

In January 1992, *Los Angeles Times* columnist Robert A. Jones offered a more detailed explanation of film's allegedly limited ability to influence its audience. "The truth is this: the power of a movie tends to last only as long as the lights are down and the screen flickers," he wrote. "While you're watching, it owns you. But as soon as you walk out of the theater and the cold air hits your face, the movie starts to evaporate, almost like it's leaking through your skin. By the time you reach the parking lot, it's mostly gone."

This reassuring notion turns up time and again in the industry's efforts to confound its critics. An especially eloquent and effective attack on those of us who try to draw a connection between media violence and its real-world counterpart came from Teller, one half of the celebrated Penn and Teller magic-and-comedy duo, who wrote an Op-Ed piece for *The New York Times* in January 1992. In it, he derided those

> who seem to think that if we stop showing rape in movies people will stop committing it in real life. Anthropologists call this "magical thinking." It's the same impulse that makes people stick pins in voodoo dolls, hoping to cripple an enemy. It feels logical, but it does not take into account that rape predates home video by thousands of years.
>
> Zealots have long tried to prove that "evil" fiction causes wickedness in the real world. But the facts fail to cooperate.... Those who want us to give up our freedom disagree. They claim people are not smart enough to tell make-believe from reality. Give us a break! When one pays seven dollars to go into a theater to see big pictures moving on a wall, one does not have to be a mental giant to realize you are watching a movie. It makes you wonder how they explain the millions of people who saw *Psycho* without stealing bankrolls or bumping off blondes.

With this elegant flourish, the magician brought off a rhetorical sleight of hand, imputing to his ideological opponents opinions that they do not hold and demolishing positions that they had never advanced.

To the best of my knowledge, none of the prominent participants in the current national debate on media values has ever suggested that "if we stop showing rape in movies people will stop committing it in real life"; nor has anyone seriously suggested that "people are not smart enough to tell make-believe from reality."

Instead of confronting the substantive concerns of those who question Hollywood's excesses, what Teller and the other commentators quoted above have done is to set up convenient and highly vulnerable straw men. Naturally, their self-contained debate against these phantoms allows them to achieve a magnificent victory, with a final score reading Hollywood 4, Straw Men 0.

Essential Distinctions

In an attempt to avoid the application of such deceptive tactics to the arguments advanced in this book, I want to leave no room for confusion about what I *am* saying—and what I am *not* saying—about the popular culture's impact on society.

All future disputants in this controversy, please take note:

• I do not claim that media messages *cause* destructive behavior, but I do contend that they *encourage* it. I have never suggested that Hollywood is single-handedly responsible for America's social problems but I do believe that the entertainment industry exacerbates them and that it has become an important contributing factor in many of our current difficulties.

• At the same time, I never stress the pernicious power of *one* movie, or one TV show, or one hit song; what concerns me is the accumulated impact of irresponsible messages that are repeated hour after hour, year after year. The most significant problems of the popular culture stem from the pervasive presence of antisocial material, not from a few isolated examples of offensiveness.

With these essential distinctions in mind, I believe that some of the most outspoken critics of Hollywood's values make a serious mistake when they try to indict the industry by emphasizing a handful of shocking episodes in which unbalanced individuals injured themselves or others by imitating behavior they saw on screen.

We have all read lurid press accounts of such cases, describing the tragic toll of twenty-six people who killed themselves in games of Russian roulette shortly after *The Deer Hunter* aired on national TV; or the fourteen-year-old girl who meticulously copied the murders she saw in the movie *Heathers* (1990) by organizing a game of croquet and a picnic in which she poisoned two of her best friends; or the two sixteen-year-olds who put bullets through their heads while listening again and again to Ozzy Osbourne's "Suicide Solution"; or the four Oklahoma high school dropouts who recently gang-raped and battered two of their classmates while repeatedly playing a tape of the rap song "Gangster of Love"—which specifically glorifies just such an assault.

These and many similar incidents are most certainly dramatic and disturbing, but the lawsuits and public controversy surrounding them only serve to distract attention from the more significant questions about Hollywood and society.

The most profound problem with the popular culture isn't its immediate impact on a few vulnerable and explosive individuals, but its long-term effect on all the rest of us. The deepest concerns about Hollywood go beyond the industry's role in provoking a handful of specific crimes and involve its contribution to a general climate of violence and self-indulgence.

A Clear Consensus

The entertainment establishment responds to these concerns by supplementing its standard rhetorical tricks with a few laughably bald-faced lies. On May 18, 1992, Barbara Dixon, Jack Valenti's colleague as spokesperson for the Motion Picture Association of America, told the *Los Angeles Times:* "We have dealt with this issue for a long time and have looked at a number of studies. According to the First Amendment lawyers who have handled the issue for us, none of [the studies] say that motion picture violence affects the behavior of people."

If Ms. Dixon has accurately summarized the report she received from her lawyers, then she should immediately seek more competent legal representation: in fact, more than three thousand research projects and scientific studies between 1960 and 1992 have confirmed the connection between a steady diet of violent entertainment and aggressive and antisocial behavior.

In a comprehensive 1982 report, published along with five thick volumes of social science surveys, the Surgeon General of the United States concluded that "there is a clear consensus among most researchers that television violence leads to aggressive behavior." Or, as the American Psychological Association declared in a 1991 resolution following a five-year task-force investigation: "The conclusion drawn on the basis of twenty-five years of research . . . is that viewing televised violence may lead to increases in aggressive attitudes, values, and behavior, particularly in children."

Scientific and academic support for this conclusion has increased year after year, with official statements linking media messages and antisocial conduct from the American Academy of Pediatrics, the American Medical Association, the National Institute of Mental Health, the National Commission on the Causes and Prevention of Violence, the U.S. Public Health Service, the National Parent-Teacher Association, the U.S. Attorney General's Task Force on Family Violence, and the National Education Association. Professor Aletha Huston of the University of Kansas recently declared: "Virtually all independent scholars agree. We keep pumping children with the message that violence is the way to solve their problems—and some of it takes hold."

In light of the nearly universal support for this viewpoint, it is increasingly difficult to understand how Jack Valenti and other industry insiders can continue to claim that the notion of the media's destructive impact is somehow an "open question" in the scientific community. It is an unsettled issue only in the sense that every hypothesis remains perpetually on trial, always subject to further research and review. In the social sciences, nothing can be proven beyond all doubt, and even the best-established theories and assumptions attract occasional challenges. When it comes to the proposition that the popular culture exerts a harmful influence on our children, however, remaining doubters have been recently deluged by a wealth of new studies that leave little room for confusion.

In November 1990, twenty-five leading academics and media researchers gathered in Pittsburgh for a conference on "The Impact of the Media on Children and the Family." Participants included distinguished faculty members from universities ranging from Yale to Northwestern, from Duke to Michigan State, from Rutgers to the University

of Wisconsin, and they presented more than thirty papers and work-
shops in the course of the three-day program. Barbara Hattemer, one
of the organizers of the conference, reported, "Given the diversity of
participants, they reached a surprising consensus that values in much
of the mass media, especially in violent and sexually explicit materials,
are on a collision course with traditional family values and the protection of children."

As a follow-up to the discussions in Pittsburgh, Hattemer under-
took a systematic review of all the available literature on the impact of
the most brutal and graphic elements in the media. "This review found
harmful effects in 86 percent of the studies and ends the debate about
whether or not there is harm," she wrote.

Research Perspectives

Highlights from research reports released by an array of scholars
over the past several years offer some intriguing insights on the way
that media messages alter our perspective:

• Dr. Jennings Bryant of the University of Alabama declares that
"some of the most durable and important effects of watching television
come in the form of subtle, incremental, cumulative changes in the way
we view the world." He describes these changes as "stalagmite
effects—cognitive deposits build up almost imperceptibly from the
drip-drip-drip of television's electronic limewater." These cumulative
effects are particularly potent for adolescents who are going through a
"turbulent time of life in which very insecure people struggle with their
self-concepts and their values on a daily basis . . . when values appear
to be quite frail and very malleable." Dr. Bryant cites three carefully
constructed research studies which indicate that "heavy exposure to
prime-time programming featuring sexual intimacy between unmarried people can clearly result in altered moral judgment."

• American teenagers most certainly receive that "heavy exposure"
to sexual messages in the media. Dr. Bradley S. Greenberg of Michigan
State University reports that adolescents take in some three thousand
to four thousand references to sexual activity in movies and television
each year. If they happen to watch MTV, the total goes even higher.

"One hour per day of viewing MTV," Dr. Greenberg concludes, "would add 1,500 more video-sex experiences on an annual basis to the teenager's imagination." He also points to several research projects which show that sexually explicit material leaves most viewers notably "less satisfied with their partners—with their affection, physical appearance, and sexual performance."

• In September 1991, the Centers for Disease Control reported a crisis in the teen suicide rate—which has increased by more than 400 percent since 1950. In one twelve-month period, more than a million teenagers attempted suicide, with 276,000 sustaining injuries serious enough to require medical attention. In a CDC survey of 11,631 students, an astonishing 8.3 *percent said they had actually tried to commit suicide* at some point in their lives. Both the National Education Association and the American Medical Association have pointed to popular music as a significant contributing factor in this crisis. During the summer of 1990, the AMA issued an official statement condemning the harmful themes exploited by many rock 'n' roll artists. Dr. William C. Scott, chairman of the AMA Council on Scientific Affairs, explained that certain types of music "may present a real threat to the physical health and emotional well-being of especially vulnerable children and adolescents." Examples of self-destructive messages abound, including the hit song "Suicide Solution," by Ozzy Osbourne, which tells his fans:

Suicide is slow with liquor,
Take a bottle, drown your sorrows.

More recently, in the spring of 1992, the critically acclaimed band The Jesus and Mary Chain released a single called "Reverence," in which the artists declared:

I wanna die just like Jesus Christ . . . and go see Paradise.
I wanna die just like JFK . . . on a sunny day.

Studies conducted at Columbia University and the University of California at San Diego, and reported in the *New England Journal of Medicine*, indicate that such suicidal messages have an especially potent and immediate impact. Researchers reported that television programs and news reports on the subject of teen suicide produced a measurable increase in the rate of adolescents taking their own lives in the one week immediately following such broadcasts.

• Caryl Rivers, professor of communications at Boston University, suggests that teenagers in the inner-city community are especially vulnerable to the media's glorification of brute force. "When you tell young males that violence is glamorous, that it's wonderful to be macho and that you should get away with whatever you can to get what you want, this is a dangerous message," she says. While middle-class kids may channel their media-roused aggressions into educational or economic competition, "ghetto kids don't have those avenues available to them . . . so they take out their aggressions and try to satisfy their ambitions in the streets. . . . . Research studies have shown that people who view violent movies and TV do become desensitized to violence and their attitudes become more permissive."

• Violent messages in the media are aimed with particular intensity at the very young and have become a major feature of so-called children's programming. Dr. George Gerbner, former dean of the Annenberg School of Communications at the University of Pennsylvania, authored an alarming study entitled *Violence Profile 1967–1989: Enduring Patterns,* in which he reported that more than 90 percent of all programs offered during children's prime viewing hours are violent. For the Saturday morning time slot during which so many parents entrust their little ones to the tender care of the tube, children's programming contains an average of more than twenty-five violent acts per hour. "Young viewers who watch a lot of TV are more likely to agree that it is almost always right to hit someone if you are mad at them for a good reason," Dr. Gerbner reports.

• In its monitoring of more than 350 children's cartoon episodes between 1990 and 1991, the National Coalition on Television Violence found that 72 percent of them contained more than ten acts of violence per hour. Many titles, such as "Cookie's Cartoon Club," "Dragon Warrior," "GI Joe," and "Toxic Crusaders," contained more than sixty moments of mayhem per hour—or one each minute. In terms of violent messages, children's movies are often even worse than the programming on television. *Teenage Mutant Ninja Turtles* featured 194 violent acts; its sequel offered a still impressive 179. These motion pictures helped to teach their enthusiastic young viewers such valuable skills as punching, kicking, throwing, bashing, socking, poking, and choking. The heroes not only use their nunchakus to damage their opponents, but also demonstrate their resourcefulness by adapting innocuous items (sausages, a yo-yo) for violent purposes. After the release of the first *Turtles* movie, a team of professors from Wheelock and Lesley colleges in Massachusetts polled seventy-three educators in nineteen states and found that 95 percent of the respondents could identify examples of classroom aggressive behavior linked to the film.

• Dr. Thomas Radecki, research director of the National Coalition on Television Violence, points out that the destructive impact of the popular culture is "not just a kids' issue. There is overwhelming evidence that adults as well as children are affected by the glamorization and promotion of violence. TV-watching adults are more likely to purchase handguns, support military solutions to world problems, and overestimate the amount of violence in the real world." Dr. George Gerbner's twenty years of research at the University of Pennsylvania confirm that the impact of the entertainment industry reaches into every age, education level, and income group in the society, though people respond to its messages very differently. Susceptibility to a given television program with sexual or violent content varies greatly, with the majority of people feeling no short-term effects from what they see, but 20 to 30 percent of those viewing the same program or film becoming fearful or depressed, and seeing themselves as the victim. Most alarmingly, 7 to 11 percent of those viewing the program or film will "mainline" what they see and want to go out and replicate some of the actions of the characters.

• Dr. Brandon Centerwall, a psychiatrist at the University of Washington, spent several years assessing the impact of television by analyzing the incidence of violence in various communities before and after TV was introduced. He achieved what Dr. Joseph Strayhorn, child psychiatrist at Allegheny General Hospital, termed "impressive results . . . that demonstrated that the introduction of television into communities resulted in increases in violent and aggressive behavior." Dr. Centerwall, who published his conclusions in the June 1992 issue of *The Journal of the American Medical Association,* reported that our prolonged exposure to violent television programs produces ten thousand extra murders every year in the United States, and suggested that our overall crime rate would be half what it is today had TV never been introduced. Dr. Centerwall further identified violent television programming as a "causal factor" in some 70,000 annual rapes and 700,000 injurious assaults.

Corporate Arrogance

In a stunning display of corporate arrogance, the major entertainment conglomerates disregard the conclusions of all the leading researchers and continue to insist that their work has no harmful impact on society.

With almost ritualized regularity, their official representatives repeat the claim that scientific investigations show "mixed" results on the question of media influence. "There are so many yesses and nos in the literature that it's confusing," declared CBS vice president David Blank in one typical statement in 1978. In a striking demonstration of wishful thinking, he then added, "I'm not sure anyone will ever solve the problem."

Meanwhile, the entertainment industry greatly encourages the confusion described by Dr. Blank by spending literally millions of dollars to commission its own studies which—surprise!—usually demonstrate that the media exert no influence on anyone. CBS, ABC, and NBC have all sponsored such projects with great fanfare, and the resulting research is regularly dusted off and trotted out whenever the industry wants to demonstrate divided opinion among the experts on the question of the pop culture's impact.

The fact that such studies are taken seriously at all is itself a scandal: the industry-originated surveys deserve no more respect or consideration than we grant to all the many research reports commissioned by the tobacco industry to prove that the Surgeon General is wrong and that cigarette smoking is actually good for you.

The claims that Hollywood's messages do nothing to shape attitudes and behavior are equally ludicrous, and on occasion the truth is so obvious that not even the generous expenditure of industry funds can guarantee the research results the moguls desire. In 1978, CBS invested $290,000 on a six-year study on the effect of television on teenage boys conducted by the Survey Research Centre of the London School of Economics. William Belson, who supervised the project, concluded from his examination that "the evidence is very strongly supportive of the hypothesis that long-term exposure to violence increases the degree to which boys engage in violence of a serious kind. The same goes for violence of the less serious kind, such as swearing and the use of bad language, aggressiveness in sport or play, threatening to use violence on another boy, writing slogans on walls, and breaking windows."

Predictably enough, when confronted with these unexpected and unwelcome results, CBS managed to keep its enthusiasm firmly under control. The network's embarrassed spokesman, David Blank, did his level best to downplay the value of the findings his own company had financed, announcing that "Belson's study was interesting, but has come along after a lot of other work has been done and adds nothing of consequence from our standpoint."

The Height of Hypocrisy

As representatives of the television business continue to stonewall, insisting that their programming has no power whatever to influence the public, no one seems to have noticed that this utterly implausible position contradicts the most basic assumptions of their industry.

In 1982, ABC released a commissioned study in which the hired-gun experts declared that "the research does not support the conclusion that television significantly cultivates viewer attitudes and perceptions of social reality."

If the executives at ABC sincerely believe this nonsense and agree that their broadcasts fail to "cultivate viewer attitudes," then the network should prepare to refund all the billions of dollars of advertising revenue that it has collected under false pretenses.

The mighty mechanism of commercial television is based entirely on the premise that broadcast advertising can alter the buying behavior of a significant segment of the huge viewing audience. That is why hardheaded corporations will gladly invest millions of dollars in a few thirty-second commercials, secure in the knowledge that even this sort of fleeting exposure can make an important difference in the public's point of view.

It is the height of hypocrisy that the same network executives who accept—and demand—this lavish payment for the briefest moments of broadcast advertising simultaneously try to convince us that all their many hours of programming do nothing to change the attitudes of the audience. In short, they have adopted the outrageously illogical assumption that a sixty-second commercial makes a more significant impression than a sixty-minute sitcom.

On the one hand we're told that an hour of television programming does nothing to shape the sentiments of the public, and on the other we're asked to believe that the brief spots that interrupt this program are powerful enough to change perceptions of anything from canned goods to candidates. The underlying idea appears to be the bizarre notion that the average viewer ignores or shrugs off the televised entertainment he has chosen to watch, while sitting up in his chair and paying close attention only when the commercials come on.

The industry simply cannot have it both ways: if it claims a near magical ability to sell products or politics, planting lasting images in just a few quick seconds, then it must acknowledge the long-term impact of its prime time programs, with their frequently violent and antisocial themes.

The motion picture business faces a similarly absurd internal contradiction in its refusal to acknowledge the influence of the movies it makes.

In recent years, what Hollywood calls "product placement" has played an increasingly prominent role in the production process, with corporate logos and brand names frequently displayed in the course of every major film. This process helps the producers defray the astronomical costs of filmmaking, as the advertiser provides props or sets or costumes, or agrees to help sell the film by mounting a tie-in promotional campaign at the time of its release. As the *Wall Street Journal* reports: "Friendly producers send scripts . . . weeks and even months before filming starts, and the company analyzes them scene by scene to see if it can place a product—or advertising material, a billboard perhaps—on, under, or behind the stars."

According to most estimates, these efforts result in several million dollars in benefits to the producers of a typical major studio film. Writing in the *Atlantic Monthly,* Mark Crispin Miller reports that the 1989 James Bond entry, *License to Kill,* featured a scene in which 007 ostentatiously smokes Larks—a magical moment for which Philip Morris paid $350,000. In the Michael Keaton comedy *Mr. Mom* (1983), Miller identified plugs for McDonald's, Domino's pizza, Terminix exterminators, Folger's coffee, Lite beer, Jack Daniel's, Van Camp's chili, Ban deodorant, Windex, Tide, Spray 'n Wash, Borax, Clorox 2, and Downy fabric softener.

Corporate marketing experts invest considerable effort and expense in these placements because their research indicates that they are highly effective. Even if the viewer registers the name of the product only in an unconscious manner, the association between a familiar brand and a glamorous star will make a measurable difference in future sales.

This is an established principle in the motion picture business—accepted without question when it comes to taking the money of eager advertisers. At the same time that everyone agrees that a two-second glimpse of a box of Tide can help the manufacturer, there is no acknowledgment that two hours of graphic gore can hurt the audience.

Imagine a forthcoming feature film with a torrid sex scene between two charismatic stars. On the night stand beside the bed is a subtle product placement—say a bottle of mouthwash, with its label turned toward the camera. The current logic of the motion picture business suggests that the typical member of the audience turns his eyes away from two naked, gorgeous bodies in transports of passion and instead focuses all attention on the bottle of mouthwash at the edge of the frame. How else can one explain the assumption that the mouthwash label will influence the viewers' future behavior, but the vivid sex scene will not?

In short, the industry's position is both flagrantly dishonest and lavishly illogical.

A Fun-House Mirror

A Second Line of Defense

Whenever Hollywood's refusal to acknowledge its own influence begins collapsing under the weight of its own absurdities and contradictions, the industry's apologists shift their ground and retreat to a second line of defense. Their first contention—that no proof exists for a connection between between screen images and real-world consequences—flies in the face of both a massive accumulation of evidence and ordinary common sense, but this second argument provides them with a more sophisticated, secure, and defensible redoubt. It concedes the obvious fact that some connection exists between disturbing movie themes and our most pressing social problems, but insists that the problems shape the themes, rather than vice versa. In other words, change flows in only one direction: America influences Hollywood, but Hollywood never influences America.

This argument has been effectively and concisely stated by any number of observers both inside and outside the entertainment community. During a 1991 forum on movie violence sponsored by a group of leading liberal activists, director Paul Verhoeven (*Robocop,*

Basic Instinct) declared: "Art is a reflection of the world. If the world is horrible, the reflection in the mirror is horrible."

Along similar lines, Verhoeven's colleague Sydney Pollack (*Tootsie, Out of Africa*) told the American Enterprise Institute: "I share your nostalgia for some of those lost traditional values, but attempting to reinstill them by arbitrarily putting them into movies when they don't exist in everyday life will not get people to go to movies or put those values back into life."

A young veteran of Operation Desert Storm, with no personal connection to the entertainment industry, echoed these sentiments when he wrote me in response to one of my articles questioning Hollywood's messages and their impact. "I happen to enjoy today's movies and popular music," declared Private First Class Daniel Hopson. "As for the movie industry influencing and changing our society, I think the movie and music industries are more influenced by the world around them. They portray what they see in America today. . . . Instead of pointing the finger at the entertainment industry, why don't you point it at the politicians who refuse to do anything about our drug problem, our homeless, and the crime rate in America?"

In response to Private Hopson, I can only assure him that if I were a political writer, I would most certainly point my finger at our politicians, whose pathetic performance unquestionably contributes to our current difficulties. As it happens, however, my beat is the entertainment industry, and I am convinced that this industry makes its own significant contributions to what is going wrong in our country and to the prevailing atmosphere of despair that has become a destructive feature of our national life. The fact that our governmental leaders may be selfish and irresponsible in no way absolves the most powerful people in Hollywood from the same charges; there is, unfortunately, enough blame to go around.

Nor can the purveyors of the popular culture dodge that blame by claiming that their violent and sex-drenched entertainments merely reproduce the grim realities of contemporary life.

It is ironic that Paul Verhoeven, of all people, stands among those who insist that "art is a reflection of the world." Which world does his 1992 box office smash *Basic Instinct* reflect? In what way does its portrayal of four different lesbian or bisexual characters as homicidal nut cases mirror the current realities of gay life? Numerous gay organizations properly pointed out that taken as group, lesbians actually display one of the lowest rates of violent crime of any segment of the society. Mr. Verhoeven is surely entitled to bring to the screen his warped and feverish fantasies (just so long as the studios support him in these endeavors), but it strains credibility for him to suggest that *Basic Instinct*—or *Total Recall* or *Robocop*, for that matter—simply recreate the horrors of everyday life.

Actually, Verhoeven's recent body of work demonstrates Hollywood's own basic instinct, which is to paint America with a decidedly dark palette in which the favorite color is always a deep red. A previous chapter noted the fact that the industry's bloody obsessions bear little resemblance to reality, and that the world portrayed both on television and in motion pictures is vastly more violent than even our meanest streets. After twenty years of studying media mayhem at the Annenberg School of Communications, Dr. George Gerbner and his associates concluded that on prime-time programming as a whole (including such "innocuous" fare as sitcoms, family dramas, game shows, and so forth) "there are between six and eight acts of violence an hour with two entertaining murders each night." This means that violent acts occurred on television some *fifty-five times more frequently than they did in the real world.*

This emphasis on brutality leads to a hugely disproportionate focus on male characters, since men are more readily associated with physical force of every kind. According to Gerbner's research, in the world of television in 1988, major male characters outnumbered females by three to one. Meanwhile, those women who do appear are generally younger than their male counterparts, but they age faster. Those who claim that Hollywood accurately represents the society it serves may find it difficult to explain a television universe that is some three-quarters male—or a movie world that seems similarly weighted toward leading men over leading women. Authoritative statistics compiled by the Screen Actors Guild in a 1989 study show that 70.9 percent of *all* roles in feature films—and 64.6 percent of *all* TV roles—go to men.

The gross overrepresentation of violence, and of the male protagonists who perpetrate it, constitute only two of the more obvious areas in which the entertainment industry's vision of America savagely distorts our current realities. If, as some maintain, Hollywood is a mirror held up to the larger society then it is, at best, a fun-house mirror—throwing back grotesque and misshapen images that tell us next to nothing about the everyday actuality that surrounds us.

Isolated Too Long

Some of those who defend the popular culture as an accurate reflection of our society seem themselves to have fallen victim to that culture's characteristic distortions; in the course of their immersion in the entertainment industry they have lost touch with the American mainstream. When a thoughtful, serious, and decent director like Sydney Pollack can describe "those lost traditional values" that "don't exist in everyday life," one can only assume that he has been isolated too long among the entertainment elite in Los Angeles and Manhattan. Though it may come as news to him, traditional values are alive and well, and thriving in a neighborhood near you.

Surveys on every significant issue in contemporary life show that the values and attitudes of the majority of Americans have changed far less substantially than Hollywood honchos believe that they have.

Recent studies show that

- 87 percent of our fellow citizens "never doubt the existence of God" and 77 percent say "prayer is an important part of my daily life" (*Los Angeles Times,* 1991);
- 80 percent consider "spousal sexual fidelity" a "key to a good marriage," while 85 percent of married people say they would marry the same person again (Louis Harris Associates, 1987);
- 78 percent of high school seniors say that having a good marriage is "very important" to them (Survey Research Center, University of Michigan, 1990);
- 67 percent of all Americans say they are "very satisfied" with their own family lives (Massachusetts Mutual Survey, 1991);
- 67 percent consider "their own hard work" the most important factor in "getting ahead," while only 13 percent list "luck" (National Opinion Research Center, 1991);
- 89 percent of all workers agree with the statement "I am proud

to be working for this organization" (National Opinion Research Center, 1991);

- only 25 percent of teenagers support the legalization of marijuana, compared to a near majority in 1970 (*National Opinion Research Center*, 1991);

- 57 percent "agree strongly" that "the rich deserve what they have" (*Los Angeles Times*, 1991);

- 90 percent "feel safe and secure at home at night," compared to 81 percent in 1975 (Gallup Organization, 1990);

- 64 percent believe the police are doing a "good" or "excellent" job (National Victims Center, 1991), while 76 percent are "generally satisfied" with police protection in their neighborhoods (CBS News/*New York Times*, 1991);

- only 6 percent have ever "been held up at gun or knife point," and only 9 percent have "tried cocaine" (Roper Organization, 1990);

- only 19 percent list "rock" as the "kind of music I like to listen to most," while 34 percent say "easy listening," 21 percent say "country," and a startling 14 percent say "classical" (*USA Today*, 1990);

- 75 percent say that "patriotism" is "in"; only 15 percent say it is "out" (Roper Organization, 1990);

- 88 percent say they are "satisfied with their own lives and their communities" (*Los Angeles Times*, 1991).

While it is also true that most Americans express dissatisfaction with our political leadership and worry about the general direction of the country, the figures cited above (and the results of countless other studies) can hardly be said to portray a nation that is seething with embittered and alienated citizens.

If anything, the direction of public opinion involves a return to and renewal of traditional values, rather than any embrace of the radical alternatives so frequently promoted by Hollywood. The research firm Mellman & Lazarus conducted two intensive studies of twelve hundred Americans for the Massachusetts Mutual Life Insurance Company, in 1989 and 1991. Measuring the changes in that two-year span, the researchers concluded that "Americans show a deeper sense of 'core family values' . . . Americans feel more responsibility for providing for their families . . . and Americans make more time for family." According to this study, 80 percent said "they would not miss a major family holiday, such as Thanksgiving, even for $1,000."

Considering the emphasis on faith, family, and traditionalism that emerges so unmistakably from all available surveys, it is hardly surprising that such an overwhelming percentage of the populace expresses distaste for Hollywood's messages and values. One can only surmise that the number of Americans who might agree with Paul Verhoeven's judgment that "the reflection in the mirror is horrible" only because "the world is horrible" would prove to be remarkably small.

In previous sections of this book I have provided considerable detail to demonstrate the ways in which Hollywood goes out of its way to trash the cherished values of most Americans, including their commitment to religion (Part II), their belief in the nuclear family (Part III) and their preference for common decency, traditional heroes, and passionate patriotism (Part IV). In none of these areas could the preoccupations of the entertainment industry possibly be traced to the priorities of the public. In fact, the show business community remained so stubbornly oblivious to life in the real world that its projects never registered some of the more notable trends of recent years. On a number of defining issues, the themes of Hollywood and the values of the public actually headed in opposite directions.

- While marriage rates have increased and divorce rates have declined on a regular basis since 1982, the movie business focused almost entirely on single characters and began portraying the nuclear family as an outmoded, nightmarish institution.
- In a period when the most conservative elements in Christianity—and in Judaism—gained influence and adherents, and the press began writing of a religious revival, Hollywood ignored religion altogether, or else attacked it with unprecedented ferocity.
- While crime rates *declined* slightly but steadily throughout the 1980s, the incidence of violence in films and television showed a spectacular increase, as the popular culture took its obsession with brutality and bloodshed to new levels of depravity.
- At the same time that Americans provided record-breaking levels of support for Ronald Reagan, the nation's most prominent proponent of military power, and then offered a huge outpouring of pride

over the achievements of our troops in the Persian Gulf, movies and television shows displayed a critical new perspective of their portrayal of the armed services and America's role in the world.

Rather than following the course of events or the shifts of public opinion, the entertainment industry pursued its own decadent and self-destructive agenda. In view of this consistent failure to reflect major changes in the social and political climate, it is ludicrous to suggest that the popular culture merely responds to developments in the larger society. Anyone who claims that today's movies, TV, and music offer a faithful reflection of American life is either out of touch with America, or else ignorant of what Hollywood sends out to the world.

Getting the Message

The gap between the viewpoint of the entertainment elite and values of ordinary citizens is so huge and so obvious that it raises new questions about Hollywood's ability to influence the rest of us. To some observers, the stubborn and surprising strength of traditional values in towns and neighborhoods throughout the land suggests that the power of the entertainment industry may have been greatly exaggerated.

"If *Studs* glorifies premarital sex," asks Karlyn Keene, editor of *The American Enterprise,* "why is it that 86 percent of young people say that premarital sex for teens is always or almost always wrong? . . . If American culture is corrupting us, I would expect some evidence of that to show up in the survey data." She raises a significant challenge to those of us concerned about the consequences of the popular culture's dark obsessions. If the influence of the entertainment industry is as substantial as we say it is, then why have the leaders of that industry been unable to bring the rest of America in line with their attitudes?

Part of the answer to that question involves the slow but steady nature of media influence. According to all available research on the subject, the most significant aspects of that influence are gradual and cumulative, not immediate, and they occur only after extended exposure. The alienated and antisocial themes in so much of today's Hollywood entertainment are a relatively recent development; the violent, sexual, and degrading elements have become far more intense in just

the last few years. Those changes have been particularly dramatic—
and recent—on television, which is the element of the popular culture
that reaches by far the largest audience. What this means is that the full
impact of today's media messages will only be felt some years in the
future. Considering the determined and energetic nature of Hollywood's assault on reigning conventions, there is good reason to question whether core values will remain as firmly implanted in years to
come as they are today.

The research on the impact of popular culture by George Gerbner
and others demonstrates that members of the public differ dramatically
in their susceptibility to the ideas and standards which that culture
transmits. A small minority will be quickly transformed by the media
fantasies they watch; others will feel the impact more gradually and
subtly; still others will remain largely unaffected.

Despite the stalwart optimism of commentators like Karlyn Keene,
there is considerable evidence that the most vulnerable segment of the
population has already felt the consequences of Hollywood's irresponsible excesses.

While Ms. Keene may be correct that 86 percent of teenagers dis-
approve of premarital sex, and that prevailing attitudes of adolescents
are far more conservative than media moguls will acknowledge, the
Centers for Disease Control reported that 25 percent of American
females have engaged in intercourse by age fifteen—five times the percentage that prevailed as recently as 1970.

At the same time, the national rate of out-of-wedlock births has
increased 500 percent since 1960, the rate of teen suicide is up 400
percent since 1950, and the number of fourteen- to seventeen-year-
olds arrested for crimes of violence rose a mind-boggling 3,000 percent
between 1950 and 1990.

It is no coincidence that the segment of society that displays the
most self-destructive and irresponsible behavior is the same group that
most avidly and insatiably consumes the products of our popular culture. Teenagers are especially threatened by the influence of the entertainment industry because of the inherently unsettled circumstances of
adolescence, and the sheer volume of music, movies, TV, and videos
they devour. Their current troubles and tragedies suggest that while we
wait for the long-term impact of media images on the rest of the population, millions of American teens have already gotten the message.

Redefining Normal

The transmission of that message isn't magical or mysterious: the power of the entertainment industry to influence our actions flows from its ability to redefine what constitutes normal behavior in this society.

The popular culture now consumes such a huge proportion of our time and attention that it has assumed a dominant role in establishing social conventions. The fantasy figures who entertain us on our TV and movie screens, or who croon to us constantly from our radios and CD players, take the lead in determining what is considered hip, and what will be viewed as hopelessly weird. In every society, ordinary folk have been able to cultivate a sense of style by aping the airs of the aristocracy; in this stubbornly democratic culture, the only aristocracy that counts for anything is the world of "celebrities" who appear on the tube and in the tabloids.

Young people in particular take these role models seriously, and a pop culture personality with enough clout can single-handedly initiate a national trend. Imagine what might have happened had some suburban fourteen-year-old independently decided that she would start wearing lingerie as outerwear: she surely would have been ridiculed by her peers for such embarrassing behavior and perhaps sent by her worried parents to consult a therapist. The fact that it was Madonna who launched this fashion folly made all the difference: the practice of wearing a black studded bustier in place of a blouse achieved instant legitimacy across the country. Parents and school authorities may have been less than thrilled with this new trend, but for the most part they grudgingly accepted it as one more inevitable and unstoppable expression of an always rebellious popular culture. Through the transforming power of the mass media, a bizarre and illogical idiosyncrasy suddenly became normal—and the thing to do.

The popular culture's ability to promulgate instant new rules on what makes for acceptable or amusing conduct is so obvious that it strongly suggests its potential for influencing more significant standards. In the opinion of many observers, television demonstrated some of that potential in its provocative coverage of the recent Los Angeles riots. According to press accounts, a significant percentage of the many thousands who looted stores and shops throughout the city initially got the idea to participate in this activity by watching other looters on TV. Those images not only communicated the small likelihood of interference from police, but they also redefined looting as common behavior. With so many others helping themselves to new VCRs and groceries, why be a chump and miss the fun? By repeatedly showing huge crowds of people engaged in this endeavor, television took outrageous behavior and made it look routine.

If a few glimpses of televised hysteria could help to stoke the fires of Los Angeles, how can we doubt that the fourteen hundred hours the typical American watches every year will permanently affect the way he thinks and feels? By the time the average teenager graduates from high school, he or she will have witnessed more than 15,000 murders on the tube. Thanks to this sort of extended exposure to violence and cruelty, the entertainment industry changes our view not only of what is accepted, but what is expected.

Most American children begin watching television before they can even talk. By the time they are six, typical kids will have invested more hours communing with the tube than they will spend speaking with their fathers in an entire lifetime. Media images are especially important in these early years, since children have so few alternate sources of information about the way that most adults talk, dress, work, play, and relate to one another. The mass media provide young people with their most significant impressions of the larger world beyond the family circle. Even the most dim-witted child will be sure to notice that in that larger world, many good-looking grown-ups like to shoot each other with guns or squeeze each other in bed.

"All the secrets that a print culture kept from children—about sex, violence, death, and human aberration—are revealed all at once by media which do not, and cannot, exclude any audience," writes Neil Postman, professor of media ecology at New York University.

One of the reasons for the unparalleled potency of the media in shaping attitudes and values arises from the absence of countervailing forces. "There are many influences on the life of a young person," explains former Secretary of Education William Bennett. "We can handle television and popular culture to a much greater degree if we think other institutions are doing their job.

"We worry that many children today are being raised by the popular culture. There is no influence in society that competes for their attention. Many schools are starting to imitate the popular culture rather than to counter it. There are schools in this country that start the day with heavy metal. That is a serious problem."

The lack of competing influences in the lives of many children parallels the lack of alternate images within the media mix. The problem isn't just the presence of all the antisocial signals, it is also the absence of opposing messages that might promote goodness, unselfishness, deferred gratification, and—dare I say it?—respect for authority.

Carol Tavris, a social psychologist and columnist, pointed out in 1991: "People are affected not only by what they see but also by what they don't see. They don't see counterbalancing stories of what used to be called character. They don't see problems solved other than by violence. They rarely see stories of real people—the kind who know each other longer than two minutes before they jump into bed or commit murder with chainsaws."

Of course, dedicated families can work effectively to counteract these influences, but why should parents be forced to fight this battle in the first place? Within memory, the popular culture served to reinforce the messages that children received at home; it is only in recent years that most mothers and fathers have come to believe that the entertainment industry undermines those lessons. In the 1991 Massachusetts Mutual survey, less than 2 percent of the respondents identified "movies and TV" as a source of positive values such as "helping your community or neighborhood," "having a happy marriage," or "earning a good living." More and more parents view the popular culture as a powerful enemy in an ongoing war for the souls of their children.

The Poison of Pessimism

One of the most significant battlefields in that war concerns the vision of the future that we will pass on to the next generation.

Most parents believe in the power of hope and try to encourage the old idea that hard work and wholesome values will help make tomorrow better than today. In one recent survey, 72 percent of a representative sample of our fellow citizens agreed with the statement "people like me and my family have a good chance of improving our standard of living" (National Opinion Research Center, 1987).

Hollywood, on the other hand, is transfixed by nightmares of doom and corruption. From the popular culture's invariably pessimistic perspective, all our major institutions—family, church, business, government, police, and the military—have been hopelessly compromised. Critics and other industry insiders reserve their warmest praise for those motion pictures (*The Silence of the Lambs, GoodFellas, Blue Velvet, Bugsy, My Own Private Idaho, Dances with Wolves, JFK, Naked Lunch*) that provide the harshest, darkest views of American life. In the industry's most highly touted "serious" and "artistic" entertainments, the present is always brutal and dire, and the future is bound to be even worse.

These gloomy expectations emerge whenever Hollywood presents its fatalistic fantasies of what awaits us in the years ahead. The three fabulously successful *Star Wars* films (1977–1983) now seem almost quaint in their enthusiasm for a future of high-tech heroism; their unabashedly boyish spirit is far closer to *Buck Rogers* or *Flash Gordon* than to any of the industry's more recent apocalyptic visions. Some of these visions urge us to prepare for a world of rampaging mobs, rusting machinery, scarce resources, grime, poverty, and hideous brutality (the *Mad Max/Road Warrior* movies, *Blade Runner,* the *Robocop* films, *Alien Nation, Cyborg, Split Second,* and many more) while other predictive pictures emphasize a future that is dominated by evil corporations and fascistic governments that work to stamp out every scrap of individuality (*Brazil, Alien 3, The Handmaid's Tale, Total Recall, Liquid Dreams, The Running Man,* and the *Terminator* films). None of these ominous explorations of the territory ahead could possibly be confused with "The Jetsons." In recent years, the only big-budget futuristic films to maintain an even mildly optimistic tone were entries in the *Star Trek* series—which managed to escape the prevailing gloom only because they were so firmly rooted in a fondly remembered 1960s TV show.

For years, Hollywood explained this bleak perspective on the present and the future by invoking the ubiquitous specter of The Bomb. Various experts told us that the grim themes that often appeared in movies or in popular songs stemmed chiefly from the fact that we all lived under the ghastly shadow of nuclear destruction. Knowing, as we did, that the entire world might blow itself up at any moment, how could we expect the artists of our era to offer optimistic themes? Fear of nuclear devastation helped to explain anything that needed to be explained—from apathy to passionate activism, from random violence to hedonistic self-indulgence to a frightened inability to face the world.

One of the most revealing aspects of the entertainment industry's present inclination toward pessimism is that it has changed so little in response to epochal international events. Now that the Cold War is over, the Soviet Union dismantled, the Iron Curtain eliminated, and The Bomb removed as any imminent threat, why has the prevailing gloom in the popular culture not lifted accordingly? While freedom makes dramatic progress almost everywhere, from Prague to Pretoria, from Managua to Moscow, Hollywood's morbid point of view about our world and its future has brightened not one bit.

This failure to reflect the more hopeful occurrences of recent years stands as incomparably eloquent testimony to the fact that the popular culture expresses the inner compulsions of the isolated artists who shape it, rather than responding to historical developments among the rest of humanity. It is especially enlightening to watch the ease with which moviemakers manage to adjust their fearful fantasies of the future to the inconvenient disappearance of the nuclear threat. In several recent projects they have simply removed references to "nuclear holocaust" and replaced them with descriptions of "environmental holocaust" without missing a beat.

These expectations of imminent ecological catastrophe began turning up several years ago. In May 1988, the ABC situation comedy "Head of the Class" aired an episode in which Mr. Moore (Howard Hesseman) asked his incredibly bright advanced placement students to speculate on what life might be like in fifty years. One student, Maria, immediately took up the challenge. "What is fun about toxic waste, or acid rain, or even nuclear war?" she wailed. "Economic collapse is right around the corner. There's depression, there's famine, there's war."

At that point, Dennis, the class science whiz, added his sage perspective. "Science today is just a tool in the hands of the superpowers," he explained to his classmates and to the TV audience. "All they want to do is build things like Star Wars and lasers and beam weapons in space. I have just come to the realization that those people out there are using me, using me for their evil ends. Well, I'm not going to have any part of it."

This sort of corrosive cynicism, appropriately packaged for kids, is more and more typical of the bleak visions the popular culture promotes. "Miami Vice" offered an especially elegant example of the industry's effectiveness in advancing its agenda. In the world of the show, the rugged, unshaven hero found corruption and hypocrisy everywhere around him; he might fight the good fight for an hour each week, but with no real hope of making headway against the prevailing decadence. As television writer and commentator Ben Stein wrote in 1985: "'Miami Vice' is extremely cynical about more than minorities, women, business, and government; it is cynical about the human condition generally speaking. Take the attitude of a typical 'film noir' of the late 1940s, mix in a good healthy dose of Hobbes and Spengler, and you have the worldview of 'Miami Vice' . . . a bouquet of racism, nihilism, and despair, wrapped perfectly in a Hermès silk square."

More recently, major stars of the music business have begun promoting dire predictions of their own, with an emphasis on the imminence of race war and genocide. In 1991, the rap group Public Enemy created a controversial video that depicts the musicians leading a bloody, fiery, apocalyptic assault on the Arizona state capitol—to punish the state for refusing to endorse the Martin Luther King holiday! Meanwhile, their colleague, Sister Souljah, released a highly publicized single and video called "The Final Solution: Slavery's Back in Effect." This graphic minidrama, set in 1995, begins with terrified African-Americans gathered around TVs and radios to listen to an unnamed President announcing the reinstitution of slavery. With the cooperation of Congress and of "Vice President Duke," the Chief Executive then orders troops and police to hunt down and manacle all blacks who remain at large; those who attempt to escape, including a mother and a frightened child, are shot in cold blood.

Defenders of such shocking material insist that it serves the same useful purpose as all of Hollywood's pessimistic predictions—it can rouse people from their apathy and mobilize them to become a force for necessary and overdue change.

Recent history suggests, however, that these gloomy messages have produced precisely the opposite effect, encouraging a sense of hopelessness and cynicism that further disenfranchises the public. If we are all doomed anyway, powerless to challenge the gigantic conspiracies and "invisible government" that ruthlessly block all prospects for improvement, then why should we bother with meaningless rituals like voting or voluntarism? If I have no hope for advancement in a sick and terminally racist society that only wants to enslave me, then why shouldn't I loot and burn the stores in my neighborhood?

Year by year, the numbers show an alarming erosion of public participation in both the electoral process and community causes, indicating that the poison of pessimism has already begun working its way through the body politic.

"Pessimism is, unfortunately, more than just a posture," writes Martin E. P. Seligman, professor of psychology at the University of Pennsylvania.

> It has consequences for the mental health of the nation, its economy and productivity. . . . A pessimistic nation, like a pessimistic individual, will have lower achievement than its resources warrant. A pessimistic nation will have rampant mental depression among its people and a high suicide rate among its teenagers. A pessimistic nation, like a pessimistic individual, will not persist in the face of troubles. . . .
>
> Hundreds of studies over the last twenty years involving hundreds of thousands of people have shown . . . the mechanisms of optimism are not a mystery. It works simply through increased persistence in the face of problems. When defeated at any stage, the pessimist tends to give up, while the optimist keeps trying.

We all have a vested interest in the hope that America, and Americans, will keep trying. In this context, Hollywood's dark distortions about who we are and where we are going, amount to more than annoyance or insult: they represent a serious threat to the well-being of our children and our country.

"The Most Effective Weapon Known to Man"

When it comes to the perils of pessimism, or to any other dangers arising from the proclivities of the popular culture, Hollywood's facile defenders have a final glib answer ready to hand.

"Nobody is forcing you to see these movies," they say. "If you don't like their messages, don't go. If you hate the lyrics to some popular song, don't listen to it. And if you're bothered by what they're doing on some TV show, you can always turn it off."

In the words of Jack Valenti: "When people say, I don't like that kind of film, I say, you have the most effective weapon known to man— don't go to see it."

Unfortunately, responding to the penetrating power of today's popular culture is seldom so simple.

In this connection, I vividly recall an ill-fated family outing in the spring of 1990.

In the middle of our week-long Passover holiday, we took an afternoon excursion to a lake in the mountains near Santa Barbara. The weather couldn't have been more perfect—with puffy clouds floating fat and lazy in a clear, cool April sky. When we pulled into the public park at the lake shore, our little girls, aged one and three, began babbling excitedly about the family of ducks they saw at the edge of the water. For any parent, one of the most endearing aspects of time spent with your kids is watching the way that simple things—like a mother duck and a half-dozen fuzzy ducklings—can thrill them beyond all measure. As our daughters got out of the car and began running full tilt toward the birds, the one-year-old reached out with her chubby little arms and urgently shrieked, "Duckie! Duckie!" My wife and I beamed at each other because it happened to be one of the first words she had ever pronounced with unmistakable clarity.

Within minutes, our pride gave way to concern as a group of teenagers, mostly thirteen- to fifteen-year-olds, walked up to the lakeside picnic area. They happened to be white suburban boys, wearing long hair and occasional earrings, together with colorful, loose-fitting clothes. They also carried an enormous boom box, and emerging from that shiny chrome machine came the sounds of a rap song that featured lyrics of simply unimaginable ugliness.

To this day, I don't know for certain if the number they played represented the work of NWA, or 2 Live Crew, or Ice Cube, or some lesser known creative giant. But I do know that it featured an angry series of obscene shouts describing rape and feces and oral sex, blasted out into the mountain air at near-deafening volume.

Naturally, our little girls reacted in terror. I doubt if they understood the words of the song, but they certainly felt the painful power of its explosive, throbbing bass line. The one-year-old, interrupted in her pursuit of ducklings, suddenly began to cry, and her older sister soon joined her. Within minutes, we had our hands full trying to comfort two frightened little girls.

Eventually, I walked over to the young gentleman who held the boom box, sitting at a picnic bench with his head bobbing back and forth in time to the music. Trying to make myself heard over the din, I asked him as politely as I could if he wouldn't mind turning down the volume because it was scaring my girls. In response, he offered a silent smirk and then cranked up the sound level even further, to the point of the ear-splitting maximum his machine could provide.

I suppose we could have stayed and made a scene, but I don't happen to carry assault weapons in my trunk. Instead, my wife and I did the only sensible thing, loading our kids into the car and driving away. We gave up our planned picnic, the sparkling lake, and the beautiful day, abandoning the scene to these brutish kids and their triumphant noise.

The point is that there is no refuge today from the ubiquitous presence of the popular culture. Even those who make a personal decision not to partake of its products will find its influence inescapable. You can put your TV in the closet, avoid movies altogether, and use earplugs to spare your ears from the sounds of rap or heavy metal, but these forms of entertainment will still change your life through their influence on everyone else in this society. Though you may struggle to protect your own kids from material that encourages violence or irresponsible sex, you can't possibly protect them from all the other kids in your community who have received full exposure.

The attitudes and images of the entertainment industry are everywhere around us and they seep into every corner of our daily lives; receiving Hollywood's message is no longer a matter of choice. I imagine that some readers of this book may never have purchased a Madonna record, or attended one of her sold-out concerts, or even watched one of her controversial videos on MTV. Nevertheless, you will know plenty about this public figure—who she is, how she dresses or dances, who she dates, and what she sings about. Even if you never chose to make Madonna's face and form part of your personal consciousness, there she is—on countless magazine covers and talk shows, discussed endlessly in news stories and at dinner parties, an inescapable force in the world around us. In considering this phenomenon, ABC's "Nightline" even elected to broadcast her bisexual, sadomasochistic "Justify Your Love" music video in its uncensored entirety. Whether you like it or not, this woman is a part of your cultural environment.

Movie images are now similarly inescapable. I know many people who would never dream of spending $7.50 to go see *Basic Instinct,* but they can nonetheless describe much of its content with reasonable accuracy. The same is true of *The Hand That Rocks the Cradle,* or *White Men Can't Jump,* or *Fatal Attraction,* or *JFK,* or most other hit films. TV and newspaper ads, as well as frequent discussions in print and on the air, make sure that people receive key messages even from movies they choose not to see.

No one remains entirely untouched by what goes on in Hollywood and its attitudes penetrate even the most isolated enclaves on the continent. During a trip to New York a few years ago, I walked through an exclusively Hasidic neighborhood in Brooklyn and stopped to watch a group of ten-year-olds playing stickball in the street across from a religious school. They all wore skullcaps and side-curls and the traditional fringes dangling over their belts. As they shouted encouragement and insults at one another, they could have all been characters in a Chaim Potok novel—except for the fact that one of the boys sported a yellow-and-black *Batman* sweatshirt. I sincerely doubt that his presumably pious parents had actually let him see the film, but he nevertheless put its logo on his chest as a symbol of something potent and exciting.

Technological advances only add to the imperial reach of the popular culture. Heavy metal music now blares out of boom boxes, Walkmans, and car CD players, recent movies play on airplanes and in hotel rooms, and television turns up absolutely everywhere. I recently rode with a cab driver who terrified me by zipping in and out of traffic while avidly watching "Wheel of Fortune" on a tiny portable TV perched on his dashboard. Later that same day I discovered a section of the airport that helpfully provided special chairs with attached television screens that could be rented for a few quarters. It is increasingly possible to remain connected to Hollywood's input every moment of our waking lives. In elevators and in shopping malls, in doctors' offices and even in school classrooms, the sights and sounds of the popular culture assault our senses. For many Americans, television and radio have become an essential accompaniment to a wide range of daily activities; they enjoy its offerings while they are jogging or cooking, cleaning the car, doing homework, eating dinner, or making love.

In short, the popular culture is now as unavoidable as any airborne pollutant. To say that if you don't like it you should just tune it out makes as much sense as saying that if you don't like the smog, stop breathing. As the great Joe Louis said, you can run, but you can't hide.

That is why the perspectives of the popular culture are an appropriate issue for all of us, not just for the members of the entertainment elite.

Some representatives of that leadership have candidly acknowledged the importance of what they do and their substantial contributions to our present problems. In November 1981, George Lucas, one of the most successful filmmakers in Hollywood history, spoke at a ground-breaking for new facilities at the USC Film and Television School. "Film and visual entertainment are a pervasively important part of our culture, an extremely significant influence on the way our society operates," he said. "People in the film industry don't want to accept the responsibility that they had a hand in the way the world is loused up. But, for better or worse . . . films and television tell us the way we conduct our lives, what is right and wrong. It's important that the people who make films have ethics classes, philosophy classes, history classes. Otherwise, we're witch doctors."

Unfortunately, nothing has occurred in the last ten years to achieve the attitude adjustment that Lucas suggested. Some of his colleagues believe it is already too late for minor changes to make a difference. Addressing a forum on movie violence in November 1991, the Oscar-nominated actor and activist Edward James Olmos solemnly declared, "Nothing that we can do will ever stop the damage that we've done."

He may be right, but concerted efforts inside and outside the entertainment industry, and a better understanding of how we came to our present predicament, may help us to avoid even more devastating damage in the years ahead.

PART VI

BELOW THE BOTTOM LINE

What Went Wrong

Hollywood's Dirty Little Secret

Any serious effort to promote more positive values in the popular culture must begin with an exploration of the origins of the current crisis.

At the heart of the problem is the alienation of the audience—the tendency of increasing numbers of potential patrons to view the products of Hollywood with suspicion and resentment. When—and how—did the entertainment elite begin to lose touch with the American mainstream?

Of course, some of the industry's defenders object to the very premise of the question. They insist that there is no long-term crisis, and they recite some reassuring box-office figures to prove their point. While everyone acknowledges that total revenues have dipped in the last three years, industry advocates remind us that 1989 represented a peak period for the motion picture business. During those twelve months—described with much fanfare in the trade press as "the best year in Hollywood history"—American films set an all-time record by earning $5,033,400,000 at the domestic box office.

In view of this impressive performance, the entertainment oracles declare that their business is basically sound and faces no deep-seated difficulties in connecting with the mass of American moviegoers.

Unfortunately, this argument rests on faulty logic—and faulty figures.

In fact, I am increasingly convinced that industry leaders deliberately emphasize the numbers on "box office grosses" in order to mislead the public (and themselves) and to disguise the depth of their dilemma.

It is Hollywood's dirty little secret that these highly touted figures tell us nothing at all about the actual size of the movie audience; *what they reflect most significantly is the incessant and excessive rise in ticket prices.*

Those prices have shot up nearly 70 percent since 1982—nearly twice the rate of inflation in the overall consumer price index. The price increases hide the ongoing decline in the size of the movie audience, allowing Hollywood to report higher gross receipts even though their movies draw dramatically fewer people.

For instance, Hollywood's much-ballyhooed "Golden Year" of 1989 actually attracted a *smaller* audience than did the unheralded seasons of 1984, 1983, or 1982.

The only numbers that accurately reflect the industry's ability to connect with the general public are figures on "admissions"—the total number of American moviegoers who actually go to the theaters and pay to see Hollywood's product. These statistics, as published at the end of each year by the Motion Picture Association of America, tell a dismal tale of an industry that has needlessly and stupidly sacrificed the majority of its available audience.

Missing Moviegoers

A quick review of the last few decades of Hollywood history makes it surprisingly easy to identify when—and how—the entertainment establishment lost those missing moviegoers.

The advent of television delivered the first blow.

Between the years 1948 and 1953, as the tube entered more and more American homes, motion picture attendance collapsed, dropping from a weekly average of 90 million down to a level of 46 million.

At that point, however, the situation stabilized—much to the relief of the major studios. With television already well-established across the country in 1953, the overall size of the movie audience showed remarkably little variation for the next twelve years, remaining fixed in the 40 million–49 million weekly range.

Then, after 1965, Hollywood faced another turning point—and the levels of motion picture attendance showed another sudden and disastrous decline. In terms of the percentage of the audience they estranged, the developments of the late 1960s proved even more cataclysmic than the introduction of television.

The numbers reveal the scope of the catastrophe: weekly attendance figures plummeted from 44 million in 1965 to a pathetic 17.5 million in 1969. In the brief span of four years, some unanticipated and still unidentified hydrogen bomb exploded on Hollywood—wiping out more than 60 percent of the previously stable audience.

Unfortunately, the impact of this explosion has proven permanent: Hollywood has never recovered from the debacle of the late '60s. Since 1965, industry-wide weekly attendance never again rose above the level of 23 million (which it achieved in 1984); by 1991 it had slipped again to an anemic 18.9 million.

What was the hidden force that wiped out moviegoing as a comfortable American habit?

Despite hand-wringing by some industry insiders, the development of home video and cable television had nothing to do with the disaster. These technological breakthroughs arrived on the scene more than ten years *after* the mass movie audience had already disappeared, and their introduction had far less impact than expected on ticket sales at the theaters; weekly attendance hovered near the 20 million mark during the entire period (1980–1990) that videocassette recorders penetrated most American homes. No one can plausibly point to the VCR as the culprit in the unsolved mystery of the missing moviegoers.°

Nor can anyone explain away what happened by citing demo-

°For most people, home video has developed as an alternative to television, rather than a threat to the already severely diminished audience for feature films. The experience of watching a video at home has far more in common with viewing TV than it does with the process of going to the theater to see a new movie. Enjoying a home video requires far less commitment in terms of money, travel time, inconvenience, and discomfort than choosing a feature film; as a result, the audience demands far less of the titles it sees in this format. This helps to explain the seemingly contradictory phenomena of the emergence of a huge new home video audience at the same time that survey data shows overwhelming public disgust and disillusionment with Hollywood's current offerings. People will rent videos to watch at home even when they don't expect to find them par-

graphic or financial factors. The years in which audiences initially abandoned the theaters represented a period of overall economic *expansion*
for the nation at large; moreover, the flat attendance figures since 1969
have shown no tendency whatever to respond to the sharp ups and
downs in the economy. If demographics alone determined destiny, the
period 1965 to 1969 should have brought record audiences for the film
business as multitudinous members of the baby boom entered precisely those ages (fifteen to twenty-five) in which all prior experience
showed them most likely to buy movie tickets. The fact that they failed
to do so—that these kids joined their elders in staying away from the
theaters in droves—indicates the depth of the industry's problems of
the period.

"Emancipate Our Films from Morality!"

What went wrong with the movie business in the late '60s had little
to do with external influences and everything to do with altered attitudes in the industry itself. As a result, untangling the enigma of the
evaporating audience involves answers that are both obvious and
uncomfortable. The injury originated at the very heart of Hollywood—
with the values of the people who produced the pictures, and the messages in the movies they made.

The distance the movie business traveled in a few short but disastrous years can be measured by the titles it chose to honor with Oscars
as Best Picture of the Year.

In 1965, the Academy selected *The Sound of Music*.

Four years later, it chose the X-rated saga of a homeless hustler,
Midnight Cowboy.

Is it entirely coincidence that in the year of *Midnight Cowboy*
(1969) Hollywood films drew *scarcely one-third* the number of paying

---

ticularly satisfying; like television, the video market serves most consumers as an antidote to boredom rather than a source of enchantment or inspiration.

In serving these lowered expectations of the audience, the newly developed video industry
has managed to keep Hollywood's struggling studios from financial collapse: the American people
spend more than twice as much money renting and buying home videos as they do on buying tickets for feature films at their local theaters. The wide range of options available at the video store
most certainly contributes to the popularity of the new format. Video consumers can select
favorite musicals, classic films from Hollywood's past, family and children's entertainment, along
with recent titles that have piqued their interest, rather than confining themselves to the narrow
(and often dreary) choices offered at the nearest multiplex.

customers who had flocked to the theaters in the year of *The Sound of Music*?

To put the matter as directly as possible:

Between 1965 and 1969 the values of the entertainment industry changed, and audiences fled from the theaters in horror and disgust.

Those disillusioned moviegoers have stayed away to this day—and they will remain estranged until the industry returns to a more positive and populist approach to entertaining its audience.

For some twenty-five years, Hollywood's leaders have ignored—or denied—this painfully obvious pattern. They stubbornly refuse to face the historical evidence or to acknowledge the connection between the changing content of motion pictures and the diminished enthusiasm of the mass audience.

At the time of the industry-wide upheaval that shook Hollywood in the late '60s, only one member of the old guard grasped the full scope of the revolution in values and accurately anticipated its hugely destructive impact on the business he loved. Frank Capra, three-time Oscar winner and creator of several of the best-loved motion pictures ever made, walked away from the business at age sixty-four because he refused to adjust to the cynicism of the new order. In his 1971 autobiography, *The Name Above the Title*, he wrote of the altered attitudes that made his continued participation impossible:

> The winds of change blew through the dream factories of make-believe, tore at its crinoline tatters. . . . The hedonists, the homosexuals, the hemophilic bleeding hearts, the God-haters, the quick-buck artists who substituted shock for talent, all cried: "Shake 'em! Rattle 'em! God is dead. Long live Pleasure! Nudity? Yea! Wife-swapping? Yea! Liberate the world from prudery. Emancipate our films from morality!". . .
>
> There was dancing in the streets among the disciples of lewdness and violence. Sentiment was dead, they cried. And so was Capra, its aging missionary. *Viva* hard core brutality: *Arriba* barnyard sex! *Arriba* SHOCK! Topless-shock! Bottomless-shock! Mass intercourse, mass rape, mass murder, kill for thrill—shock! Shock! To hell with the good in man. Dredge up his evil—shock! Shock!

Industry insiders may prefer to dismiss Capra's complaints as the reactionary rantings of an embittered old man, but now, twenty-one years after he penned these words, they seem positively prescient as a description of Hollywood's reigning aesthetic. The emphasis on "lewdness and violence" and the desire to "dredge up man's evil" serve as guiding principles for many of today's most honored filmmakers. Perhaps even Capra might not have guessed that just a few months after his death in 1991, a pitch-dark thriller about transvestite and cannibalistic serial killers would equal the achievement of his *It Happened One Night* by sweeping all the major Oscars as a representative of the industry's highest achievements. The great director's derisive mention of "barnyard sex" may have been hyperbole in 1971, but two decades later MGM announced plans—previously noted in this book—for a picture about the President of the United States having sex with a cow. Can anyone doubt that the transformations of twenty years ago that Capra described so scathingly still hold sway in the Tinseltown of today?

Its Own Curious Time Warp

Of course, those revolutionary changes in Hollywood mirrored simultaneous shifts in other segments of society, as the social and political convulsions of the '60s uprooted old conventions and experimentation emerged as the order of the day. For a time, radical new thinking seemed to triumph in every arena of American life, but nowhere did its victories prove so sweeping—or so permanent—as they did in the entertainment industry.

Long after the rest of the country had abandoned its flirtation with freakiness, the entertainment elite maintained its countercultural perspectives. By the mid-1980s, social scientists noted a nationwide "return to traditionalism" among the population at large; with Ronald Reagan riding high in Washington, heavy majorities recognized the dangers of recreational drug use and recreational sex, while asserting the importance of hard work, traditional family life, a strong national defense, and material acquisition. Millions of aspiring professionals and new parents gave up their warm and fuzzy Summer of Love sentiments along with their bell-bottoms and patchouli oil. The once trendy tenets of major philosophers such as Timothy Leary and Abbie Hoffman were discredited everywhere—except in Hollywood and some of the more cloistered corners of academia.

To a remarkable extent, the leaders of the entertainment industry remained true to the irreverent attitudes of their youth—maintaining antifamily, antireligious, antibusiness, and antimilitary biases long after they had ceased to be fashionable in the country at large. The flood of feature film and television projects about Black Panthers, doomed rock stars, Vietnam atrocities, aging hippies, Native American militants, CIA conspiracies, environmental activists, and assorted revolutionaries on the run glorified both the "idealism" and paranoia of the '60s in outrageously uncritical terms. These projects reflect the shallow but unrepentant radicalism of an industry lost in its own curious time warp, its outlook permanently frozen in the worldview of the sour summer of '69, set in amber somewhere between the release of *Easy Rider* and the messianic mudfest at Woodstock.

"An Anachronistic Piece of Censorship"

The counterculture's comprehensive conquest of Hollywood involved more than an enduring alteration of the attitudes of the elite, but also included the outright abolition of one of the industry's most powerful and well-established institutions.

Beginning in 1922, the major studios came together to establish a full-time office designed to regulate the content of all movies produced in Hollywood. After 1930, this so-called Hays Office (named after its first administrator, former Postmaster General Will H. Hays) enforced the provisions of a detailed Production Code which placed specific restrictions on obscene language, sex, violence, religious ridicule, ethnic insults, drug abuse, and other potentially offensive elements in movies.

From the outset, Hollywood's most powerful moguls planned these self-policing efforts as a response to public pressure concerning immorality in movies: by pointing to internal efforts to control motion picture content the industry managed to avoid the very real threat of state or federal censorship.

In practice, the day-to-day workings of the Hays Office proved far more lenient than the written strictures of the Production Code might suggest; nevertheless, for more than forty years this operation exerted a powerful influence that reached every corner of the popular culture.

Its very existence reminded moviemakers of the need to work within broadly accepted standards of decency and good taste. Critics of the Production Code Administration (PCA) suggested that its regular review of movie scripts and its required approval on all final cuts amounted to an intolerable interference in the creative process. Defenders of the system insisted that in order to keep the confidence of the mass audience and to avoid potential offense or outrage, the industry had to impose its own clear-cut standards on the products it presented to the public.

The debate ended in 1966, shortly after Jack Valenti assumed the leadership of the industry-wide organization of major producers. "The first thing I did when I became president of the Motion Picture Association of America," Valenti proudly recalled a quarter century later, "was to junk the Hays Production Code, which was an anachronistic piece of censorship that we never should have put into place." Instead of the old guidelines declaring certain elements altogether out of bounds for Hollywood movies, the industry initiated a new policy that would allow anything that the filmmaker chose to present, but would rate every new picture in terms of its suitability for family viewing. With several relatively minor modifications, that rating system remains in place today.

Needless to say, the new procedure drew unanimous praise from the creative community as a liberating step totally in keeping with the adventurous spirit of the times. Industry leaders predicted that the demise of the outmoded Production Code would lead to two immediate benefits for the motion picture business—uplifting the artistic quality of films by providing greater freedom to the filmmakers, at the same time that the exciting new offerings sure to result would draw an eager and greatly enlarged audience.

One needn't be a fan of the old Hays Office, with all its hypocrisies and inefficiencies, to recognize that its elimination never produced the desired results. In terms of the aesthetic excellence of motion pictures, the long-term impact proved dubious; in terms of the expansion of the audience, it was downright disastrous.

The years immediately following the change most certainly produced a flurry of superb, challenging, and highly original films (*They Shoot Horses, Don't They?*, 1969; *Five Easy Pieces*, 1970; *A Clockwork Orange*, 1971; *The Godfather*, 1972) in which brilliant filmmakers reveled in their newfound artistic freedom, but few observers would suggest that the *overall* quality of motion pictures has improved since the removal of the Production Code. Considering all of the films of the '80s and '90s, for instance, and comparing them to the Hollywood product of the '30s and '40s, it is difficult to imagine that anyone could claim that the increased latitude for filmmakers has brought about a more distinguished body of work. While many of the specific rules in the old Production Code look thoroughly ludicrous by today's standards, it is instructive to recall that Alfred Hitchcock and Howard Hawks, John Ford and Billy Wilder, George Cukor and Frank Capra and Orson Welles all somehow managed to create their masterpieces under its auspices.

However one might argue the aesthetic impact of Hollywood's new directions in the late '60s, there can be no question of the reaction of the mass audience: Americans overwhelmingly rejected the dark themes and shocking elements that audacious filmmakers introduced in the films of the period. While individual examples of the countercultural trend might achieve respectable box office returns (*Bonnie and Clyde,* 1967; *Easy Rider,* 1969; *Midnight Cowboy,* 1969; *M°A°S°H,* 1970), the general distaste for the industry's emphasis on sex and violence provoked an unprecedented flight of the mass audience.

In 1967, the first year in which Hollywood found itself finally free to appeal to the public without the "paralyzing" restrictions of the old Production Code, American pictures drew an average weekly audience of only 17.8 million—compared to the weekly average of 38 million who had gone to the theaters just one year before! In a single twelve-month period, more than half the movie audience disappeared—*by far* the largest one-year decline in the history of the motion picture business.

There is no way to test the extent to which these appalling numbers represent a direct response to the closure of the Hays Office, but the statistics nonetheless definitively deflate the notion that liberating the industry from its established standards would help it to win a huge new audience. The suspension of the Production Code may have contributed to some extent to the alienation of the public, but it seems unlikely that it constituted a primary cause of the crisis. Rather, the removal of the code and the collapse in movie attendance both represented *symptoms* of the same underlying illness that afflicted the popular culture in the late 1960s.

An Unmistakable Message from the Hinterlands

The seriousness of that sickness is shown by the fact that it prevented the entertainment industry from responding in a normal way to the forces of the marketplace. Even as Hollywood marched merrily into the fever swamps of alienation and self-indulgence, indications abounded that the new directions made no commercial sense.

In April 1973, the chairman of the National Association of Theatre Owners blamed "a commensurate drop in the morality quotient of films for much of the erosion in patronage." In a passionate speech reported in depth by the *Hollywood Reporter,* industry leader B. V. Sturdivant declared that Hollywood's problems originated "some three years ago, when the scatalogical stench permeated so many production circles, and obscenity coupled with violence threatened to explode beyond acceptable limits. . . ." Noting that movie attendance had recently plunged to an all-time low, the veteran theater owner saw scant hope of recapturing the confidence and enthusiasm of the mass audience unless the industry returned to more traditional values. "So long as we have producers, distributors, and exhibitors who seek the dirty dollar as panderers of filth . . . the outlook for reconciliation is dim."

The most surprising characteristic of these "panderers of filth" and their energetic pursuit of "the dirty dollar" is their chronic inefficency in achieving their goals. At the very moment that the new countercultural values won their first great triumphs in Hollywood, the moviegoing public sent powerful signals of its unfriendly attitude toward the revolution. *Variety's* review of the movie business for the turning point year of 1969 featured the revealing headline: YEAR'S SURPRISE: "FAMILY" FILMS DID BEST. In the accompanying article, Robert B. Frederick pointed out that the Disney comedy *The Love Bug,* hardly a work of hard-hitting social criticism, turned out to be the year's box-office champ. Despite the enormous attention lavished on *Easy Rider* by the press, *Oliver, Funny Girl,* and *Chitty Chitty Bang Bang,* all holdovers from the previous year, easily earned more money at the box office. "If there was a surprise in the year-end check of the big business pix," Frederick wrote, "it was that the real whoppers of $10 million and above were, with a single exception (*Midnight Cowboy*) what could easily be considered 'family' fare."

With truly suicidal disregard of the public's preferences, Hollywood responded to this unmistakable message from the hinterlands by steadily *reducing* the number of family and children's offerings in its movie mix. In 1968, the first year of the new ratings system, 41 percent of all American releases earned the mildest available designation—the "G" rating. By 1977, despite the "Top 5" box-office performance of movies like *Benji* (1975) and *The Bad News Bears* (1976), the number of these "general audience" films had fallen to 13 percent of Hollywood's offerings. In 1991, "G" movies accounted for only 2.3 percent of the product that the industry offered the public—a total of just fourteen titles—but two of those fourteen placed among the year's Top 20 box-office leaders!

The prevailing contempt for the family audience could never be explained in terms of rational self-interest. One "circuit booker" described by *Box Office* magazine as "an aggressive, young, with-it film buyer" reported: "People are shopping for good, clean entertainment—and we see them—young and older patrons alike. . . . It's time the film companies took a cue from all this and began to make clean, solid, entertaining movies again."

Amazingly enough, he made the comments more than twenty years ago—in October 1970. In the same article, *Box Office* concluded that "the steamy, 'contemporary' motion picture has begun to sour at the box office . . . the now thing seems to have run its course and the nudity-sex thing is a cipher all of a sudden." The piece ended with a few words of sound advice to the studios: "In a nutshell, clean 'em up and clean up!"

Anyone who has checked the recent offerings at the neighborhood multiplex or read the dismal attendance figures in current issues of the trade press knows how completely Hollywood has ignored this sage suggestion.

18

Motivations for Madness

Following the Money?

If nothing else, an honest account of the entertainment industry's tortured path to its present predicament should shatter, once and for all, and beyond any question, one of the most enduring myths about the movies: the peculiarly persistent notion that Hollywood gives us sleaze and violence only because we demand it.

Recent history shows conclusively that whatever motivations pushed the motion picture business to its current obsessions, financial self-interest was not among them. How could an industry that radically changed its focus and thereby permanently sacrificed nearly two-thirds of its audience be described, in any serious sense, as "following the money"? In presenting the bleak and bloody visions that trouble so many of our fellow citizens, the popular culture isn't responding to some primitive blood lust of the American people; it is, rather, following its own warped conceptions of artistic integrity, driven by some dark compulsion beyond simple greed.

This idea is so revolutionary, so disturbing, so counterintuitive, that most analysts refuse to take it seriously—despite an overwhelming accumulation of evidence.

Consider, for example, the universally accepted assumption that Hollywood grinds out so many "R"-rated films only because these features make more money at the box office. This proposition cannot possibly survive even a brief inspection of the readily available figures from accepted industry sources.

• Looking over *Variety's* list of the Top 10 box-office films of the decade of the 1980s, only one—*Beverly Hills Cop*—happened to be rated "R," even though "R" films accounted for more than 60 percent of all titles released in this period.

• At the same time, "PG" films represented less than 25 percent of all titles—but occupied *six* of the Top 10 places on the list of the decade's leading money-makers.

• If you expand the calculations to consider the twenty leading titles in terms of domestic box-office returns between 1981 and 1990, 55 percent were rated "G" or "PG"; only 25 percent were "R" films.

• An analysis of all 1,010 domestic releases logged into the comprehensive data base at Robert Cain Consulting Associates between 1983 and 1989 demonstrates a dramatic and unmistakable public preference for family-oriented material. During this period, all "G" films achieved a median box office gross of $17.3 million, while "PG" titles earned a median figure of $13.0 million. For "PG-13" releases, the numbers dipped sharply to $9.3 million, while "R" pictures returned an even more pathetic median gross of $8.3 million.

In response to this consistent trend throughout the decade, one might reasonably expect that Hollywood would adjust its approach and reduce the levels of sex, violence and gutter language so that fewer films would earn the "R" rating. Instead, official figures from the Motion Picture Association of America show that the percentage of "R"-rated movies dramatically *increased*—from 46 percent in 1980, to 67 percent in 1989.

Bringing this analysis up to date, the self-destructive pattern only repeats itself:

• In 1990, Hollywood produced more than four times as many "R" films as "G" and "PG" films combined (64 percent of all titles compared to 14.3 percent); nevertheless, the annual Top 20 included the same number (seven) of "PG" and "R" titles.

• Most recently, in 1991, "R" films comprised 61 percent of all titles, but only 30 percent of the Top 20 hits; "G" and "PG" films, with 16.5 percent of total releases, represented 40 percent of the commercial leaders.

• This means that the statistics for the last two years—and for the entire decade of the 1980s—show stunningly similar results, with a disproportionately large number of the relatively rare "G" and "PG" films performing well at the box office, while a far smaller percentage of the much more common "R"-rated pictures emerge as major commercial winners. *Taken together, the numbers since 1980 show that a given "G" or "PG" film is nearly five times more likely to place among the year's box-office leaders than an "R" film.*

Good Reason to Reexamine their Assumptions

When I presented these surprising calculations to a gathering of entertainment executives and journalists in June 1992, one of Hollywood's most respected leaders took passionate exception to my conclusions.

"Do you really think we're nincompoops?" asked this dynamic chairman of one of the major studios. "Your numbers are interesting, but they only deal with box office home runs. When you're running a studio, you're looking for solid singles most of the time, and you're always worried about striking out. Maybe you're right that 'PG' pictures stand a better chance of hitting it big than 'R' pictures, but I'm sure they also have a much better chance of turning into big flops.

"That's why we go with 'R' pictures so much of the time. We need pictures that have teeth to them, that have an edge, that stand out from all the stuff people see on TV. You've got to understand that the TV ads are crucial when it comes to getting people to go out to see a picture and 'PG' films don't cut it because they're soft—the audience just confuses them with stuff that's already on the tube. That's why hard-edged pictures are a much safer bet—because they cut through the TV haze and get attention. It's not like we're committed to blood and guts and language, but that's what you need today to open a film. If you take another look at the numbers, I'm sure you'll see what I mean."

Intrigued by his argument, I accepted his challenge to "take another look at the numbers" and to pursue further investigation of the relationship between a film's M.P.A.A. rating and its chances of box-office success.

In this endeavor I enlisted the able assistance of Robert D. Cain, an entertainment industry consultant and the Director of Research for the Screen Actors Guild. At my request, he analyzed 221 films "representing virtually all of the domestically-produced theatrical films for which 1991 box office figures are currently available. . . . Box office revenue figures were prepared by Entertainment Data Inc., and are considered highly reliable."

The results of this research proved entirely consistent with the trends I had previously discovered going back to 1980—and showed that the preponderance of "R"-films in each year's release schedule makes no logical sense whatsoever.

As Mr. Cain concluded, "By almost every measure, 'R'-rated films are less likely to succeed at the box office than their 'G,' 'PG,' and 'PG-13' counterparts. R-rated films generate substantially less revenue, return less profit, and are more likely to 'flop' than films aimed at teen and family audiences."

The specific figures should give the studio head and his colleagues good reason to reexamine their assumptions.

• Concerning his contention that "hard-edged pictures are a much safer bet," *41 percent of all "R"-films generated less than $2 million in box-office receipts—compared to only 28 percent of "PG" pictures.*

• At the other end of the spectrum of success, "R" films are similarly disadvantaged. Thirty-eight percent of all "PG" films exceeded $25 million in box-office gross in 1991—while only 19 percent of "R" films reached that level of revenue. In other words, "R" films proved less than half as likely as "PG" releases to reach the "respectable" box-office plateau of $25 million.

• In 1991, the median "PG"-rated picture grossed $15.7 million in domestic box office, *almost triple the median "R"-picture gross of $5.5 million.* Meanwhile, the few "G" pictures registered the highest returns of all—a median box-office gross of $18.5 million.

As Robert Cain reported, "These general patterns held true for independent as well as major studio releases."

These figures do not mean that a new "PG" film is guaranteed commercial success any more than they signify that a forthcoming "R"-rated title is a sure-fire failure.

But they do destroy the argument that the industry's long-standing and hugely unbalanced emphasis on "adult" fare is dictated by financial self-interest.

When the typical "PG" film generates nearly three times the revenue of the typical "R" bloodbath or shocker, then the industry's insistence of cranking out more than four times as many "R" titles must be seen as an irrational and irresponsible habit.°

Of course, no one would suggest that a "PG" rating automatically indicates that a motion picture is appropriate for kids, or instantly qualifies its makers for sainthood. Under our famously flawed rating system, many PG movies (like *Kindergarten Cop*) include graphic material that would horrify most parents. Nevertheless, "R" films generally feature even more intense elements—and more to the point, they *promise* those elements to the public. Even when a rating provides no accurate description of what a movie contains, it still reflects the way that picture is promoted and perceived. With moviegoers consistently choosing titles labeled "PG" over those labeled "R," it's ridiculous to suggest that they are somehow clamoring for the gory or graphic extremes of what Hollywood misleadingly calls "adult entertainment."

For a long time, the American people have been trying to send the message that they want more wholesome entertainment. Whenever they are asked their opinion by pollsters (as they were in a comprehensive Associated Press survey in 1989), overwhelming majorities indicate

---

°In response to these calculations some industry analysts will properly point out that the figures cited above reflect only domestic box-office receipts and provide no information on the increasingly significant overseas markets—where hyperviolent "action" films often fare well. A scene in which a grunting, muscular hero picks up a submachine gun and blows away two dozen of his enemies requires neither subtitles nor dubbing; in this way brutality, not love, has become the international language of cinema.

This may help explain how struggling producers of "R"-rated material manage to stay afloat, despite their disadvantage in domestic competition with "PG" material, but it cannot account for the fatal attraction of a risky strategy that relies on the enthusiasm of moviegoers in Beirut to overcome the indifference of moviegoers in Boston. For one thing, the films that achieve the most conspicuous success in foreign markets are generally the same titles that did best in the United States; the extent of promotional support and press coverage that a movie receives overseas is largely dependent on its popularity during its prior American release.

Furthermore, the acceptance of violent material by audiences abroad tells us nothing about the underlying attitudes of audiences at home. Statistics on foreign market receipts therefore shed no light at all on the question of whether or not an industry that consistently focuses 60 percent of its efforts on an "R"-rated product accurately reflects the preferences of the American public.

that they want less violence in movies (82 percent), less sexual content (72 percent), and less foul language (80 percent). Their recent box-office behavior indicates that when they express such opinions, the members of the mass audience might actually mean what they say.

Beyond Simple Greed

Greed can explain many things in Hollywood, but it cannot explain everything.

Would anyone suggest that a lust for profits motivated what *Los Angeles Times* critic Charles Champlin called "the trendy moral anarchy" of the movies? Writing in 1973, the veteran industry observer noted the increasing tendency for "letting the bad guys win" and saw that "the pendulum has swung so far (and frozen there) that now the surprise is when the good guys win, virtue triumphs and when something is understood to be right or wrong." The pendulum has remained frozen at the same peculiar point for twenty years now and motion picture attendance remains anemic. Is this the result of calculating producers assuming that by stressing moral ambiguity and downbeat resolutions in their most "serious" cinematic statements they would somehow rake in the big bucks? Not even the most obtuse studio executive could possibly be so stupid.

Nor could they assume that they would possibly make money on the constantly escalating infatuation with foul language, discussed in some detail in Chapter 11 of this book. More gutter speech turns up in mainstream movies year after year, month after month, *despite* innumerable surveys that show that huge majorities of potential moviegoers resent this kind of talk. I know of no scientific study of audience preferences, and no analysis of box-office returns, that has ever been able to demonstrate a desire on the part of the public to hear their favorite actors or actresses repeatedly pronouncing the "F-word." Nevertheless, this juvenile emphasis on unnecessary obscenity continues to characterize every sort of new film and to contribute to the ongoing alienation of the audience.

There is simply no way that the single-minded pursuit of profit can account for Hollywood's ongoing war on traditional values—for the never-ending stream of film and television indictments of organized religion described in Part II, or the similarly crowded parade of anti-marriage message movies discussed in Part III, or the relentless and embittered assaults on America's past and present place in the world enumerated in Part IV. Nearly all of these projects proved to be box-office poison, but future plans from the major studios show their intention to continue investing vast resources in similarly risky fare. When it comes to material that challenges some of the public's most cherished ideals and institutions, the entertainment industry displays unexpected and irrational recklessness while stubbornly repeating its own mistakes.

In a sense, this surprising tendency to take chances on unpopular messages demonstrates that the entertainment establishment is actually less greedy and more idealistic than its critics—or even its supporters—are ready to admit.

The Hollywood community wants respect even more than it wants riches; above all, its members crave acceptance and recognition as serious artists. Money is not the main motivation for their current madness. The leading figures of the popular culture, insecure and uncertain like all creative personalities, are driven by a deep-seated need to reassure themselves as to the significance of their own work. Contempt for "mere" commercial considerations is frequently expressed by those who long to view themselves as something more than entertainers or businessmen.

As Oscar-winning director Sydney Pollack told the American Enterprise Institute in 1992: "You have to remember that most of us who are doing this got into it for the romance, the glory, the applause, the chance to tell stories, even to learn, but rarely for the money." After examining the record compiled by Mr. Pollack and his colleagues, one is compelled to believe him.

Craving Esteem and Immortality

Michael Jackson, one of the prime potentates of the popular culture, provides a powerful illustration of the incurable craving for esteem and immortality that motivates so many efforts of the entertainment industry. He may have won worldwide admiration for his singing and dancing, but it is not enough to satisfy his deeper ambitions. "I wanted to do an album that was like Tchaikovsky's *Nutcracker Suite*," he told *Ebony* magazine (May 1992) in discussing his latest opus, *Dangerous*. "So that in a thousand years from now, people would still be listening to it. Something that would live forever. I would like to see children and teenagers and parents and all races all over the world, hundreds and hundreds of years from now, still pulling out songs from that album and dissecting it. I want it to live." You may recall that the work for which Mr. Jackson expressed such cosmic aspirations happened to be the same album that was introduced to the world with a music video showing the artist repeatedly grabbing his own crotch and attacking a parked car with a crowbar. While some might question the impact of such images on Jackson's young fans, the shy superstar disclaimed ultimate responsibility for the visions and music he created. "I'm just the source through which it comes," he insisted in the same interview. "I can't take credit for it because it's God's work. He's just using me as the messenger."

Other Hollywood figures may stop short of claiming the status of divine messenger but they still describe their work in incongruously high-minded terms. Filmmaker Oliver Stone, for instance, characterized his movie *JFK* as nothing less than "a battle over the meaning of my generation with the likes of Dan Quayle, a battle between official mythology and disturbing truth."

Even those producers who ply their trade in the populist precincts of network television feel a similar need to ascribe higher purposes to their projects. In a recent radio interview, Linda Bloodworth-Thomason, creator of "Designing Women" and "Evening Shade," compared her mission to that of Mark Twain and Herman Melville. "What I'm doing in my shows," she told the listening audience, "is exactly what they were doing a hundred years ago." When questioned over the deeper similarities between "Evening Shade" and *Moby Dick,* she retreated to a more modest analogy. "Actually, it's Louisa May Alcott who's my personal model. I think anybody could see that *Little Women* and 'Designing Women' are really the same thing."

In addition to her high-flying literary aspirations, Bloodworth-Thomason is noted for her political activism and the liberal messages she inserts wherever possible in her television programs. For several years, such attempts to raise the consciousness of the audience have represented the ultimate goal for many leading producers. "With varying successes we did the story of a homosexual rape, an unwed father, unwed mothers, abortions, drug addiction, indecent exposure," boasted David Victor, a writer-producer for "Marcus Welby, M.D.," in a 1983 interview for the book *The Producer's Medium.* "I'm proud of that. I think I educate as well as entertain."

Leonard Goldberg, creator of shows such as "Fantasy Island" and "Starsky and Hutch," also asserted "educational" ambitions that go well beyond ratings success. "I think it is the responsibility of television not only to entertain, but to present contemporary problems facing our society and to offer some guidance. . . ."

"Up on a Soapbox"

The nature of that "guidance" invariably involves a rejection of the established order and the need to reshape American society and its institutions. In their ground-breaking 1983 study of more than a hundred of the most influential and successful television producers in the business, media analysts S. Robert Lichter, Linda Lichter, and Stanley Rothman discovered that a full 66 percent of them agreed with the statement "TV should promote social reform." "This is perhaps the single most striking finding in our study," the researchers wrote. "According to television's creators, they are not in it just for the money. They also seek to move their audience to their own vision of the good society."

With that vision in mind, the entertainment elite takes particular pride in those instances when it can defy convention and present its own perspectives to the American people. In a 1987 interview televised on PBS, Philip DeGuere, creator of "Simon & Simon," explained: "When the business community . . . [made] public their grievance that they were being constantly treated like villains on television shows it hit me like a sledgehammer. I said, 'Yes, that is exactly what I've been doing personally.' . . . And I'm going to do it even more."

At times, major powers in the TV business are remarkably candid in acknowledging that key elements in their shows derive from their own attitudes and experiences. Diane English, the brilliant producer of "Murphy Brown," told the Associated Press in March 1992: "Murphy expresses a quite liberal point of view. It's also my point of view . . . [Murphy's] a dyed-in-the-wool Democratic liberal." Along similar lines,

"L.A. Law" executive producer Patricia Green told *The New York Times*, "I'm stronger on the issue shows. I love to get up on a soapbox."

Personal encounters as well as political perspectives inevitably find their way to prime time. Peter Noah, executive producer of "Anything but Love," explained to *Time* magazine that a 1991 episode in which the two romantic leads spent nearly the whole half hour frolicking under the sheets "was entirely drawn out of my passionate relationship with my wife. We have also had plenty of fights, and if I get my way, every one of them is going to end up on television." Don Reo, creator of "Blossom," noted the growing number of shows, including his own, that feature shattered families headed by single fathers. "Most of them are created by guys who are divorced," he said. "The reason they do them must be wish fulfillment. They're subliminally trying to kill their ex-wives."

These private pecularities and opinions play an increasingly prominent part in shaping the content of popular entertainment, often overriding cold-hearted commercial calculation. In their 1991 book, *Watching America*, Lichter, Lichter, and Rothman concluded: "Far from always following in the wake of popular tastes, the fictional world of prime time can be sharply at odds with public sentiment. More often, it tries to guide middle-American tastes in the direction of intellectual trends emanating from New York and Los Angeles."

Ignorance and Arrogance

Those trends originate with a leadership elite of shockingly small size and abiding insularity. *Time* reporter Jordan Bonfante noted that since the early 1970s, television "has become more and more a captive of Los Angeles. It is especially dominated by a small but powerful group of L.A.-based writer-producers who year after year create the lion's share of successful prime-time programs. Numbering no more than 150, they act as the industry's permanent bureaucracy, remaining in place while studio chiefs and network honchos come and go."

The members of this enduring establishment display an almost tribal solidarity whenever their achievements or attitudes are attacked—or even questioned—by outsiders. They resent all suggestions that their slant on society might be distorted, and they cling defiantly to the peculiar vision that television writer Ben Stein described in the title to his 1979 book as *The View from Sunset Boulevard*. Stein came to consider "the TV production community as part of a small but extremely energetic and militant class. . . . The TV people see certain classes as their enemies from long ago. Moreover, they still see those people as enemies, except that now a sea change has occurred. Instead of having to work out of nothing to become something, the TV people are now in a position to dominate society. They can contend with the businessman class, with the military class, with small-town gentry, with *anyone* for the leadership role in society."

This new self-confidence leads to an impatient and contemptuous dismissal of the values of the majority of their countrymen; for most members of the Hollywood establishment, America is a strange, backward land that you are forced to traverse on your way between Manhattan and the Coast. Novelist and *New York Times* sportswriter Robert Lipsyte writes: "The people we fly over, those noncoastal heartland Nielsen families maddened by the wintry prairie winds, may produce more than their share of CEOs and TV anchors, but they rarely see their visions affirmed on the national fantasy loop."

This disregard for Middle American visions stems from both ignorance and arrogance. Ignorance, because the members of the Hollywood elite lead complex and often chaotic lives that leave them thoroughly isolated from the daily concerns and circumstances faced by most members of their mass audience. Arrogance, because they never question the viewpoints of the pampered and tightly sealed little world in which they live, even when confronted with survey data and other indications demonstrating that those values are rejected by overwhelming majorities of their fellow citizens. It makes little impact when you prove to princes of the popular culture that more than 40 percent of the nation at large attends church or synagogue every week; in response to such figures they will merely smile and shake their heads, unshakably certain that their own rejection of religion merely *proves* that they are more enlightened than their backward and superstitious neighbors.

This line of reasoning can make for some frustrating conversations. I recently spent an hour arguing with a powerful agent over the surprisingly hostile attitude in recent films and television programs toward the institution of marriage. While acknowledging the trend, he insisted that it reflected current realities and expressed the American public's overwhelming desire to "move beyond" the limitations of the nuclear family. When I trotted out a wealth of census figures and survey data suggesting that most Americans remain deeply and stubbornly attached to the old mores and family ideals, my friend deftly changed the basis for his defense. "Maybe we *are* a little bit ahead of the curve on this one," he acknowledged. "But sometimes that's what you've got to do. You've got to take special risks to help that audience evolve to the next level of consciousness."

That sense of mission has become a powerful force in Hollywood, since the people who produce the popular culture aren't nearly as individualistic or independent as they pretend to be. They feel free to defy the values of the public at large, but at the same time they are powerfully influenced by the attitudes and ideologies of one another. The more they are estranged from realities of ordinary Americans, the more they are subject to the pressures and priorities of their own self-enclosed community. This is a common phenomenon among "cutting edge" artists and thinkers who strive to challenge the reigning conventions of their society. In his fascinating book *Intellectuals* (1988), the historian Paul Johnson writes: "Intellectuals, far from being highly individualistic and nonconformist people, follow certain patterns of behavior. Taken as a group, they are often ultra-conforming within the circles formed by those whose approval they seek and value. That is what makes them, *en masse*, so dangerous, for it enables them to create climates of opinion and prevailing orthodoxies, which themselves often generate irrational and destructive courses of action."

An Insatiable Need for Reassurance

Public performers are especially inclined to adopt these irrational courses of action because of their desperate and insatiable need for the approval of their colleagues.

Anyone who has spent time with actors or actresses—even of the amateur variety—understands how painfully exposed they feel whenever they stand in front of strangers and pretend to be someone else. Little in life can leave you so vulnerable—or so hungry for the message from someone you respect that you haven't irretrievably embarrassed yourself.

A few years ago I interviewed an ambitious and glamorous young actress who had become intensely depressed over the critical drubbing she had received for one of her first films. I tried to encourage her by saying the commercial success of the picture indicated that the public appreciated her work, despite the skeptical reviews. This argument made no headway: she felt convinced that the enthusiasm of ordinary moviegoers had nothing to do with her artistic abilities and everything to do with one extended nude scene. "They didn't like my acting," she sighed. "They just liked my rear end."

The need for approval from other industry indsiders helps to explain the yearly obsession with the Oscars. When Sally Field received the Best Actress award for her performance in *Places in the Heart* (1984), her tearful declaration "You like me! You really like me!" expressed this all-consuming and almost touching eagerness for endorsement by associates. Ms. Field had already achieved the pinnacle of professional success—earning millions of dollars each year and enjoying the affection of legions of fans around the world. Nevertheless, the fact that a majority of the four thousand members of the Academy expressed their admiration by voting her a second Best Actress award touched her insatiable need for reassurance and unleashed her emotions.

The annual, industry-wide insanity over the Oscar process provides a powerful rebuttal to the idea that financial success is all that matters in the movie business. In handing out its most coveted honors, Hollywood makes a major point of looking below the bottom line; the Academy has recently shattered the old unwritten rule that only hit movies would be considered for major awards. As critic Richard Grenier points out, "Suddenly, in 1980, the pattern broke with Robert Redford's *Ordinary People,* which, only an indifferent success commercially, won three of the top Academy Awards, including Best Picture and Best Director. From then on the Academy has behaved more like the awards committee for the Nobel Prize, the Pulitzer Prize, or the MacArthur Foundation. The unwashed public be damned. The Academy now honors what it considers to be the artistic, the idealistic, and the socially progressive no matter how mediocre the movie's record at the box office."

In fact, too much profit can actually impede a picture's prospects of winning the industry's most prestigious awards. In 1982, for instance, most observers considered *E.T.* the early front-runner for the Academy Award for Best Picture of the year until its runaway success at the box office (and with merchandising tie-ins) helped tilt Oscar voters toward *Gandhi.* When *Ghost* won a surprise Best Picture nomination in 1990, all commentators agreed that it stood no chance at all of upsetting *Dances with Wolves* and actually winning the award: it seemed unthinkable that the Academy would anoint the year's top money-maker.

Meanwhile, no one has ever suggested an alternate awards ceremony—or even a yearly luncheon—in which major stars would hand out trophies for the biggest box-office winners. The only show that even comes close to such an enshrinement of popular preferences is the televised "People's Choice" awards, which tabulates millions of votes from the public at large rather than surveying the opinions of critics or the creative community. Needless to say, this annual exercise is held in contempt by the Hollywood establishment, and receives considerably less attention than honors awarded by only a few dozen journalists or reviewers—such as the L.A. Film Critics Awards, the Golden Globes, the N.Y. Film Critics Awards, and the National Board of Review. In the curious culture of Hollywood, peer respect can count for more than public response.

In contrast to the widely held assumption that an ability to generate profits is the only source of power in the entertainment industry, a number of Hollywood's most esteemed and sought-after directors have built huge reputations without once creating a spectacular commercial success. Martin Scorsese, Woody Allen, Roland Joffe, Alan Parker, Spike Lee, Terry Gilliam, Joel Coen, David Lynch, and Gus Van Sant receive unequivocal admiration from the industry elite and lavish support from producers despite the fact that none of them has ever made an unqualified smash hit that finished in a yearly list of the box-office Top 10.

If you speak to ambitious young directors eager to carve a place for themselves in the business, you will find precious few who say they dream of emulating populist hit makers like Robert Zemeckis (*Back to the Future, Who Framed Roger Rabbit?*) or Ron Howard (*Splash, Cocoon*), but many will talk of following the paths of Martin Scorsese or Gus Van

Sant. Aesthetic ambition and artistic integrity, as defined by industry insiders, are more highly prized than popularity with the public. Members of the creative community never apologize when they create a project that is clearly out of step with the prevailing currents of public opinion; instead, they point with pride to their courage in daring to go against the grain in a noble effort to shock the mass audience out of its complacency. If a film contains the right ideological or aesthetic elements, even the most abject failure at the box office is considered no disgrace.

The Myth of the Alienated Artist

This readiness to accept—and finance—"noble flops" reflects the increasingly common idea that the people who create our popular culture are artists, not just entertainers.

To reinforce this notion, they adopt a self-consciously adversarial position toward the nation's institutions and traditions—thereby conforming to contemporary expectations that all "serious" artists are somehow alienated from the less sensitive masses. As Norman Mailer recently declared, "Great artists are almost always in opposition to their society."

The only problem with this sweeping assertion is that it totally misrepresents several millennia of Western culture.

As my colleague Richard Grenier usefully points out, "Any art historian should know that none of the titans of past centuries—neither Michelangelo nor Rembrandt nor El Greco nor Shakespeare—was ever free to insult and/or belittle the fundamental beliefs of his church and people. Nor until modern times did many of them even want to. . . . Yet despite these political inhibitions Shakespeare and Chaucer managed to produce works generally thought to have artistic merit."

In his indispensable book *Capturing the Culture* (1991), Grenier reminds us that the concept of the alienated artist is a recent development that marks a radical departure in the course of civilization.

The author of the *Song of Roland,* an early version of which was chanted to Norman troops before the Battle of Hastings, did not see himself as marginal, adversarial or alienated in any way from his lord and sovereign, William the Conqueror. . . . The author of the *Nibelungenlied* did not secretly think Siegfried was a putz. Homer did not think Achilles was a putz. Corneille did not think Le Cid was a putz. Cimabue and Fra Angelico were not secret atheists, painting this religious trash because the church paid them big commissions.

Dante, whose *Divine Comedy* pictures a changeless universe ordered by God, its theme the gradual revelation of God to man, was a nobleman and officer of the Florentine cavalry that routed the Ghibellines at the battle of Campaldino. Cervantes, for all his mockery of the medieval romance in *Don Quixote,* fought as an officer of Spain against the infidel Turk at Lepanto, one of the greatest sea battles of history. Spain's greatest playwright, Lope de Vega, for the true church and that most Christian king, Philip II, sailed to conquer England in the Spanish Armada. . . .

The simple fact is that, until the French Enlightenment, Romantic movement, and the American and French Revolutions of the eighteenth century, the artist saw himself as a celebrant of his society and all its values, which to him—if not to aesthetes of today—were noble and heroic.

Discussing Dante and Fra Angelico in the same context as Arnold Schwarzenegger and Guns n' Roses may seem a bit of a stretch, but the changes in the high culture cast significant light on recent changes in the entertainment industry. Until the revolution of the 1960s, the leaders of the popular culture served the artist's old purposes as a "celebrant of his society and all its values," but since that time Hollywood has cast itself in an increasingly alienated role.

Some measure of the change can be seen in the personal commitments of major stars.

In 1941, James Stewart had just emerged as one of the world's most popular big-screen performers. Winner of the Best Actor Academy Award in 1940 (for *The Philadelphia Story*), he stood at the peak of popularity and promise. Nevertheless, he turned his back on the money and the fame to enlist in the Army Air Corps at the outbreak of World War II. He made it a point to refuse publicity or special treatment based on his celebrity, and instead worked for several years as a bombardier instructor. In 1943 he went to Europe as commander of an Eighth Air Force bomber squadron and flew twenty-five missions over enemy territory. He rose to the rank of full colonel, and earned an Air Medal, a Distinguished Flying Cross, and the Croix de Guerre. For twenty-three years after the war he remained active in the air force reserve, holding the rank of brigadier general.

Stewart's friend Henry Fonda held dramatically different political views (as a lifelong Democrat and committed supporter of the New Deal) but shared a sense of obligation to his country. In 1942, Fonda suspended his high-flying Hollywood career and left behind his two small children (Jane and Peter) to enlist in the U.S. Navy. He served with conspicuous gallantry as an assistant operations and air combat intelligence officer, rising to the rank of lieutenant and receiving a Bronze Star and a presidential citation.

At the same time, Frank Capra, who had already established himself as the industry's most acclaimed and successful director, gave up four years at the height of his powers to serve in the armed forces. He had previously fought as a second lieutenant in the First World War, but during World War II, Colonel Capra devoted himself to creating the *Why We Fight* series—some of the most inspiring and effective documentary films ever made—that helped to rally millions of soldiers and civilians to the Allied cause.

The wartime heroics of so many of Hollywood's major figures reflected their sense of themselves as grateful members of a good society—and defenders of its values and interests. The distance between these patriots and the pampered principals of today's popular culture is almost immeasurable. Could anyone begin to imagine Bruce Willis or Tom Cruise interrupting *their* careers and romances to fight in the Gulf War—or to serve their country in any other capacity? The entertainment industry's estrangement from the concerns and commitments of mainstream America is so well understood and so widely accepted that no one even remarked on the total lack of Hollywood participation in the recent hostilities in the Middle East.

"Reptiles Slithering on the Ground"

The attitude of alienation on the part of leading entertainers is communicated not only through the creative work that they place before the public but by endless accounts in the popular press of their off-screen idiosyncrasies. Where the all-powerful moguls who once ruled Hollywood tried to hide eccentric behavior behind a veneer of respectability, today's show business community seems to revel in its own exquisite weirdness. In the words of director Terry Gilliam: "The problem with movies is that you're in the most bizarre group of people." No less an expert in outlandish excess than Madonna herself emphatically agrees with him. "The actors and singers and entertainers I know are emotional cripples," she told a 1991 MTV interview. "Really healthy people aren't in this business, let's face it."

The assumption that only "emotional cripples" belong in Hollywood echoes the fashionable claim that only wounded and disaffected spirits can create worthwhile art. This mind-set leads some of the wealthiest and most powerful figures in the entertainment establishment to strike occasional poses as haunted desperadoes; they will take enough time away from their jacuzzis and their car phones to pretend that they are actually dangerous rebels, living life on the fringes of society and the edge of sanity. In 1991, at the time of the release of *The Doors,* his monumentally depressing meditation on the life of rock star Jim Morrison, Oliver Stone told the press: "I believed in Morrison's incantation. Break on through. Kill the pigs. Destroy. Loot . . . all that shit. Anything goes. Anything."

With this ideal in mind, the purpose of popular entertainment has been redefined to emphasize its ability to disturb and discomfit the audience. Gus Van Sant, the acclaimed director of *My Own Private Idaho,* offered a memorable statement of his own artistic credo in the fall of 1991: "I believe the properly manipulated image can provoke an audience to the Burroughsian limit of riot, rampant sex, instantaneous death, even spontaneous combustion," he wrote. ". . . The raw materials of inspiration include elements as primal and potentially frightening as violence, sex, and death—which have haunted us since we were reptiles slithering on the ground. Only in our dreams can we make the journey back through labyrinthine, DNA-encoded history to our fiery, barbaric origins. But the primitive world of blood and flame is still with us."

"The primitive world of blood and flame" is most certainly with us on our motion picture and television screens—whether we welcome it or not. The alienated artists who helped bring about a revolution in pop culture sensibilities have enabled the media of mass entertainment to "catch up" with the other arts in their bleak and angry view of the world.

As a result of those changes, the entertainment industry now faces the prospect of permanently estranging its audience and following the path of other artistic endeavors that have rendered themselves increasingly irrelevant to the lives of ordinary citizens.

In his book *A World Without Heroes,* Dr. George Roche describes the process through which the spiritual emptiness of contemporary culture has undermined the West's artistic traditions. "A more precipitous cultural decline than ours is hard to imagine," he writes. "From the old masters to splatters and splotches and worse; from literature to pornography; from Bach to rock. . . . Denying that beauty lay beyond themselves, they killed it with their hands and brushes and words, and call ugly things beautiful. Thinking to set the arts free in a brave new world, they tore down all the signposts. In place of joyous music and paintings to lift our souls, they give us steel hulks that tell us life is a wearisome joke."

As the aspiring artists of the entertainment industry define their own aims in ever more grandiose terms, they litter the Hollywood landscape with celluloid hulks that convey the same dismal message.

The Contribution of the Critics

The agonies and excesses of the popular culture presented the members of the critical community with a major opportunity. As a group, we could have raised a higher standard and decried the process of degradation, thereby helping to deflect the entertainment industry from its destructive course. Instead, the weight of critical opinion has encouraged every self-indulgent impulse and greatly assisted Hollywood along the path to its present predicament. To paraphrase Eldridge Cleaver: we haven't been part of the solution, and so we've definitely become part of the problem.

This negative role reflects no malicious or conspiratorial intent, but arises from the sad fact that most of us spend too much of our time in the dark. We are required to see more movies than even laboratory animals should be forced to endure, and this extended exposure often warps our perspective. For the last eight years I've averaged at least six screenings a week, and some of my colleagues attend even more.

The main impact of this ongoing ordeal—aside from making one feel like a glorified sewer inspector—is to create an irascible and vaguely resentful attitude whenever the lights go down. I've discussed with several of my colleagues the difficulties we face in forcing our eyes to stay open through particularly predictable projects—especially if we're viewing them as the second or third screening in a given day. The sounds of snoring are not at all uncommon in critics' screenings organized by the major studios.

What all this means is that we are inordinately appreciative whenever a movie comes along that breaks the tedium: it need not be high art as long as it wakes us up. Novelty becomes an especially treasured attribute, and any film that is different and daring will earn automatic gratitude from weary and bored reviewers. One of the critical commendations of *Bugsy* (1991), quoted in the early newspaper ads for the film, explicitly communicated this longing for the offbeat and the unsettling. "Our biggest need right now is to be appalled, shaken up—by movies, by our public life in general," wrote Richard Schickel of *Time* magazine, one of our most thoughtful and articulate film journalists. "For a couple of riveting, dislocating hours, *Bugsy* does just that."

This preference for the unpredictable is, to some extent, an unavoidable occupational hazard, but we should be able to place it in its proper perspective. We should remember that average moviegoers are looking for a good time at their local theater rather than hoping for some stunning new aesthetic breakthrough; they will probably be far less enthusiastic than we are about "riveting, dislocating hours" in the dark with material that's strange or shocking.

This built-in divergence between the critical perspective and the interests of the general public helps to explain why most Americans happily disregard all recommendations of reviewers. Over the years, many journalists and marketing analysts have tried to demonstrate the box-office influence of major critics—particularly those of us who appear on national TV—but the evidence is hardly flattering to our sense of self-importance. The recent past provides innumerable examples of movies that received devastatingly negative reviews and still drew huge numbers of moviegoers, and other instances where we unanimously cheered a new title but audiences steadfastly refused to venture anywhere near the theaters. The conclusion is inescapable that those occasions when public and critics end up liking the same movie represent nothing more than comfortable coincidence.

Ironically, Hollywood remains the one community in the country where movie critics are taken seriously. Within the industry, top executives harbor few illusions as to the impact of our opinions on nationwide box-office performance but they acknowledge the significance of those reviews to the tender egos of filmmakers and performers. The breathless endorsement quotes that decorate ads for even the most irredeemably awful motion pictures may or may not lure unsuspecting audiences to the theaters, but they do reassure the insecure moviemakers that *someone* appreciates their work.

In this way, a sheaf of genuinely positive reviews can remove some of the sting of even the most thoroughgoing rejection by the public. A combination of critical praise and audience indifference can encourage the creator of Hollywood's latest shocker about Christian cannibals or incestuous CIA men to assume the fashionable pose of the alienated artist; the sympathetic notices prove that this courageous filmmaker is simply too innovative and too honest to achieve "cheap" popularity.

Of course, the critics have their own stake in promoting these upscale aesthetic pretensions in the motion picture business. If motion pictures are viewed as artistic statements rather than pieces of popular entertainment, then our role as arbiters of excellence becomes more prestigious and significant. We can aspire to positions as disinterested cultural mandarins, calmly dispensing our approval or rebuke according to some abstract and objective standard, rather than playing a part as popular tribunes who predict whether a given project will please the people. This ambition leads to a consistent preference for pictures that are audacious, artistic, and unusual, and a disposition to dislike any piece of work that too obviously panders to the public. By following this understandable and perhaps inevitable tendency, the critics of this country make a subtle but significant contribution to Hollywood's increasingly contemptuous attitude toward the tastes and values of the mass audience.

Co-opting the Bosses

Against all logic, that arrogant attitude has begun to spread from the creative community to the corridors of corporate power. To a remarkable extent studio executives have come to share filmmakers' fashionable disdain for the sensibilities of ordinary American families.

During Hollywood's Golden Age, the mighty moguls kept a tight rein on any tendency on the part of writers or directors toward self-indulgence or sermonizing. The late Samuel Goldwyn famously declared, "If you want to send a message, go see Western Union." He and his colleagues defined their mission as entertaining an audience, and they summarily dispensed with any attitudes or ideologies that interfered with their single-minded pursuit of that purpose. One of the enduring images of old-time Hollywood (most recently dramatized in *Barton Fink*) shows some sensitive soul arriving in Tinseltown to toil in the vineyards as a writer or director, only to see his shining ideals corrupted by the ruthless commercialism of the benighted bosses. According to this cherished cliché, an artist's youthful altruism is inevitably compromised by his exposure to the brutal realities of the studio system.

Today, to the amazement of all (and to the delight of many), the entertainment industry has managed to reverse the process. It's now the top executives who find themselves co-opted by the prevailing culture of the creative community, the hardheaded businessmen whose practical priorities are gradually undermined by the idealism and artistic ambition of the tender spirits surrounding them. The old struggle between art and commerce has tilted decisively in the direction of art as the movie business takes itself more seriously with each passing year; today, even the heads of major studios assert that making significant statments—not crafting entertainment—is the essence of what they do.

In terms of movie messages, Sam Goldwyn might be surprised to see that today's major studios increasingly resemble Western Union offices.

Shortly after he took over as production chief at troubled Columbia Pictures in 1991, Mark Canton gave a revealing interview to the *Los Angeles Times* in which he seemed positively apologetic about his own past triumphs at Warner Brothers:

> I shouldn't be tarred because of my success with *Batman* and *Lethal Weapon*. They weren't derivative—or if they were, they took the genre to another level. . . . But I went on to do *Hamlet, Accidental Tourist*—developing complex films and, more important, films that not only entertained but which could, potentially, make a difference. *Lethal Weapon 2* dealt with apartheid; *New Jack City* said something.

Given the world we live in—Anita Hill taking on Clarence Thomas one day and a guy driving his truck into a Texas cafeteria the next—I'd like to try to give something back to the community.

It may not be immediately apparent how Mr. Canton's gifts "back to the community" will assist society in dealing with the twin horrors of televised Senate hearings and crazed killers in Texas, but his good intentions are obvious and commendable. At the same time, one can only marvel at the fact that the executive who shaped one of the top five box-office hits in movie history (*Batman*) must justify this achievement by reminding us that this project was "not derivative" and "took the genre to another level." Even among the most powerful studio brass, financial success is no longer sufficient to guarantee respectability in Hollywood.

The tendency for popular filmmakers to dismiss their own crowd-pleasing work and to long for more "socially significant" projects is nothing new in Hollywood. In 1941, Preston Sturges made a splendidly wise and entertaining film called *Sullivan's Travels*, about a leading comedy director (Joel McCrea) who dreams of moving beyond cinematic frivolity to create bitter, downbeat dramas that emphasize human suffering. In the 1940s, the moguls applied practical business principles to counteract such self-indulgent impulses and to keep their filmmakers in touch with the mass audience. Today, Mark Canton and his colleagues would never be so crass; they echo the desire of the writers and directors to create "serious art" that will please the critics and impress the industry elite.

In a sense, the new pretensions reflect fundamental changes in the social and educational backgrounds of the people who run Hollywood. Fifty years ago, former furriers and junk dealers, onetime salesmen and nickelodeon entrepreneurs wielded great power in the movie business, while eastern intellectuals and members of America's established elites generally looked down on their all-too-popular endeavors. Today, the entertainment industry's top executive offices are crowded with graduates of the most prestigious Ivy League universities—gifted and often privileged individuals who have been trained from childhood to nurse noble and world-changing ambitions. The brutish, cigar-chomping, money-grubbing mogul is an outmoded and irrelevant stereotype; the leadership of the most important entertainment companies has moved decisively upscale.

These altered executive attitudes correspond with the demise of the old studio system, and the permanent shift in power from corporate officials to big-name stars and filmmakers. The days have long since ended when an imperious executive could plausibly threaten a rebellious actress by telling her, "You'll never work in this town again!" Today, she would simply smile, call her agent, and instantly ink a three-picture deal with Paramount. In the Hollywood of the 1990s, the major studios need established talent far more than these artists need the studios. As a result, well-known performers and creative personnel enjoy an unprecedented ability to influence the content of their motion picture projects.

It has therefore become a matter of self-interest and self-preservation for leading executives to adopt the values, attitudes, and aspirations of the intense and pretentious personalities who actually make the movies. If you want your company to get Paul Verhoeven's next project, or Dustin Hoffman's or Robert De Niro's or Oliver Stone's, you can't afford the reputation of a boss who frets over motion picture content or worries about potential offense to a mass audience. To increase their own clout with the big-name artists who dominate the business, studio brass deliberately cultivate the image of daring and integrity— which means that you never second-guess a filmmaker on an abundance of "F-words" or a brief episode of incest. You certainly don't want to become known as a timid nerd who runs away from those searing "indictments of society" so beloved of today's writers and directors.

This fear of dissenting from the dominant orthodoxies of the entertainment establishment leads to business decisions that often bear little connection to the pressures of the marketplace. "Obviously, no Hollywood producer shoots a movie consciusly thinking, 'This baby's going to lose money all right, but it's a blow for peace and social justice,'" writes Richard Grenier in a 1991 article in *The National Interest*. "But self-deception is a constant factor. A producer is persuaded by a star actor or director that such and such an idealistic movie will make money, too. And after all, the producer already has his bankable star."

At times, leading executives manage to deceive themselves even without the help of bankable stars; they have been so thoroughly co-opted into the assumption that they bear some solemn obligation to challenge the conservative instincts of the mass audience that they will personally initiate insanely unpromising projects. The guiding force behind 1992's *Radio Flyer*, for instance, was Columbia Pictures' then co-chairman Jon Peters—despite the fact that a shocking melodrama about two boys reacting to brutal child abuse with escape fantasies that may (or may not) be suicidal hardly qualified as a slam-dunk money-maker. According to one studio source who discussed the subject with the *Los Angeles Times* in March 1992: "The child abuse was more potent than any people's love for the movie. I think a lot of people knew it would be tough for this movie to work. A vast majority knew that at the studio." Nevertheless, Peters ran the show and dismissed the doubts of his subordinates, telling one meeting of senior executives that the theme of the film related to his own troubled childhood. "This was a script Jon loved more than life itself," one of his colleagues recalled.

As it turned out, Peters's act of love resulted in a disaster of truly monumental proportions: while Columbia spent $41 million to produce and market *Radio Flyer*, the picture earned a grand total of $4.2 million at the box office. Conveniently enough, at the time of its debut the visionary executive had already moved on from his position as co-chief of the studio.

The insistence that business leaders in the entertainment industry must look beyond profit and loss when it comes to issues-driven or "artistic" material has become so powerfully pervasive in Hollywood that it has even infected the executive suites of the major television networks. Though not generally identified as eleemosynary institutions, the networks have demonstrated a stunning willingness to sacrifice millions of dollars in advertising revenue in order to make politically correct statements approved by the Hollywood community.

In 1990, for example, NBC lost several hundred thousand dollars when it proved unable to sell all the available advertising time on its controversial docudrama on the abortion issue, *Roe vs. Wade*. ABC took an even bigger hit by sanctioning the inclusion of a scene in "thirtysomething" in which two gay male characters appear in bed together, talking about the one-night stand they've just enjoyed. This brief sequence cost the network more than $1 million in lost revenue, but following the fiasco top corporate officials assured "thirtysomething" producers that "they would fully support any future exploration of the gay characters' lives." True to their word, they authorized another show in the next season (1991) in which the same two characters exchange a midnight kiss at a New Year's party. This time, advertiser withdrawals cost the network more than $500,000. "I am grateful that ABC was willing to air the program at a loss," said Ed Zwick, co-creator of the critically acclaimed series. Robert A. Iger, president of ABC Entertainment, told the press that his support for the embattled episode reflected his "social and creative responsibilities."

Along similar lines, NBC aired a January 1992 edition of "Quantum Leap" about a heroic homosexual cadet who becomes the victim of gay-bashing aimed at a naval college. Four months before the broadcast, NBC executives had asked Universal Television, producers of the series, to accept liability for any lost advertising revenue associated with the episode's controversial content, but in the end they relented and agreed to swallow the loss themselves. The predictable result of this noble decision: a setback for the network estimated by official sources as "about $500,000."

This pattern—repeated on several other shows in recent years— could be applauded as a courageous example of unselfish devotion to principle, or it could be condemned as a stubborn refusal to respond to public and advertiser concerns over highly sensitive materials. In any event, it demonstrates that in today's Hollywood, the famous bottom line is not always the bottom line.

The Myth of a Gay Conspiracy

The willingness of the networks to accept major losses on gay-theme programming raises the sensitive but unavoidable issue of the impact of Hollywood's powerful homosexual community.

Some of the popular culture's most outspoken critics contend that the overrepresentation of homosexuals in every corner of the creative community leads directly to the entertainment industry's antifamily bias and its obsession with violent and deviant behavior. According to this theory, gay writers, directors, producers, and stars inevitably impose their own values on projects in which they participate, portraying marriage as a restrictive and outmoded institution, or wallowing in sadomasochistic and promiscuous excess.

These charges offer a one-dimensional and misleading explanation of a complex phenomenon, and should be rejected by all fair-minded people. Those who look for evidence of some huge "gay conspiracy" at the heart of Hollywood will be frustrated in that search, for the simple reason that no such conspiracy exists. Some militant gay rights organizations may indeed pursue a radical agenda in their efforts to influence the messages of the popular culture, but homosexual performers and filmmakers are far from unanimous in advancing that agenda in their work.

The gay men and lesbian women who play prominent roles in the entertainment industry are as diverse and dissimilar as their straight colleagues. They are involved on every side of every significant issue that currently divides the popular culture. While some of them certainly turn out work that denigrates traditional values and glorifies ugliness, others create wholesome entertainment that Middle America embraces with grateful enthusiasm.

In fact, gay artists have been associated with some of the finest and most uplifting family entertainment of recent years. The late Howard Ashman, who died of AIDS in 1991, wrote the award-winning lyrics to *Beauty and the Beast*. When it comes to profound, moving, and impeccably tasteful motion pictures for adults, no one has compiled a more distinguished record among contemporary filmmakers than director James Ivory (*A Room with a View, Howards End*), and his longtime partner, producer Ismail Merchant. During Hollywood's Golden Age, director George Cukor made little secret of his homosexuality, while creating such timeless classics as *Dinner at Eight, Camille, The Philadelphia Story,* and *A Star is Born.* Today, many writers, directors, and stars who make no particular point of their gay identity contribute to stirring outdoor adventures, touching family dramas, patriotic crowd-pleasers, stylish and insightful comedies, and some of the few films of recent years to treat organized religion with affection and respect.

An artist's homosexual orientation in private life doesn't mean that his work will assault traditional values—any more than an artist's heterosexuality guarantees that his work will defend those values. Without question, a huge majority of the most powerful promoters of violent, self-destructive, and antisocial messages in movies, TV, and popular music happen to be heterosexual.

While "gay control" of the movie business is a myth, gay influence is very much a reality. No one could deny that the formidable gay presence in the entertainment business encourages industry leaders to take a far more sympathetic view of homosexuality than does the public at large. In a 1990 study of "Hollywood opinion leaders" by University of Texas government professor David F. Prindle, 68 percent said they supported "gay rights," compared to only 12 percent who endorsed that position in a 1987 national *Times Mirror* poll. More recently, an impressive array of the Hollywood establishment's most influential figures have provided support for leading gay rights organizations. In August 1991, top executives from all four television networks and from the eight largest movie studios served together on the host committee for a gala dinner to benefit the National Gay and Lesbian Task Force.

This off-screen encouragement, however, in no way insures positive on-screen treatment of homosexual issues or individuals. For every motion picture that offers an approving view of a gay character, it's easy to find one that emphasizes negative stereotypes—portraying homosexuals as crazed killers or swishy objects of ridicule.

The angry demonstrators at the Academy Awards of March, 1992 expressed their rage over a perceived proliferation of antigay characterizations, and focused especially on the transvestite killer in *The Silence of the Lambs.* The film they protested then went on to sweep all the major awards—hardly demonstrating iron control of the industry by gay activist groups. Surprisingly enough, homosexual performers and filmmakers have played prominent roles in some of the projects most harshly criticized as gay-bashing, while a number of the more sympathetic gay portrayals on television and at the movies have been created entirely by heterosexuals.

In short, the role of the gay community in Hollywood is too complicated—and even contradictory—to conform to anyone's simplistic conspiracy theories. The urge to hold homosexuals responsible for the popular culture's many problems represents one more example of the unfortunate and seemingly irresistible temptation to single out scapegoats rather than searching for solutions.

Blaming the Jews

This brings us to the other group most commonly blamed for all of the negative aspects of today's entertainment industry—the Jews.

Over the years I've gotten mail from viewers and readers in all regions of the country who suspect that the disproportionate number of Jews in Hollywood leadership positions might somehow account for the alienation of the industry elite from the American mainstream. Some of these letters appear to be sincere attempts by basically well-meaning people to understand what's gone wrong with the popular culture. Others reflect anti-Semitic attitudes of the most poisonous and pernicious variety.

In 1991, for instance, I received copies of a slickly packaged book and video called *The Other Israel* by an Oregon-based activist named Ted Pike. His "extensive research" convinced him that Hollywood's destructive messages represented only the latest attempt by "Talmudic Judaism" to advance its timeless and evil agenda of child abuse, promiscuity, and satanism. In his effectively edited video documentary, the earnest, handsome Pike talks directly to the camera and guides the viewer through a wealth of contemporary and historical images meant to dramatize more than three thousand years of Jewish plots against decency, culminating with an impassioned denunciation of today's mass media.

These charges follow a familiar pattern in Jewish history: in every generation, in every corner of the globe, paranoid agitators have ascribed secret powers and purposes to the Jewish people. Fringe fanatics like Ted Pike deserve serious attention only when the dark fears they articulate begin turning up in the mainstream, among responsible and intelligent people who can't be dismissed as irrational hate-mongers.

That is the situation at this moment in American history, as questions about Jewish influence on Hollywood move well beyond extremist groups. No business in the world is so firmly associated in the public mind with the Jewish people as the American entertainment industry; when substantial segments of society begin to view Hollywood as some hostile, heedless force, it's unavoidable that some of those who hold this attitude will try to explain the situation with reference to the Jews.

In this context, I vividly recall an emotional conversation with a best-selling author and popular television commentator who appeared with me as part of a well-attended public discussion on media accountability. During the session, we agreed on nearly everything—particularly Hollywood's hostility to all forms of organized religion—but afterward he asked if I could spare a few minutes to speak with him confidentially.

"Maybe you can help me understand something," he began, as we adjourned to his private office. "You're right on target when you talk about what Hollywood's been doing to this country. But you're also part of the Jewish community. And what I don't get, when I look at Hollywood, is why is it that so many of the people who are responsible for all the worst garbage turn out to be Jews? It's sort of become an obvious question, but nobody likes to talk about it, because nobody wants to sound like a bigot. But this is supposed to be the people of The Book, isn't it, God's chosen people? How come they're so set on trashing everything that the rest of us still care about? I'm afraid we've got more and more people out there—decent people—who are wondering about the same thing."

To hear this sophisticated and dynamic public figure draw a connection between Jewish involvement in Hollywood and the current degradation of our popular culture hit me with the force of a blow to the chest. No one could ever accuse him of anti-Semitism; for many years he had compiled an admirable record of service to Jewish causes and he'd made several trips to Israel. As uncomfortable as I felt in confronting the issue, I thanked him for his candor in raising it with me, and for his consideration in doing so in private. I felt he deserved an answer in the same constructive spirit in which he had asked the question.

That approach remains appropriate in addressing the matter here.

When considering the notion that some distinctive Jewish input helps to shape the most destructive aspects of the popular culture, there is an easy and logical way to test that proposition.

The historical record can settle the question. If Jewish influence in Hollywood is responsible for the most despicable messages emanating from the entertainment capital, then we would expect to see the industry at its very worst whenever Jewish pull is at its height—delivering an absolute maximum of vile and violent content.

When Jewish clout decreases, on the other hand, this theory demands that the hateful intensity of Hollywood's messages must also decrease, and the industry should become more wholesome.

Of course, the last half century of Hollywood history utterly confounds these expectations—and fatally undermines the suggestion that

Jewish participation is responsible for what's gone wrong with the world of show business.

By all accounts, Jewish influence in the entertainment industry reached its high-water mark in the 1930s and early 1940s—during the period often described as Hollywood's Golden Age. At that time, seven of the eight major studios were owned and operated by Jewish families who managed to create what Hollywood historian Neal Gabler aptly describes as *An Empire of Their Own*. According to one 1936 study, "Of eighty-five names engaged in production, fifty-three are Jews. And the Jewish advantage holds in prestige as well as numbers."

The Jewish studio bosses who built this mighty industry most certainly had their faults and foibles, but they managed to create motion pictures that appealed to a huge audience transcending all boundaries of ethnicity, religion, age, and social status. In 1940 some 80 million paying customers went to the theaters *every week*—more than 60 percent of the national population. They flocked to see images created by Hollywood's Jews, visions that represented the immigrant entrepreneurs' own extravagant love affair with their new country. Gabler describes the moguls as celebrating "an America where fathers were strong, families stable, people attractive, resilient, resourceful, and decent. This was *their* America, and its invention may be their most enduring legacy." The overwhelming majority of Americans felt comfortable with that legacy and believed that they saw their own deepest values reflected on screen.

When it came to religious themes, the movie industry offered films like *Sign of the Cross* (1932), *Angels with Dirty Faces* (1938), *Boys Town* (1938), *The Song of Bernadette* (1943), *Going My Way* (1944), *It's A Wonderful Life* (1946), and so many others—all of them warmly respectful of the Christian faith. If the Jews who used to run Hollywood nursed some burning passion to trash Christianity, then they most certainly missed their chance at the moment of their peak influence.

Today, in stark contrast to the 1940s, no clear-sighted or responsible observer could possibly view Hollywood as a Jewish empire. None of the major studios are Jewish family businesses in the way they once were: two have been purchased by enormous Japanese corporations (Columbia and Universal), one by Australian interests (Twentieth Century Fox), and one (MGM) has been passed back and forth among a flamboyant Armenian-American entrepreneur, a cable TV king from Atlanta, and a shadowy Italian tycoon. The other studios have all been gobbled up by gigantic and decidedly non-Jewish conglomerates, including Gulf and Western (Paramount) and the notoriously WASPy Time, Inc. (Warner Brothers). The same situation applies with television networks, where takeovers by larger companies have seriously diluted "Jewish influence." As any viewer of "Late Night with David Letterman" already knows, the huge General Electric Corporation now owns NBC, while ABC has been operated for some years by Capital Cities Communications, an upstate New York outfit originally cofounded by onetime CIA chief William Casey.

Though Jews are still prominent in many areas in the Hollywood creative community, talk of Jewish "domination" is increasingly ludicrous. For instance, of all the fifteen Oscars handed out by the Motion Picture Academy for acting and directing since 1989, not one has gone to a Jewish performer or filmmaker.

In other words, the agitators who warn of the dangers of Jewish influence have already gotten their wish—"Hebraic Hollywood" is a mere shadow of its former self, and Jewish "control" of American entertainment now stands at an all-time low. This means that the period in which Hollywood's values turned sour happened to coincide with the period in which Jewish power decisively *declined*. According to classic anti-Semitic reasoning, show business should now be more wholesome, more life-affirming, more mainstream than ever before— and the obvious fact that this is not the case serves to blow that reasoning out of the water.

From the beginning, allegations about the corrupting role of Jewish influence have relied not only on historical ignorance but on a fundamental misunderstanding as to the nature of Jewish identity among some of the leaders of today's entertainment industry.

Many non-Jews assume that anyone with a Jewish name, or with even a hint of Jewish ancestry, can automatcially be counted as a self-conscious spokesman for his faith and his people. This is ridiculous, of course—especially as it applies to show business celebrities who are, as a group, disproportionately detached from their own heritage.

On a recent Friday night my wife and I welcomed a gifted, prominent, and prolific movie director to our home as a guest for our weekly Sabbath dinner. He expressed wonder and delight at all the ancient traditions we follow as a matter of course—the glowing candles over a white tablecloth, the blessing of the wine, the formal washing of hands and breaking of bread, a benediction for each of our two children, and so forth. In the course of the dinner conversation that followed, the fifty-year-old filmmaker emotionally confessed that this occasion represented the first time in his entire life that he had ever participated in a traditional Sabbath meal. Having grown up in a home of committed atheists, he had never seen anything like it before—and he had always assumed that these rituals, of which he understood nothing, had disappeared long ago.

His position is altogether typical of the disaffiliated Jews who work in Hollywood as producers and performers, writers and directors. These people no more represent a "Jewish point of view" than Brian De Palma and Al Pacino reflect the viewpoint of the Vatican, or Paul Verhoeven and Paul Schrader express the outlook of the Dutch Reform Church. When a Jewish producer or director perpetrates some especially degenerate piece of work, it makes as much sense to explain that outrage with reference to his family's religious heritage as it does to blame Madonna's latest music video on her years in Catholic parochial school. In both cases, the questionable material involves a rejection—not an assertion—of the artist's own tradition.

In terms of spiritual outlook and religious practice, the privileged personalities who make up the entertainment elite—of Catholic, Protestant, and Jewish background—have far more in common with one another than they do with traditional believers in the faiths they left behind. Whatever their origins, former Christians and former Jews are now indistinguishable: they share a common commitment to secularism. The best available study of the industry establishment (for *Public Opinion,* 1983) shows that 93 percent of these people attend no religious services of any kind.

The most significant difference between the Jews and non-Jews who participate in the entertainment industry is that the Jews are even more ill-informed concerning the fundamentals of their faith. Since we live in an overwhelmingly Christian nation, even those Gentiles with the most minimal religious backgrounds pick up something about the basic practices and beliefs of Christianity. Jews, on the other hand, represent only 2.4 percent of the American population. A Jew who happened to be raised in a nonreligious home (like the Sabbath guest described above) may well grow to maturity knowing something about bagels and Woody Allen, but nothing at all about Torah and tradition.

This overall lack of religious identification points out the incomparable insanity in suggesting that Hollywood's Jews are following some supersecret script for world domination laid out for them in the Talmud some fifteen hundred years ago. At times, any normal person may reasonably wonder how writers and directors come up with the ideas for the unspeakable junk they create—but it's a safe bet that they didn't get them from the codification of the Jewish oral law written down (in Aramaic) in fifth-century Babylonia. I can speak with some authority in declaring that all the Hollywood personalities who have ever studied even a single page of Talmud at any time in their lives could be comfortably assembled in one very small kitchen; most of the industry's Jews wouldn't recognize a volume of Jewish sacred text if it rose up and bit them. If one wants to blame a particular book for implanting all the strange ideas that have recently taken hold among the members of the industry elite, one should at least select a tome that most of them have read—say, *What Makes Sammy Run?* or *Dianetics* or *The Leadership Secrets of Attila the Hun.*

The shortage of information about even the most basic teachings of Judaism suggests that Hollywood today suffers not from too *much* Jewish influence, but from too *little;* a deeper exposure to the traditional Torah emphasis on family responsibilities, self-discipline, and respect for others could only serve to improve and enrich the industry's values.

Attempts to establish a new voice for substantive Judaism within the entertainment community, pursued simultaneously with parallel efforts to enlarge the Christian presence, have already begun. They represent one thrust of the ambitious programs launched by would-be reformers both inside and outside the Hollywood community.

With the entertainment establishment confronting an ongoing crisis that threatens both its economic well-being and its sense of self-respect, the time has never been better for bold initiatives to alter its directions.

Before reviewing the progress that's been made to date, and considering new approaches that might work for the future, it's essential to address some of the frequently mentioned pseudosolutions that serve as both a delusion and a distraction for many of those who yearn to transform the popular culture into a more positive force in the society at large.

"The End of the Beginning"

The Censorship Temptation

Mounting frustration over the degradation of our popular culture leads some otherwise thoughtful citizens to propose simplistic solutions to a complex problem.

Censorship is the most popular of these quick-fix prescriptions—and it is also the most dangerous.

In any discussion of Hollywood's destructive impact, the censorship issue serves as a huge distraction. No sooner does the prospect of governmental interference rear its ugly head than the focus instantly shifts from an examination of the industry's values to an assertion of its constitutional rights. The fear of Big Brother is so potent—and so appropriate—that it often overshadows public concern about the messages of the media.

Conservatives in particular should understand that fear—and should resist the old-fashioned liberal temptation to try to solve every problem with a new government program. I am always surprised at right-wing activists who argue passionately that bureaucratic solutions will never eliminate poverty, or improve medical care, or end racism overnight, but who nonetheless believe that a governmental initiative can magically succeed in the delicate task of raising the moral tone of the popular culture.

Official censorship is not the answer, and attempts to move in that direction will always prove counterproductive. As soon as the government attempts to crack down on some purveyor of slime he is quickly transformed into a defender of the First Amendment.

The 1990 Florida obscenity arrest of 2 Live Crew offers a depressing demonstration of this process. While America's most celebrated poets of the perverse performed at an adults-only club, going through the motions for a handful of masochists who had actually paid money to listen to their feebleminded filth, the police appeared to apprehend the stars of the evening and to cart them away in handcuffs.

This much-publicized prosecution turned thugs into overnight folk heroes. The leader of the group, Luther Campbell, enlisted the support of no less than Bruce Springsteen, who authorized free use of his most famous song as the basis for a new "protest single" by Campbell, "Banned in the USA." This contribution to political discourse, promoted with an image depicting the frightened face of the artist gagged with an American flag, achieved impressive sales figures. So did 2 Live Crew's album, *As Nasty as They Wanna Be*, which had already sold more than a million copies before the obscenity case, but which received an additional boost through trial-related publicity. Luther Campbell bragged to *Rolling Stone* about the rewards he had received in just a few short months, including "a corporate empire that includes three labels, a recording studio, a construction company, three discos, and an investment portfolio brimming with mutual funds and real estate. He owns a Jaguar, a BMW convertible, a Westwind jet, and a new home." Another magazine estimated his personal income as $11 million in 1990 alone. In short, the would-be censors made no visible progress when it came to restricting this group's message or impeding its success. As Talleyrand commented about Napoleon's 1804 killing of the duc d'Enghien: "It was worse than a crime. It was a blunder."

Advocates of censorship emphatically disagree, and make the argument that even if their efforts achieve nothing else, they at least put pressure on Hollywood to clean up its own act. They point to the fact that leaders of the entertainment establishment seem to be well aware of the more than 350 pieces of proposed legislation recently introduced in Congress and in various state legislatures that are designed to curb media excesses.

Unfortunately, these pending political squabbles only fuel Hollywood's us-vs.-them mentality and encourage the industry to view any challenge to its license as an attack on its liberties. In order to enlist allies within the industry it is essential that advocates for more wholesome values manage to shift the terms of the debate from a focus on *rights,* to a broader question of *responsibilities.* One can agree that a movie company has every *right* to make a film glorifying the mutilation of young women, at the same time that you argue that they have a *responsibility* not to do so.

Resurrecting the Code?

In one memorable attempt to reestablish that sense of responsibility, Cardinal Roger Mahony of the Archdiocese of Los Angeles challenged Hollywood to think about the unthinkable: to consider reinstituting the old Production Code that guided the content of feature films for more than thirty years.

Addressing a public forum at the Hollywood Roosevelt Hotel on February 1, 1992, the Cardinal commended the efforts of his Protestant colleagues at the Atlanta-based Christian Film and Television Commission in updating and revising the old Hays Code. "Perhaps the time is ripe for the entertainment industry to consider the advisability of having such a code," His Eminence somewhat tentatively announced, though he stopped well short of offering a specific endorsement. ". . . I would encourage the media to look upon calls for reform not as a censorship issue, but, rather, as an issue of human rights and dignity."

Despite the cautious and moderate tone of his remarks, Mahony's statement provoked an explosion of hysterical—and entirely predictable—criticism from the Hollywood community. The American Civil Liberties Union ran an ad in *Daily Variety* under the headline "WHAT! BACK TO SEPARATE BEDS?" in which it claimed (inaccurately) that the Cardinal demanded that "all movie and television shows needed a church seal of approval before they were ever made" and warning of "a list of moral rules that would return us to the 1950s." The

ACLU ad included a request for the public to write to Mahony asking him to "withdraw" the code that he had never formally endorsed in the first place. "The only way to stop attacks on free speech is to speak out!" the organization concluded.

At this point, with the controversy raging at full boil in print and on the air, the *Los Angeles Times* began searching for someone in Hollywood, for *anyone*, who would be foolhardy enough to say a kind word about Mahony.

Naturally, they found me.

Like Mahony himself, I had serious reservations about the feasibility of actually enforcing the new/old code, but I certainly believed that the wide-ranging discussion provoked by this proposal served a useful purpose. "One needn't support the specific plan, nor endorse the details of the proposed code, to recognize that the Cardinal has performed a courageous public service," I wrote in an Op-Ed column on February 6. "After all, in his public statement, Mahony declared, 'I do not propose that this is the only possible means of achieving the end of reforming movies and television, but I do ask the industry to consider that something must be done.' An overwhelming majority of Americans clearly agree with him."

Inevitably, a few careless journalists for various publications managed to misinterpret (or distort) my column and to report that a certain "renegade film critic" had outraged his colleagues by actually backing the hated Hays Code.

While I'm always delighted to outrage my colleagues, I don't like seeing my position misreported. My personal attitude toward the code has remained entirely consistent and might best be described as sympathetic skepticism: while I understand—and applaud—the concern that gives rise to such a proposal, I don't believe that a new production code could ever work in today's Hollywood.

The problem is that changes in the fundamental structure of the movie business now make it altogether impossible for a handful of executives to impose a self-policing scheme on the entire industry. Before World War II, the concentration of power in the eight major studios allowed their omnipotent bosses to compel colleagues in every corner of the entertainment community to go along with the Hays Office restrictions. If a film violated those standards and failed to receive a "Motion Picture Code Seal," it wouldn't be shown, period.

After the war, when the Justice Department dismembered the old Hollywood system by forcing the studios to sell off the theaters that they owned across the country, code enforcement became far more difficult. The Production Code Administration faced a series of significant challenges to its authority before the Motion Picture Association of America terminated the Hays Office operations altogether in 1966. Any effort to reestablish a centralized source for movie standards would provoke even sharper challenges in today's altered climate. Even if all the major studios agreed, by some miracle, to abide by a new code, any number of independent producers or upstart companies would happily defy them and continue efforts to sell sleaze and gore to the public. The new importance of the home-video business further complicates attempts at industry self-censorship. While some theater owners and theatrical chains might be persuaded to cooperate with a new effort by Hollywood to clean up its act, winning significant compliance from the thousands upon thousands of video outlets across the country is hard to imagine.

In any event, the fact that a new code would be largely unenforceable doesn't mean that the introduction of this issue by Cardinal Mahony and his colleagues represented some dire threat to the American Way of Life, or a mean-spirited attempt to prevent consenting adults from sleeping in the same bed. Mahony spoke for tens of millions of citizens who are fed up with the content and messages of popular culture and want some sign that the entertainment industry cares about their concerns. Even if Hollywood can't possibly reestablish formal, binding guidelines for movie content, that doesn't mean that it should altogether abandon its obligation to accept responsible standards for its own activities.

In fact, a public acknowledgment of that obligation by the leading studios and production companies could send a useful signal to the segment of the mass audience that is seriously disenchanted. The one element of the old code that could—and should—win present-day approval by all major players in Hollywood is the expression of principles in its preamble: "Motion picture producers recognize the high trust and confidence which have been placed in them by the people of the world. . . . They recognize their responsibility to the public because of this trust and because entertainment and art are important influences in the life of a nation."

The 1930 code went on to provide a capsule summary of its under-lying idea in two simple sentences that touch the fundamental concerns of all those who worry over the impact of the popular culture. "No picture shall be produced which will lower the moral standards of those who see it," declared the code's first General Principle. "Hence the sympathy of the audience shall never be thrown to the side of crime, wrongdoing, evil, or sin."

Shouldn't it be possible for all self-respecting entertainment executives to sign on to some such statement? Of course, the unpopular words "evil" and "sin," with their unmistakably religious overtones, would have to be dropped and perhaps replaced with more politically correct terminology like "self-destructive and anti-social behavior."

Whatever specific wording the industry may choose, some general statement of principles and purposes, some far-reaching acknowledgment of its responsibilities to the public, could represent an important step in the right direction. If nothing else, it would offer a clear basis for shaming major corporations if they authorize projects that depart from the broad principles of decency to which they have publicly subscribed.

Watchdog Organizations

The ability to employ the power of embarrassment and to pressure the entertainment industry toward a more wholesome posture presupposes the establishment of institutions devoted to that purpose. Fortunately, many such organizations already exist and play a vital part in the continuing combat over the values of the popular culture.

All of these operations—like all individuals—are inevitably imperfect and occasionally irresponsible, subject to serious errors in judgment or implementation; by mentioning specific groups I intend no endorsement of everything they do. Nevertheless, I believe that these controversial "media watchdog" organizations have made a constructive contribution to the national debate on accountability in the entertainment industry. Meanwhile, their ongoing efforts provide concerned citizens with opportunities for personal involvement.

• The Christian Film and Television Commission in Atlanta, Georgia, under the leadership of the tireless and articulate Ted Baehr, has established an especially ambitious agenda for influencing Hollywood and opening up a full-time liaison with the entertainment industry.

• The American Family Association, based in Tupelo, Mississippi, has attracted an abundance of both resentment and support and made its president, the Rev. Donald Wildmon, an enormously controversial public figure.

• The Media Research Center in Washington, D.C., provides a valuable monitoring service on both news and entertainment programming, and publishes a lively newsletter called *TV, etc.*

• With offices in Champaign, Illinois, Los Angeles, and other cities, the National Coalition on Television Violence (NCTV) concentrates on scientific investigations on the impact of media images and detailed evaluation of a wealth of popular entertainment.

• Other associations that work to promote more positive and responsible messages in the media include Focus on the Family, in Colorado Springs, Colorado; the Dove Foundation, in Grand Rapids, Michigan; Christian Leaders for Responsible Television (CLeaR-TV), in Wheaton, Illinois; The Parent's Music Resource Center in Washington, D.C.; the New York–based Morality in Media; the Michigan-based Americans for Responsible Television; and the Delaware-based Concerned Citizens for Quality Television.

To no one's surprise, these organizations have won few friends or admirers within the media establishment. In July 1990, *Newsweek* derisively dismissed them as "artbusters" and "a new breed of bluenoses." Gary David Goldberg, creator of such well-received television shows as "Family Ties" and "Brooklyn Bridge," speaks for many of his colleagues in expressing his outrage at activities of the various watchdog groups. "I resent terribly the feeling that we as a profession need a group monitoring us to make us more responsible than we already are," he told *Channels* magazine. "As a member of the community, as an adult person living in the world, I have a right to put my ideas into the marketplace."

Goldberg most certainly deserves that right, but he ought to acknowledge that Ted Baehr and his colleagues deserve it as well. Many members of the Hollywood community seem to believe passionately in free speech for all Americans except for those who use that freedom to attack Hollywood. As Donald Wildmon told *Time* in June

1989, "I'm not infringing on anybody's rights. I have as much right as any other individual in this society to try to shape society. I have as much right to try to influence people. I have as much right to create what I consider to be a decent, good, clean, wholesome, moral society. I'm very cognizant of other people's rights. All I'm asking is for them to be cognizant of mine."

One may oppose the media watchdog groups, and lambaste their leaders as "American Ayatollahs," but even their most controversial activities amount to nothing more than an impassioned and appropriate participation in the give-and-take of the free marketplace of ideas.

Why is it inherently less valid for the American Family Association to try to pressure the networks to feature *fewer* homosexual characters on prime-time TV than it is for the Gay and Lesbian Alliance Against Discrimination (GLAAD) to try to pressure the networks for *more* such characters? Both groups are engaged in totally legitimate efforts to influence major TV producers to broadcast images that correspond with their own views of what constitutes a good society.

For many years, organizations representing the interests of gays and lesbians, African Americans, Latinos, Jews, Native Americans, people with disabilities, and many other groups have lobbied Hollywood to provide more sympathetic and sensitive screen portrayals of their communities. All such initiatives are pertinent and positive, and occasionally enjoy striking success; if nothing else they help to keep the entertainment establishment in touch with the concerns of significant segments of its audience. It is impossible to argue that the viewpoints and interests of conservative Christians should be viewed any differently. By what double standard do CLeaR-TV's worries over negative portrayals of members of the clergy represent a more serious threat to freedom of expression than concern by the National Federation of the Blind over negative portrayals of people who are blind? The latter group organized a well-publicized national boycott in October 1991 to protest the ABC show "Good and Evil" and its inclusion of a blind character who consistently displayed "ineptitude and stupidity"; within weeks, ABC had canceled the failing show.

The fact is that leaders of the entertainment establishment are instinctively more sympathetic to blind people, or to members of other "disadvantaged" groups, than they are to churchgoers from the Midwest. In part, this stems from the perennial preference for the underdog, but it also reflects the obvious distance between the unconventional personal lives of the Hollywood elite and the far more traditional values of most American families. This gap calls for more activity by religious watchdog groups, not less: those organizations can actually help the members of the Hollywood community connect with the sensibilities of an important but often forgotten constituency. As Warner Brothers executive Bruce Berman somewhat sheepishly confessed to *The Hollywood Reporter* in April 1991: "Hollywood filmmakers may not understand Middle America. They're not very well equipped to deal in that context."

Activists in defense of traditional values can provide some of that missing equipment and can help Hollywood to understand the heartland. With the entertainment industry at a crossroads, pushed and pulled in several directions at once by powerful and competing forces, Americans who care about the content of the movies and TV we consume should weigh in with their opinions.

"Ominous or not, the lobbying of television is a fact," writes Patricia E. Bauer of *Channels* magazine. "And it should be of special concern to those who care about what they view but don't lobby. Put another way, those who remain silent have much in common with those who fail to vote: They won't be heard because they have disenfranchised themselves."

The Boycott Weapon

One of the important instruments for gaining the attention of the entertainment establishment is the threat of sponsor boycotts.

The very term "boycott" has become a dirty word in Hollywood—one of the few dirty words the industry is actually reluctant to pronounce. The tactic arouses fear and fury precisely because it carries such obvious force and logic when it is applied to the world of commercial television.

The entire purpose of buying advertising time on TV is to create a positive public perception of your particular product. If the programming that you pay to sponsor ends up offending a significant segment of the audience, then you've undermined the entire basis of your advertising investment. Sponsor boycotts are a way for interest groups to let the advertiser know they are offended and that they resent the corporate decision to support a certain kind of television. If the boycotting group speaks for only a small percentage of the public, then the sponsor can ignore its protests with impunity. If, however, the objecting organization can mobilize enough people to support its cause, then it can produce financial consequences that force the advertiser to sit up and take notice. When those consequences—or threatened consequences—are serious enough, they may even persuade major corporations to rethink their attitude toward the future television programming they choose to finance.

There is nothing dictatorial or intolerant or undemocratic about any of this. A boycott is nothing more than an attempt to deploy private buying power to serve a public purpose. Most often, this means organizing consumers in order to discourage what a substantial group of citizens view as irresponsible corporate behavior. One group may boycott products to condemn pollution or apartheid; another will protest the sponsorship of televised sleaze.

This approach hardly represents some radical departure; it has been employed for a wide range of causes over the course of several hundred years. Letter-writer Alan Kaufman helpfully reminded the readers of the *Los Angeles Jewish Journal* "that our American colonists refused to buy British goods after passage of the 1765 Stamp Act; that in 1905 the Chinese boycotted U.S. goods because of miserable treatment of the American Chinese; that Gandhi's 'passive resistance' program featured boycott as one of its main weapons; and that in our time, Cesar Chavez has relied heavily on the grapes boycott."

Al Sikes, chairman of the Federal Communications Commission, echoed this point on a Washington panel in March 1992 when he condemned "people in Hollywood who boycott lettuce and grapes but cry censorship" when interest groups organize against TV programs. Mr. Sikes reported that the FCC receives "an extraordinary outpouring of frustration" from parents who are distressed over today's television programming.

The intensity of this frustration creates a vast reservoir of potential support for organized efforts to curb the excesses of the mass media. An independent survey in October 1991 demonstrated that a surprising number of Americans specifically endorse the idea of using economic boycotts as a means of advancing causes they care about. The Barna

Research Group reported that 14 percent of a representative national sample said that in the previous month they had "avoided buying a specific product or brand because it is being boycotted by a group or cause" they support. This 14 percent translates to over 25 million Americans participating in one boycott or another during a single month.

When asked to respond to the statement, "Participating in a boycott of products or companies doesn't really accomplish anything" only 12 percent agreed strongly, while 67 percent disagreed. George Barna, who conducted the study, commented: "With the markets for most consumer goods becoming increasingly fragmented and market share levels dropping in many product categories, boycotts may have a significant effect on the boycotted product or company. With 25 million people involved, losing sales from even a small proportion of this group could have a devastating impact on a company."

A month after publication of Barna's survey, one major American enterprise showed that it understood his arithmetic. On November 4 and 5, 1991, Burger King Corporation ran "An Open Letter to the American People" in several hundred newspapers across the country. "Burger King wishes to go on record as supporting traditional American values on television, especially the importance of the family," the ad stated. "We believe the American people desire television programs that reflect the values they are trying to instill in their children. We pledge to support such programs with our advertising dollars."

This half-page newspaper spread served as a response to a threatened boycott by CLeaR-TV, which had previously cited Burger King as a "leading sponsor of network TV sex, violence, profanity, and anti-Christian bigotry" during May ratings sweeps.

"As soon as we learned about the boycott, we started having meetings with CLeaR representatives," Burger King spokesman Michael Evans told the *Los Angeles Times*. The company then assured the watchdog group that it would prescreen programs that it planned to sponsor and would avoid supporting shows that contained potentially offensive material.

Howard Rosenberg, the distinguished television critic of the *Los Angeles Times*, condemned this meeting of the minds and criticized the resulting ad as "echoing the tone of loyalty oaths" from the early '50s. "The case has all the earmarks of a corporation choosing profits over principle by gutlessly caving in to a pressure group," he wrote, without ever naming the higher principle he wanted Burger King to defend. On what basis should a hamburger company feel some higher obligation to risk a national boycott by defying a group of some sixteen hundred religious leaders and continuing to sponsor television programming that many of its customers might find objectionable?

Rosenberg's complaint reflects the common Hollywood assumption that any attempt by viewers to participate in organized efforts to combat violent and sexual excesses in the media is dangerous and fascistic. This viewpoint ignores both history and logic. Nowhere in the Constitution is it written that TV viewers must sit quietly on their couches and passively accept whatever the industry chooses to place on the air; the right to protest degrading material is not limited to those favored few who are asked to report their viewing on a Nielsen box.

Inside Moves

In addition to efforts to reform Hollywood through the force of outside pressure, a number of groups have begun working inobtrusively but effectively inside the entertainment industry to introduce a more traditional outlook to some of the individuals who make up its working core. These highly personal approaches follow the assumption that the best way to change the values of the popular culture is to change the values of the people who shape it.

Most of the organizations pursuing this strategy are, of course, religious in nature. They recognize the spiritual hunger among entertainment professionals that has led many of them to follow trendy if tortured paths to enlightenment, ranging from Scientology to est, from Shirley MacLaine's mind-boggling body of beliefs to Hollywood's latest rage—Marianne Williamson's "Course in Miracles." With so many industry insiders trying to use spiritual teachings to make sense of their lives, it seems reasonable to assume that some of them might even find satisfaction in the tenets of Christianity and Judaism.

These initiatives by "movieland missionaries" began in earnest only twelve years ago and since that time they have succeeded beyond anyone's expectations. Several groups of show business believers now assemble for regular seminars, social events, and networking sessions, though fear of the industry's abiding allergy to organized religion leads them all to maintain a low public profile.

Dr. Larry Poland, a hearty midwesterner of formidable intelligence and enormous charm, helped launch Hollywood's current wave of religious outreach when he established a ministry called Associates in Media in 1980. That effort soon spawned Premise, described as "a dynamic group for young writers, directors, and producers . . . that helps Christian believers grow in their faith, encourage one another in a somewhat hostile spiritual environment, and hone their professional skills for greater penetration and success in the industry."

More recently, Dr. Poland has concentrated his efforts on individual counseling and small-group training through his Mastermedia organization. Recognizing the widespread fear that open religious identification could hamper career advancement, this operation offers "confidential Christian fellowship" and counts among its regular participants top executives at Disney, Paramount, MGM, and all four television networks.

Intermission, founded by a charismatic stage and television actor named David Schall, has become the most visible and energetic expression of the industry's quiet religious revival. Under the operational umbrella of the Hollywood Presbyterian Church, Intermission's quarterly meetings draw four hundred to five hundred participants from every branch of the business, featuring a sprinkling of big-name producers and stars together with a host of ambitious younger artists. The two features that all members of the group somehow seem to combine are an absolutely infectious sense of mission and extraordinary good looks. No one who attends an Intermission meeting can fail to be impressed by the intoxicating energy and confidence of these determined idealists.

This group also sponsors the Actors Co-op, which operates its own highly professional (and critically praised) theater troupe and provides fellowship, encouragement, and artistic growth for Christian performers.

In order to encourage more religiously committed young people to pursue careers in the media, the recently established Los Angeles Film Studies Center offers a "Hollywood Semester" for promising students from Christian colleges across the country. The program provides direct contact with the production process, as well as an intensive seminar on "Exploring a Christian Perspective on the Nature and Influence of Film."

In parallel to the burgeoning Christian presence in Hollywood, a number of Jewish religious institutions have begun their own outreach efforts to the disaffiliated Jews so common in the entertainment industry. Pacific Jewish Center, an organization to which I've volunteered my time for some fifteen years, offers a wide range of classes, discussion groups, and special "Learners' Services" that introduce Sabbath and High Holiday observances to people with limited religious background. We've also conducted a series of standing-room-only sessions called "Celluloid Judaism," exploring the competing claims and messages of Hollywood and Jewish tradition. Over the years, large numbers of producers, agents, directors, actors, and writers have reconnected with their heritage through participation in these programs.

Aish HaTorah Jerusalem, an international educational network with a flourishing center in Los Angeles, has launched its own aggressive and effective outreach to the Hollywood community. This campaign has already produced dramatic results: following his personal study with one of the Aish HaTorah rabbis, an award-winning television producer introduced into his current weekly series the first *observant* Jewish character in the history of prime time.

This experience highlights the fact that the entertainment industry remains one area of endeavor in which a single gifted individual can still make an enormous difference. Bringing about a revolution in Hollywood's values by no means requires the transformation of all personnel who work in the media of mass entertainment. The quiet religious revival currently at work in the industry aims instead at the far more realistic goal of reaching enough people to create a viable minority community within the larger establishment. That revival makes no attempt to *replace* the present secular perspectives, but merely hopes to *balance* them.

The same emphasis on expanding rather than reducing the range of available alternatives characterizes the many ambitious enterprises initiated by religious believers to produce new movies that reflect more traditional values. More than a dozen companies, partnerships, and foundations have sprung up to achieve this goal, with persistent producers prepared to go outside the normal production channels to show

Hollywood that more wholesome forms of entertainment can reach a significant audience. Some of these rebel projects feature explicit religious messages, but most of them do not. Present plans call for big-budget film versions of the best-selling novels *Christy*, by Catherine Marshall, and *This Present Darkness*, by Frank Peretti, in addition to a wide range of lesser-known, values-based stories for both children and adults.

One pioneering production along these lines has already achieved impressive success: *China Cry* (1990), financed by the Trinity Broadcasting Network and starring the gifted Asian-American performers Julia Nickson Soul and Russell Wong. No one would describe this earnest low-budget film as an unqualified artistic triumph, but its emotional impact is undeniable; both times I've watched it, audience members wept openly at its true story of a young mother who undergoes a religious conversion while suffering brutal persecution at the hands of the Chinese Communists.

The biggest surprise about this off-beat production involves its remarkable performance at the box office: without well-known stars or any promotion budget to speak of, *China Cry* drew an amazing response from the public and averaged more than $6,000 per screening in its first month of release. This means that in the multiplex theaters where it played alongside major studio releases, it easily clobbered films such as *Rocky V* or *GoodFellas* or *Predator II*. The picture ultimately played in some nine hundred theaters, sold over 200,000 video units, and earned more than double its initial production cost of $5 million. Much of the credit for its success goes to its coproducer, Tim Penland, a well-respected Hollywood insider who resigned his position as a consultant at Universal in the midst of the controversy over *The Last Temptation of Christ*. Penland notes that *China Cry*, produced and distributed for a mere fraction of the cost of *Last Temptation*, and with none of the attendant national publicity, still reached significantly larger audiences in both its theatrical and video releases. If future undertakings originating in the religious community manage to achieve comparable success, the major studios will be forced to take notice and perhaps to make room for similar projects under their aegis.

In view of the scope and seriousness of Hollywood's present problems, the small victories and new beginnings described above may seem irrelevant and insignificant. It remains to be seen whether the newly minted religious commitment of a few key players will ultimately reduce the levels of violence and degradation in our popular culture, or whether the commercial success of a handful of off-beat projects can persuade Hollywood to alter its underlying attitudes.

Moreover, some observers might find a conspiratorial and slightly menacing aspect to the ardent but unpublicized recruitment efforts for organized religion. "My God, it sounds like the Hollywood Communists in the 1930s!" laughed one entertainment journalist after I described some of the recent endeavors of traditional believers in the industry. "It's like they're organizing into all these secret little cells and trying to sneak some of their own people into power positions. One way or another, they want to take over everything, and then you can bet they'll get rid of all the infidels."

This is hardly the intention of the relative handful of committed Christians and observant Jews who hope to change some of the underlying attitudes of the entertainment industry. What they seek is the acceptance of their own point of view, rather than the exclusion of anyone else's. Even with the progress of recent years, religious people still face formidable obstacles to full participation in the Hollywood mainstream. I am directly acquainted with the case of a bright and capable junior-level executive at one of the major studios who lost her job because she made the mistake of using company stationery for a private letter with religious content. In another instance, Columbia Pictures recently banned a Bible study group from meeting on its premises—despite the fact that Alcoholics Anonymous, AIDS support organizations, and many other groups assemble regularly on studio property. One of the banished Christians wryly commented on the company's need to protect the sacred "separation of church and studio."

No one wants that situation to change to the extent that any movie company will *require* Bible study or morning prayers, but we ought to be able to reach a point where such activities are *permitted*.

If Hollywood manages to move in that direction it will amount to a continuation of the single most positive trend in the recent history of the entertainment industry. That trend involves the establishment's recent openness to outlooks and experiences that had been tragically excluded in the past.

Everyone applauds the arrival of a new generation of exciting and self-assured African-American filmmakers who are bringing fresh perspectives to an industry sorely in need of them. Hollywood also gains by providing greatly increased opportunities for the female writers, directors, and producers who are overcoming long-entrenched obstacles to bring their distinctive contributions to the screen. The business can only benefit when it expands the variety of viewpoints available in its movie mix.

In this context, the religious community constitutes the one group that is now most seriously underrepresented among the entertainment establishment. In part, this reflects the sad fact that talented individuals with traditional convictions or religious scruples have too often shunned active involvement in show business because of that arena's long-standing reputation for sleaziness. Now that growing numbers of the faithful have overcome that bias and declared their passionate interest in the entertainment industry, Hollywood should view that development as an opportunity, not a threat. Talented individuals who are personally committed to traditional values have demonstrated an increasing willingness to roll up their sleeves, to dirty their hands, and to get to work—outside the mainstream, if necessary—to change the direction of the popular culture. In any event, they are ready to play the game and their energetic efforts can assist the industry in reconnecting with lost elements of the mass audience.

Capable of Change

Despite promising efforts by groups both inside and outside the Hollywood community, some skeptics remain convinced that no significant improvement is possible in the popular culture. They refuse to recognize the abundant indications that the industry is capable of change in its approach to some of the most significant issues of our time.

The altered approach to drugs offers the most obvious example. Before 1984, Hollywood turned out a wealth of projects depicting the use of marijuana and even cocaine as sexy, exciting, and altogether enjoyable. Cheech and Chong became major stars based entirely on their thoroughly convincing impersonation of a pair of lovable, addle-brained pot heads. In movies, and even in a few TV shows, emotional liberation and sexual ecstasy generally followed a character's initiation into the glories of marijuana.

In the mid-'80s, the attitude in the entertainment industry changed substantially along with the opinions and practices of the nation at large. Despite occasional throwbacks like Mel Gibson's role as a charismatic coke peddler in *Tequila Sunrise* (1988), most drug dealers and users suddenly became villains and losers. Hollywood even turned out a series of powerful, challenging antidrug message movies such as the Michael Keaton vehicle *Clean and Sober* and the James Woods/Sean Young melodrama *The Boost* (both 1988).

The dramatic adjustment in the industry's approach reflected not only its perception of prevailing popular trends but a heightened sense of social responsibility. After years of complaints from various groups about Hollywood's persistent promotion of drug and alcohol abuse, the message finally managed to get through. As former federal drug czar William Bennett recently recalled: "Hollywood is persuadable on some things. They were persuadable on the drug issue. They stopped, for the most part, making movies that glorified drug use. In *Pretty Woman*, there is a very important scene in the beginning when Julia Roberts is holding something behind her back and Richard Gere tells her that if it's cocaine, he wants nothing to do with her. It turns out that what she has is a toothbrush. The subliminal message is if you want a guy like Richard Gere, don't fool around with cocaine."

The current compulsion to include condom references in every imaginable motion picture, television show, and popular song represents another instance of the industry's acknowledgment of the real-world impact of the images it purveys. This trend unquestionably arises out of Hollywood's sincere desire to use its enormous power for a positive purpose—in this case helping teenagers and other Americans reduce the threat of AIDS infection and unwanted pregnancies.

At times, these good intentions lead to some reasonably bizarre manifestations, such as the insistence by the Top 10 R&B vocal group TLC on wearing condoms prominently pinned to their baggy, psychedelic-colored outfits whenever—and wherever—they perform. "It's our fashion statement," says group leader Left Eye (real name: Lisa Lopes). "Kids listen to performers and we have a duty to give them certain critical information. We wanted something eye-catching, so when kids see the condoms, they ask why do we wear condoms and talk about condoms. That brings up the issue of safe sex. The point is to make condoms something kids aren't afraid of or ashamed of."

The group, creators of the hit single "Aint 2 Proud 2 Beg," feels so strongly about its unusual accessories that it has elected to skip TV shows that have insisted that they remove the decorative prophylactics as the price of performing on the air. The politically correct Arsenio Hall made no such demands and welcomed TLC as his guests—with their talismanic trademarks proudly on display.

Members of the entertainment industry have recently demonstrated similar devotion and high-mindedness on a number of other issues that they have chosen to embrace. In 1987 the Harvard Alcohol Project set out to deglamorize drunkenness and to insert references to designated drivers wherever possible; within three years this concept turned up in more than one hundred television episodes. Since 1989, the Entertainment Industry Council has enjoyed similar success in convincing television and movie writers and producers to insert both subtle and obvious endorsements for the regular wearing of seatbelts.

Ecological responsibility has become the latest fad in the entertainment capital. Rain forests are disappearing everywhere around the world except on motion picture screens: *The Emerald Forest* (1985), *At Play in the Fields of the Lord* (1991), *Medicine Man* (1992), and the expensive kiddie cartoon *Ferngully: The Last Rain Forest* (1992) all featured strong "Save the Rain Forests" themes. Despite the fact that each of these films flopped at the box office, the major studios have made the noble, unselfish (and foolhardy) commitment to at least a dozen more projects on similar themes in the next two years.

To some extent, these plans demonstrate the astonishing effectiveness of environmental activists who began their organized efforts to influence Hollywood in 1988. The Environmental Media Association based its strategy on numerous "briefing sessions" that it provided for directors, writers, producers, agents, and stars. In carefully orchestrated one-hour meetings, the Hollywood heavies met with various experts to talk about polluted oceans, toxic waste, or the perils of nuclear power. The environmentalists never tried to suggest specific story lines or subject matter for movies or television shows, but they invariably offered themselves as sources of information if the creative personnel ever wanted to take on an environmental theme.

These educational sessions and the appeals to the industry's social conscience achieved an almost immediate impact. Television producers not only provided occasional references on popular series to the importance of recycling or the need to avoid Styrofoam, but also devoted entire shows to environmental education.

One such program of "The Simpsons"—"Two Cars in Every Garage, and Three Eyes on Every Fish"—won the 1991 award from the Environmental Media Association as the best episode of television comedy. In accepting the honor at a gala banquet at Sony/Columbia studios, series creator Matt Groening noted that he had received a letter from a nuclear-power lobbying group saying his show "confused and frightened the American public." Groening noted that this "was a sign that we're doing the right thing. . . . We at 'The Simpsons' will continue to confuse and frighten the American public!"

The elegant crowd that cheered his words and ate pesticide-free vegetables and fish-farm salmon at the "Organic Oscars" featured an impressive array of Hollywood royalty, including Sony Pictures CEO Peter Guber, Creative Artists Agency Chairman Mike Ovitz, Norman Lear, Robert Redford, Barbra Streisand, Ted Turner and Jane Fonda, Sting, Chevy Chase, Ted Danson, Daryl Hannah, Diane Sawyer, George Hamilton, Shirley MacLaine, Ed Begley, Jr., and many others. As Begley waited for the parking attendant to drive up in his environmentally correct electric-powered car, he told *Los Angeles Times* reporter Bill Higgins: "The media is essential for getting the message across. There's not time to go door-to-door."

One point becomes abundantly clear to all participants in any such gathering: these are, by and large, fundamentally decent and well-intentioned people. Their eagerness to do good as they understand it, to win respect as both artists and citizens, is genuine, touching, and almost childlike. No one who knows the members of the industry elite can doubt their sincere commitment to issues that have aroused their interest. If they seem unconcerned about the degrading and antisocial messages in so much of the entertainment they offer, it is because they have not yet been convincingly confronted with the destructive impact of what they are doing.

Sustained public and private pressure can help to open their eyes. The industry must finally be forced to recognize that if the media are capable of real-world influence when it comes to encouraging socially responsible behavior like recycling, then they are also capable of encouraging antisocial behavior, like rape and looting and gang violence.

At the moment, the environment is Hollywood's most fashionable issue. The fight to stop nuclear power is far more trendy than the fight to save the nuclear family; reducing the level of pollution seems to be a higher priority than reducing the level of teenage promiscuity.

Nevertheless, these other concerns should be addressed with the same patience and sophistication with which the environmental activists raised Hollywood's consciousness. An industry that has committed considerable resources to saving the rain forests might be persuaded of the comparable importance of saving the institution of marriage. If producers are willing to repeatedly endorse condoms, is it ridiculous to suggest that they might also encourage hard work in school or even respect for teachers?

During the controversy over the loathsome lyrics of 2 Live Crew, George Will wrote, "America today is capable of terrific intolerance about smoking or toxic waste that threatens trout. But only a deeply confused society is more concerned about protecting lungs than minds, trout than black women. . . ."

Industry apologists may tremble at the thought that this line of reasoning leads inevitably to the dreaded prospect of "self-censorship," but they ignore the fact that this exercise of self-restraint is already well-established in Hollywood.

No studio will make a project glorifying the Ku Klux Klan, or blaming a Jewish conspiracy for World War II, or urging Americans to slaughter all our remaining wolves before they pounce on a few more cattle. It wouldn't matter who proposed such projects, or how many past successes they had achieved: certain ideas will be instantly censored, not by the government or by some industry ratings board, but by executives themselves and their own sense of taste and responsibility.

The most important priority in the struggle for the soul of the popular culture is expanding that sense of responsibility.

We have recently accepted the notion that giant companies must pay more attention to what they are doing to pollute our air and water. At the same time, it is reasonable to ask the entertainment conglomerates to assume greater responsibility for their pollution of our popular culture—for fouling the moral and social atmosphere that we all breathe.

Consider the case of the rock group known as W.A.S.P. (We Are Sexual Perverts). It employs saws, axes, skeletons, and gallons of fake blood in its act, while the group's leader dances for the crowd wearing a codpiece with a circular saw blade attached. "We spit blood and throw raw pieces of meat into the crowd," boasts one of his associates. Capitol Records chose to reward such inventiveness by signing the band to a $1.5 million recording contract.

Could this conceivably be described as a responsible corporate decision? Does it in any way amount to censorship to suggest that Capitol should have taken social considerations into account and invested its money elsewhere? As it turned out, their commitment to the group proved to be a bad move financially as well as philosophically; despite heavy promotion, W.A.S.P. failed to catch on with its intended teenage audience.

By contrast, the controversial rapper Ice Cube caught on all too well: his album *Death Certificate* proved to be one of the best-selling records released in 1991. It drew intense criticism at the time of its debut for its inclusion of a song called "Black Korea," which featured the lyrics, "So pay respect to the black fist/Or we'll burn down your store right down to a crisp." The artist described the song to the *Los Angeles Times* as "a warning to Koreans—in strong, threatening terms. If things don't get better, we're going to burn their stores down."

Six months later, angry crowds of rioters did precisely that—with several hundred Korean-American stores torched in the Los Angeles disturbances. In prophetic words at the time of the song's release, Gary Kim of the Korean American Coalition asked, "If a Korean-owned store gets burned down, I wonder if Ice Cube is going to accept responsibility for such actions." In the final analysis, it's not the rapper who should accept responsibility: it's Priority Records, the company that made the disastrous decision to record and distribute his song.

As Ice Cube himself said in November 1991, "As long as I keep selling records that's all they care about. Give them a Nazi record, and if they can make money off it, they will."

Somehow, major companies must be held to a higher standard.

As Charles P. Alexander argued in an important essay in *Time* mag-

azine (May 7, 1990): "There will always be filth on the fringes of entertainment. The problem arises when filth becomes mainstream, when it
is mass-marketed. A few giant corporations, including Disney, Fox,
MCA, Paramount, Time-Warner, Britain's EMI, West Germany's Ber-
telsmann, and Japan's Sony, produce a huge proportion of our children's entertainment. Many parents feel that these companies should
take the lead in setting the standards for everyone."

To paraphrase Malcolm X, the fight to establish such standards
should proceed "by whatever means necessary."

In addition to the boycotts, letter writing, and public shaming that
should be part of the process, we should also use stockholder meetings
of the major entertainment enterprises to raise key issues in the popular culture. Environmental activists regularly challenge huge corporations over their most dubious practices in front of shareholders,
investors, board members, and the press. Entertainment activists can
employ the same tactics to combat pop culture pollution. The conglomerates that produce the bulk of our mass-audience entertainment
ought to be reminded that bad messages are often bad business.

In the words of George Gerbner, former dean of the Annenberg
School of Communications: "What we need is a new cultural environmental movement in which we achieve some degree of citizen participation in cultural decision-making. This has never happened before."

"Renewal, Honor, and Optimism"

The chances for a successful launch of such an unprecedented
"cultural environmental movement" have never been better.

The restive public feels increasingly and unmistakably dissatisfied
with Hollywood's current directions. Among a significant proportion of
our countrymen, disenchantment has begun to give way to a sense of
rage and betrayal.

If nothing else, the financial impact of this alienation of the audience can no longer be safely ignored. In every component of the popular culture—from motion pictures to rock 'n' roll music to prime-time
TV—economic problems are persistent and perilous. Already, the most
sensitive and farsighted figures within the show business community
freely acknowledge that their industry may be facing long-term trou-

ble. "Nothing works anymore," wailed one major producer at a recent dinner party at his Beverly Hills home. "It's not just a case of fine-tuning the machine. Maybe we've got to rethink the whole approach and figure out what we're doing wrong."

In this unsettled atmosphere, anything is possible.

The movers and shakers in the mass media may begin to hear the message that their underlying problem in connecting with the public involves the substance of their projects, not the competence of their execution. Instead of exploiting our nightmares, they could cultivate the best dreams of our hearts. Perhaps they might even entertain the notion that America deserves a popular culture as decent and as hopeful as the spirit of her people.

The alternative to the present madness in no way requires a reversion to infantilism or the dreaded simplifications of "Ozzie and Harriet" and Norman Rockwell. No one wants an entertainment industry that would gear *all* its offerings to small children—but that doesn't mean that we must accept the other extreme, with its relentless emphasis on the most brutal and horrifying aspects of human nature. Somewhere between the childish pabulum that the industry elite fears and decries, and the current concentration on degradation and despair, lies an appropriate balance.

Miraculously, the movie business of fifty years ago managed to get the mix just about right. To look back on the incomparable films of Hollywood's single greatest year, 1939, is to feel a dull ache over what we have lost—and over the tragedy of an industry that's lost its way. When you watch *Mr. Smith Goes to Washington, Gone With the Wind, Wuthering Heights, The Wizard of Oz, Ninotchka, Of Mice and Men, Goodbye, Mr. Chips, Stagecoach, Young Mr. Lincoln, Drums Along the Mohawk, Beau Geste,* or *Gunga Din,* it is obvious that no one could describe them as saccharine, simple-minded, empty entertainments—nor are they shocking and grotesque visions of the meaningless cruelty of life. The finest films of the past—along with a handful of the most noble cinematic achievements of the present—manage to find a middle course and to show that great popular art isn't an either/or proposition.

They also demonstrate that it is possible to create entertainment of enduring worth without assaulting the fundamental values of the people.

The current debate on the values of the entertainment industry involves far more than abstract aesthetic issues; the stakes for all of us are intensely personal. In his *Time* essay, Charles Alexander reflects, "I realize I can shelter my boys for only so long. As they grow older, I will lose control of them, and they will eagerly sample the forbidden fruit. I hope that by then they will have internalized my values. But I fear that pop culture and peer pressure may overwhelm my influence."

That is what all parents fear today, and as I watch my own sleeping children, hugging each other in the bed they share with the blankets tangled around their feet, I experience a terrible sense of powerlessness when measured against the protective instincts that I feel. Their bedspread features a cheerful pattern with kittens and butterflies; my younger daughter clutches a purple-plush dinosaur who resembles the singing, dancing main character in a home video she particularly enjoys. The girls are now five and three years old, respectively; we expect our third child, God willing, just two months after I write these words and conclude this book. I know that these children cannot sleep this sweet sleep forever; they will some day face a world that delivers its moments of shock, darkness, and despair. But not now, please. Not yet. May the frights and the furies of our current cultural malaise let them sleep—and play—in peace awhile longer.

In the final analysis, I worry over the impact of media messages not only on my children but on myself—and on all the rest of us. No matter how sophisticated we believe that we are, or how determined our best efforts to counteract their influence, the poisons of the popular culture seep into our very souls. A well-known slogan of the 1960s declared, with reasonable accuracy, "War is unhealthy for children and other living things." Today, one might similarly observe, "The popular culture is unhealthy for children—and other living things."

In 1990, Australian writer Richard Neville gave memorable expression to the challenges we face:

> In much of the world . . . where dictators are dumped and walls crash down, the picture seems brighter, but in my local video store, I see teenagers stockpiling at least ten hours of horror, porn, and pain for the weekend. . . .
>
> Alone in a darkened space our moral sensibilities are no match for the Tinseltown hype and the whiz-bang reviews. . . . As surely as toxic

residue kills the fish and the fowl, so the sloth of our mean-spirited film-makers and writers kills our spirit. It is renewal that is needed now, honor and optimism.

We can find grounds for that optimism in the commitment to change from so many good people, both inside and outside the entertainment community. The struggle for the soul of the popular culture promises no quick or easy victories; all progress will be measured in subtle increments.

Nevertheless, the battle has been joined and the groundwork is there for new offensives. In the words of Winston Churchill, spoken fifty years ago at an early turning point in the most costly war in human history: "Now this is not the end. It is not even the beginning of the end. But it is, perhaps, the end of the beginning."

Notes on Sources

PART I: THE POISON FACTORY

Chapter 1: A Sickness in the Soul

Alienating the Audience

Media General/Associated Press Poll #26, May 5–13, 1989;

Parents Poll, "Should TV Be Censored?", *Parents* magazine, April 1990, p. 34;

Gallup Poll, 1991; cited in *Los Angeles Times/Calendar*, November 3, 1991, p. 81;

Time/Cable News Network Poll (conducted by Yankelovich Clancy Shulman), June 1, 1989;

Los Angeles Times survey; September 14–19, 1989.

"This Simply Cannot Go On"

John Neal, quoted in *Los Angeles Times*, December 4, 1991, p. F8;

Network audience and profit figures from *Three Blind Mice: How The TV Networks Lost Their Way*, by Ken Auletta, Random House, 1991, p. 3;

Gene DeWitt quoted in "Goodbye to the Mass Audience" by Richard Zoglin, *Time*, November 19, 1990, pp. 122–23;

Mike Royko, "On TV, Even the High Quality Trash Is Becoming Boring," *Detroit Free Press*, November 27, 1988;

Cal Thomas, "TV Continues Slide into Sewer," *Human Events,* November 24, 1990;

National Association of Broadcasters survey, cited in "Why People Are Turned Off by Television", *U.S. News & World Report,* February 13, 1984, p. 49;

"The New TV Viewer," *Channels* magazine, September 1988, p. 61;

Surveys by the Gallup Organization, the latest that of August 16–19, 1990, published in *The Public Perspective: A Roper Center Review of Public Opinion and Polling,* Volume 2, Number 5, July/August 1991, p. 91;

"Recession or Creative Stagnation?: Execs Ponder Lower Music Shipments," *Billboard,* November 2, 1991, p. 3;

Rock's share of music industry's total take, cited in "Rekindling the Fire," by Robert Hilburn, *Los Angeles Times/Calendar,* October 27, 1991, p. 8; Bill Graham quoted p. 9;

"Country Tops Top 40 as No. 3 Format," *Billboard,* November 9, 1991, pp. 1, 17;

Bob Lefsetz, interview with author, December 10, 1991;

Motion Picture Association of America, "Incidence of Motion Picture Attendance Among the Adult and Teenage Public," January 1991;

Gallup Organization/*Newsweek,* May 30, 1990; Gordon S. Black Corporation/*U.S.A. Today,* June 12, 1990; Barna Research Group, 1990; Media General/Associated Press, May 5–13, 1989;

"Hollywood Pulls Curtain Down on Theatre Chains," by John Lippman, *Los Angeles Times,* September 15, 1991, p. D9;

"Home Video Faces 'A' Title Drought: Hollywood Slump is Challenge to Suppliers," by Paul Sweeting, *Billboard,* November 9, 1991, pp. 1, 49;

"Hollywood Hits a Dry Spell as Films Falter," *Billboard Home Video,* November 2, 1991, p. 61;

"No Easter Basket for Box Office," by David J. Fox, *Los Angeles Times,* April 20, 1992, pp. F1, F6;

Daily Variety, February 25, 1992;

"The Teachings of Chairman Dekom," by Charles S. Fleming, *Variety,* September 16, 1991, p. 109.

Sleaze and Self-Indulgence

David Puttnam, quoted in *Bill Moyers: A World of Ideas,* Doubleday, 1989, p. 320;

Grover Lewis, "The Wild One" (review of *Bloody Sam* by Marshall Fine), *Los Angeles Times Book Review,* December 8, 1991, p. 2;

Jeffrey Katzenberg, quoted in *Los Angeles Times/Calendar,* October 20, 1991, p. 26, and October 13, 1991, p. 24;

Gene Kirkwood, quoted in *Los Angeles Times/Calendar,* December 8, 1991, p. 24;

I. A. L. Diamond, quoted in *New York City Tribune,* June 24, 1987,

"Bucks Have Replaced Art as Impetus for Today's Screenwriters," Mark Evans, p. 14;

Julia Phillips quoted in *People*, March 18, 1991, "A Hollywood Outcast Treats the Stars to an Acid-Dip Memoir," by Joyce Wadler and Doris Bacon, p. 104;

Michael Sragow, "Gross Projections: The True Story of How Reagan and Television Ate Hollywood's Brain," *Mother Jones*, January 1990, p. 22.

"A Performance Piece by Michael Jackson"

"A Dangerous Game," reports by Alan Citron, Chuck Phillips, and Daniel Cerone, *Los Angeles Times*, pp. F1, F7–10;

"Michael Jackson: Is He Still a Thriller?", by Edna Gunderson, *U.S.A. Today*, November 25, 1991, pp. 1A, 2A;

"Michael's Video Takes Beating; 4 Minutes Cut" by Daniel Cerone, *Los Angeles Times*, November 16, 1991, pp. F1, F18;

"A New Video Opens the Michael Jackson Blitz" by Jon Pareles, *New York Times*, The Arts, p. 13.

A Traitor to the Industry

Theodore Roszak, *Flicker*, Summit Books, 1991, p. 1.

Chapter 2: A Bias for the Bizarre

One Small Skirmish

Caryn James, "Peter Greenaway's Elegant and Brutal 'Cook,'" *New York Times*, April 6, 1990, p. C12;

Richard Corliss, "X Marks the Top," *Time*, April 9, 1990, p. 95.

"Incompatible Worldviews"

Michael Hudson quoted in *Daily Variety*, "Left and Right Square Off During Panel on Censorship and Government Arts Funding," by Kathleen O'Steen, November 20, 1991, p. 1;

Jack Valenti quoted in *Los Angeles Times*, "Exhibitors Convene Amid War, Recession," by David J. Fox, February 6, 1991;

Mary Schmidt Campbell, quoted in "This is the Battle for America's Soul," by Patrick J. Buchanan, *Los Angeles Times*, January 25, 1990;

Congressman Henry Hyde quoted in *Movieguide*, Vol. V (10), 1990, "Sour Grapes," by Ted Baehr, p. 3;

Pat Buchanan, "This is the Battle for America's Soul," *Los Angeles Times*, January 25, 1990;

Dr. James C. Dobson and Gary Bauer, *Children at Risk: The Battle for the Hearts and Minds of Our Kids*, Word Publishing, 1990, p. 19.

Excretion and Masturbation

Irving Kristol, "It's Obscene but Is It Art?", *The Wall Street Journal*, August 7, 1990;

James F. Cooper, "Art Censors: A Closer Look at the NEA," *New Dimensions: The Psychology Behind the News*, June 1991, pp. 26–30.

"Life Stinks"

Mel Brooks quoted in *Los Angeles Times/Calendar*, "Does This Mean the Video Isn't Coming Out Soon?", by Andy Marx, October 13, 1991.

Choice, Not Repression

Official Statement in press release by Time-Warner in response to CLEAT (Combined Law Enforcement Associations of Texas), June 11, 1992.

"Malign Propaganda"

Penelope Spheeris, quoted in *Time*, "Dirty Words: America's Foul-Mouthed Popular Culture," by Richard Corliss, May 7, 1990, p. 94;

David Puttnam, quoted in *Bill Moyers: A World of Ideas*, Doubleday, 1989, p. 327.

PART II: THE ATTACK ON RELIGION

Chapter 3: A Declaration of War

"Father, Forgive Them"

Larry W. Poland, Ph.D., *The Last Temptation of Hollywood*, Mastermedia International, 1988, pp. 188–96;

Russell Chandler, "25,000 Gather at Universal to Protest Film," *Los Angeles Times*, August 12, 1988, p. 1;

Mike Duffy, "Yahoos Create Unholy Row Over Film About Christ," *Detroit Free Press*, August 10, 1988.

Stonewalling

Ad by Universal Studios, "An Open Letter to Bill Bright," *Hollywood Reporter*, July 21, 1988, back page;

Pastor Richard G. Lee, quoted in Poland, op. cit., p. 173;

Press statement by Motion Picture Association of America, July 1988, quoted in Poland, op. cit., p. 136;

Terry Pristin, "The Filmmakers vs. The Crusaders," *Los Angeles Times/Calendar*, December 29, 1991, pp. 7–8, 28–33;

Don Rosen, "Temptation, Rage and Wasserman," *Los Angeles Herald-Examiner,* July 21, 1988;

John Dart, "2 Step Back from Film Protest Over Anti-Jewish Tone," *Los Angeles Times,* Part II, pp. 1, 4.

Solemn Stupidity

Mickey Rooney, quoted in "Mickey Rooney Speaks Out Against Hollywood Values," *Between the Lines,* January 11, 1991, p. 1;

Marshall Fine and Joel Siegel, quoted in Poland, op. cit., pp. 251, 255;

David Ehrenstein, "Nothing Forsaken in 'Last Temptation,'" *Los Angeles Herald-Examiner,* August 12, 1988, p. 9

Chapter 4: Comic Book Clergy

Bashing the Born-Agains

Margaret Atwood, quoted in "If Puritans Ruled ... Atwood's Story on Screen," by Gerald Perry, *Los Angeles Times/Calender,* 1990, p. 3;

Michael Tolkin, quoted in *TV, etc.,* December 1991, p. 6;

Michael Tolkin, radio interview with Jim Svejda, KNX Radio, November 1991.

Chapter 5: Forgetting the Faithful

The People's Religion

George Gallup quoted in *TV Guide,* March 11, 1989, p. 15; additional information in *Los Angeles Times,* March 14, 1992, pp. F18–19, "Gallup Says Media Should Focus on Religion—the 'New Frontier'";

Linda S. Lichter, S. Robert Lichter, and Stanley Rothman, "Hollywood and America: The Odd Couple," *Public Opinion,* December/January 1983, pp. 54–56;

Kenneth Woodward, "Talking to God," *Newsweek,* January 6, 1992, p. 39;

Time/CNN Poll, conducted by Yankelovich Clancy Shulman, *Time,* December 9, 1991, p. 64;

U.S. News and World Report, December 9, 1991, "The Retro Campaign," by Kenneth Walsh, p. 33.

Reinforcement from Rock

John Lennon quoted in *The Love You Make: An Insider's Story of the Beatles,* by Peter Brown and Steven Gaines, McGraw-Hill Book Company, 1983; pp. 212–13;

Sinead O'Connor, interview in *Spin* (November 1991), cited in "Soundbites of the Year," *TV, etc.,* January 1992, p. 4.

God on "The Tonight Show"

Lloyd Billingsley, "TV: Where the Girls Are Good Looking and the Good Guys Win," *Christianity Today*, October 4, 1985, p. 38;

Dan Wakefield, "We Need More Religion in Prime Time," *TV Guide*, March 11, 1989, p. 15;

Barbara Grizzuti Harrison, "Is Religion an X-rated Subject?", *Mademoiselle*, January 1983, "Private Eye" column, p. 44;

"Religion Found to Play a Minor Role in TV Shows," *Los Angeles Times*, February 15, 1992; pp. F16–17;

S. Robert Lichter, Linda S. Lichter, and Stanley Rothman, *Watching America: What Television Tells Us About Our Lives*, Prentice Hall Press, 1991, p. 277;

Amanda Donahoe, interview in *Interview* (September 1991), cited in "Soundbites of the Year," *TV, etc.*, January 1992, p. 4.

"Sunday Dinner"

Norman Lear quoted in *New York Times*, May 26, 1991, "Is TV Ready for Norman Lear? Was It Ever?", by Larry Rohter, p. 23;

National Council of Churches Study, cited in Reuters News Service, "Study: Church Membership Up," October 7, 1991;

Norman Lear quoted in Rohter, op. cit.

An All but Irresistible Target

Boston Globe, "Plagiarism and Poor Taste," unsigned editorial, July 6, 1991.

PART III: THE ASSAULT ON THE FAMILY

Chapter 6: Promoting Promiscuity

A Curious Inconsistency

Massachusetts Mutual Life Insurance Company, *The 1991 Study: A Return to Family Values*, Study by Mellman & Lazarus, Inc.;

Gallup Poll, cited in *U.S. News and World Report*, December 9, 1991;

"Everyplace, Enemies of the Family," by Nina J. Easton, *Los Angeles Times*, March 3, 1991, pp. 1, 24;

Ellen Goodman, "Blessed Be Feasting in Kinship," *Los Angeles Times*, November 28, 1991.

Popular Music: As Nasty as It Wants to Be

Terry Higgins, quoted in "Hate Music: Who's Peddling It. And Who's Buying It," by Greg Kot, *Chicago Tribune*, "The Arts," section 13, p. 5;

Bob DeMoss, "Rap Group 2 Live Crew Found Guilty of Recorded Obscenity," *Focus on the Family*, press release, June 7, 1990;

Nona Hendryx quoted in Kot, op. cit., *Chicago Tribune*.

Charges of Racism

Luther Campbell quoted in *Los Angeles Times*, "Today They're Trying to Censor Rap, Tomorrow . . . ," November 5, 1990;

Henry Louis Gates, quoted in *The New Republic*, "Notebook," November 12, 1990, p. 8;

Dr. Benjamin Hooks, Press Release by NAACP, June 1990;

Clarence Page, "Public Enemy Descends on Arizona," *Los Angeles Times*, January 17, 1992;

David Samuels, "The Rap on Rap," *The New Republic*, November 11, 1991, pp. 24–29.

"Rotten to the Core"

Robert Hilburn, "Prince's Flawed 'Diamonds, Pearls,'" *Los Angeles Times/Calendar*, September 29, 1991;

Steve Simels, "My Madonna Problem (And Yours)," *Stereo Review*, April 1991, p. 95;

Joni Mitchell, quoted in "A Conversation with Joni Mitchell," by David Wild, *Rolling Stone*, May 7, 1991, p. 65;

Bob DeMoss, *Learn to Discern*, Zondervan Publishing House, 1992, pp. 54, 135;

Time, May 7, 1990, "Dirty Words: America's Foul-Mouthed Popular Culture," by Richard Corliss, p. 94;

Allan Bloom, *The Closing of the American Mind*, Simon & Schuster, 1987, pp. 74–75, 81.

Titillation on the Tube

Steve Weinstein, "A TV Ratings Hunk," *Los Angeles Times*, November 12, 1991, pp. F1, F7.

"A Potpourri of Tangled Love Affairs"

Lichter, Lichter, and Rothman, op. cit., pp. 25–28;

Cal Thomas, "TV Continues Slide Into Sewer," *Human Events*, November 24, 1990, p. 13;

Cynthia Crossen, "Is TV Too Sexy?", *McCalls*, October 1991, pp. 100–102;

Planned Parenthood Study cited in *New York Times*, January 27, 1988;

Terry Louise Fisher quoted in *New York Times*, March 8, 1987, p. H29;

Joyce Sprafkin and Theresa Silverman, "Update: Physically Intimate and

Sexual Behavior on Prime-Time Television, 1978-1979," *Journal of Communication*, Winter 1981, p. 37;

American Family Association, "Prime Time Viewing: Spring Sweeps, April 28–May 25, 1991," *AFA*, Spring, 1991; cited in *U.S. News and World Report*, June 8, 1992, "The War Over Family Values," by David Whitman, p. 36;

William A. Henry III, "Is TV Getting Better or Worse?", *TV Guide*, March 12, 1988, p. 5.

"TV Virginity Week"

Michael Weithorn quoted in *Los Angeles Times,* "The Young and the Randy," by Dennis McDougall, September 18, 1991, p. F1;

Marlene Goland quoted in "End of the Innocence," by Michael C. Byrne, *TV, etc.,* October 1991, pp. 1–2;

USA Weekend Poll by ICR Associates, conducted November 15–24, 1991, results published in *USA Weekend,* December 27–29, 1991, p. 5.

A Surprisingly Conservative Streak

Marcel Omohundro, letter to *Los Angeles Times,* October 5, 1991, p. F2;

Shannen Doherty quoted in Michael C. Byrne, op. cit., p. 2;

Michael A. Carrera quoted in "What Teen Boys Think About Sex," by Sey Chassler, *Parade,* December 18, 1988, p. 16;

USA Weekend, op. cit.;

"Healthy People 2000: National Health Promotion and Disease Prevention Objectives," Public Health Service, September 1990;

"American Mood Hurt By Past Year's Events," by George Skelton, *Los Angeles Times,* January 1, 1991, pp. A1, A4;

RAND Study reported in "Study Shows AIDS Changing Sexual Behavior," by Claire Spiegel, *Los Angeles Times,* August 17, 1991, p. A1.

"Double-Entendre City"

Jay Martel, "The Schlock of the New," *Rolling Stone,* October 3, 1991, pp. 127–30;

Perry Simon and Glen Gordon Caron, quoted in "Titillating Talk Tests the Limits," *USA Today,* November 18, 1986, p. D-1;

Howard Rosenberg, "Emmycast Down and Dirty—and Funny," *Los Angeles Times,* August 26, 1991, pp. F1, F12;

Claudio Letelier, letter to *Los Angeles Times,* September 7, 1991.

"A Love Crash"

Faye Wattleton quoted in "Television's Sexual Messages Leave Consequences Unexplored," by Eleanor Blau, *New York Times,* January 29, 1988;

Peggy Charen quoted in "Is TV Too Sexy?", Cynthia Crossen, op. cit., p. 104;

Joseph Mankiewicz quoted in "All About Joe . . . " by John Anderson, *Los Angeles Times,* May 6, 1991, p. F1.

Chapter 7: Maligning Marriage

Deadly Delusions
Susan Faludi, *Backlash: The Undeclared War Against American Women,* Crown, 1991, p. 137.

Husbands and Wives in Short Supply
Jacqueline Simenauer and David Carroll, *Singles: The New Americans,* Simon & Schuster, 1982, pp. 321–25.

Innocent Illusions and Grim Realities
H. Ross Perot quoted in "Perot Once Chastised 'Doogie Howser,'" by Alan C. Miller, *Los Angeles Times,* June 6, 1992, p. A21;

Harry F. Water, "Whip Me, Beat Me . . . ", *Newsweek,* November 11, 1991, p. 74.

The Myth of the Fifty-Percent Divorce Rate
Louis Harris, *Inside America,* Vintage Books, 1987, pp. 87–90;

Conversation with Alan Rivlin, Massachusetts Mutual Life Insurance Survey, March 4, 1992;

Daniel Lynch, "AIDS: The Real Story About Risk," *Cosmopolitan,* March 1992, p. 197;

"Advance Report of Final Divorce Statistics," *Monthly Vital Statistics Report,* Volume 39, number 12, Supplement 2, May 21, 1991, U.S. Department of Health and Human Services, Public Health Service, p. 1.

"The Last Married Couple in America"
"Monitoring the Future," Survey Research Center, University of Michigan, 1990;

Simenauer and Carroll, op. cit., p. 351;

Harris, op. cit., p. 87;

Massachusetts Mutual Life Insurance Company, op. cit.

Underlying Attitudes
Production Notes, *Crooked Hearts,* MGM, 1991, pp. 1–2;

Production Notes, *Cape Fear,* Universal Studios, 1991, p. 3.

Chapter 8: Encouraging Illegitimacy

Challenging Family Pieties

Jessica Lange quoted in *Glamour,* 1988;

Nancy Meyers quoted in "Writing Couples Who Write About Couples," by Jan Cherubin, *L.A. Herald-Examiner,* April 30, 1985, p. B4.

"Pregnancy Has Replaced Weddings"

Caryn James, "A Baby Boom on TV as Biological Clocks Cruelly Tick Away," *New York Times,* October 16, 1991, pp. B1, B7;

Mona Charen, "Happily Unwed Moms," Creator's Syndicate, September 30, 1991;

Jordan Bonfante, "How L.A. Captured Prime Time," *Time,* November 18, 1991.

A Trap That Lasts a Lifetime

David Stewart, quoted in Bonfante, ibid.;

Roslyn Heller, quoted in "Hollywood Thinks Small," by Susan Spillman, *USA Today,* September 20, 1991, p. D1;

Vital Statistics, "Summary of 1990 Census Data," Census Bureau;

Stanford University Center for the Study of Youth Development, study cited in Joe L. Frost, "Children in a Changing Society," *Childhood Education,* March/April 1986, p. 244;

David Whitman, "The War Over 'Family Values,'" *U.S. News & World Report,* June 8, 1992;

Charen, op. cit.

Chapter 9: Kids Know Best

The Ultimate Source of Wisdom

Victoria A. Rebeck, article in *Christian Century,* cited in *Television Quarterly: The Journal of the National Academy of Television Arts and Sciences,* Volume XXVI, Number 1, 1991, p. 93;

Kenneth Turan, review of *Radio Flyer, Los Angeles Times,* February 21, 1992, p. F12;

Richard Zoglin, "Troubles on the Home Front," *Time,* January 28, 1985, p. 65;

Axl Rose, quoted in "Run 'n Gun" by Robert Hilburn, *Los Angeles Times/Calendar,* July 21, 1991, p. 7.

"And a Little Child Shall Lead Them"

Beth Austin, "Pretty Worthless: Whatever Happened to Making Movies That Make a Difference?", *Washington Monthly,* May 1991, p. 35;

Peter Rainer, review of *Little Man Tate*, *Los Angeles Times*, October 9, 1991, p. F7.

A Legacy of the '60s
Neil Hickey, "Its Audience Is Aging . . . So Why Is TV Still Chasing the Kids?", *TV Guide*, October 20, 1990, p. 22.

Harder Than It Has to Be
Irving Kristol, "The Future of American Jewry," *Commentary*, August 1991, p. 25;
Steve Allen, "TV Humor: Barbarians Are Storming the Gates," *Los Angeles Times*, September 17, 1990.

PART IV: THE GLORIFICATION OF UGLINESS

Chapter 10: The Urge to Offend

This Lurid Freak Show
Stephen Farber, "Why Do Critics Love These Repellent Movies?", *Los Angeles Times/Calendar*, March 17, 1991, p. 5;
David Puttnam quoted in *Bill Moyers: A World of Ideas*, Doubleday, 1989, p. 318.

The Cannibalism Compulsion
Robert Watts, quoted in "Film Clips/In The Works," by Andy Marx, *Los Angeles Times/Calendar*, May 10, 1992, p. 14.

Incestuous Excesses
Mick Garris quoted in Production Notes, *Sleepwalkers*, Sony/Columbia Studios, 1992.

Interspecies Intercourse
David J. Fox, "Film Clips/Nothing's Sacred," *Los Angeles Times/Calendar*, February 9, 1992, p. 15.

Vomit and Urine
Henry Allen, "The Retched Excesses of Film," *The Washington Post*, March 14, 1988, pp. G1, G10–11;
Betsy Sherman, Boston Globe, cited in movie ad for *Shakes the Clown*, *Chicago Tribune*, March 13, 1992, section 7, p. K.

Roaches and Maggots

Inger Lorre quoted in "Nymphs Singer Lorre Dares to Be Audacious," by Dennis Hunt, *Los Angeles Times,* January 23, 1992, p. F7;

Jonathan Gold, "Grind!", *Los Angeles Times/Calendar,* June 2, 1991, pp. 55, 62–64;

"Artistic Freedom Defense Flushed," *Los Angeles Times,* August 26, 1991, p. F3;

Jonathan Gold, op. cit., p. 64.

Chapter 11: The Infatuation with Foul Language

Media General/Associated Press Poll #26, May 5–13, 1989, op. cit.;

Ann Landers, "Filthy Talk Tarnishing the Silver Screen," *Los Angeles Times,* May 15, 1989;

Rebecca Ross Albers, "Moviehouse Watchdogs," *Miami Herald,* April 23, 1991, p. 1C;

Entertainment Research Group, *State of the Arts: How Would You Rate Hollywood,* February 1992;

Entertainment Research Group, *Graphical Illustrations of Selected Data as a Percentage of Total Movies by M.P.A.A. Ratings, 1991 Movie Edition Reports,* February 1992;

Bill Bruns and Mary Murphy, "Dirty Words, Dirty Pictures: Is TV Going Too Far?", *TV Guide,* November 10, 1990, p. 13;

Delbert Mann, quoted in "TV Standards" by Rick Du Brow, *Los Angeles Times/Calendar,* November 3, 1991.

Chapter 12: The Addiction to Violence

"Definitely a Causal Connection"

Daniel Linz and George Comstock quoted in "Gore Galore" by Sean Mitchell, *USA Weekend,* July 12–14, 1991, p. 4;

Drs. L. Rowell Huesman and Leonard Eron quoted in cover story "Violence Goes Mainstream," *Newsweek,* April 1, 1991, p. 51.

Shocking and Dangerous in Their Time

Review of *Public Enemy,* quoted in "Now at a Theatre Near You: A Skyrocketing Body Count," by Vincent Canby, *New York Times,* July 16, 1990, p. C11;

Tim Appelo, "Ultraviolence: Why Has This Been the Bloodiest Summer in Movie History?", *Entertainment Weekly,* August 3, 1990, p. 51.

"An Insatiability for Raw Sensation"

Alan J. Pakula quoted in Appelo, op. cit., p. 51;

Rob Bottin quoted in ibid., p. 53;

Vincent Canby, "Now at a Theatre Near You: A Skyrocketing Body Count," *New York Times,* July 16, 1990, p. C11;

Entertainment Research Group, op. cit.

Irrelevant Ratings

Entertainment Research Group, *Number of Movies Released in 1991 in Which Identified Potentially Objectionable Item or Conduct Appeared,* January 1992;

Walter Berns, "Popular Culture and Popular Government," conference paper, American Enterprise Institute, March 10, 1992, p 5.

Sadistic Laughter

"Betsy" quoted in Appelo, op. cit., p. 53;

Todd Gitlin, "Who are the World?", conference paper, American Enterprise Institute, March 10, 1992, pp. 8–9;

Mark Crispin Miller, "Hollywood, The Ad," *Atlantic Monthly,* April 1990, p. 53;

Martin Scorsese quoted in *Los Angeles Times/Calendar,* November 10, 1991, p. 5;

Robert H. Knight, "Hollywood, You Slay Me," *The Wall Street Journal,* October 5, 1989.

Music and Mayhem

National Coalition on Television Violence, "MTV and Other Music Video Violence Increases," press release, November 8, 1991;

Senator Robert Byrd quoted in *Electronic Media,* September 30, 1991;

Mike Muir quoted in "Getting Emotional . . . With a Bang," by Jonathan Gold, *Los Angeles Times/Calendar,* February 17, 1991, p. 64;

Leonard Pitts quoted in DeMoss, *Learn to Discern,* op. cit., p. 70;

Steve Hochman, "Rock 'n' Roll 'n' Violence," *Los Angeles Times/Calendar,* December 25, 1988, p. 66.

Vastly More Violent Than the Streets

Stuart Gordon quoted in "Gore Galore" by Sean Mitchell, *USA Weekend,* July 12–14, 1991, p. 5;

Lichter, Lichter, and Rothman, op. cit., pp. 185, 187–89;

Howard Rosenberg, "Television's Criminal Tendencies," *Los Angeles Times,* September 26, 1991, p. F1;

James Q. Wilson, lecture at "Hollywood Salon," October 26, 1991.

"Untying the Fabric of Our Society"

Bill Clinton quoted in "Clinton, Bush Step Up Debate on Family Values," by Ronald Brownstein, *Los Angeles Times,* May 22, 1992, p. A22;

Marian Wright Edelman quoted in "Kids Say Adults Should Get Real," *USA Today,* March 16, 1992, p. 1D;

Leonard Eron quoted in Sean Mitchell, op. cit., p. 5;

L. Rowell Huesmann quoted in *Newsweek,* op. cit., p. 51;

Martin Scorsese quoted in ibid., p. 48;

David Puttnam quoted in Moyers, op. cit., p. 320.

Chapter 13: Hostility to Heroes

Smaller Than Life

"In: Evil/Out: Good," *US,* January 1992, p. 34;

Armand Assante quoted in "Armand Assante Beats the Drums for 'Mambo Kings,'" by Anemona Hartocollis, *Los Angeles Times,* February 29, 1992, p. F6;

Billy Crystal quoted in "Mr. Monday Night," by Kirk Honeycutt, *Los Angeles Times/Calendar,* March 29, 1992, pp. 29–30;

James Toback quoted in profile by Stephen Rebello, *Movieline,* October 1991, p. 36.

Trashing Icons

Ian Whitcomb quoted in "The Fabric and Role of American Popular Music: Interviews with John Brennan and Ian Whitcomb," *The Public Perspective,* July/August 1991, pp. 14–15.

Creeps and Killing Machines

National Coalition on Television Violence Poll, cited in "Freddy Krueger: The Nightmare Continues," *Parental Guidance,* October 1991, p. 1;

Aileen Carol Wuornos case, cited in "A Mother's Love," by Mike Clary, *Los Angeles Times,* December 17, 1991, p. E1.

Stupidity and Selfishness

Jan Stuart, "Read My Lips, Make My Day, Hasta La Vista, Baby: Pop-culture Teenspeak and Our National Mean Streak," *FanFare,* September 29, 1991, p. 7.

"Aiming Far Too Low"

Charles Champlin, "Frank Capra's Wonderful Life," *Los Angeles Times,* September 5, 1991, p. F1;

George Roche, *A World Without Heroes: The Modern Tragedy,* Hillsdale College Press, 1987, pp. 191, 194.

Chapter 14: Bashing America

"We Have Become the Enemy"

Susan Sarandon quoted in *The Washington Times,* May 22, 1991;

Sean Penn quoted in "A Cannes Curiosity," by Jack Mathews, *Los Angeles Times,* May 20, 1991, p. F6;

Oliver Stone quoted in "Oliver Stone Takes Stock," by Alexander Cockburn, *American Film,* December 1987, pp. 25–26;

James Bernard, "Rap Panther," *Mother Jones,* May/June 1991, p. 9.

Antipathy to the Military

Stanley Rothman, David J. Rothman, and Stephen P. Powers, "Hollywood Views the Military," *Society/Transaction,* Volume 28, I (November/December 1990), pp. 79–84.

Evil Industrialists

Lichter, Lichter, and Rothman, op. cit., pp. 131–32, 203–4;

Stephen P. Powers, David Rothman, and Stanley Rothman, "Hollywood Movies, Society and Political Criticism," *The World & I,* April 1991, p. 579.

Corrupt Cops

Ibid., p. 578;

Lichter, Lichter, and Rothman, op. cit., p. 21.

"America on Trial"

Powers, Rothman, and Rothman, op. cit., p. 581;

John Powers, "Bleak Chic," *American Film,* March 1987, p. 48.

Poisoning the Past

Tom Shales quoted in *TV, etc.,* August 1991, "Politically Acclaimed," p. 2;

Richard Grenier, "Hollywood's Foreign Policy: Utopianism Tempered By Greed," *The National Interest,* Summer 1991, pp. 76–77.

Vicious Vets, Pristine Protesters

Matt Tabak quoted in "The-'60s-Aren't-Dead File: There Are *Five* Black Panther Movies in the Works," by Nina J. Easton, *Los Angeles Times/Calendar,* July 21, 1991.

Exporting Ugliness

James G. Robinson quoted in *Los Angeles Times*, "Hollywood Goes Boffo Overseas," by Alan Citron, March 30, 1992, p. A1;

Richard Grenier, "Does Madonna Yodel?", conference paper, American Enterprise Institute, March 10, 1992, p. 2;

Ben Wattenberg, "A Bumper Sticker for Our Time: Cultural Neo-Manifest Destiny," conference paper, American Enterprise Institute, March 10, 1992, p. 4;

David Puttnam quoted in Moyers, op. cit., p. 317;

Irving Kristol, "Does the Spread of American Popular Culture Advance American Interests?", conference paper, American Enterprise Institute, March 10, 1992, pp. 4–5.

PART V: AN INESCAPABLE INFLUENCE

Chapter 15: Denial Behavior

A Cultural Nuthouse

A. M. Rosenthal, "If Not Now, When?", *New York Times*, May 5, 1992;

Jack Valenti quoted in transcript of conference on "Global Impact of American Popular Culture," American Enterprise Institute, March 10, 1992;

Mike Medavoy quoted in "Screen Violence Would Stop if It Didn't Sell Tickets, Filmmakers Say," by Bob Pool, *Los Angeles Times*, November 3, 1991, p. B6;

Robert A. Jones, "Coast Letter: Mr. Stone's Not So Fine Adventure," *Los Angeles Times*, January 12, 1992, p. A3;

Teller, "Movies Don't Cause Crime," *New York Times*, OP-ED, January 17, 1992.

A Clear Consensus

Barbara Dixon quoted in "Soul-Searching on Violence by the Industry," by Terry Pristin, *Los Angeles Times*, May 18, 1992, p. F12;

U.S. Department of Health and Human Services, *Television and Behavior: Ten Years of Scientific Progress and Implications for the Eighties*, 1982, cited in "Researching Television Violence," by Alan Wurtzel and Guy Lometti, *Society*, Volume 22, September/October 1984, p. 23;

Terry Pristin, "Soul-Searching on Violence by the Industry," *Los Angeles Times*, May 18, 1992, p. F12;

Aletha Huston quoted in *Hollywood's Reel of Fortune*, by Ted Baehr, Coral Ridge, 1991, p. 9;

Barbara Hattemer, letter of June 13, 1991.

Research Perspectives

Barbara Hattemer, *Summary: Conference on the Impact of the Media on Children and the Family,* Pittsburgh, Pennsylvania, Novemer 9–11, 1990;

Marlene Cimons, "Study Shows a Million Teen Suicide Attempts," *Los Angeles Times,* September 20, 1991, pp. A1, A26;

Dr. William C. Scott quoted in DeMoss, op. cit., p. 8;

Caryl Rivers quoted in "Does 'Warrior' Mentality Feed the Rise in Violence?", by Suzanne Gordon, *Boston Globe,* July 8, 1990;

Dr. George Gerbner quoted in "When TV Becomes a Killing Poison," by Randall Murphee, *American Family Association Journal,* August, 1991;

"Cartoon Violence: Monitoring Results, September 2, 1990 to March 25, 1991," *National Coalition on Television Violence News,* Volume 12, Numbers 3–5, June–August 1991, pp. 7–8;

"Turtlemania Strikes Again," *Parental Guidance,* Volume 1, Number 11, May 1991, p. 1;

Dr. Thomas Radecki quoted in "Is TV Stealing the Days of Our Lives?", by James Breig, *U.S. Catholic,* February 1988, p. 9;

Dr. Joseph Strayhorn, "Strategies for Reducing Exposure to Violent Movies: Questions Answered and Unanswered," *National Coalition on Television Violence News,* Volume 12, Numbers 3–5, June–August 1991, pp. 4–5;

Dr. Brandon Centerwall, "Television and Violence: The Scale of the Problem and Where to Go from Here," *The Journal of the American Medical Association,* June 10, 1992, Volume 267, Number 22, p. 3061.

Corporate Arrogance

David Blank quoted in "Teenage Violence and the Telly," by Howard Muson, *Psychology Today,* Volume 11, March 1978, p. 50;

William Belson quoted in ibid.

The Height of Hypocrisy

Alan Wurtzel and Guy Lometti, "Researching Television Violence," *Society,* Volume 22, September/October 1984, p. 23;

Wall Street Journal cited in "Hollywood, The Ad," by Mark Crispin Miller, *Atlantic Monthly,* April 1990, p. 46;

Ibid., p. 44.

Chapter 16: A Fun-House Mirror

A Second Line of Defense

Paul Verhoeven quoted in "Screen Violence Would Stop if It Didn't Sell Tickets, Filmmakers Say," by Bob Pool, op. cit., p. B6;

Sydney Pollack "The Way We Are: Keynote Address," *The American Enterprise,* May/June 1992, p. 95;

Private First Class Daniel Hopson, Bamberg, Germany, letter to *American Legion Magazine*, September 1991;

George Gerbner quoted in "Is TV Stealing the Days of Our Lives?" by James Breig, op. cit., p. 9;

Gerbner statistics cited in "When TV Becomes a Killing Poison," by Randall Murphee, op. cit;

Roger Lateiner and Tony Phipps, "The Female in Focus: In Whose Image," *Screen Actor Magazine*, Fall 1990, p. 12.

Isolated Too Long

1991 Times Mirror Survey cited in Appendix 4B, "Religious America: Still A Big Exception," conference paper, American Enterprise Institute, March 10, 1992, p. A20; *Los Angeles Times/World Report*, September 17, 1991;

Louis Harris, *Inside America*, Vintage Books, 1987, pp. 88–89;

"Monitoring the Future," Survey Research Center, University of Michigan, 1990.

Massachusetts Mutual Survey, op. cit.;

Survey by NORC, February/April 1991 cited in Appendix 3, "The Ideology Shows Its Pull Across Class Lines," conference paper, American Enterprise Institute, March 10, 1992, p. A15;

Survey by NORC, February/April 1991 cited in "Public Opinion and Demographic Report," *The American Enterprise*, May/June 1992, p. 113;

cited in "The New Global Popular Culture," op. cit., p. 82;

Los Angeles Times/World Report, op. cit.;

Gallup Organization Surveys, September 10–11, 1990, cited in *The Public Perspective: A Roper Center Review of Public Opinion and Polling*, Volume 2, Number 5, July/August 1991, p. 75;

Survey by Schulman Ronca Bucuvalas the National Victim's Center, March 8–17, and CBS News/*New York Times* Survey, April 1–3, 1991, cited in "Rating and Ranking the Police," *The Public Perspective*, op. cit., pp. 76–77;

Survey by the Roper Organization, July 14–21, 1990, *Roper Reports* 90–7;

Survey by Gordon S. Black Corporation for *USA Today*, March 22–28, 1990;

Survey by the Roper Organization, October 20–27, 1990, *Roper Reports* 90–10;

Los Angeles Times Poll, reported in "American Mood Hurt by Past Year's Events," by George Skelton, *Los Angeles Times*, January 1, 1991, p. A1;

Mellman and Lazarus surveys reported in Massachusetts Mutual Life Insurance Co., op. cit.

Getting the Message

Karlyn Keene quoted in "The Controversy About Popular Culture," *The American Enterprise*, May/June 1992, p. 82;

Marlene Cimons, "Study Says More Young Women Have Sex," *Los Angeles Times,* January 1, 1991;

Delores Kong, "Teens and Sex," *Detroit Free Press,* March 9, 1989, pp. 1B–4B.

Redefining Normal

William Bennett quoted in "The Controversy About Popular Culture," op. cit., pp. 80–81;

Carol Tavris, "America is Still Shockable—Barely," *Los Angeles Times,* August 9, 1991;

Massachusetts Mutual Survey, op. cit.

The Poison of Pessimism

National Opinion Research Center Survey, cited in Appendix 5A: "The U.S. and Other Countries Compared: Liberal Individualism," conference paper, The American Enterprise Institute, March 10, 1992, p. A23;

Media Watch, Volume 2, Number 5, May 1988;

Ben Stein, "Miami Vice: It's So Hip You'll Want to Kill Yourself," *Public Opinion,* October/November 1985, p. 43;

Martin E. P. Seligman, "To the Optimists Will Go the World," *Los Angeles Times,* September 27, 1991.

"The Most Effective Weapon Known to Man"

Jack Valenti quoted in "The Controversy About Popular Culture," op. cit., pp. 82–83;

George Lucas quoted in "U.S.C. Breaks New Ground for a Film-TV School," by Aljean Harmetz, *New York Times,* November 25, 1991, p. C16;

Edward James Olmos quoted in "Screen Violence Would Stop if It Didn't Sell Tickets, Filmmakers Say," by Bob Pool, *Los Angeles Times,* November 3, 1991, p. B6.

PART VI: BELOW THE BOTTOM LINE

Chapter 17: What Went Wrong

Missing Moviegoers

All figures on weekly movie attendance from the Motion Picture Association of America (research by Opinion Research Corporation of Princeton, New Jersey), cited in *Reel Facts: The Movie Book of Records,* by Cobbett Steinberg, Vintage Books, 1978, pp. 370–71; more recent figures from "U.S. Economic Review 1990" and "U.S. Economic Review 1991," by M.P.A.A., New York office.

"Emancipate Our Films from Morality!"

Frank Capra, *The Name Above the Title,* 1971, pp. 480–81, 486.

"An Anachronistic Piece of Censorship"

Jack Valenti quoted in "The Controversy About Popular Culture," op. cit., pp. 82–83.

An Unmistakable Message from the Hinterlands

B.V. Sturdivant quoted in "'Dirty Dollar' Chase Held Bar To Church Support of Movies," by Will Tusher, *Hollywood Reporter,* April 11, 1973;

Robert B. Frederick, "Year's Surprise: 'Family' Films Did Best," *Variety,* January 7, 1970, p. 15;

Cobbett Steinberg, *Reel Facts,* op. cit., p. 478; M.P.A.A. "C.A.R.A. Ratings," 1991;

"'Now' Films Stumble in Minneapolis As Patrons Favor Familiar Reissues," *Box Office,* October 12, 1970.

Chapter 18: Motivations for Madness

Following the Money?

"All-Time Film Rental Champs" (by decade) compiled by Lawrence Cohn, *Variety,* May 6, 1991, p. 82;

"C.A.R.A. Ratings: Summary of Yearly Percentage Reports, 1980–1991," Motion Picture Association of America, New York office, FAX Transmission to author, May 27, 1992;

"Top Grossing Films of the Year," from *Hollywood Reporter,* January 8, 1992, and January 1991;

Research Report and Analysis for the author, "The Relative Financial Performance of R-Rated Films," by Robert D. Cain/Entertainment Industry Consulting, July 1, 1992.

Beyond Simple Greed

Charles Champlin, "Moral Tale for an Amoral World," *Los Angeles Times,* March 9, 1973, "Calendar" p. 1;

Sydney Pollack, "The Way We Are: Keynote Address," *The American Enterprise,* May/June 1992, p. 94.

Craving Esteem and Immortality

Michael Jackson *Ebony* Interview (May 1992) quoted in "Jackson's Off-the-Wall Ebony Interview," *Los Angeles Times/Calendar,* May 10, 1992, p. 52;

Oliver Stone quoted in "Oliver Stone Builds His Own Myths," *Los Angeles Times/Calendar,* December 15, 1991;

Linda Bloodworth-Thomason, radio conversation with the author, and David Beckwith, on KCRW-FM, June 16, 1992;

David Victor and Leonard Goldberg quoted in *The Producer's Medium* by Horace Newcomb and Robert S. Alley, Oxford University Press, 1983, pp. 73, 91.

"Up on a Soapbox"

Linda S. Lichter, S. Robert Lichter, and Stanley Rothman, "Hollywood and America: The Odd Couple," *Public Opinion,* December/January 1983, p. 58;

Phillip DeGuere quoted in "Hollywood's Favorite Heavy," PBS documentary by Manifold Productions, 1987;

Diane English, Associated Press Interview, cited in "Murphy to the Rescue," by Donald P. Tosatti, *TV, etc.,* April 1992, p. 8;

Patricia Green, *New York Times* Interview (July 30, 1991), cited in "And now, a word from the stars . . . ," *TV, etc.,* September 1991, p. 3;

Peter Noah and Don Reo quoted in "How L.A. Captured Prime Time" by Jordan Bonfante, *Time,* November 18, 1991, pp. 93–94;

Lichter, Lichter, and Rothman, *Watching America,* op. cit., p. 4.

Ignorance and Arrogance

Jordan Bonfante, "How L.A. Captured Prime Time," op. cit.;

Ben Stein, *The View from Sunset Boulevard,* Basic Books, 1979, p. 135;

Robert Lipsyte, "A Lot of Hubba-Hubba," *Book Review/Los Angeles Times,* December 15, 1991, p. 4;

Paul Johnson, *Intellectuals,* Harper & Row, 1988, p. 342.

An Insatiable Need for Reassurance

Richard Grenier, "Hollywood's Foreign Policy: Utopianism Tempered by Greed," *The National Interest,* Summer 1991, p. 70.

The Myth of the Alienated Artist

Richard Grenier, "Modern Artists Forget Their History," *The Wall Street Journal,* June 1, 1990;

Richard Grenier, *Capturing the Culture: Film, Art, and Politics,* The Ethics and Public Policy Center, 1991, pp. xxii–xxiii;

Lawrence Christon, "James Stewart's Wonderful Life," *Los Angeles Times/Calendar,* May 10, 1992, p. 81.

"Reptiles Slithering on the Ground"

Madonna, MTV Interview, quoted in "Perplexing Perspectives," *Parental Guidance,* Volume 2, Number 1, July 1991, p. 2;

Terry Gilliam quoted in "Gilliam in the Lion's Den," by Harlan Ellison, *Book Review/Los Angeles Times,* December 8, 1991;

Oliver Stone quoted in "Popular Culture and American Values" by Robert H. Bork, conference paper, American Enterprise Institute, March 10, 1992, p. 6;

Gus Van Sant, "Free the Reptile," *LA Style,* December 1991, p. 139;

George Roche, *A World Without Heroes: The Modern Tragedy,* Hillsdale College Press, 1987, pp. 190, 205.

The Contribution of the Critics

Richard Schickel, quoted in full-page newspaper advertisement for *Bugsy, Los Angeles Times/Calendar,* December 8, 1991, p. 10.

Co-opting the Bosses

Mark Canton quoted in *Los Angeles Times/Calendar,* November 10, 1991, p. 26;

Richard Grenier, "Hollywood's Foreign Policy," op. cit., pp. 70–71;

Robert Welkos, "On the Ropes: Columbia Execs Under Fire Over Costly Flops 'Gladiator,' 'Radio Flyer,'" *Los Angeles Times,* March 17, 1992, p. F9;

Steve Weinstein, "When Gay Means Loss of Revenue," *Los Angeles Times,* December 22, 1990, pp. F1, F5;

Howard Rosenberg, "NBC Takes Hit Over Gay Issue on 'Leap' Show," *Los Angeles Times,* January 17, 1992, p. F1.

The Myth of a Gay Conspiracy

David F. Prindle study cited in "Is Hollywood Ruining America," by Robert Welkos, *Los Angeles Times/Calendar,* June 21, 1992, p. 7.

Blaming the Jews

Ted Pike, writer and producer, "The Other Israel," video distributed by "The National Prayer Network," Oregon City, Oregon, 1987;

Neal Gabler, *An Empire of Their Own: How the Jews Invented Hollywood,* Crown, 1988, pp. 2, 6.

Chapter 19: "The End of the Beginning"

The Censorship Temptation

Luther Campbell interview with *Rolling Stone* quoted in "1st Amendment: Last Resort," by Larry Canale, *CD Review,* October 1990, p. 5.

Resurrecting the Code?

"Cardinal Mahony Calls For Reform in Motion Pictures and Television Productions," Press Release, Archdiocese of Los Angeles, February 1, 1992;

Amy Wallace, "ACLU Attacks Code Backed by Mahony," *Los Angeles Times,* February 7, 1992, pp. B1, B3;

Michael Medved, "A Sickness of the Soul Replaces the Tinsel," *Los Angeles Times,* February 6, 1992, p. B7;

"The 1930 Production Code" full text in *Reel Facts* by Cobbett Steinberg, Vintage Books, 1978, pp. 460–75.

Watchdog Organizations

Tom Mathews, "Fine Art or Foul?", *Newsweek,* July 2, 1990, p. 48;

Gary David Goldberg quoted in "Hollywood Inc.: How to Win Friends and Influence TV," by Patricia E. Bauer, *Channels,* p. 69;

Donald Wildmon quoted in "Bringing Satan to Heel," interview by Don Winbush, *Time,* June 19, 1989, p. 55;

Bruce Berman interview in *The Hollywood Reporter* cited in "The Christian Film & Television Commission: Why, What & How," by Ted Baehr, *Religious Broadcasting,* December 1991, p. 22.

The Boycott Weapon

Alan Kaufman, letter to *The Jewish Journal* (Los Angeles), November 29, 1991;

Al Sikes quoted in "Sikes Supports Advertiser Boycotts," by Dennis Wharton, *Variety,* March 16, 1992;

Barna Research Group cited in "New Research Shows Effectiveness of Boycotts," by Randall Murphee, *American Family Association Journal,* October 1991;

Howard Rosenberg, "Burger King Bows to TV Watchdogs," *Los Angeles Times,* November 14, 1990, p. F1.

Inside Moves

Larry Poland, Ph.D., letter to the author, January 14, 1992.

Capable of Change

William Bennett quoted in "The Controversy About Popular Culture," *The American Enterprise,* May/June 1992, p. 83;

Dennis Hunt, "Condom Fashions Are a Political Statement," *Los Angeles Times/Calendar,* April 26, 1992;

Robert Epstein, "An Awards Show with a Social Conscience," *Los Angeles Times,* September 26, 1991, pp. F1, F8–9;

Bill Higgins, "'Wolves,' 'Simpsons' Lauded at Environmental Awards Fete," *Los Angeles Times,* October 2, 1991, p. F8;

"We Are Sexual Perverts" quoted in review by Fred Barnes, of *Raising Kids in an X-Rated Society* by Tipper Gore, *The American Spectator,* September 1987, p. 42;

George Will, "America's Slide into the Sewer," *Newsweek,* July 30, 1990, p. 64;

Craig Rosen, "Webs Refuse to Drop Ice Cube Set," *Billboard,* November 16, 1991, pp. 5, 91;

Charles P. Alexander, "A Parent's View of Pop Sex and Violence," *Time,* May 7, 1990, p. 100;

George Gerbner quoted in "The Controversy About Popular Culture," op. cit., p. 80.

"Renewal, Honor, and Optimism"

Richard Neville quoted in "Take a Lesson from David Puttnam," by Joseph Farah, *Movieguide,* Volume 5, Number 24, November 28, 1990, p. 3.

Index